SONS IN THE SADDLE

THIS BOOK IS DEDICATED TO
THE MEMORY OF MY GRANDFATHER
PATSY'S 'SONS IN THE SADDLE' AND
TO THOSE WHO RODE WITH THEM

CONTENTS

ACKNOWLEDGEMENTS

During the writing of this book I have tapped many sources apart from family and company records, and have received much needed information from a number of people.

Among those to whom I am especially indebted are Miss Margaret Medcalf and her assistants at the Battye Archives of Western Australia, who have helped me in so many ways throughout the years.

I am also deeply grateful to the Australian Research Grants Committee whose fellowship award enabled me to secure secretarial and research assistance. It is largely to this body that I owe the experienced services of Miss Constance Hooker who faithfully assisted me for a number of years, and also the help of Mrs Ros Golding who has been of great support in the latter stages of this book. For researching much of the background I have also to thank Miss Ruth Allender and Mr John Lee.

To my dear friend Dame Ida Mann D.B.E. I owe more than I can say for her assistance with the abstraction and summary of diaries and letters. I would like to acknowledge, too, the helpful interest of Professor G. C. Bolton whose thesis on the Kimberley Pastoral Industry from 1885 has been an invaluable source of reference.

Among those who kindly made photographs available, I would especially like to thank Mrs S. B. Edwards of Victoria for photos taken in the early 1900s by her relative, A. J. Campbell.

I have been in touch throughout with a host of relatives in all States of Australia who kindly provided details relating to their various branches of the family. I am especially indebted to my cousins Ken Davidson, who assisted with legal aspects of the story; Kathleen McArthur, daughter of Kit Evans *nee* Durack who figures herein; Ambrosine Wyles, daughter of Mr and Mrs Ambrose Durack; and her son Tony.

In addition I am much obliged to those families other than my own who made available relevant material, much of which has been quoted with, I hope, due acknowledgement.

Old-timers in the Kimberley district were all most cooperative, among them being my Aboriginal friends Johnnie Walker and Ernie Chapman who not only shared with me their own memories, but organized group discussions to obtain a consensus of opinion on more contentious issues.

These acknowledgements would not be complete without mention of Airlines of Western Australia (formerly MacRobertson-Miller Aviation Company) and the Department of the North-West for the generous help they have extended to me over the years.

M.D.

FOREWORD

The writing of this documentary began for me when I found myself in possession of the family and company records of over one hundred years. This was soon after my father's death in September 1950 when I had gone with my mother, sister Elizabeth and brother Kim to clear out the Connor, Doherty & Durack office, 20 Howard Street, Perth, for the incoming tenants.

We were aware of the family tendency to hoard but were taken aback by the formidable accumulation in those office cupboards, safes, and drawers. Opinions were divided concerning how we should deal with it. Should everything be kept and stored? Should we sort and keep only the more personal and interesting items, or simply instruct the cleaners to dispose of the lot? The latter had been Mother's suggestion for in undertaking numerous moves in her day she had found a 'clean sweep' to be the only practical course. Otherwise posterity would be left with more junk than living room. Going through old letters was a long sad task as she well knew and who now had time for it, anyway? We finally packed up all the diaries, letter-books, documents, and newspaper-cutting books with the intention of depositing them in the State archives where an experienced staff could decide what was of possible interest for research purposes. I thought however that I should first browse through the material and provide a few explanatory notes.

This task proved more absorbing and extensive than I had foreseen and finally lured me into writing a documentary covering my grandfather's lifetime from 1834 to 1898. A foreword to the book that was eventually published, *Kings in Grass Castles*, concluded in this way:

> Although Grandfather ceased some years before his death to be the controlling force in his family, an era ended with his life and only another volume, upon which I feel I have neither the heart nor the perspective to embark, could properly cover the rest.

Thereupon as originally intended, I deposited all the documents in the Battye Archives of Western Australia.

It was not until the early 1970s, as I watched the waters of the dam rising over the site of the Argyle homestead and the fertile valley of the Ord, that I felt impelled to take up the task again before too much unrecorded history had likewise disappeared. On my return to Perth I retrieved from the Battye all the relevant material, by this time indexed and in much better order than when it had left my hands, and began unravelling the tangled story from where I had left off. My most urgent task was to obtain as much inside information as possible from the remaining old-timers whose ranks were dwindling year by year.

Operating from Kununurra, town-centre for the Ord River irrigation project on what had been part of our Ivanhoe station property, I got down to work with notebook and tape-recorder. My white informants usually preferred me to take notes, but the Aborigines were happier with the modern device. As one of them put it: 'How do we know what you're writing down there? Might be anything. Better you turn on that recorder and we all know where we are.' Truth to tell, they enjoyed hearing themselves played back, but they were also anxious that individual versions should be checked in group discussion. I found their memories remarkable and perhaps typical of a people whose culture has been perpetuated from time immemorial by the spoken word. I was often moved by the objectivity of their interpretations and by their understanding not only of the *djoalung* (black man) but the *guddea* (white man) point of view. Remarkable also were their accounts of so many I had known and whom they recalled with true-to-life imitations of characteristic mannerisms, modes of speech, and tone of voice.

I have tried to be likewise objective and to present as balanced a picture as possible of black and white relationships.

The actual writing of the book was a slow process, interrupted by many other projects and pressures for which I was obliged to set it aside for extended intervals. The task was also complicated by there being so much more material to hand than had been available for the previous book. The continuing saga, if less romantic than in its earlier stages, was certainly more diversified and covered a considerably broader canvas of city and bush life, urban and outback business ventures, hopes and disappointments, family and inter-family relationships, against a background of local and world events, politics, and contemporary issues of all kinds.

The Durack brothers and their partners were very much men of their time and travelled widely throughout Australia and abroad. The development of their characters could have been more effectively handled in a novel than in the more constricting medium of a documentary, but it is to be hoped that some impression of their individual traits and different methods of handling mutual interests will emerge from this account.

My father, generally referred to as 'M.P.', being the most consistent chronicler and reared to become head of his family, inevitably takes centre stage in this narrative, as did Grandfather in the last. He was a man of considerable versatility, at home in stock camps and salons, experienced in the handling and judging of stock, an able company director, and for some years a conscientious politician.

His life in the bush was full of the stark exigencies of a hard land, especially before the advent of modern amenities. He was a coroner at many an inquest and presided over numerous burials, including those of close relatives. On the other hand he enjoyed his constant travelling on horse-back, by buggy, or by motor-car between the company properties. He took pleasure in acting as judge at race-meetings and extending to visitors to Wyndham and the stations his customary courteous welcome.

In the city his life was more conventional but never dull, his home and the company office being a rendezvous for the business and political figures of the day as well as for many relatives and friends. The diaries he left us are invaluable not only as an explanatory background to letters, cables, and legal documents, but for their reference to contemporary people and the issues or incidents with which they were involved. The inclusion of these together with explanatory notes would have led too often from the main stream of the narrative into a confusion of side channels—hence the fairly expansive References which the reader can take or leave as his time and interest dictate.

M.P. had a keen sense of history and realised that the recording of even one man's daily round, though often seemingly humdrum and repetitive, might still be of some significance in what he termed 'the Good Lord's mysterious scheme of things'.

JOHN DURACK
of County Galway, Ireland
m 1806 Amy Forde 'Mammie Amy'

MICHAEL
b 1808
m Bridget Dillon
to Australia 1853
d 1853 Goulburn

DARBY
b 1819
m Margaret Kilfoyle
to Australia 1849
d 1873

BRIDGET
b 1848 at sea
m Michael Cahill
d 1934 ↓

JOHN
'Big Johnnie'
b 1849
d 1886.

PATRICK
'Mantinea' or 'Black Pat'
b 1851
m Susan Downes
d 1933

MICHAEL
'M.J.' or 'Long Michael'
b 1854
m Bertha Levinson
d 1936

CATHERINE
b ?
m John Nesbit
d ?

THOMAS
b 1857
d 1922

WALTER
b 1904
d 1975 ↓

LANCE
b 1905
d 1982 ↓

AUSTIN
b 1907
d 1973 ↓

BILL
b 1913
d 1973 ↓

MARY
b 1833
m Denis Skeahan
d 1920

PATRICK
'Patsy'
b 1834
m 1862 Mary Costello
d 1898

MARGARET
b 1837
m 1860 John Bennet
d 1864

BRIDGET
b 1839
m Patrick Scanlan
d 1873

SARAH
b 1841
m Patrick Tully
d 1914 ↓

ANNE
b 1845
m John Redgrave
d 1874

MICHAEL
'Stumpy'
b 1846
m 1873 Catherine McInnes
d 1895

JEREMIAH
'Galway Jerry'
b 1853
m 1879 Frances Neal
d 1901

MICHAEL
b 1862
d ?

PATRICK
b ?
d ?

JOHN
b 1871
m Emily Woodland
d ? ↓

JERRY
b 1875 (?)
d 1905

AMBROSE
b 1875
m Nancy Tiddy
d 1954
Ambrosine
b 1916 ↓

MARGARET
b 1877
m Marchant
d 1953

BARBARA
b 1879
d 1901

MARY
b 1863
d 1865

MICHAEL
'M.P.' 'Miguel'
b 1865
m Bessie Johnstone
d 1950

JOHN
'J.W.'
b 1867
d 1936

JEREMIAH
b 1869
d 1869

PATRICK
'P.B.'
b 1870
m Eva Hughes
d 1933

MARY
b 1872
m James Davidson
d 1948

BRIDGET
'Bird'
b 1874
d 1949

JEREMIAH
'Dermot'
b 1877
m Diana Wentworth
d 1956
Patrick
b 1920 ↓

SHEILA
b 1903
d 1990 ↓

CECIL
b 1906
d 1957 ↓

ERIC
b 1908
d 1992 ↓

VINCENT
b 1914 ↓

KENNETH
b 1901
d 1993 ↓

DOUGLAS
b 1903
d 1974 ↓

LORNA
b 1904 ↓

REGINALD
b 1911 ↓

MARY
b 1913
d 1994 ↓

ELIZABETH
b 1915 ↓

KIMBERLEY
b 1917
d 1968 ↓

WILLIAM
b 1918 ↓

DAVID
b 1920
d 1982 ↓

The entries in this abbreviated Durack family tree are limited to those members who are contemporary with this story.

JEREMIAH 'J.B.' b 1858 m Agnes O'Hara d 1952	MARGARET b ? m Gus McEvilly d 1938	MARYANNE b 1862 d 1939	JAMES b 1863 d 1907	LAWRENCE b 1865 d 1933	SARAH b 1867 m J. Stokes d 1925	WILL b 1869 d 1911

MADELINE b 1909 ↓	GERALD b 1911 d 1975 ↓	NOEL b 1914 d 1983	NANCY b 1919 d 1983

CATHERINE 'Kathleen', 'Kit' b 1881 m Dan Evans d 1951	JESSIE b 1883 m Helion d 1916	CHRISTINA b 1884 d 1978	SARAH b 1885 d 1947	CLARE b 1887 d 1940	FERGUS b 1889 d 1915	FLORA b 1892 d 1968(?)

JANE b 1880 d 1883	BRIDGET b 1881 d 1884	PATSY b 1882 m Lillas Mulligan d 1933	ANNIE b 1884 d 1898	JACK 'J.P.' b 1888 m Rowe d 1978	NEAL b 1892 m Imelda Sellenger d 1920	MOLLIE b 1894 m Leslie Brockman d 1962	VERA b 1896 d 1898	FRANK b 1901 m Wertheimer d 1972

NEAL b 1923 d 1974 ↓	PATSY b 1928 d 1936	PETER b 1926 ↓	AUVERGNE b 1919 d 1996 ↓	NANCYE b 1921

JOHN
b 1911

LESLIE b 1928 d 1996 ↓	WARREN b 1930 d 1996 ↓	MOYA b 1932 ↓	DENHAM b 1934 ↓

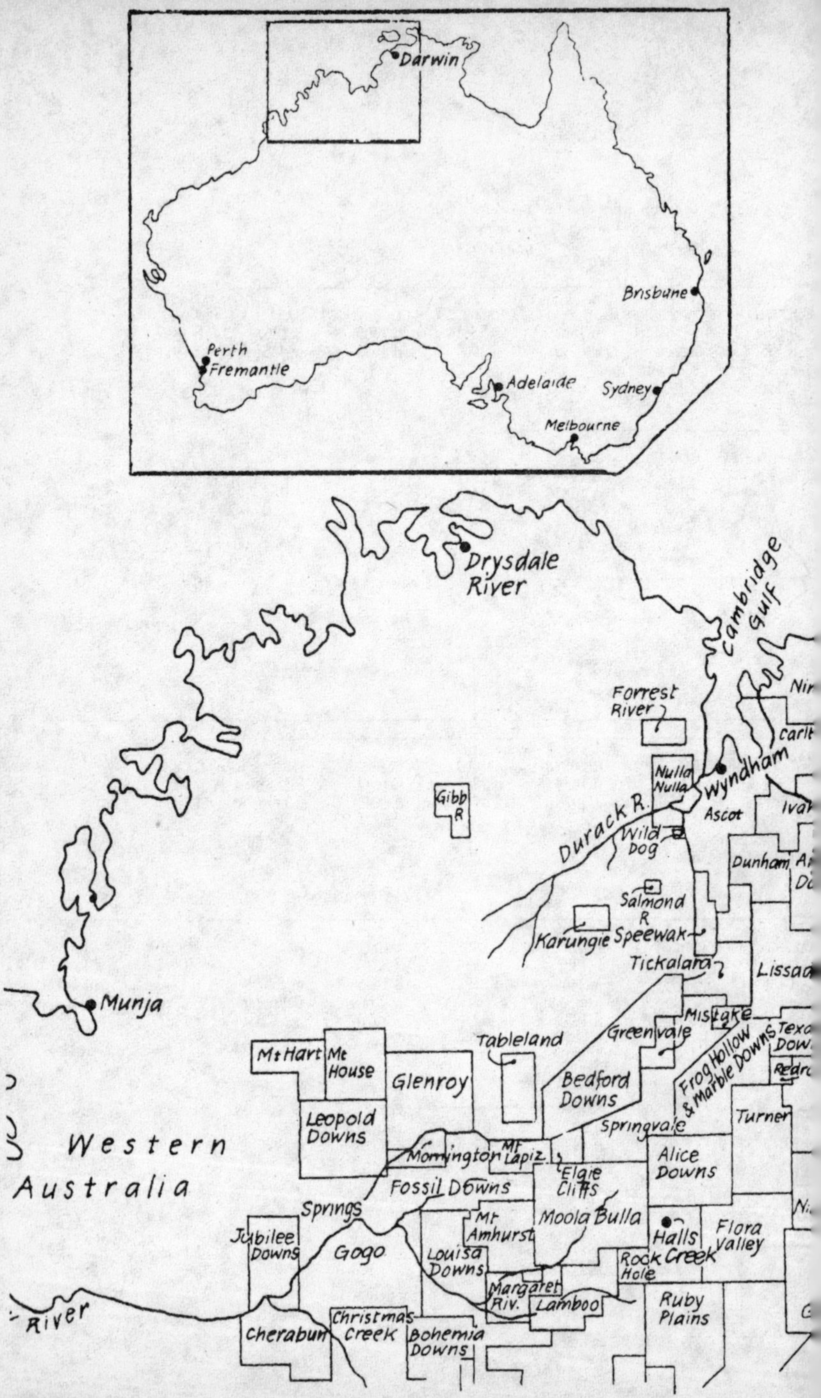

Darwin
Brisbane
Perth
Fremantle
Adelaide
Sydney
Melbourne
Drysdale River
Cambridge Gulf
Forrest River
Wyndham
Nulla Nulla
Ascot
Gibb R
Durack R.
Wild Dog
Dunham
Salmond R
Karungie
Speewak
Tickalara
Munja
Mistake
Greenvale
Tableland
Frog Hollow & Marble Downs
Mt Hart
Mt House
Glenroy
Bedford Downs
Leopold Downs
Springvale
Turner
Western Australia
Mornington
Mt Lapiz
Elgie Cliffs
Alice Downs
Fossil Downs
Springs
Mt Amhurst
Moola Bulla
Halls Creek
Flora Valley
Jubilee Downs
Gogo
Louisa Downs
Rock Hole
Margaret Riv.
Lamboo
Ruby Plains
River
Christmas Creek
Cherabun
Bohemia Downs

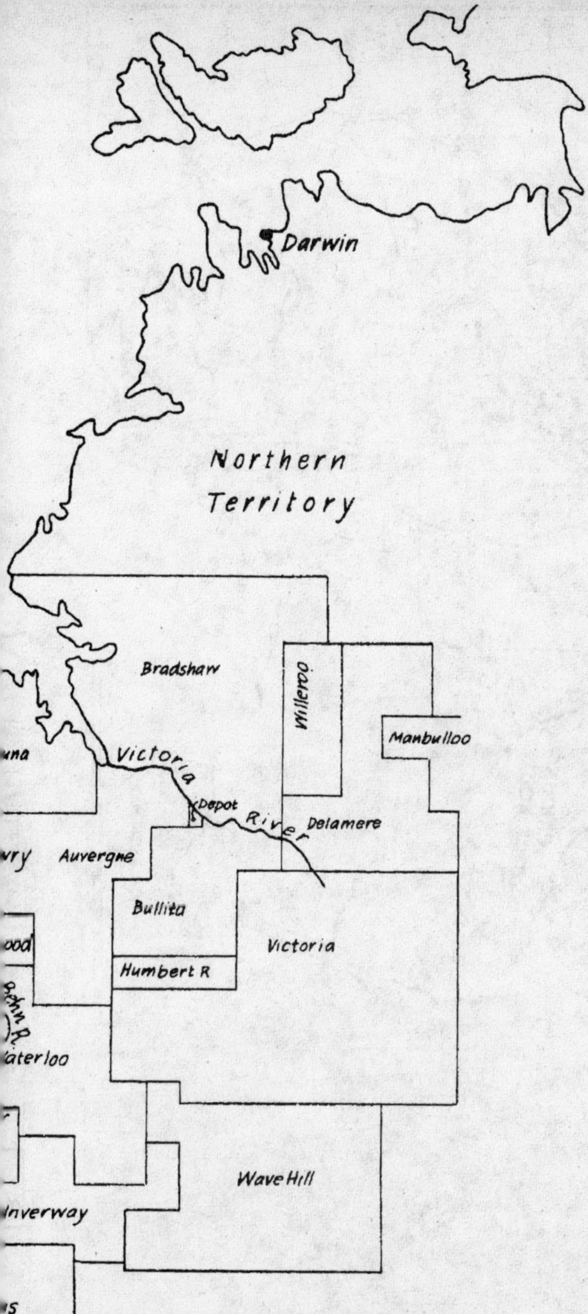
Darwin
Northern Territory
Bradshaw
Willeroo
Manbulloo
Victoria River
Depot
Delamere
Auvergne
Bullita
Victoria
Humbert R
Wave Hill

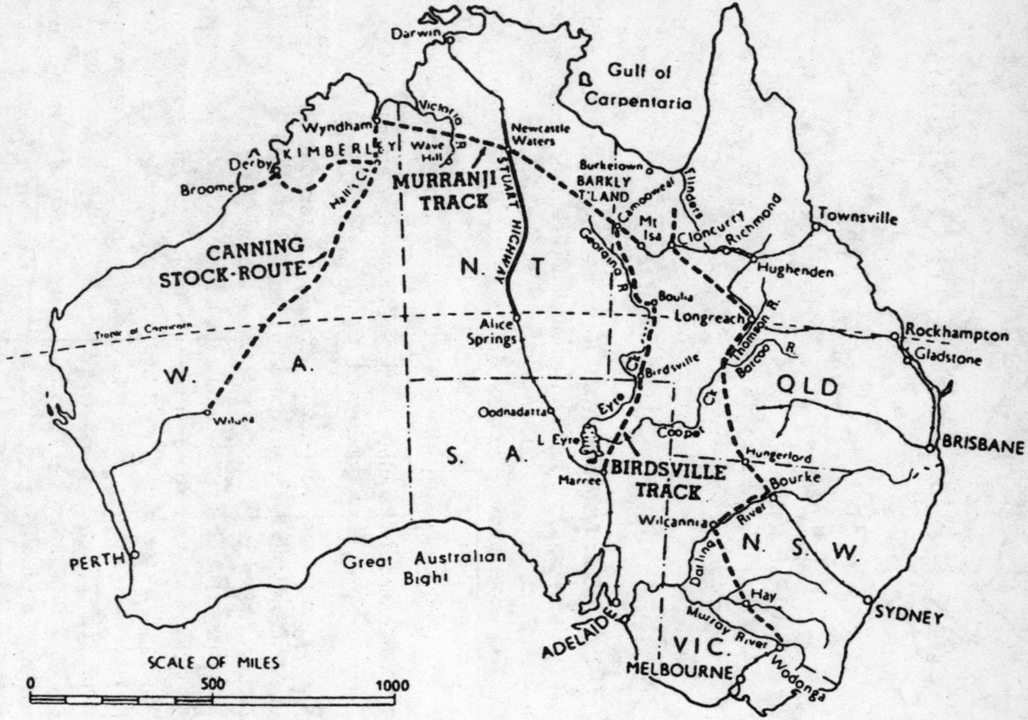
Darwin
Gulf of
Carpentaria
Wyndham
Victoria
Newcastle
Waters
KIMBERLEY
Derby
Broome
Wave
Hill
MURRANJI
TRACK
STUART HIGHWAY
Burketown
BARKLY
T'LAND
Camooweal
Flinders
Mt
Isa
Cloncurry
Richmond
Townsville
Hughenden
CANNING
STOCK-ROUTE
N.
T
Georgina
R
Boulia
Alice
Springs
Longreach
Thomson R.
Rockhampton
Gladstone
Birdsville
Barcoo
R.
W.
A.
QLD
Wiluna
Oodnadatta
Eyre
L Eyre
Cooper
BRISBANE
S.
A.
BIRDSVILLE
TRACK
Hungerford
Marree
Bourke
Wilcannia
River
Darling
N.
S.
W.
PERTH
Great
Australian
Bight
Hay
SYDNEY
Murray River
ADELAIDE
VIC.
MELBOURNE
Wodonga
SCALE OF MILES
0
500
1000

1

AN END AND A BEGINNING

1898

One day I will be leaving ye in the saddle, so to speak, and I hope in God ye will know enough for to take the right direction when that time comes.

Thus Grandfather wrote in a letter to his sons then at St Patrick's College, Goulburn in 1882. He had no doubt written figuratively but it was in fact from the saddle—at Anthony's Lagoon in the Northern Territory—that my father received that fateful bundle of telegrams (none of them ever destroyed) on 4 February 1898.

The first he opened had been sent from Fremantle two weeks previously:

> Father died this morning. His last words were for his boys. I am heart-broken. Your loving sister Mary.

The sad news was not easy to accept, for the old man's recent uncharacteristically low spirits had been thought due to the loss of his life's partner rather than an indication of failing health. After all, at sixty-four, he had more than fulfilled the family condition for achieving longevity, its having been a saying among them that Duracks lucky enough to survive to fifty years were destined for a ripe old age. Few enough of them had done so, for fate in one baleful form or another had lain in wait for most before that half-century milepost.

Grandfather himself had become head of his family at seventeen years old when, soon after their arrival in Australia in 1853, his father, aged forty-five, had been killed in an accident with a horse and cart. Patsy Durack's story had thereafter been in something of the rags-to-riches genre. He had had his setbacks, problems, and heartbreaks, to be sure, but his long-range plans, however seemingly improbable, had, at least until his latter years, shown a remarkable capacity for working out.

Who would have believed that a penniless Irish boy, setting forth from Goulburn to the Victorian goldfields bent upon earning £1,000 to set his family up on a small farm, would have done just that within eighteen months? Who could have credited the steady expansion of his holdings and his herds until, by 1862, he could no longer be rejected as an unworthy suitor for the girl of his dreams, the daughter of well-established Irish settlers of earlier migration?

Many predicted his downfall when, in 1867, he set off with his family to take up unsurveyed land in the remote south-west of the new colony of Queensland. As it happened he not only prospered but, with his brother-in-law John Costello, pioneered a thriving frontier settlement centred around their main stations—Thylungra and Kyabra.

In 1879, attracted by the explorer Alexander Forrest's report on the Kimberley district of Western Australia, Grandfather Patsy went into partnership with the Goulburn banker and landholder, Solomon Emanuel, to finance a further investigation of the area. The expedition they mounted, under the leadership of Patsy's younger brother Michael, returned with an optimistic view of the potential of this 'land of neither drought nor flood'. The promoters therefore decided to move in on its river frontages and rich natural pastures without delay. While the Emanuels took up large lease-holdings along the Fitzroy River to the west, the Duracks secured the grazing rights to the rich valley of the Ord and in no time one of the longest cattle drives in world history had been organized and sent upon its way in charge of several of Patsy's younger relatives.

Deciding that the time had now come to retire from active pioneering, Patsy built a fine house at Albion above the Brisbane River and settled down to the life of a city gentleman. The cattle which set out in May 1883 were held up by bad seasons, devastating floods, and the outbreak of stock disease, but the surviving drovers reached the Ord at last with half the original 8,000 head in September 1885.

Early in 1886 Michael (M.P.) and John (J.W.)*, the two eldest of Patsy's four sons, just out of college, left by ship to take over the vast Kimberley estate their father had registered in their names. When people asked Patsy where he expected them to sell their beef so far from the marts of trade, he replied confidently that outlets would soon open up. Even his optimistic

* Owing to the redundance of Michaels, Johns, Patricks and Jerrys in various branches of the Durack family they were mostly known by their initials snd sometimes nicknames. My father was generally known as M.P. and as 'Miguel' to his family and other close associates. The Aborigines rendered his initials as 'Umpy', though after his father's death he inherited the various terms of respect by which they had referred to Grandfather—*Yamagee* ('old man'), *Ngirragull* or *Goorung* (big-boss-belong-me and all-about).

imagination, however, could hardly have invented a gold-rush—the first in the western colony—coinciding in the Kimberley district with the arrival of the stock. By the middle of 1886 miners were flocking to the newly established ports of Derby and Wyndham and making their way with feverish haste to Hall's Creek, approximately 140 miles south-west of the Durack base at Argyle. Instead of their having to find a market, as had been expected, a market had found them. On his twenty-first birthday, in July 1886, my father weighed out £1,200 in raw Kimberley nuggets for bullocks at £17 a head.

News of the gold strike would no doubt have been too much for Patsy even without the persuasion of the faithful Aboriginal Pumpkin who, anxious for the welfare of the boys he had helped to rear, pleaded earnestly to join them. They soon afterwards took ship together for Wyndham, leaving Grandmother in Brisbane with the younger members of the family.

Since the alluvial gold had, by that time, begun to peter out and the miners to drift away, Patsy, anxious to retain this lucrative local market, pegged out a claim of his own and set to work on it with heavy crushing machinery. His efforts had met with little success when news of an impending bank crisis forced him to return to Brisbane. His own financial ruin was prelude to the general crash of '91. Only a few possessions in his wife's name survived the rush of creditors, and were brought along with them to the little mud-brick house at Argyle. After the first cold shock Patsy accepted his misfortune as one of the lower troughs in the ups and downs of life. Sooner or later, he believed, times would improve as they always did, markets would open up again, and settlement would follow as it had elsewhere.

His views were echoed by his two up-and-coming friends and countrymen, Francis Connor and Denis Doherty, who had started in partnership in 1886 when they set out from Sydney with merchandise for the recently publicized Kimberley gold strike. For twelve to eighteen months their business, with Connor transporting goods 285 miles from the port to the mining centre at Hall's Creek, and Doherty in charge of affairs at their Wyndham base, had fairly boomed. The tent with which they started was soon replaced by a roomy iron shack, complete with bolts and bars and burglar-proof safes stuffed with bags of undeclared gold, either purchased from the diggers or traded in exchange for goods.

The gold boom was short-lived but Connor and Doherty had faith enough in the district to hold on. It might also be said that they had put down too many stakes in the country to pull out. Connor declared, in a report of the time, that Kimberley was unsurpassed anywhere as a cattle-raising country and was capable of carrying millions of head. He also believed that its mineral resources, as yet scarcely tapped, were superior to those of any other part of Australia. As signal to the sincerity of such statements, the partners set about the acquisition of pastoral leases and sank a considerable sum of money into the Ruby Queen mine which they purchased from Grandfather at the time of his financial downfall.

Though somewhat daunted by the discovery of rich gold deposits in the Coolgardie area, which shattered all hopes of the return of a prospecting population to Kimberley, they at once began organizing the export of beef cattle to cater for a dramatically increased southern market. However suspect their terms might seem to local growers in time to come, Connor and Doherty, riding the countryside with cheery greetings and confident mien, were welcomed as the harbingers of prosperity, the heralds of hope. Cattle purchased on contract were to be delivered at, and shipped from, Derby, and the long, hard droving trip was a small price to pay if it proved to an indifferent government the urgent need for a loading jetty in Wyndham.

Little wonder that in the following year Connor was elected unopposed to the East Kimberley seat left vacant on the death of W. L. Baker, first member for the district. Truth to tell, the residents, preoccupied with the exigencies of their daily lives, isolated from the rest of the world and mostly from each other, took little interest in politics. Few of them even bothered to register on the electoral roll. There was, however, nothing *laissez-faire* in Connor's attitude to his new office. Largely owing to his influence, a jetty suitable for the loading of cattle was completed at Wyndham in 1894, and the partners, who had chartered three ships in advance from the Adelaide Steamship Company, lost no time in putting it to use. In 1888 they had secured the leasehold of an improbably large chunk of country extending east from the Western Australian and Territory border, which they had named Newry after the Irish seaport of their mutual origin. When, eight years later, they purchased from Macartney and Mayne[1] the adjoining and considerably larger Auvergne run, their position appeared, to the inexperienced eye, to be substantially strengthened; but Auvergne had a bad name in the district as a wild and intractable property on which too many stockmen had come to an untimely end.

Immediately after this transaction both Connor and Doherty transferred themselves, with their wives and young families, to a headquarters near Fremantle, then the business centre of the colony, where they soon established a land and shipping agency and an auctioneering business.

Included in a collection of contemporary biographies, the partners were presented in colourful terms as having by this time fought a tough frontier battle to an enviably successful conclusion.

> For their fearlessness in investing capital in North Western Australia the two old schoolfellows merit unstinted praise, for by these means the wealth of the colony has been considerably augmented; they have paved the way to the development of much hitherto waste country ... No better stamp of men for an advance guard of civilization could be obtained. Truly these partners sowed in tribulation and discomfort and they now reap in joy the rich harvest so carefully tilled ... [*History of Western Australia*, W. B. Kimberly, Melbourne, 1897]

The fact remained, however, that for all their busy expansion and enterprise, they were still not strong enough to enter into effective competition with Forrest and Emanuel of West Kimberley, an alliance of entrenched West Australian and wealthy Jewish families who represented a formidable threat to the two blow-in Irishmen. No one could have known better than Connor and Doherty themselves that their hold in the north was extremely precarious. Their Wyndham store and agency had naturally declined when the departure of the gold-diggers reduced the population to a handful of townspeople, station owners and bush workers. Where their pastoral properties were concerned, they were in even worse case. Connor's youthful service in his father's auctioneering and stock-selling business in County Down had provided him with little useful experience in the raising of cattle in a savage country; while Doherty's apprenticeship in a linen factory in the same district had equipped him with none at all. At the mercy of unsupervised managers, they sometimes feared, in fact, that the treacherous Aborigines whom they were quoted as declaring 'impossible to civilize and tame', stood a good chance of winning back the territorial rights to which they still, so unreasonably, laid claim.

The partners had already been forced to suspend operations on their first property, a modest 60,000-acre selection about twenty miles from Wyndham where they planned to breed pedigree horses as remounts for the Indian army and which, in a moment of euphoric optimism, they had named Ascot. It was not so much they who had abandoned the experiment as the experiment that had abandoned them, for the horses, with no respect for the unfenced boundary of their lawful domain, had at once proceeded to 'run brumby' in the outlying ranges.

The obvious solution to their problems had seemed to be amalgamation with the Durack brothers who not only owned the 2,000,000-acre runs of Argyle and Ivanhoe which adjoined their own estates, but who seemed to take the management of stock under the open-range conditions of that untamed country in their matter-of-fact stride. Since their arrival in Kimberley the partners had naturally established a friendly relationship with the Durack family, and in 1896 had suggested that they combine forces to their mutual advantage.

Grandfather's two eldest sons had seen much to be derived from this move, for whatever experience Connor and Doherty lacked in certain respects they more than made up for in their business perspicacity and drive. Their education, at St Colman's College in their home country, was much on a par with that dispensed by the Irish religious at St Patrick's College, Goulburn. Their general knowledge of the world, however, was impressive compared to that of the bush-reared brothers who had not yet crossed the seas that insulated their native land and confined the vision of its inhabitants. Besides these factors, there was the position of both Connor and Doherty as Members of Parliament—surely a useful balance of power to that of Alexander Forrest's long-standing office as a member of the Legislative Council for Kimberley, to say nothing of his brother John's status as first Premier of the colony. Nor was their influence in the contentious cattle-tick[2] question to be overlooked for, from seeming to East Kimberley pastoralists a matter of only mild concern, this had by now become a political weapon that was being used to promote the interests of Forrest and Emanuel.

It was indeed an ironic turn of fate by which *Ixodes bovis*, this blood-sucking little parasite, blind, deaf, and dumb, should have come to challenge the future of a major industry and to expose the human weaknesses of so many prominent and supposedly upright colonists. Seldom had any issue aroused such blatant self-interest and unprincipled double-talk. Seldom had contenders in the same trade so accurately analysed each other's motives while remaining conveniently blind to their own.

The controversy had started reasonably enough when, in 1896, Francis Connor, as member for East Kimberley and partner with Denis Doherty in a storekeeping and cattle-dealing business in Wyndham, sensibly concerned himself with the possible danger arising from cattle-tick being introduced from infested areas in the Northern Territory and Queensland. Connor figured prominently in a deputation representing this problem to the Commissioner for Crown Lands, A. R. Richardson, with the result that in 1897 an ordinance was passed prohibiting the importing of cattle from the Northern Territory.

This might seem to indicate a commendably disinterested attitude on

Connor's part. He had, however, made sure that properties adjoining or extending over the Western Australian border, from which he and Doherty were drawing cattle for the Fremantle market, were not included in the ordinance. This proviso had been made on the grounds that these holdings, namely Wave Hill, Ord River, and Connor and Doherty's own stations Newry and Auvergne, were virtually tick-free and were moreover topographically identified with East Kimberley. It also served to put a spoke in the wheel of Forrest and Emanuel who were bidding, far afield of their own area, for trade with East Kimberley and Territory pastoralists.

It was not long, however, before West Kimberley cattle-growers, genuinely concerned about the spread of tick to their area, had, with the strong backing of Forrest, Emanuel & Co., successfully clamoured for the tightening of quarantine restrictions against all cattle being introduced from the Northern Territory. This meant that the Wyndham cattle-buyers could operate only from their immediate area and that the growers, realising their predicament, could bargain for higher prices. Connor now opposed the whole quarantine barrier on the grounds that there were by this time as many tick on one side of the border as on the other. Much as it suited Forrest and Emanuel to deny this, it was no doubt true. Connor, nonetheless, overstated his argument by maintaining that stock-inspectors had been hard put to find *Ixodes bovis*, as distinct from other harmless species of tick, in East Kimberley, and that in any case no relationship had been established between tick and redwater fever. His parliamentary diatribes on the absurdity of the regulations and the unscrupulous motives of rival interests in urging them, while failing to convince the majority of his fellow members, impressed the Durack brothers and convinced them that a combination of interests would greatly strengthen their position.

Grandfather himself was not in favour of the partnership but having placed the Kimberley estate in his sons' hands in 1886 he could do no more than proffer his advice. Talk of consolidating against 'jealous and unscrupulous rivals' in West Kimberley reminded him that but for Alexander Forrest's initial exploration of the district they would probably never—for better or worse—have taken up country in Kimberley to begin with. He and his brother, on their visit to Perth in 1881 to enquire into the newly proclaimed area, had been received with the warmest cordiality by Forrest whom they summed up as a first-rate explorer and an astute and fair-minded businessman. Nor could Grandfather forget that Forrest's partners, Sydney and Isadore Emanuel, seen by Connor and Doherty as hard and wily opponents, were the sons of a man whose generosity he credited with having started him on his career and who had remained one of his best and staunchest friends. He envisaged a multitude of calamities arising from what he described as 'this amalgamation'. He saw friendships degenerating into feuds, 'castles in the air' vanishing like rainbows. It was moreover his contention, as a man of much experience in the assessment of pastoral country, that Argyle was worth all Connor and Doherty's assets put together, including their two stations and the Wyndham and Fremantle businesses. His third son, Patrick (P.B.) agreed with him, and did his best to persuade his elder brothers to continue on their own. The youngest son, Jerry (J.J., later generally known as Dermot) was then completing a science degree at the Sydney University and was evidently thought too far removed from local problems to be consulted.

During their protracted arguments, Grandfather was careful to point out that he had nothing personally against the two Wyndham partners. In fact he found them extremely congenial and could enjoy a night out with either or both of them better than could any of his boys. His contention was that whereas the two companies should certainly co-operate in trade, they should not become associated in a close-knit business relationship. He knew that, although of Irish parentage, his Australian sons understood neither the strengths nor the weaknesses of the Irish-born. He, too, could appreciate Connor's stirring eloquence and boundless optimism. He could even enjoy, for what they were worth, the visions Connor conjured up of millionaire pastoral estates supporting them in elegant mansions far removed from the rugged Kimberleys. Such things might happen of course: had he not seen, for a time at least, the realisation of such a far-fetched dream? But although by nature optimistic, he was sceptical of 'wild flights of fancy' and financial juggling tricks. Men who had reached their goals in the Australian outback had done so, in his experience, through clear thinking and what he termed 'working along steady'.

Connor's stirring, oratorical style, Doherty's witty and persuasive tongue—heady stuff in a humdrum outback town—were common enough fare in the old country. They were nonetheless a formidable combination. Connor, forty years old in 1897, had a dash and charm that impressed men and women alike. Doherty, three years his junior, was of stockier build with chiselled features softened by a natural affability. He was the shrewder of the two, less given to forthright public declamations, more consistent in argument. Both were of essentially urban tastes and it was clear to Grandfather that, for all their professed belief in the future of Kimberley, they had no inclination to settle there. In fact, as he pointed out to his sons, their desire for the amalgamation had much to do with the chance it offered them of comfortable family life in the temperate south.

This, where his sons were concerned, seemed if anything a point in favour of the partnership. They had no objection whatever to Connor and Doherty running the firm's business in Fremantle, thus leaving the Duracks in charge of affairs in the north. And so, after much discussion, an agreement was at last drawn up under which M.P. was appointed general manager of the four stations, in control of the movements of the cattle, P.B. was manager in charge of stock on the stations, and J.W. was manager of the Wyndham mercantile business, at salaries of £500, £300 and £300 respectively.

Grandfather pointed out that this arrangement might not seem so appropriate if his sons were to marry, for women given any possible alternative did not appear to relish the idea of permanent homes in the north. At the beginning of Kimberley settlement he had tried hard to encourage family life in the district, as he had done with such success in Western Queensland, but he was now forced to admit that there were adverse factors here that had not applied to the other area. Life in that region, though remote enough, had been suburban by comparison. There was, moreover, as he had learned to his great personal sorrow, a disease in this country that had not menaced them out east on Cooper's Creek. Call it what they would—malaria, dengue, or simply the fever—it was a killer at worst and at best was a waster of vital time and human energy.

It was something of a relief to his elder sons that when the company was finally registered Grandfather, recently bereaved, was persuaded to take a long-deferred trip to Ireland. They regretted having to argue with their old man, but it seemed clear to them that although so practical in many respects he had 'no head for business'. How otherwise, they asked each other, could he have let a considerable fortune slip so easily through his fingers? They had apparently forgotten that many of Australia's reputedly most astute businessmen had fared no better at that time, and that their father had at least had the foresight to assure their ownership of his Kimberley interests before the crash came.

Early in 1897, apart from the tick question which, thanks to Connor's forthright representation, seemed soon to be satisfactorily answered, prospects for the newly formed company of Connor, Doherty & Durack appeared extremely bright. Labour, at that time mostly white, was cheap and not hard to come by. Cattle in East Kimberley, then estimated at some 58,528 head, were multiplying rapidly on their open range and were fattening on the good natural pastures. Despite quarantine regulations, upwards of 7,000 head were being shipped each year from Wyndham to southern markets. Once the ban was lifted on the import of cattle from the Territory, what with the prospects of a lively trade with South Africa and the opening of Asian markets, it seemed that the sky would be the limit to their activities.

Encouraged by Connor's optimistic reports from Fremantle, M.P. set off for the Territory to purchase cattle and hold them for shipment from Wyndham as soon as the battle of the border had been successfully concluded. With 500 head being held at Anthony's Lagoon and another 436 at Brunette Downs, he waited from August to February with what patience he could command. The weeks of anxious waiting and uncertainty dragged by on leaden feet, M.P. keeping in touch with his men, ever vigilant lest they go on the grog, watching the condition of the cattle decline as the rains held off.

> ... The stock in hand in fair condition but the stench of dead beasts unbearable along the track—many just alive propped for support against the trees. The crows thick everywhere, chanting, as it were, their funeral dirge ...

Many times he rode with high hopes to Newcastle Waters and Anthony's Lagoon, only to be informed once again: 'Sorry M.P.—no letters—no wires.'

With what eagerness, therefore, did he at long last snatch up the bundle of telegrams that, after all, contained nothing but bad news on both personal and business fronts. Besides the sad message from his sister Mary, there were several others in the same vein from relatives and friends, including his partners, Connor and Doherty. Connor's brief message of condolence added that he and his wife had taken the sorrowing Mary into their own home in Fremantle. Doherty, with no concession to telegraphic economy, spread himself in typical Irish rhetoric over several forms:

> Your father died this morning brave to the last a heart like a lion no complaint despite his sufferings his thoughts with you and your brothers' success. I have cabled Ireland. My father will break the news to Bird.* I will wire all your people in Queensland and elsewhere the passing of a generous relative and stalwart pioneer. Follow his course. Be up and doing. He has left you a priceless heritage an unblemished name.

* Bird, Patsy's youngest daughter, was then on a visit to Ireland with Mrs Doherty and family.

2
A World Without Time

November 1897–July 1898

M.P., while appreciating Doherty's sentiments, would surely have considered his admonition to be 'up and doing' somewhat uncalled for. When, indeed, had he not been up and doing except when trapped, as at present, by depressing circumstances beyond his control? What would he not give to be up and doing—off and away from this sweltering land of lost men and blighted hopes? Then thirty-three years of age, he was more accustomed to giving advice than taking it. In fact he had been reared as an heir apparent to the expectation of command, though it stands to his credit that he neither flaunted nor abused his authority. He could appreciate a challenge to his views and enjoyed an honest argument but those who opposed him in what he deemed an uncivil or unreasonable manner found that he could effectively defend his point of view, if necessary even with his fists.

His present frustration was typical of all his experiences to date with the Territory, that 523,620-square mile problem foster-child of South Australia. He recalled his first visit when he and Tom Kilfoyle had pioneered a 350-mile stock route from Argyle to the gold-mining centre at Pine Creek. Since no one had been prepared to buy their cattle, they had set up their own butchery under a bough shed and disposed of the beef at a price about level with costs. As there was no alternative market at that time, they made six further trips to Pine Creek with fresh supplies before the opening of the Wyndham jetty provided a more lucrative outlet. And now, just as their fortunes appeared to have taken a promising turn, this 'tick fiasco' had set them—for the time being at least—back where they started.

Little wonder that M.P., for all his characteristic optimism, saw the Territory at that time through somewhat jaundiced eyes. That it had boundless potential he did not doubt. 'But', he asked of his diary, 'will this promise be realised in our own lifetime?' He would no doubt have been depressed to read Ernestine Hill's description of the Territory written over half a century later:

> ... a colony in quicksand ... Black men wandering and white men riding in a world without time where sons do not inherit and

> money goes mouldy in the pocket, where ambition is wax melted in the sun, and those who sow may not reap ... the Northern Territory of Australia ... land of an ever-shadowed past and an ever-shining future, of eternal promise that never comes true ...
> [*The Territory*, Ernestine Hill, Sydney, 1951]

M.P.'s Territory associates of the time shared his frustration, for since the decline of their local mining centres they looked anxiously westward for a market. Not only station owners were concerned but managers, stockmen, book-keepers and other station hands whose jobs depended on the continuation of the industry. Wages, at £4 to £5 a week for a station manager, £2 10s for a head stockman, £1 to £2 'all found' for other hands, seem pitiful by present standards but the bush workers of that time prized their jobs and knew that had they stuck out for better conditions they would have been replaced easily enough. Some of them were educated men, some were barely able to read and write, and others quite illiterate. A number were operating under assumed names, anxious, for one reason or another, to evade some aspect of their past. Others, influenced by tales of America's rapidly developing back country, were awaiting a similar outcome for Australia's pastoral frontier. Others again, reared to the saddle on restricted southern properties, had made for the Territory and the Kimberleys in search of a wider range and a freer rein. Most aimed to establish runs of their own and a few were to achieve this ambition—for a while at least. Many, their hopes too long deferred, already talked of getting out when they had made enough to start elsewhere, but few would ever escape the curious hold of that aptly dubbed 'never-never' country, or would acquire anything more substantial as a result of their labours than a local identity.

The homesteads of the Territory and Kimberleys of that time were for the most part desolate bachelor establishments—mud-brick or pisé shacks with corrugated iron roofs and earthen floors. There was usually an inner room or two surrounded by a verandah where most of the living was carried on. Chairs were lengths of canvas slung on wooden structures with extended sides to accommodate saddle-weary legs. Beds were timber frames crisscrossed with strips of greenhide. Water bags swung from the corner beams, alongside saddles and packs. Most of the places had Chinese cooks operating from separate quarters with the help of a few Aboriginal women. Some kept excellent gardens in the cooler months of the year and produced surprisingly good fare from limited ingredients and under primitive conditions.

M.P. was made very welcome at the lonely Territory outposts, for even in adverse times he had an infectious zest for life and was both a good talker and a good listener. His manner, in whatever place or company, was one of courteous formality that, although fair game for bush mimics, was impressive and subtly flattering. He was not of the 'hail-fellow' fraternity. Christian names and nicknames did not come readily to his lips and he made it clear without even trying that he had no taste for the bawdy or the profane. He had, however, inherited something of his father's gift for drawing into conversation even the most reserved and limited of men. His interest in their ideas, activities, backgrounds, and places of origin, was quite genuine and his memory for people met at any time or under any circumstances never seemed to fail him. He often spoke of the men he knew in the Territory at this time and was later to jot down more detailed notes on people mentioned briefly in his daily record.

It was part of the unwritten etiquette of the country that one did not question a man about his background, but 'biographies', apocryphal or substantially true, were built up from hearsay, snippets of first-hand information, and a deal of quiet detective work. A case in point was a young man giving his name as Charlie Biondi, at that time stock-riding on Alexandria Station. He was said to hold the title of a once rich and powerful Italian family and to have heard of the Territory as a place where he might restore the Biondi fortunes and build up a new principality. While working as a humble jackeroo, he was believed to be investigating local conditions with a view to the purchase of property. Whether or not the tale was true M.P., droving stock from Alexandria to Newcastle Waters with the assistance of 'the Count', found him excellent company. He could converse fluently on European classics and history, and would enliven the long rides and night camps with operatic excerpts rendered in a fine tenor. M.P. understood that he intended soon returning to present a report to his family, but he seems never again to have left the Territory. A year or two later he was packing the mail from Camooweal to Borroloola and thereafter he took possession of the store at Anthony's Lagoon on the track from Queensland to Kimberley. His hopes of its developing into an important town site came to naught, but by that time Biondi had, in Aboriginal parlance, been 'sung' or spell-bound like so many others to end his days in that lonely land. He lived to become one of the Territory's famous characters, his hospitality a legend and his exquisitely plaited goods—stockwhips, belts and hatbands—prized as a local art form. Married to a part Aboriginal woman, he produced a family of four daughters and three sons to carry on the Biondi name[1].

Then there was Harry Redford, whom M.P. found 'a right good old social character, willing at all times to entertain with stories of his youthful prowess'. This was none other than the man on whose exploits Rolf Boldrewood had based his classic *Robbery Under Arms*, the daredevil 'Captain Starlight' himself who had driven 1,000 head of stolen cattle from Western Queensland down the desert track to market in Adelaide in 1870. When M.P. had reminded him that it was his Uncle John Costello of Kyabra who had been responsible for setting the police on his trail, Redford responded heartily: 'I'm proud to think it took one of the best bushmen in Australia to dub me in. Those greenhorn police would have been hunting for me yet!' M.P., meeting him now in his later years, could readily understand how Redford as a young man had captured public sympathy, and although caught red-handed had been declared 'Not Guilty' at his famous trial in Roma. He told M.P. how he had afterwards struck out for the Territory with 3,000 head of cattle from the Barcoo to form Brunette Downs, this exploit 'all square and above board'.

His subsequent adventures could have filled many books and there is no doubt that, although sometimes on the shady side of the law, he contributed as much as anyone to the early settlement of the Territory. In the late '80s when the Pine Creek gold boom had begun to peter out, Redford, leading the way on horseback, piloted a big party of Chinese prospectors, carrying supplies and swags on bamboo poles, from Katherine to Camooweal, a distance of some 800 miles. Much of their track lay over the treeless Barkly Tableland and also through the tribal country of hostile Aborigines. It was terrain on which hundreds of unescorted Chinese are reputed to have perished while making either to or from the Territory goldfields. Those who accompanied Redford proceeded from Camooweal by Cobb & Co coach to the Queensland coast, from whence they took ship back to China.

Now too stiff in the joints for regular cattle work, Redford[2] had set himself up in a solitary camp on Armchair Creek near Anthony's Lagoon, lending an occasional hand to travellers for payment of a handout of tucker and tobacco and an attentive ear. In this way he attached himself to M.P. during his unwilling sojourn in the Territory and helped him pass the dreary weeks of waiting and suspense.

James Hutton, manager of Brunette Downs, was another associate of that period. An avid reader, Hutton waged a continual battle with the cockroaches for possession of his well-stocked library and was the proud possessor of a hand organ on which he ground out musical recitals as a change from nightly games of cribbage and baccarat.

Old Bill Blair, one-time accountant and book-keeper on Alexandria, was then employed as an odd-job man at Brunette. Though regarded by many as a religious crank, Blair was an erudite scholar and his Biblical dissertations shamed M.P. into admitting his own superficial knowledge of the Great Book. Reading it for the first time from cover to cover, he recorded his appreciation of its power and poetry, while finding its application to his own day sometimes disconcerting:

> 12.4.98: Absorbed until the early hours with the law laid down by Moses whose opinions on land rights would seem to be in line with those of the labouring classes of the present day!

The Bible digested, he was plied with Emerson's essay, 'Man the Reformer', thoughts from which he jotted down for future reference on the fly-leaves of his journal:

> 13.4.98: 'Selfishness, not kindness has been the history of our age for these thousand years. By our distrust we make the thief, the burglar, the incendiary and by our court's jail we keep him so. The sentiment of love is the one remedy for all ills, the panacea of nature ...'
>
> Emerson insists that the State must consider the small man and urges us to contemplate the mushroom as a symbol of the power of kindness, breaking through the frosty ground lifting a hard crust on its head ...

At the time of recording these lofty sentiments, M.P. believed implicitly that the best means of helping the small men of his district lay in his company's becoming big enough to outmanoeuvre the bigger men seeking to frustrate their enterprise. On this subject he gave vent to his feelings in long letters to his brothers in East Kimberley and to Connor and Doherty in Fremantle.

> ... It appears a crying shame that people should be suffering from lack of meat supply when they have here on the Tablelands any amount of splendidly conditioned animals going to waste for want of market ... As for the question of tick and tick fever, it is here but a subject for ridicule and banter ... I hear from the telegraph that our Premier is back in W.A. [from a Colonial Conference in London] and I am now anxiously expecting to hear that the border question has been properly settled. Were he to see the question in the true light he would surely be prepared to admit that the introduction of cattle from the N.T. has been vetoed by a lot of southern pastoralists unscrupulous of the truth and studying only

> their personal aggrandisement at a loss to the country and starvation to the miner. [M.P.D., N.T., to J.W.D., Wyndham, 18.9.97]

In November of the same year he wrote soliciting the support of a stock inspector in Camooweal:

> . . . It is to dispel the fear and try to prove to our authorities that the country from which we take those cattle is free from fever producing tick that I write to you. The route by which we will travel those cattle will be out by Newcastle and thence through the head of Victoria River thereby avoiding the possibility of picking up tick on the way out. Seeing the great devastation that tick fever has made amongst so many herds in Queensland it most certainly behoves us in our own interests to guard against the introduction of tick fever into our herds in W.A., but from my own experience of the question I am now assured that there will be no danger of the outbreak of fever in our colony from the introduction of cattle from the Tablelands. [Letter from M.P.D. to stock inspector, Camooweal, November 1897]

The stock inspector at Camooweal supplied a letter upholding the writer's case. In the meantime, however, the support that Connor and Doherty had rallied on the parliamentary front was frustrated by the discovery of tick, supposedly shipped with cattle from Wyndham, in the stockyards at Fremantle. This caused a genuine scare among stock-breeders throughout the colony and resulted in the banning of all livestock from East Kimberley until such time as the Chief Inspector should declare it free from tick or Parliament be again consulted.

Only Charles Moran, member for East Kalgoorlie and a friend and countryman of Connor and Doherty, raised any doubts about this resolution, his contention being that leaving the Kimberley trade to Forrest, Emanuel would bring about inflated prices and cause hardships to the consumers. His objection over-ruled, he suggested that the area of stock inspection be extended to West Kimberley where he had no doubt there were by now as many tick as in the East. This move, as might be expected, was blocked by members with interests in the former district.

At much the same time, news of the tick problem in North Australia reached South Africa and a ban was placed on the import of cattle to that area. Connor and Doherty, characteristically sanguine, saw this as little more than another move in the game but it meant that for the time being their operations had reached a stalemate. A telegram informing M.P. of the impasse was delivered to him with the wires advising of his father's death.

According to his diary, 'Bacchus' was at that time in control at Anthony's Lagoon and M.P. was in no mood for the drunken condolences of his white associates. Only the three Aborigines holding the cattle were in their right minds, and of these old Pumpkin was so consumed with grief as to present a problem of another kind. Since claiming Patsy Durack as his brother in Western Queensland nearly thirty years before, Pumpkin had loved and served him and his family with unfaltering devotion. M.P. thought that he might find some consolation in a visit to his own tribal country but this idea Pumpkin firmly dismissed. His home, he said, was now in Kimberley with his late 'brother's' relatives, to whom M.P. was no doubt anxious to dispatch urgent letters. Although the normal means of sending mail to East Kimberley was by ship from Darwin, M.P. at once engaged a stockman to take Pumpkin's place and sent Pumpkin off with letters to his brothers, P.B. at Argyle and J.W. in Wyndham.

After much negotiation with Queensland stock inspectors and cattle-buyers, he at last arranged for the sale of one mob at Hughenden and the other at the Endeavour Meat Export Agency that was due to open in Burketown in May that year. The mobs had no sooner moved off with their respective drovers than news reached M.P. by special messenger that the new processing works had been completely destroyed by fire. He hurried to the border town of Camooweal where he learned that there was a market for the cattle in Adelaide if he could obtain a clearance for entry into South Australia. This was a complicated process involving long discussions with stock inspectors and numerous letters and telegrams assuring authorities in both Brisbane and Adelaide that the mob had been declared 'clean' and was meanwhile being held on the border at great expense.

On this occasion the waiting around that M.P. usually found so irksome passed very pleasantly. In progress at Camooweal was a racing carnival to which people had flocked from all directions. Participants included his Costello relatives from Lake Nash, who made sure that he was well accommodated and introduced to all. Sympathies in the loss of his father, and special courtesies, were pressed upon him on all sides. He was appointed judge at the race-meeting, invited to present the trophies, and given friendly advice concerning the disposal of his cattle.

During the meeting, to M.P.'s great delight, Nat Buchanan turned up. Then seventy-two years old, this hardy pioneer had long since earned the reputation of having settled more new country than any other man in Australia, without, for one reason and another, having acquired anything of permanent value for himself. Although Buchanan had been a close friend of his father, M.P. had met him on only a few previous occasions and wrote enthusiastically of this Camooweal encounter which was to be their last:

> Buchanan was making his way on to Dalgonelly Station from the west and pulled up for lunch at the Georgina River crossing close by the township with his native assistant. When packing up to move on he heard that I and two or three others known to him were in town so he called at our quarters. Conversation flowed freely and although intent on going on that day, Buchanan ended up staying the night. After midnight, our companions having retired, he and I continued talking until 3 a.m.[3]

At the end of the racing carnival, word came through that the cattle were cleared to proceed to Adelaide, and they were immediately headed south in charge of W. Walsh, a competent drover who was to take them down the Georgina River and thence to Kapunda via the Birdsville track. At about the time M.P. received wires from his partners urging him to give evidence at a commission into the tick problem being set up by Premier Forrest. This request decided him to proceed to Fremantle via the eastern capitals, for he was confident that with the evidence he had already acquired, together with what he hoped to gather on his way around, he would soon be able to settle the frustrating tick question for good and all. His Camooweal friends hastily organized a farewell party that took the form of a dinner-dance at which his health was drunk in champagne, 'with many eulogisms and kindly words'.

3

Golden Opportunities

July–September 1898

The journey from Camooweal to Richmond—350 miles as the crow flies, considerably more by the roundabout bush tracks and mail stages of that era—was an eight-day ordeal by Cobb & Co coach. M.P., however, was an ardent traveller. Country, spectacular or monotonous, was all of interest to his perceptive eye. He recorded faithfully the general topography and quality of the land, the condition of stock and of natural pasture, making special comment on people met at remote stations and in dusty outpost towns. One pictures his eager interest enlivening over a brief encounter their drab and isolated existences.

> 3.7.98: On eastern side of McKinlay range passed small post office serving also as a school. Mrs. Russell (*nee* Hutton) in charge—11 children (3 her own). Receives £25 a year, all found, including clothing. Good garden, milk and butter with meals . . .
> 8.7.98: Into Cloncurry. Put up at Prince of Wales Hotel. The landlady its only recommendation. A dance at night drawing representative types including a sprinkling of half caste women. General standard of behaviour rough and ready to say the least.
> 12.7.98: Left Richmond 5.30 a.m. Bitterly cold. Secured privileged box seat in front. Pretty soon found the driver swaying and nodding off to sleep—not surprising after the amount he imbibed last night! I suggested he gave me the reins and this he did—watched me for a few minutes, said 'Oh, you're alright,' then concealed himself in a large box that was used for storing parcels from which sanctuary he did not emerge until after 4 p.m. Cobb & Co.'s new driver was challenged at different stages but explained that the man usually in charge was temporarily indisposed. No further questions.
>
> At one stage we took on a police officer with a sealed box presumably containing gold. He also went to sleep.
>
> Travellers greeted us with friendly salutations: 'Good day! How's things? Any mail for me?' Being given the individual's name I searched the loose letters compartment under the seat. Satisfied

> or disappointed each took his leave with a cheery: 'Thank you! So long!'

In additional notes on this journey made at a later date, M.P. wrote of 'one person worthy of special comment—a woman—tall, gaunt-looking and with bright red hair', who helped him rummage for her mail and with the customary salutations rode on her way. He learned that she went under the sobriquet of Red Jack and was known on many stations in those parts as an efficient stockwoman. She was also an expert with her stockwhip which she effectively used on any of her fellow workers who ventured to press upon her their unwelcome attentions. No one seemed to know anything about her private life or background, her horse Mephistopheles being apparently her only close friend and confidant[1].

Late in the afternoon the coachman emerged and took over once again but had not gone far when the pole horses floundered, fell over some rough going and almost capsized the coach. Things were put to rights by the passengers but it was well after dark—and no one in attendance—when they clattered up to the Hughenden post office. The unloading of mail and other cargo fell to M.P. and the police officer who remarked that the driver was by no means typical of Cobb & Co employees, most of whom were noted for their reliability and initiative.

M.P. caught the train from Hughenden to Townsville where he was met by an old school-mate named Jack Dwyer and elected an honorary member of the North Queensland Club. He had a more than casual interest in the two local meatworks, for it was already the dream of East Kimberley cattlemen to have a meat-processing works set up in Wyndham—a move they believed would solve all their marketing problems while putting an end to the tick controversy. M.P. embarked on his tour of inspection with typical enthusiasm, taking careful notes for presentation to the Government of Western Australia. Of the Alligator Works he wrote:

> Cattle put through at a rate of 320 a day—about 2,000 head a week. Everything saved and processed ... Highly efficient and economical ...

Having taken ship to Brisbane, he pursued his investigations into various aspects of the meat industry, witnessing experiments in inoculation at Indooroopilly and making appropriate contacts.

> Mr. Chataway, Minister for Agriculture, read me a telegram he had recently received from John Forrest re the tick question. Mr. C. states that he sees no sense in the harassing restrictions put on

> pastoralists: 'We have spent £35,000 trying to arrest the invasion of ticks without any result.'
>
> Mr. Murray, Minister for Works and Railways, agrees with him. He says: 'You now have our experience and by all means profit by it. With all our restrictions and prohibitory regulations what have we effected? Nothing beyond having almost crippled one of our most stable industries—the cattle.'

Met at the train in Sydney by his sister Mary, recently arrived from Fremantle, and his youngest brother Jerry, M.P. was escorted at once to Kimberley House in York St, a comfortable hotel run by Darby Durack's widow and daughters which was for many years the family headquarters in that city. Of all the relatives he met over this period, M.P. found Jerry the most changed, for the shy, gawky boy of their last meeting was now six feet tall and at twenty-one years old very much a young man of the world.

> He not only expressed disapproval of my unmodish apparel but suggested that I get some specialist to dispel the strong aroma of gum leaves and 'possoms from my personality. He took me to a tailor to be measured for new clothes and to purchase a few items to add at least a touch of respectability to my appearance. Only then was I permitted to visit my old friends the McEvillys and to meet various members of the smart set with whom young Jerry is acquainted.

Despite the strong bond of affection and mutual esteem between Grandfather's eldest and youngest sons, there was already an element of envy in their relationship. As far as M.P. was concerned, Jerry was fortunate in having been free to embrace the academic career that J.W. and he himself would have espoused from choice. It had been made clear in their case that their duty lay in carrying on the pastoral business established by 'the pater', and in accepting this role they had found their lot cast in a tough country where men were judged by standards of physical endurance and adaptability to local conditions. It was also a country of strong local mores based less on conventional moral, and intellectual standards than on those of sheer brute survival. M.P., riding a rugged land in the saddle he sat so well, saw his job as lonely and mundane indeed compared with life in the ordered but mentally stimulating precincts of a university, where men could talk with academic detachment of such things as ethics, human rights, and the government of man.

Jerry on the other hand, encouraged in his choice of a university career by his father and elder brothers, had also found his lot a lonely and arduous one in the intervening years. A bush-born boy, deeply attached to his family circle, he of them all had been obliged to go it alone in city surroundings that were not, for a long time at least, his natural environment. M.P., J.W., and P.B., even during their hardest and most isolated periods in the bush, had had for the most part each other's company. They had also been fortunate enough to share their parents' last years. Apart from his personal deprivations, Jerry desperately missed what he remembered as a carefree station life where time was gauged by the seasons and the sun. He believed, moreover, that of all his brothers and cousins he had the most genuine feeling for horseflesh, for whereas they thought of horses as tools of trade, he loved them to a point of passion for their own sakes. He was an excellent rider and in the midst of his studies found any excuse to visit the training paddocks and offer his services gratis.

Lack of cash was another factor that had irked him sorely, for although after his father's financial ruin Jerry's brothers had continued to pay his university and college fees, they had been far from lavish with spending money. Every year it had been the same story—they were all short of ready cash but prospects were promising and they should very soon be better off. When that time came he would receive his full share of their prosperity but in the meantime he must manage as best he could.

M.P. took the opportunity of their meeting to explain his brother's financial position. Jerry's university expenses which had been debited against his shares in the Durack Brothers' business were to be written off in consideration of his paying the five other members of his family 1,000 each of his 10,000 shares in the new company of Connor, Doherty & Durack. The trend of these discussions is clearly indicated in a follow-up letter, written by M.P. shortly after his return to Kimberley.

> Taking everything into consideration I think you will consider this fair.
>
> Your position now shows on a much better standing than did ours at your present age.
>
> The 12 or 13 years that we have put into the establishment of our present position will I am sure be acknowledged by you to be commensurate with the demands we have set forth above.
>
> Seeing that the support of the two girls, Mary and Bird, for the past 6 or 7 years devolved upon us and still falls as a liability upon our shoulders until such time as their shares begin to pay dividends, I think you can offer no objection on this point.

> We have viewed the matter in this wise:- by your giving the girls 1000 shares each we have waived our right to any extra consideration we would have been justly entitled to for our lengthy period of management under conditions I must say most trying and circumstances the most adverse.
>
> Should you elect to follow a course of your own at the termination of your university career we will finance you, hitherto debiting you with the amount which would stand against your shares were there no dividends declared.
>
> Of course we have a very uphill battle to fight this year and much depends upon how the ticks are going to treat us . . . Should everything go all right however we should be able to declare a dividend of 10% . . .
>
> We would much prefer you to come into our business for there is ample scope and it must develop into large proportions with the advent of a little prosperity.
>
> What office you would have to fill in Fremantle we cannot exactly say but Jack [J.W.] tells me that he finds he cannot control the whole of our business in Wyndham and would like to have you here . . . The work is rather erratic—a great rush on the arrival of a boat and thereafter fairly slack . . .
>
> I need not tell you further about the conditions of life up here. As I have said—the climate is trying, little in the way of recreation except you indulge in duck shooting, and socially no one to meet . . .

But there were matters of far wider significance to claim their attention at this time. M.P.'s arrival in Sydney coincided with a vital stage in the history of an issue which had been under heated debate since 1883 when Henry Parkes had suggested the formation of a Federal Council of Australian States. Following Parkes' death in 1895, Edmund Barton had taken over his role as leader of the Federal Party in New South Wales and at the convention of 1897–8 urged that the proposed union be termed the 'Commonwealth—the grandest and most stately name by which a great association of self-governing people can be characterized'.

As a result of this convention a bill was drawn up with which G.H. Reid, Premier of New South Wales, took issue on several points. Of these the most important was a clause providing that the seat of government should be determined by the Parliament, for, backed by a large body of opinion in Sydney, Reid believed that the capital of the Commonwealth should be in New South Wales, the oldest, richest, and most populous colony in Australia. Barton saw Reid's objections as unnecessary obstacles to the realisation of his ideal of 'a nation for a continent and a continent for a nation'.

A few hurriedly jotted notes in M.P.'s diary recall the fierce party and public frenzy engendered by the last-minute referendum debates.

> 25.8.98: With Jerry and McEvilly to hear Reid in the city. A great enthusiastic meeting. My companions were Barton's champions and engaged in a good deal of heckling and banter which Reid parried with clever jest and formidable logic.
> 27.8.98: Polling day. Sydney seething with excitement. Crowds milling around the booths. Immense gatherings around the 'Herald', 'Telegraph', and 'Star', offices. Witnessed an exciting scene between the rival champions Barton and Reid.

The result of the referendum, a disappointing one for M.P. and his associates, meant the frustration of the federal union for another two years, but the ideal of an Australian Commonwealth had by this time taken firm hold of the Australian people. A small population of common origin cut off from the rest of the world, their strength and inspiration clearly lay in a constitution such as had already been attained in the United States of America.

While her brothers were taken up with matters of personal business and national politics, Mary, still in mourning for her father, had found comfort in recalling to friends and relatives the sorrowful details of his passing. She and her sister Bird had left school in Goulburn to join their family at Argyle after their mother's death in '93, and this was the first time she had returned to the east. An emotional but commonsense enough girl, she shared with the menfolk of her family their love of movement, of renewing old acquaintances and adding new links to an endless chain of relationships encircling the continent. Now en route to Melbourne with her brother, she must take tearful leave of her Sydney connections and brace herself for the even more intimate associates of the Goulburn area.

At the Convent of Mercy where she and her sister had spent ten of their most formative years, she was swept into the embrace of her beloved nuns. There were more tears, more heart-to-heart post-mortems, Masses, Benedictions, rosaries, and special prayers for the repose of the faithful. One gathers that it was all a little much for M.P., though he appreciated the loving concern made manifest in the rituals of his faith. Cross-examined by the Reverend Mother concerning the future of his sisters, he explained that their father had left his four sons jointly responsible for the girls' maintenance and general welfare until such time as they should marry or enter a convent. Bird had been for some time strongly disposed to follow the latter course and it was possible that she might reconsider it. M.P. was sure the good sisters would agree with his action in having, two years before, opposed her marriage to a man whose reputation as a former associate of the unfortunate Oscar Wilde had been made known to him only just in time. He explained that 'the poor girl' had soon afterwards gone off for a trip to Ireland with the wife and young family of their new partner Denis Doherty, and that they were then on their way back to Australia.

A visit to their grandmother, Mrs Michael Costello, living on a family property outside Goulburn caused M.P. to ruminate on the unpredictability of life. There was the old woman, hale and hearty at eighty-six, her memory, except for what she chose to forget, apparently unimpaired, while his mother (her cherished daughter) and his father (of whom she had often disapproved) were both no more. Now she recalled only the happier memories of her association with her son-in-law. Ignoring what she had once seen as his reckless and inconsiderate ambition, she praised his farsightedness, his kindness and generosity, his abiding faith in God and his fellow men. Delighted to hear of M.P.'s recent contact with her son John and his family at Lake Nash and Camooweal, she spoke of her fear that what was left of their once-widespread pastoral empire would not long survive the combined threat of drought and falling markets. With this in mind, she had held on to their own comparatively small family property with its comfortable homestead overlooked by the church that had been the gift of her husband and herself to the Wheeo parish[2].

M.P., anxious to catch the S.S. *India* from Adelaide, curtailed his sister's extensive visiting list and hustled her on to the express to Melbourne. In a week they were in Perth, met at the train from Albany by J.W. who had recently arrived from Wyndham. This was the first time since their father's death that the two brothers had been together, but after the many letters they had exchanged there was not much left to be said on that sad subject. On the business front, however, there was much to be discussed. Between sittings of the tick commission, during which M.P. and his partners contributed to 'animated and sometimes acrimonious debate', they had time to consider the range of options open to them in the near future. That they would win their case with the government they had no doubt, for John Forrest, by this time returned from abroad, had indicated his intention to view the matter with a completely open mind. The scare created by the discovery of *Ixodes bovis* in the Fremantle cattleyards had died down, since no report had been received of its further spread in southern areas. In order, however, to demonstrate their concern, C.D. & D. had surveyed a site near Owen's anchorage where their cattle could be held in quarantine until certified clean by local stock inspectors.

The opening of a market in South Africa also seemed worth reinvestigating in view of hostilities seen as likely to break out between Britain and the Boers. Fighting forces would surely need all the meat they could get, and the authorities in that colony were less likely, in the event of war, to be worried by introduction of a few cattle-tick.

At this stage it occurred to the partners that they should acquaint themselves personally with activities on the goldfields, paying special attention to the sundry butchery businesses on which their main market depended. Accordingly, M.P. and Frank Connor set forth by train for an action-packed round of the fields. For all M.P. had heard of the diggings, he was surprised to find in the desert waste of the west so much of the lively atmosphere of 'the other side'. The population of Kalgoorlie and Boulder was by this time more than 20,000, and the broad main thoroughfare, Hannan Street, boasted twenty-five hotels, the largest of which had no less than fifty rooms. Of this edifice M.P. reports:

> We were greeted on arrival at 'The Palace' by Brownlow, the manager, who showed us over the premises—all most elaborate, the fittings and furnishings having cost £17,000 and the building itself £27,000. The rooms are quite sumptuously fitted up with electric light and fans operated from the hotel's own machinery. Brownlow himself in receipt of a weekly wage of £90!

M.P. found Sunday in Kalgoorlie very different from the conventional Sabbaths of Perth and Fremantle:

> Here, all religious denominations appear to carry on their various avocations at the one time and whilst the R.C. laiety are devoutly engaged the Salvation Army band accompanies their meditations with stirring strains. Meanwhile, the Fire Brigade next door, not to allow a wanton waste of God's good time, rings out with busy hammers the praises of the Lord. Emerging at last one's attention is captured by the devotional exercises of Wesleyan and Anglican.

Attending the same church service that day was J. W. Kirwan, editor of the *Kalgoorlie Miner*[3], who with Irish eloquence extolled for the visitors the glowing future of the fields under the banner of approaching federation.

As spokesman for the majority of the goldfields' residents, Kirwan was strongly in favour of the Constitution Bill that had received such a setback at the recent referendum and which a number of influential western colonists of the coastal areas had opposed. He declared, in richly pedantic phraseology, that he was prepared to take the case for the separation of the goldfields from the rest of the colony to the Secretary of State for Colonies in London, reminding him of the fact that the British Government had, by the Constitution Act of 1890, retained the right to subdivide the colony as it saw fit.

M.P., a keen Federalist, regretted that the Kimberley region had neither the wealth nor the numbers to support a similar movement. Connor, on the other hand, thought them both sadly lacking in judgement. In fact the question of federation was one of the several on which he and Doherty saw eye to eye with their business rival, Alexander Forrest.

Having inspected the mines and visited the slaughter yards and butcheries of the area, they returned to Perth, fortified in spirit, like pilgrims from a shrine, by the sheer forward-thrusting dynamism of the fields. In the meantime there had been encouraging developments for C.D. & D., by that time generally referred to as 'the firm'. The Commission's findings on the tick question indicated that although quarantine laws might check the spread of the disease they would be of little ultimate benefit in preventing its widespread dissemination. It was recommended that inoculation facilities be set up throughout the colony and that slaughter yards and a chilling works be provided at the port of Wyndham. Sir John Forrest saw little chance of raising the necessary finance for the latter proposal, but agreed to a compromise that could operate at least until such time as the suggestion might be reconsidered. From December of that year cattle could be again shipped from Wyndham. If showing signs of tick on arrival at Fremantle, they were to be slaughtered immediately, and if clean they could be trucked direct to the goldfields in special freight vans. This, while re-opening the cattle market for East Kimberley, served also to reassure these with genuine fears of tick contamination. The prohibition of cattle from the Northern Territory, including the C.D. & D. properties of Newry and Auvergne, was maintained but it was obvious to all but a few diehard antagonists that this ordinance too must soon be revoked.

It seemed a fitting time for a celebratory dinner to mark not only the reopening of East Kimberley trade but the return from abroad of Mrs Doherty with her children and her companion, Bird. This was held at De Baun's Palace Hotel in St George's Terrace, the recent opening of which M.P. had hailed as 'a welcome signal of faith in the future of our golden colony'. A palatial establishment for those times, it had at once become a favourite venue for Perth's society. During the occasion Connor and Doherty proudly displayed the new company letterhead devised, no doubt at the expense of a few headaches, by some hard-pressed commercial artist of the day. It suggested the partners' meteoric rise from humble beginnings to a position of some substance with a formidable array of business agencies and connections ranging from the capitals of Australia to London and Glasgow. Painstakingly incorporated in the design were cattle in a northern setting, the merchant business in Fremantle (fashionable carriages parked without), ships berthing at the adjacent wharf, and the stock-saleyards at Guildford, with indigenous flora as background to the design.

There can be no doubt of the warm relationship that then existed between the partners, and that they shared not only their business but their personal problems. Both Connor and Doherty had young families and comfortable homes within convenient distance of their Fremantle office. In the previous year Doherty had entered Forrest's third Parliament as member for East Fremantle, so the two men were now very much in the public life of the community with interests in a wide range of political, business and social activities. They were hospitably inclined and their homes were always open to members of the Durack family.

Since Grandfather's death they had all shared in worried discussions about the future of his two girls. Mary would have liked to return to her brothers in Kimberley: she enjoyed station life, the constant movement of men and stock, the animated talk of shipping and delivery dates, of seasons and the condition of the cattle. Her younger sister, on the other hand, had never had much liking for bush life and had even less since the unfortunate romance that had been shattered so abruptly at Argyle two years before. Bird's tastes lay in conventional surroundings, in the company of quiet-living, gentle folk. Her interest in livestock was limited to well-behaved domestic pets, and the range of her conversation to domestic issues and the affairs of friends and family. She was, however, an appealing and popular girl, with a concern for people that was by no means restricted to those of her own social circle. If the Dohertys, whose ménage in the Perth suburb of Claremont[4] she then shared, had any fault to find in her, it was her tendency to 'spoil' their servants. She would take over from the nurse-maid to allow her a few days at home with an ailing parent, or, if dinner guests were expected, forgo some social function in order to assist the harassed cook. Her small allowance was reduced to a pittance by her generosity. Forever visiting the sick or otherwise unfortunate, she went nowhere empty-handed and made so light of her largesse as to imply that money was, in her position, of little consequence. To the Doherty children, three girls and a boy, she was an adored and doting 'aunt' who pandered to their whims and defended their every peccadillo. Such devotion was a boon to the socially minded Dohertys, who were naturally anxious to keep her as a house guest for as long as possible.

Mary, being of a more gregarious and restless disposition, divided her time, over this period, between a variety of friends. M.P. refused to consider the proposition of her going north without the company of her sister, and thought it much better that things remained for the time being as they were. That both girls would marry in the near future he had little doubt but, as Denis Doherty had sapiently observed, any man with apparently suitable matrimonial qualifications in the Kimberley district (with the exception of course of themselves) was there for reasons better not too thoroughly investigated.

M.P. himself, although susceptible enough to women's charms, had not up to this time considered himself in a position to marry. In fact he had had little chance to cultivate romantic attachments, although his diaries of '94 to '96 contain occasional allusions to the 'beguiling charms' of a 'captivating brunette' who displayed 'the loftiest human feelings of her divine sex'. This paragon was one Norma Pierce, daughter of Wyndham's resident magistrate, but M.P. never proposed to her. In fact she was surprised in later years to learn that he had held her in such special regard.

During this period he and his brother J.W., caught up in the social swim of Perth and Fremantle, had become acquainted with a family by the name of Wilson living at a house called Lytton in the then fashionable suburb of Mount Lawley. M.P. makes several references to visiting 'the Wilson girls', and before long mentions driving out to Lytton 'to see Meg'. He did not, however, have much, if any, chance of seeing her alone, for she appears to have had a possessive mother and several ubiquitous neighbours. When he called to tell her that promising business developments demanded his immediate return to Kimberley, he remarked that 'conversation with the fair young lady on the verandah was rudely interrupted by old Horgan!' Meg was, however, at the wharf with his sisters to see J.W. and himself away on the *Albany* at the end of September. There had been no chance of a private farewell, but she had gone so far as to intimate that she would look forward to his promised letters and would most certainly reply to them. Far from seeming bored with his talk of the Kimberleys, she had professed to finding it of the greatest interest and she had even hinted at a desire to see the country for herself some day. Oh no, she did not at all mind the heat—in fact, she preferred the summer to any other time of the year; and as to roughing it—why, there was nothing she liked better than an alfresco meal and a long bush ramble! He watched her from the deck of the departing ship until her blue gown and frilled white parasol had 'vanished from sight, but never, never from memory'.

4

Problems and Personalities

October 1898

As the ship steamed north, M.P.'s romantic musings were mixed with anxious calculations concerning the formidable task ahead of him. The wet weather clouds would soon be building up over Kimberley, and the *Tangier* was due to collect 800 head of cattle at the beginning of December. That allowed just two months to rally the contracted numbers from various stations and get the mobs down to the port. The Northern Territory market still being closed, extra effort must be put into purchasing bullocks from East Kimberley properties. For the next few weeks therefore he must ride hard and talk with persuasive tongue to convince local growers that they would do better selling to C.D. & D. than to the interlopers from West Kimberley.

It was the custom, as a vessel drew within shouting distance of the Wyndham jetty, for passengers and those gathered to meet them to begin relaying potted versions of stories soon to be enjoyed or lamented over in full. The number of items exchanged in this way, enlivened by the give-and-take of more personal banter, depended on the length of time it took to manoeuvre the ship alongside against the tide and set the gangway in place. On the occasion of M.P.'s return with his brother J.W. custom took its usual course.

From the ship:
'The port's been opened! We can start mustering.'

From the jetty:
'Old Pethic died at Texas!'
'Cassidy had his camp looted by the blacks.'
'I can see you've been on the greenfeed down there.'
'Wait till you see the new hotel!'

In fact the hotel, being on the corner immediately opposite the jetty, could be clearly seen from the ship. It was on the site of a former hostelry, The

Custom-House, put up in the gold-rush days by the Cable family, one of whose members had married Denis Doherty in 1888. Later sold to Doherty and his partner, it had now been demolished to make way for the superior two-storey edifice that towered impressively above the lowly iron-and-timber shacks comprising the rest of the port. The supervision of this project had fallen to J.W. as manager of the Wyndham business, and he was justly proud of the result. He would have preferred that the timber had been painted white but, persuaded that the next dust-storm to come swooping down O'Donnell Street would transform it to a murky brown, he had compromised on a light tan that everyone agreed looked very well. The inside walls had been painted a dark shade of green to give a maximum impression of coolness and provide relief from the outer glare. There were spacious verandahs, a big kitchen, and an airy dining-room that would serve also as a venue for social events, from civic functions to race-balls and private celebrations. The bar opened at an inviting angle to the hot street and was adjoined by a billiard-room, a final touch of modernity being fans hung from the ceilings in anticipation of the day when machinery would be available to set them in motion. A corner of the residential area on the upper floor had been designed as a flat of sorts for members of C.D. & D. when on brief visits to the town.

All in all it was the most inspiring symbol of progress for Wyndham since the opening of the telegraph station ten years before. It also put an end, for the time being at least, to talk of moving the port to the more salubrious site for which government surveyors had drawn up an official town plan twelve years before. Prospectors attracted by the gold strike of '86 had wanted to be put ashore as close to their goal as possible, with the result that the settlement had grown willy-nilly around their landing-place near the head of the gulf. Closed in between the marshy foreshore and the rocky slopes of the Bastion Mountain, it could spread lengthwise only on either side of its single street, but once the shanty pubs and the little supply stores had been hustled up it was good enough for a population whose sole aim was to get rich quick and get out.

M.P., who had often enough criticized the unfortunate placing and dreary aspect of the town, found it unusually congenial on his return after an absence of more than a year. His brother P.B. and the two young Aborigines, Boxer and Ulysses, were at the jetty, with a number of other station hands, in town on one pretext or another, who greeted the brothers with moist, congratulatory handshakes on the re-opening of the port and heartfelt expressions of sympathy on the death of their old man. Everyone was confident that East Kimberley was at last on the threshold of the long-awaited good times, and that thanks to the forthright representations of C.D. & D. the 'tick fiasco' was soon to be satisfactorily resolved. Even P.B., who had supported his father in opposing the amalgamation, was now prepared to admit that on this issue at least there was strength in numbers, and that Connor and Doherty in their parliamentary capacities were doing a great job for both the country and the company.

At a banquet that night to celebrate the opening of the hotel and the lifting of the embargo, J.W. is reported to have spoken eloquently when proposing the toast of the town and the shipping services which where its lifeline. M.P. toasted the pastoral industry and the ministry, and 'glasses were raised to innumberable other worthy institutions and individuals'. It is not on record that anyone toasted the bush workers whose immoderate drinking habits, so often deplored, were to keep them in the country, and keep the hotel in business, through good times and bad.

M.P. and P.B., with their two attendants, were on the road next morning, calling briefly as usual at the Three Mile where C.D. & D. had taken over a butchery that supplied meat to the townspeople. They had also recently purchased a hotel at this site—a ramshackle place of bush timber and corrugated iron, the roof held down with rocks to prevent its taking off in the wind, but popular with the bushies who felt more at home there than in the comparative splendour of the new place in town.

M.P. had so far told P.B. nothing of his feelings for Meg Wilson, to whom he had posted letters from every port on his way north, for his brother was not only an incorrigible tease but would have made the subject a popular talking-point in no time at all. Reticent on issues that touched him most personally, M.P. had enjoined J.W., his most trusted and closest confidant, to silence on the same score. JW., ever anxious for the well-being of friends and relatives and eager to promote a happy outcome to the romance, agreed that at this delicate stage of proceedings the less said the better.

Where P.B.'s own romance was concerned, it was a different matter, since he welcomed any reference to the subject, teasing or otherwise. Given the slightest excuse, or none, he would launch into anecdotes dating back to his first meeting with his beloved Eva Hughes during his Nudgee college days in Brisbane, and leading up to their latest, two years before, when he had taken the first holiday of his seven years in Kimberley. They had since corresponded, and he had recently made so bold as to propose. The girl's response had been cool and to the point. Being city born and bred, she declared that she had neither the taste nor the training for life on a station in the furthermost back of beyond. She was, moreover, anxious to pursue the musical studies in which she was keenly interested. P.B., not to be so easily put off, maintained that her reaction had been based on a misunderstanding. Her life in the Kimberleys, he argued, would be anything but one of isolation and humble toil. From their headquarters at Argyle they would travel around together in the buggy, visiting friends at neighbouring stations and in the port. When at home there would be people coming and going all the time, and with a Chinese cook and several trained native women she would never be required to soil her lovely hands. There was a piano at Argyle, and several in Wyndham, on which she could keep in practice while entertaining enchanted audiences. Besides this, since the company was chartering its own ships, she could take a spell in the south as often as she liked. Any further doubts she might have had after receiving letters to this effect, Pat believed, would be readily dispelled as soon as he could get away to put his case in person.

To all of this M.P. listened as they rode along. The life Pat envisaged for Eva was very much what he had in mind for Meg, though he could foresee possible difficulties in having two brides living together at Argyle. The Territory properties, Newry and Auvergne, were far too 'way out' to be considered as headquarters, whereas Ivanhoe, only sixty miles from Wyndham, was occupied by the manager Duncan McCaully[1], his wife and small daughter. Although the place was roomy enough to accommodate visitors, it was hardly suitable for two families. The company property about fifteen miles from town on which Connor and Doherty had once planned to raise horses was now used by the company as a holding paddock and for desultory experiments in pig-raising, from which it had been inelegantly dubbed 'the piggery'. There was a homestead of sorts, usually occupied by a bachelor caretaker, which might easily, M.P. thought, be suitably upgraded, and with the property's former name of Ascot restored, it might be taken over as his official base.

With such thoughts in mind he rode around the 250 head of cattle being held here for the next shipment, noting with satisfaction that none of the beasts showed any evidence of tick. Stockmen encountered further along the road, however, had a different story. They had found six bullocks dead and others sick when mustering the day before. It is difficult to make any accurate assessment of the situation from M.P.'s cryptic entries, but it is clear that tick had by that time as firm a hold in Kimberley as in the Territory. C.D. & D.'s policy was evidently to show responsible concern but never alarm, and to continue to fight border restrictions on the entry of cattle by every means possible, including reasonable and unreasonable argument, recrimination, and ridicule. They certainly never spared themselves in disseminating propaganda to this end, nor did they intend abiding by the quarantine law while there was any way of circumventing it.

At Ivanhoe, Big Duncan McCaully, just in from the mustering camp, clasped M.P.'s hand in his iron grip and proceeded to lament the passing of the grand old man. McCaully had worked for Grandfather on Thylungra, Western Queensland, and had come to Kimberley with the Durack cattle in the early '80s. Except for a brief period as stockman on Ord River Station he had worked for the family ever since, and had during this time won the heart and hand of the accomplished little Miss Cameron who came to Kimberley in 1891 as governess to Galway Jerry's family. A Lowland Scot, Duncan claimed a border-raiding ancestry that was a fitting background, he declared, for life in the backblocks of his adopted land. Weighing fourteen stone and standing six feet tall, he was noted as a man with a tough hide and a soft heart, and now, recalling former years when his old boss rode at his side, he was not ashamed of his tears.

The journey between Ivanhoe and Argyle was, as usual, negotiated by buggy, the brothers sending Aboriginal attendants ahead with a change of horses. There was no habitation whatever over this sixty-mile stretch of country which embraced park-like, well-pastured plains and a deal of rough, scrubby country broken by ranges, creeks, and billabongs. The usual overnight camp was at Cockatoo Lagoon, half-way through 'the sands' that, although heavy going at any time, were not seriously to daunt the traveller before the advent of the motor-car.

Argyle was home base at that time to M.P. and his brothers. They had helped to build the roomy stone-and-timber house on the high bank of the Behn, and had used it since to accommodate their respective goods and chattels. Their parents had been inveterate hoarders in different categories, and had left many cases now to be gone through in search of legal documents pertaining to the old man's affairs. P.B. was in favour of keeping the relics, scapulas, Agnus Deis, blessed medals, and holy pictures that his parents had accumulated over two lifetimes of pious association, and for destroying the records that seemed to have no further bearing on life in this world or the next. M.P., with his keener sense of history, was for respectfully disposing of most of the bric-à-brac and keeping the station documents going back to early days on Thylungra. Some kind of compromise was arrived at whereby I was to inherit, in the fulness of time, several black tin trunks containing, along with an assortment of religious keepsakes, a miscellany of letters, stock records, and cash-books that were to reveal to me, over half a century later, so much of my grandfather's restless enterprise.

M.P. records that he was pleased to be back in the old place again and that although the house wanted much in the absence of his sisters, Pumpkin's wife Valley was doing her best to keep things in reasonable order. For Pumpkin he had brought the watch and chain that Grandfather had left to him, and with it a message from his sister Mary that the old man had spoken of his Aboriginal 'brother' almost with his last breath. Having seen his charges Boxer and Ulysses grown almost to manhood, Pumpkin had taken on another protégé who had been given the high-sounding name of Theology—since degenerated into Deology—a remarkably bright and attractive lad who had become a general favourite. M.P. remarks on finding him 'lively as a cricket and grown a lot, his dancing and singing a source of entertainment to all'. The following cryptic entries suggest that there was little otherwise in the way of entertainment at Argyle at that time:

> Jack Frayne from Auvergne, knocked about by a bull, though methinks Hennessy more responsible for his two black eyes . . . Cook laid up with fever . . .
>
> All hands out fighting fire in the paddock. Campbell and Beasley return and fight each other over a horse.
>
> Constable O'Keefe over from Timber Creek, looking for likely boys to take care of his camp. Reports a lot of trouble over that way.
>
> Mailman Crotty through with news that Cummins has poisoned himself at Hall's Creek. Sing, Chinese gardener, speared by blacks. Clarke died of sunstroke.

All the men here mentioned had earned local fame in one way or another. Jack Frayne, at that time employed by C.D. & D., was too valuable a stockman to be dismissed for his drinking habits. Like Jim Campbell and Jack Beasley he was a member of a steadily increasing local fraternity generally referred to as 'the battlers', most of whom had drifted across from Queensland with droving outfits operating for major pastoral companies. Singly or in partnership, they were taking up smallholdings on the borders of the unfenced big runs and were registering brands devised to be superimposed on those of their more substantial neighbours. By cross-branding and poddy-dodging (the filching of young or unbranded stock) they were gradually building up small herds and disposing of their marketable cattle to the companies from which they had originally lifted them. In the case of East Kimberley this was almost invariably C.D. & D., but, as M.P. observed, it was little use taking a man to court on a duffing charge unless he had been discovered *in flagrante delicto*. In any case, most pastoralists or managers of the time viewed the activities of the battlers with a tolerant eye since they provided a pool of experienced stock hands always willing to supplement their meagre incomes by taking occasional jobs. It was also reckoned that stock losses from a few smallholders on one's borders were less than from leaving stock open to the depredations of the bush blacks.

It is obvious that M.P. had a considerable respect for Frayne, who would carry out a job he had undertaken where others might well give it up as impossible. The writer Tom Ronan declared, in the biography of his father, *Deep of the Sky*, that he was saving Frayne's story for his next novel, but he did not, alas, live to complete this work. We are left therefore with no more than a vague picture of the tough, determined loner who was later to take up a smallholding near Montajinnie, one of the wildest corners of the Territory.

As regards Jim Campbell, alias 'Sonny Muir', one detects in M.P.'s comments no hint of respect whatever, even for his having devised as his registered brand the famous 'Diamond 40' which cleverly obliterated the brands of the major local landholders. Campbell was 'a rogue and a horse thief'. Jack Beasley was 'a young scallywag' who had teamed up with him in what was described 'a fighting partnership'. 'There is nothing Campbell has not taught Beasley,' M.P. wrote, 'except for what Beasley already knew.'[12]

Doug Moore, who became storekeeper on Ord River station in the early 1900s, wrote about many of these men in the latter years of his life.

> What rogues these chaps were! All had something against them in their past, but were otherwise nice chaps to meet and carouse with. Brennan and Madden had a small holding at Mt. John in Growler's Gully. They were working in with Jack Beasley, then head stockman on the Ord who was partner with old Billy Patterson on the Stirling run and was doing all he could on the side to stock that country up. Jack Kelly of Texas was another likeable chap but a confirmed cattle thief (thought nothing of in those days). In fact no less than six stations were stocked by shaking Ord River cattle. Most of the men employed by us were receiving wages with one hand and robbing us with the other. [D. Moore, unpublished memoirs]

Constable Edmund O'Keefe would also have loomed large in the *Who's Who of the North* at that time, had there been such a book. He had been put in charge of a small police station at Timber Creek near the Victoria River Depot landing after the narrow escape of Fred Ligar and Sam Muggleton near Jasper's Gorge in '95. The gorge was a trap for travellers, and the demand for a police escort over this part of the track had at last been met. O'Keefe was reputed to rule his district with a mixture of Irish blarney and unerring marksmanship, and had set himself up in a tidy bachelor establishment where he kept poultry and a herd of goats. He was at this time in search of some reliable boys to look after the place while he was out on patrol, and had shrewdly decided to enlist them from another district where the people would have less affiliation with his local law-breakers. There were a number of youngsters around Argyle at that time, and four of them, Sambo, Jacky, Delta, and Argyle, 'expressed themselves willing to go along with him'.

The unfortunate Cummins who, as reported by the mailman had taken his own life at Hall's Creek, was the young Englishman whose marriage to Bird had been prevented by her brothers on the eve of the ceremony two years before, when the story of his former association with Oscar Wilde had been brought to their notice. My aunt told me many years later that she had been holidaying at the time on Rottnest Island off Fremantle with her friends the Pierce girls, late of Wyndham, whose father was then Superintendent of the Rottnest Island Penal Settlement. The young people had been entertaining themselves by learning to read the Morse telegraph signals, when this tragic item of news was flashed through.

A few days at Argyle were all M.P. could spare from his urgent mission of buying up the shipload of 800 head of cattle for December. His first place of call was Dunham Station, to interview his uncle Galway Jerry about the sale of cattle and to commiserate with the family on the recent death from fever of their two-year-old Vera. He was shocked to find his uncle, habitually full of banter and good cheer, looking drawn and ill. His aunt, too, had aged in his fifteen months' absence, her once glowing red hair now almost white and her good-humoured face lined from the effects of sorrow, hardship and the pitiless sun. From as far back as he could remember—in the old days on Cooper Creek and later in Brisbane—his Aunt Fan (*née* Neal) had been the life and soul of family gatherings, her buoyant spirits and kindly, capable hands coping with any emergency. Even after the loss of two little girls in Western Queensland, the couple had had the spirit to move out and on, starting again at Ipswich, then at Rosewood on the eastern border of Argyle, and now at this lonely outpost on the Dunham River.

Their two elder boys, Patsy and Jack, were then 'down south' at college, though for young Patsy, whose help was desperately needed on the struggling run, formal schooling, of which he had had only two years, was to end in the coming December. The boy had less taste for scholarship than his younger brother Jack and seemed keen enough to return to the man's life that had begun for him when still a child. A seasoned stockman at fourteen years old, he and two Aborigines had driven a mob of cattle from the Dunham to stock Forrest River Mission in 1897. Their task was accomplished with matter-of-fact efficiency but the mission—and the cattle—were abandoned the following year owing to hostility from local tribes. As soon as he returned from school his mother planned a trip south with her three youngest children, Neal aged seven, Annie, fourteen and Mollie, four. It was hoped that Annie would not lag for too long behind her companions at a convent in Fremantle, where she had been enrolled. At that time both she and the baby Mollie were suffering from what was referred to as 'a touch of fever', and M.P., looking at their wan faces and wasted limbs, felt a sinking of the heart that his aunt's words did nothing to dispel: 'It's a hard country, Michael—all right for the men, maybe, but pity help the women and the little ones.'

He tried to cheer them with talk of rising prices and the opening of the port, and signed up for 100 head of cattle to be delivered at the Wyndham paddock in mid-December. As he rode away from the little mud-brick homestead, past the grave of the baby girl, he wondered whether his cousin Long Michael (M.J.) might after all be right in stating that any man who brought a white woman into the country was irresponsible.

M.J.'s Lissadell Station was, in fact, his next place of call in search of contracts for the coming year. The ride from the Dunham of about forty miles gave him time enough to speculate on the reception he might receive on arrival. If one of M.J.'s Argyle relatives, rebuffed on a previous occasion, failed to call in when anywhere in the vicinity, he would be upbraided for gross discourtesy. But when paid a social call, M.J. would wonder what lay behind it; and when called upon on business, he would suspect a trap. Both J.W. and P.B. shared their father's affection for this odd-man-out relative. They respected his bushmanship and his stockman's expertise, and could smile indulgently at his perversity. Try as he would, however, M.P. found it difficult to adopt a similarly understanding attitude. He could find no excuse for rudeness, especially if directed against himself or one of his own.

There was no one at the Lissadell homestead on his arrival except Ah Sooey, the Chinese cook, who was expecting his boss back the next day. M.P.'s diary, written as usual at night by the light of a kerosene lamp, gives a desolate picture of the stark bachelor establishment.

> It is over two years since I was last here. The place presents the same dismal appearance as before. Except for the old Chinaman

> not a living soul in evidence. The blacks have all cleared out after some recent disturbance—not even a dog or cat to be seen in the camp. There are a few clothes slung loosely about the empty rooms—a few old books and papers, mostly rat-eaten, a basin and a jug (a concession to civilization), in the boss's room.

M.J. rode in from the stock camp next morning with his elder brother Pat, who was at that time helping out as head stockman on Lissadell. Pat had taken up a small property near the bend of the Ord between Ivanhoe and Wyndham. This was known as Mantinea, which was his own nickname, though he was also dubbed Black Pat to distinguish him from various other Patrick relatives of fairer colouring. Both he and M.J. had overlanded with the cattle in the big trek of '83 to '85, and belonged to a local elite of 'first-footers' that did not include M.P. and J.W., who had arrived a year later. Somehow the cousins always managed to convey the impression that the Argyle brothers, with their superior college education, were new chums in the cattle game.

M.P. offered to purchase Lissadell bullocks over the coming year and named what he considered the fair price of £3.10s per head. M.J. said that Forrest, Emanuel were offering £4.10s, but when M.P., in haste to make up the December shipment, agreed to meet that figure. M.J. said he would need a week or two to think it over. He also remarked in passing that he was pleased to hear that the government had had sense enough to retain the quarantine barrier on Northern Territory cattle, and hoped that no unscrupulous parties would persuade them to the contrary. As this was hardly calculated to encourage friendly conversation, M.P. saddled up and rode back across the river to Argyle.

Another ride, this time of a mere twenty-five miles, brought him to Rosewood, where he hoped to clinch a deal with Tom Kilfoyle, uncle to the Lissadell cousins through Kilfoyle's elder sister Margaret, who was their mother. Tom had migrated from Ireland as a lad with his sister and brother-in-law, and had later gone with Patsy Durack on his first ill-fated expedition into Western Queensland in 1863. After the establishment of Thylungra on Cooper's Creek, Tom had worked fairly consistently for Grandfather, and in 1882 he had gone in the party led by Stumpy Michael Durack to explore the country from Cambridge Gulf to Beagle Bay. He had also been among the drovers of the cattle trek to Kimberley, and had soon afterwards taken up the 1,174-square mile property, Rosewood Station, in partnership with Galway Jerry Durack and Tom Hayes, another member of the big trek. That partnership was dissolved in 1896 when Hayes retired to Victoria and

Jerry Durack moved to Dunham River. Kilfoyle had thereafter gone into partnership with J. J. Holmes, member for East Fremantle.

Kilfoyle and M.P. had shared a number of expeditions, sometimes droving cattle for sale to the Territory mining centres in the early '90s, and at others exploring unoccupied country. On one such trip they had marked out a block on Auvergne which they named Kildurk, a combination of their two names; it was to pass into the hands of M.P.'s eldest son half a century later[3]. Since Tom Kilfoyle had assumed full management of the Rosewood property, M.P. and his brothers had seen many a calf with a Rosewood brand running beside an Argyle cow and had often been inclined to register formal protest. Their father, however, had felt differently. Kilfoyle, he would remind them, had been reared in a hard school: poddy-dodging had been the butter on his bread when many a time there had been precious little bread to butter. 'He's been a faithful friend and servant to this family, and I'd not now begrudge him a bit of a tarry-diddle with his branding iron.'

Kilfoyle had married rather late in life a member of the Byrne family[4] (also of long association with the Duracks), and their only child Jack had been born in Darwin in 1893. M.P. records on this visit: 'Their lives are wrapped up in the boy. He commands them at will.'

He found Tom in genial mood and willing enough for C.D. & D. to handle his cattle for the coming year. He agreed that Forrest, Emanuel should 'keep to their own backyard' and that the tick barrier was 'bosh'. M.P., expounding on the anomalies of the situation, explained that cattle were allowed in from some adjacent parts of the Territory—namely Rosewood, Ord River, and Newry Stations—duty-free, but were banned entry from Auvergne and all points east, although Newry and Auvergne cattle had been mixing for years. The 600 head he had bought in anticipation of the lifting of the ban from the Territory stations of Newcastle Waters and Hodgeson Downs had been driven to Auvergne by Fred Morch, a good man with cattle whose services he was eager to retain. Fred had been part of many epic droving-treks, and had been one of Nat Buchanan's team of seventy men who brought 20,000 head of cattle to stock Northern Territory runs for Fisher and Lyons in 1882. Of Irish-Norwegian extraction and reared in Victoria, he and his brothers Tom and Jack were held in some esteem among Northern cattlemen. He was then waiting at Auvergne for word to bring mobs across from other Territory stations, but if nothing was resolved within the next few weeks he would be forced to move on and find jobs elsewhere. 'Kilfoyle in agreement with all I have to say!'

Business completed, Mrs Kilfoyle, ever kindly and talkative, launched upon a flood of reminiscences relating to Patsy Durack and his wife—'God rest their souls!' Indeed, and it was an honoured name their children had been left to carry on, and wasn't it time they were thinking of matrimony? Mrs Tom knew all about the nice girl in Brisbane whom P.B. hoped to make his wife, but what, she asked, of M.P. and his brother J.W.? It was nonsense to say that the country was not fit for white women. Look at her own family—never as happy in their lives as when they came to Kimberley to take over the Three Mile Hotel! M.P. must of course have heard that Mantinea Pat had a fine girl in the south, and that although M.J. had not yet told them so himself it seemed that there was romance in the offing for him as well. The idea of either of his cousins, at the ripe old ages of forty-six and forty-four, being involved in romance surprised my father, though it could well explain the recent extensions to Black Pat's shack in Mantinea paddock. There had been no such signs evident at Lissadell, and it seemed highly unlikely that anyone as stubborn as M.J. would abandon his stand about bringing white women to Kimberley. M.P. mused that if his cousin intended setting up a domicile in the south, he might be considering the sale of his northern property. It would make a very valuable adjunct to the C.D. & D. estate, and also no doubt to the pastoral empire of Forrest, Emanuel. Should the rival company get such a footing in East Kimberley, it would, M.P. considered, be disastrous. He did not, however, share those thoughts with Kilfoyle and his good wife, who, friendly though they were, he knew held their nephews' interests next to their own.

5
Dreams and Realities

October 1898–July 1899

'The wet' set in before November, and the swollen creeks and rivers came tumbling down to the gulf. The spear grass sprang rank and green, and the cracked plains, turned to bog, set free a long-imprisoned multitude of exultant frogs. Locusts in their thousands flickered and flashed in the humid air, and mosquitoes descended in hungry hordes. In later years the summer season would be put in, for the most part, around the station homesteads; a time for repairing saddles and packs, making hobbles and greenhide ropes, for drawing up inventories and orders for the coming year, reading out-of-date papers and books donated by sympathetic southerners to be circulated by the Australian Inland Mission. For the first thirty-five years of settlement, however, it was a time for business as usual.

Many years later we would listen to stories of this period from Bill (W.J.C.) Jones, one of C.D. & D.'s veteran employees. Gazing from the Ivanhoe Station verandah across the steaming, rain-sodden countryside, we would ask how on earth they had contrived to muster cattle and drive them to Wyndham under such conditions. Bill, shrugging his bony shoulders and puffing on his pipe, would reply laconically: 'We had no option. There were no freezing works in the country then and beef on the hoof had to be shipped away all seasons of the year. A man will do anything if his livelihood depends on it.'

So P.B. was mustering on Argyle, McCaully at Ivanhoe, Frayne, Madden and Jim Patterson at Newry. Their mobs, with others to come in from the Dunham station, Rosewood, Lissadell, and Mantinea, were calculated to make up the required total. All was proceeding to plan until a wire from M.J. in Wyndham informed M.P. that both he and Tom Kilfoyle had decided to give their year's contract to Forrest, Emanuel. M.P., wondering in his exasperation what influence his cousin had exerted on Kilfoyle to cause this sudden change of face, swam his horses across the flooded Ord at Ivanhoe and made his way to the port with all possible haste. For the next few days the line between Wyndham and Fremantle ran hot with telegrams in Bentley's code trying to ascertain the next move. Since it was now impossible to get the necessary 800 head before the December date, the *Tangier* was at the last minute diverted on another mission and her Wyndham assignment postponed until early January. This was calculated to allow time for negotiations further afield and also for more pressure to be brought to bear in relation to the tick barrier.

It was as well that M.P. had, at this time, more congenial thoughts to occupy his mind. Awaiting him in Wyndham were two letters from Meg Wilson in reply to his several communications written from the ship. Among other items of bright chatter, she conveyed news of his sisters with whom she had, since his departure, attended concerts and bazaars, visited the new Zoological Gardens in South Perth, and viewed an exhibition of modern wonders including a self-propelled conveyance known as a 'motor car'. In replies left for the next south-bound ship, M.P. was able to enclose the first results obtained from the camera which, together with the paraphernalia for developing his pictures, had been given him by his brother Jerry for his last birthday. These would, he said, give her some idea of how greatly the northern landscape differed from that of the south, though only if some genius should one day invent colour photography would it be possible to convey the true, many-hued magnificence of that rugged land. Hesitant as yet to mention the feelings he had for her, he made so bold as to confess that the memory of their time together was the fond preoccupation of his long and lonely rides. To be sure, he explained, he seldom travelled without the company of either Boxer or Ulysses, both good, pleasant-natured boys, but their conversational range was, as she might imagine, somewhat limited.

No sooner was he back at Argyle than his urgent quest for cattle contracts took M.P., with Ulysses for company, to interview the manager of Ord River Station. This ride upriver of nearly 100 miles was an uncomfortable expedition at that time of year. Accepted casually enough by M.P. and his contemporaries of that era, it would be regarded as a Spartan ordeal today. Thirty miles a day was about the limit that a good horse could travel in that environment, with minimum time off to boil a midday billy and select a night camp in time to use the last light for hobbling out the horses, getting a fire alight (not always easy when the wood was wet), knocking up a damper and 'a bit of a feed'. If it rained during the day, the travellers simply rode on; if at night, they would take shelter of a sort under their berkmyer ground-sheets. Even nets were inadequate protection against the hordes of blood-thirsty mosquitoes that infested the sodden countryside. No traveller, however, expected to sleep soundly on the track, least of all the boss who must doze with half an eye open for the first glimmer of the morning star, when he would rouse his boy to get the horses, then stoke or relight the fire to boil the morning billy while he cut the damper and a slice or two from a chunk of salt beef.

On this occasion the tedious trip was, after all, to no avail since William Osmond, the owner of the property, had given his manager no authority to make negotiations. Osmond, a retired naval officer, had in 1884 gone into partnership with Joseph Panton, a Melbourne magistrate, in taking up the 3,365,000-acre property of which 1,000,000 acres sprawled over into the Northern Territory. The run had been stocked by Nat Buchanan, together with the Gordons and the Cahills and the redoubtable Bob Button who became its first manager. Ten years later Osmond had bought out his partner, and from his place of retirement in Stawell, Victoria, had directed a succession of discouraged managers[1] by enigmatic telegrams and autocratic letters. Where other stations were taking from £2 to £4.10s for their cattle, Osmond refused to sell at less than £7, a price which buyers would agree to only at the end of the year when desperately hard-pressed for numbers. The then manager, Charles Young, told M.P. that he suspected Osmond's only interest in the property was as a potential sales investment, and that he planned to sell out as soon as he had built up enough stock to strike a worthwhile deal. This was understandable in view of the fact that he had made little or nothing out of the unwieldy and intractable estate, but from the point of view of a conscientious manager the situation was frustrating. Osmond had clearly no interest in improving the property. He demanded regular reports but was quite unresponsive to constructive suggestions or the occasional request for some modest amenity. The few provisions made for Young's wife and two children had been put in at their own expense, while the kerosene lamp, chinaware, glass, and cutlery that graced their table were their private property. This did not surprise M.P., as he knew well enough that from the point of view of absentee owners white women and children were superfluous. If a man happened to be so encumbered, he was soon made to understand that he must expect no concessions from 'head office'.

M.P. was much impressed by Mrs Young, a refined and cheerful young woman who made light of her problems and kept up a remarkable standard in the face of so many disabilities. He approved of her insisting that the men wore coats at the meal table, regardless of the temperature, a rule that had pertained at Argyle in his mother's day and had been kept up ever since.

Here, as on all other properties he visited, the conversation turned inevitably to heavy stock losses at the hands of the Aborigines. The situation, as clearly enough stated some time before by a Government

Resident of the Northern Territory, had intensified throughout the north with every year.

> The blacks are beginning to realise that the white man ... is interfering with what they properly enough, from their point of view, regard as their natural rights. Their hunting grounds and game preserves are being disturbed and their food supply both diminished and rendered uncertain ... They can no longer, as a few years ago, travel from one watering place to another and be certain that on arrival there would be flocks of wild fowl to be snared. Nor can they, as of old, when they desired a repast of snakes, iguanas or other reptiles, set fire to the first piece of well grassed country they encounter. The stock holder uses the billabongs for cattle and very vigorously lets the blackfellows understand that it is at their peril they put a firestick to it. Naturally ... the natives will resist the intrusion of the whites. They will set the grass alight when they are so minded and, if hungry, or by way of reprisal, will spear cattle when they think they are out of range of a rifle. How to deal equably with these Aborigines, while facilitating the settlement and stocking of the country by Europeans is a problem easier to state than to solve. That settlement and stocking must and will go on is certain—that outrages will be committed on both sides is probable; but even those who do not claim to be philanthropists are not satisfied with the contemplation that the blacks are to be improved off the face of the earth ... [From the *Quarterly Report* of J. Langdon Parsons, Government Resident for the Northern Territory, Darwin, January 1885]

Reported cases of cattle speared in the Kimberley district over the current year had totalled 1,897 beasts, nearly 300 more than in the previous two years; and this was apart from the effect on the herds of being constantly harried and chased. White settlers were unanimous in the opinion that existing police action was sadly inadequate, and were urging that outpost police depots should be set up in areas where most of the marauding went on. It was also suggested that prison terms should be made more arduous, as Aborigines were evidently finding the good treatment and good tucker in the Wyndham gaol so much to their liking that they had little fear of being taken a second time. The practice that pertained on some stations, including Argyle, of killing cattle at regular intervals for the bush natives was not meeting with much success, since outside people coming in for beef were inclined to overstay their welcome and to cause trouble in the station camps, while in any case, the worst offenders—'the hardened desperadoes'—kept well out of the white man's way.

A certain element in the south, where (as the northern settlers did not hesitate to point out) the problem had long since been dealt with by military action, was given to expounding on the rights of the Aborigines. Was there nothing then to be said for the rights of the Kimberley pastoralist, struggling to set up an essential industry in an otherwise unproductive wilderness? It is hard to escape the conclusion that the 'firmer measures' generally advocated meant more ruthless shooting of offenders who were 'resisting arrest', and, for those taken into custody, more ready recourse to the lash.

In a surprisingly short time M.P. was able to report that a police depot had been set up at a place called Wild Dog, about half-way between Ord River and Argyle homesteads, and that a more frequent patrol was being carried out between the various stations. The methods used would seem to have been effective, as the estimated number of cattle speared fell abruptly in the following year, to considerably less than half. By what number the Aboriginal population fell in the process is a matter for speculation, though it is doubtful whether there were as many natives shot in police raids as is sometimes alleged. It was by no means easy to surprise the ever-vigilant tribespeople, well versed as they were in the arts of evasion and camouflage, and it should also be taken into account that whereas a police officer received an allowance for every man or woman captured and brought in, a dead body profited him nothing. Punitive expeditions organized after the spearing of a white man, and including a number of hastily recruited 'special police'—usually mates of the deceased, hot with avenging fervour—were another matter.

There is no doubt, however, that the increase of police depots and native assistants had far-reaching and tragic side-effects for the Kimberley tribespeople. Miserable processions of anything from twenty to forty natives, suspects (never discharged), and 'witnesses', chained neck to neck on their way to Wyndham, became a common sight throughout the countryside. Though the police did not always get the number of men they hoped for, they frequently came upon groups of women, children, and old people, either hastily abandoned on the approach of the patrol or awaiting the return of their men from hunting or the performance of some sacred ceremony. As the settlers were usually on the lookout for likely young helpers, the patrols were thus able to provide them with youths and young women, who as often as not settled down well enough to station life. The women, while serving an unofficial role with the white workers, became officially attached to the Aboriginal stationmen, whether or not such marriages were 'straight' by tribal law, and regardless of husbands or promised husbands left behind in the bush camps or taken into custody. Some of these alliances seem to have worked out all right; others were the cause of constant trouble and savage reprisals.

The disturbance of tribal balance also caused conflict among bush natives who, having been deprived of their own wives, looked for substitutes in other directions, the result being endless vendettas of which the white man knew and cared nothing. The Aborigines themselves attest to the fact that the number of blacks killed by whites or whites killed by blacks was nothing to the number of natives killed, from this time on, by their own countrymen. In the words of one of the oldtime Aboriginal stockmen: 'Everything in this country gone galloping wild. The black man don't know where he is.'[2]

It is clear that the Aborigines lived in fear not only of the police but of each other, and that this breakdown of trust caused the tribes to divide into warring groups or factions. Some of these, controlled by proud and strongly patriotic elders, would have no truck with the white man and his mischievous ways. There were no doubt many such long-forgotten idealists who died in defence of their sacred past or from grief at its inevitable disruption. Others, seeing like the writing on the wall those symbols of white authority slashed deep into the trunks of the boab trees, would gladly enough have exchanged submission for sustenance and security. It was soon made clear to them, however, that the privilege of the white man's patronage was granted only to the chosen few, for the time had not yet come when white workers were at a premium in the Kimberleys.

This breakdown of tribal ecology was soon reflected in the appearance of a people who not long before had been described as 'fine, sturdy specimens'. Bush natives brought in by police patrols or drifting in and out the station camps now gave a very different unpression. M.P. reports significantly about this time:

> 23.10.98: Shot a beast today for bush niggers hanging about the station—the most wretched, haggard looking lot of 38 individuals I ever saw together—all suffering from sore eyes, sickly and hopeless looking.

One detects in such contemporary jottings a note of puzzled exasperation rather than of real sympathy for these miserable dispossessed. On the other hand, the attitude of the white boss towards his Aboriginal worker was often one of genuine affection and concern. It was the sentiment he might feel towards some wild creature he had tamed and trained to useful purposes, and by whose intelligent response and devotion he was touched and gratified.

The Aboriginal worker, for his part, was pleased to be identified with a particular white master and enjoyed the prestige of being classifed as a good stockman or handyman in the new order of things. He took a real interest and pride in his job and appreciated the security it represented in times of bewildering change. In fact, his pragmatism matched that of the invading European. He accepted the taking-over of his country by the white man quite fatalistically and found that the new law, even at its hardest and most mysterious, was less so than many aspects of tribal life. As he had bowed to the law laid down by the elders, and would continue to do with some measure of compromise, so he now accepted the command of the white boss, the more definite and inflexible the better respected. His lot might have been, as can be argued, a form of slavery; for he received no money for his services, and although he was technically free to return to his people in the bush, this entailed risk and deprivations that he was not prepared to accept. There is little doubt, however, that he was happier in his servitude than his tribal-living countrymen in their liberty. He at least knew where he stood, and knew that as long as he played the white man's game he would be assured of adequate tucker, with the addition of tobacco, clothing, blankets, and other pleasing perquisites. He also knew that by a process of attrition and subtle intrigue—in which fields he excelled his white masters—he would succeed in bringing a steady stream of tribal connections into the orbit of white responsibility.

M.P.'s reasoning on the Aboriginal question was very much that of his contemporaries. It was surely the duty they owed their fellow Australians to utilize this immense area of natural pastureland, and in the process to train the country's savage children to useful occupations. If some fell victim to the folly of standing in the way of progress, it was unfortunate; but was this not the story of every confrontation of a primitive with a more developed culture? Some aspects of this situation may, however, have come harder to M.P. than to many. A man of naturally mild and scholarly disposition, he had been set down by circumstances in a region where violence of one kind or another was a commonplace of life. He never knew around what corner the next contingency or disaster awaited him—the result of accident, foul play, tribal conflict, fever, or drunken brawl.

During these months his journals are punctuated with tragic or exasperating incidents typical of the environment. The fourteen-year-old Annie Durack, whom he had earlier reported being mildly indisposed from fever, died soon after his visit to the Dunham at the end of '98. Fever was also rife at Argyle, though the only death recorded over this period was from another cause. Returning one day to the homestead after a short absence, M.P.

sensed that all was not well. Passing the native camp on the river bank, he had seen no smoke rising from the cooking-fires. There was no *yakai* of Aboriginal welcome, not so much as the bark of a dog to herald his coming. Since all the stockmen were out in the camp, there was no one on the premises except the cook, whom M.P. found in a highly nervous frame of mind. Old Annie, he was informed, had been speared to death and Pumpkin's wife Valley had been severely wounded the day before. All the camp blacks, except for the injured woman and two frightened boys, Joker and Jimmer, had cleared out, and M.P. could get little sense out of any of them beyond the fact that the culprit was, of all people, Charlie the gardener, a young man of apparently gentle and considerate temperament. The story, or as much of it as the whites would ever know, gradually emerged. Charlie had attacked the young woman first, and when old Annie had tried to interfere he had turned and speared her through the heart.

> 17.5.99: The poor old woman [M.P. records] deserved a better fate after nine years of faithful service. She will certainly be missed as an attendant of the cows, knowing them all so well as she did. She was also good at washing and ironing and proud of all the work on the place. Valley able to walk about but suffers badly.

The men returned next day and Constable O'Brien arrived fortuitously on patrol. A further diary entry leaves the end of the story unresolved.

> 19.5.99: Sent Ulysses and Joe off with O'Brien equipped with rifles and 30 rounds of cartridges each. O'Brien holding Joker and Jimmer prisoner as suspects they may be spies. Wesley Lyttleton scouting around with Pumpkin and Boxer. Saw some niggers over on the hill but they would not come down. Could hear blacks down the creek last night singing out and knocking stones. Everyone stirred up over the trouble.

M.P., like most of his contemporaries, had strong views about entrusting Aborigines with firearms but, as his diaries make amply clear, Pumpkin, Boxer, and Ulysses were regarded as exceptions.[3]

Pumpkin's having taken Valley to wife in 1893 had no doubt contravened some tribal law and left a long-smouldering resentment, over which young Charlie had been delegated to act under tribal authority. The death of the older woman would seem to have been sufficient to demonstrate the displeasure of the injured party. At all events, no further attempt was made on Valley's life or on that of her husband, whom even the most fundamental of the Mirriwung elders evidently held in awe. As for Charlie, it was not long before he was back at Argyle where, as time went on, he earned the respect of both Aboriginal and white, and was generally accepted as head of the native camp.

Among many other setbacks and annoyances was the continual breaking down of the telegraph line between Wyndham and Broome, East Kimberley's line of communication with Fremantle, owing to the Aboriginal habit of climbing the poles and knocking off the insulators for spearheads.

Then there were the machinations of a local fraternity of horse-thieves who regarded their skill at altering and disguising brands as something of an art form, and a cause therefore for self-congratulation. Among them, besides Beasley and Campbell, was a shady character named Callaghan and one Ben Bridge, a likeable rascal and superb horseman who was said to have escaped from every gaol between Murrurundi, New South Wales, and the West Australian border. All were then employed on and off as contract drovers for C.D. & D. One encounter with the group is thus recorded:

> 1.5.99: Back to Newry to meet the drovers. I recognize one of my horses in the plant that has no right to be there. They request me to witness that it bears only the plain L but on closer inspection the letter E is clearly visible. They now admit, in simulated surprise, that there is something apparent which they did not see before. Beasley at last tells me the facts. His brother did the deed having plucked the brand with a sharp bladed knife. After I dismiss Callaghan he asks me for a letter of reference! I promise him the same if I find there is no foundation in what I have heard regarding him. He tells me he will be cruising about here for some time, which I can hardly regard as good news for our company. Beasley agrees to send the contentious gin Jenny back to O'Keefe at Argyle.

M.P. and his peers in the cattle game, while they might forgive a certain amount of poddy-dodging, could find no excuse for horse-stealing or stock-spearing. When it came, however, to circumventing a prohibition that did not suit themselves, they regarded it not as law-breaking but as rightful action against injustice and a blow in the cause of progress.

Somehow the first mobs of the year were made up, despite broken contracts and the obstructive tactics of an officious stock inspector named Stephens intent on fining the company for 'falsely alleged' breaches of the droving act. ('C.D. & D. mulched again, to the extent of £2! The R.M. had his decision prepared and read from his note book—clearly prejudiced before hearing evidence.')

On arrival at Wyndham the mobs were driven, slipping and sliding, down a steep gap in the Bastion Mountain, herded into yards below, and finally manoeuvred through a race that ran the length of the jetty to the ship. The loading was carried out at night to avoid the intense heat, and was always attended with a great deal of noise and drama. The tide, subject to a twenty-six-foot rise and fall, ran fast and strong, and the men on the job, having put in time at the hotel while awaiting their late-night call to action, were usually drunk. Beasts were crushed in the race, some broke their necks falling into the hatch, and some were prone to cause dangerous confusion by turning at the entrance to the ship and panicking the cattle behind them.

Complaints, however, were not all on the side of the pastoralists. The slowly rising confidence of Australian workers' movements in their efforts to legalize trade unions and create a new concept of fair play, by the establishment of Boards of Conciliation and an Arbitration Court (soon to be realised), was reflected in Wyndham in January 1899 by a strike of the stokers on the *Tangier*. This, where C.D. & D. were concerned, was the last straw in a desperate effort to get away the first shipment of the year. M.P. saw no validity in the demands of the 'firemen' for better pay. He records with a note of satisfaction: 'The trouble makers tried. Three sentenced to four weeks hard labour. The rest acquitted as not on the ship's articles.'

As the year went on, and C.D. & D.'s shipping programne became increasingly difficult to maintain, it is hardly to be wondered that the anomaly of the border restriction seemed ever more irksome and absurd. Waiting on Auvergne were 2,000 tick-free cattle, together with the ace drover, Morch, whose services the company was eager to retain for the introduction of a further supply of bullocks from market-hungry Territory growers. By May the temptation to evade the frustrating law had evidently become too much, and it is clear from M.P.'s guarded references that the cattle were gradually 'introduced' on to the Newry run and thence 'boxed' with other bullocks, to meet the requisite numbers. The various station brands had by this time become so mixed over the years of trading that even an astute and hostile stock inspector like Stephens could not discern which had and which had not been recently introduced.

Entries of 11 and 12 May 1899 read as follows:

> With J.W. meeting cattle on arrival Wyndham. Not a soul yet knows. Marvellous how this secret has been kept ... Cattle successfully yarded and away.

Morch, having delivered the bullocks at Ascot paddock, was by that time on his way back to the Territory for another mob. It is obvious that, although there were plenty of good stockmen available at that time, men of this calibre, experienced in every hazard of their calling and above all sober, were not so easy to come by. Carbon copies of M.P.'s meticulously kept books contain frequent letters such as one of this time to a drover named McKenzie:

> We regret to inform you that we have no further need for your services. This is the third occasion now on which you have broken faith with us re abstaining from drink while in charge of the bullocks. You will understand that you have a big responsibility to us with charge of 400 head of cattle and we could not establish a precedent for such gross negligence as has been exhibited on the last three occasions. We cannot let the matter pass however without thanking you for gentlemanly demeanour in general and the willingness with which you have always otherwise worked for us. [M.P.D., Argyle, to Jack McKenzie, 5.7.99]

Within a few weeks of his dismissal the intemperate McKenzie was back on the books, but the point had been made.

It meant a good deal to a stockman to be employed by 'the firm', and a reference from M.P.D. was as good as a note of credit anywhere in the Kimberleys or the Northern Territory. His letters of direction to his drovers had an imperious ring that sent employees on their way with a sense of working under royal command:

> You will arrive at Sturt Creek on the 9th Aug., or not later than that date . . . Mr Stretch informs us that he could supply 200 head and about the same number are to come from Flora Valley . . . You will see Mr Buchanan on your way up and he will let you know pretty definitely what number he will have . . . Mr. Joe Bridge will have a few at Turkey Creek . . . Mr. J. Durack of the Dunham writes that he has 168 head which you will get on the way down . . . [M.P.D. to F. Morch, 24.7.99]

For one drover only did he thus slightly modify his pre-emptory mode of address:

> We want you to proceed to Auvergne next Monday. If the feed and water is not good at the lower gorge you had better come straight on to the Keep . . . I expect to meet you at Auvergne and then arrange a definite date for arrival in Wyndham. [M.P.D., Argyle, to Sir A.T. Cockburn-Campbell, 23.10.01]

This was to Sir Alexander Thomas Cockburn-Campbell, Australia's only baronet, who had succeeded to the title in 1892 on the death of his father, erstwhile President of the Legislative Council and part-owner and managing editor of the *West Australian* newspaper. The young baronet, supposedly on a romantic urge to see Mount Cockburn near Wyndham which had been named for one of his illustrious forebears, had come to the port in 1898 to serve for a short term as Clerk of Courts. Soon bored by both the town and the task, he applied for a job with C.D. & D. as a means of seeing something of station life before returning to Perth.

He was a natural stockman and popular with his workmates, and when the time came for him to take his leave at the end of the year M.P. was sorry to see him go. Surprised to see him back within two or three months, he was glad enough to put him on the books again but as the years went by and he continued to return, each time after a shorter absence and ever more forthright declarations of 'getting out for good', M.P.'s welcome became less hearty. Much as he appreciated Sir Alec's reliability and his occasional company, he felt about him as he did about all men of superior education and supposedly greater potential who allowed themselves to succumb to the country's peculiar and eventually corrosive magnetism. He certainly saw no point in a man who bore one of the oldest and most distinguished titles in Great Britain[4] being prepared to accept for himself the crude conditions and uncultured company of an outback stock camp. In some respects a typical romantic of his era, no one could wax more enthusiastic than M.P. about the grandeur of the northern landscape and the wonder of its wildlife, but he was under no illusions about the 'glorious freedom' of a bushman's lot. For himself he was determined never to become enslaved by the country to the point of being unable to see it, in the final, practical analysis, as a piece of real estate. He never regarded it as the setting for a permanent way of life for his family, but rather as a means to the ultimate attainment of a more satisfactory lifestyle somewhere else. In the interim he was prepared to make the best of it and to do all in his power to further the fortunes of C.D. & D.

There can be no doubt that he was a careful and diligent steward for the firm and kept a keen eye on every aspect of station management, whether involving thousands of pounds or a few shillings. The following extract from a letter written to some imprudently open-handed employee in C.D. & D.'s Wyndham store is typical:

> I notice in your invoice per drover McKenzie some items supplied to boy Billy of Auvergne. A pair of trousers (15/6). A blanket

> (22/6). There is an overstock of blankets at Auvergne as I ascertained on my last visit. Six gin's dresses. Why six? I could understand his getting one for his lubra. Only the other day some dresses were sent to Auvergne from Argyle ... Perfume! Why in the name of goodness would you supply a nigger with perfume—unless it be that the olfactory organs in your office find it a *sine qua non*? The other items, although numerous, I find the necessity for. Trusting this will receive your earnest attention ... [M.P.D., Argyle, to C.D. & D., Wyndham, April 1899]

Other letters and diary entries pertain to building contracts and to his careful inspection of all work in progress:

> Inspecting fence being put up by Barber and Villiers. Not satisfactory. They have not stuck to their contract. I insist they butt all posts now cut, go over the fence and re-ram it, and, to compensate for bad workmanship, they must complete the job with extra strength and firmness.

In another area, M.P.'s prospects over this period had taken a satisfactory turn. Meg Wilson had responded so encouragingly to his intimations of regard that he had written soon afterwards asking her to be his wife. Her reply, dispatched from Wyndham to Argyle by special courier, reached him about a month later. Joy of joys! With many expressions of tenderness she confessed to reciprocating his feelings. She did not believe that the fact of her family's being prominent members of the Presbyterian, and his of the Roman Catholic, Church should present any serious impediment to their marriage, but she thought it prudent that they should tread discreetly for a while, letting the idea of their attachment 'grow on' their respective relatives. M.P. acceded to her request, knowing that most of his own people already knew and liked Meg, and confident that they were more broad-minded than to object to a mixed marriage. If they did, it would be just too bad, for whereas he regarded it as his right and duty to obstruct, if he saw fit, any controversial plans entertained by his younger brothers and sisters, none of them had ever ventured to oppose his own. And so, despite his problems, he rode the countryside with a lighter heart than for many years.

P.B., who had had the least breaks of the three brothers during his nine years in Kimberley, had set sail for Brisbane in January to put his case in person to his beloved. M.P. had been careful to warn him, before his departure, against painting too glowing a picture of their situation, for he knew that Pat dearly loved Kimberley and even at the worst of times, while agreeing that conditions might be improved, could find no fault with the country itself. 'Where else on earth,' he once asked of his fellow stockmen, 'would a man see a sunrise like that?' 'Where else on earth,' a cynical member of his team rejoined, 'would a man have to be on the job before sunrise, anyway?'

By July P.B. was back, the news of his engagement to Eva Hughes having preceded him by excited telegram some time before. Always in good spirits, he was now quite euphoric. 'The bushies,' he declared, 'won't know what's struck them when a girl like Eva turns up in Kimberley!' It apparently did not occur to him, M.P. confided to his diary, that a girl like Eva might be equally nonplussed by the bushies. Nor did P.B. realise that he was treading on delicate ground when he touched on the religious aspect of his romance. Having always contended that 'marriages were made in heaven', Pat considered his prospective union to be a case in point. Eva was the good Catholic daughter of a Catholic family, otherwise much as he admired her he would never, he declared, have let their attachment lead to the altar.

M.P., smiling quietly at his brother's simple outlook on life, pondered the tender endearments in his Meg's most recent letters. She had at last decided to confide the fact of their attachment to her mother, feeling by this time more confident of her approval. M.P. did not have long to wait for Mrs Wilson's reactions to news of their romance.

> 4.7.99: A telegram from Meg this morning. Am quite at a loss to understand its meaning. Wired her at once requesting an explanation but her reply rendered me no wiser. Am totally nonplussed. P.B. having now returned from Brisbane I made up my mind to start down direct. Saw the cattle down the race and on board myself just before the ship's departure. Confident that Meg will explain all to me on my arrival.

6

A Bid for Empire

July–December 1899

Connor and Doherty assumed that M.P.'s unannounced arrival betokened his eagerness for first-hand information about their latest business developments. They bore him off immediately to inspect the firm's new slaughterhouses and abattoirs adjacent to the port, talking enthusiastically the while of glowing prospects opening up in various directions. The metropolitan and goldfields markets were increasing steadily, the railway line now extending from Kalgoorlie to Menzies and soon to link up with the further meat-hungry populations of Leonora and Laverton. All that was required to establish C.D. & D.'s ascendancy in the cattle trade was a steady supply of beef from the Northern Territory. The border was still officially closed but it was deemed unlikely that the government would or could enforce its manifestly unreasonable law. It was now up to M.P. to secure as much cattle from Territory properties as possible, and in the process to have a good look over Victoria River Downs, for Connor had received inside information that Goldsbrough Mort, who had taken over this property ten years before, were in financial straits and anxious to sell out at a reasonable figure. Connor believed that Victoria River's main problems had been due to lack of markets and poor prices but that with the present promise of expansion these difficulties should be overcome in the near future. If the firm could make a successful bid, they would be in possession of the biggest cattle empire in the world, and as such would become indeed a name to conjure with.

Unlike his partners, M.P. was never romantically impressed by the sheer size of a pastoral property, for he knew well enough that, in North Australia at least, it bore little necessary relationship to productivity. He had, moreover, seen a good deal of 'the big run' over the past few years and had formed the impression that 12,060 square miles (7,718,400 acres) was more than one manager and a handful of assistants could be expected to control effectively. He believed it would have been better broken up into several associated runs such as comprised their own estate, which was almost the same total size: but this operation called for more capital outlay than was then at the firm's disposal. Nonetheless, he agreed to do his best on all counts and to carry out the proposed investigations with an open mind. Excusing himself from more prolonged discussion and 'in a state of mind betwixt hopefulness and foreboding', he took a cab to the Wilsons' Mount Lawley residence.

> 17.7.99: My visit to Lytton a complete surprise [he records]. I am met at the door by a neighbour, Mrs. Humphries, who announces to Meg my arrival. We meet but, alas, not as we parted. She receives me with studied coldness. We sit down together but I fail to arrive at any explanation for her behaviour beyond that she now sees there could be no surety for our mutual happiness, she being firm in the profession of her own belief in the Scottish Church and I in mine. I had thought she realised that I am committed, as a Catholic, to our marriage being attested in my own Church, a proposition to which her mother strongly objects. I return abruptly to the Doherty residence where I am staying. Mrs. Doherty and self discuss the problem up to 3 a.m.

One pictures this concerned family friend explaining to the distraught young man the reality of Catholic and Protestant relationships in Perth society. Catholics in the colony's earlier decades had been synonymous with poor Irish immigrants, ex-convicts, or their descendants, of no social standing and little public influence. Admittedly the situation had changed since the gold-rush era which had attracted Catholics of higher educational status, many of whom had become prominent in business, press and parliamentary circles. The fact remained, however, that local society was largely dominated by the descendants of its genteel and staunchly Protestant pioneers. Catholics were blackballed from its exclusive Weld Club (ironically enough named for the colony's only Catholic Governor), and were quite unacceptable as suitors for the daughters of established families—not necessarily on personal grounds, but in view of the untenable prospect of acquiring 'Romanist' descendants. Mrs Doherty insisted that it was no use M.P.'s waiting for Meg to change her mind, for her mother's convictions were manifestly too strong for her. He should face the facts and keep his eyes open for a nice Catholic girl. M.P. had been inclined at last to agree with her, but at ten o'clock next morning he was handed a telegram asking him to call at Lytton again that day and signed 'with fondest love'. He set out post-haste with hope again high in his breast.

> 18.7.99: But alas for the varying mood of womenkind! How truly the poet describes them as 'variable as the shade by the light of

> quivering aspen made.' . . . So we meet once again to talk over our separation of the past ten months and the feelings we have expressed that are for me certainly the same. She but reiterates, however, her decision of yesterday. I take a late train back to Claremont where I talk with Mrs. D. and the two girls [his sisters] until the early hours.

M.P.'s disappointment was not the only subject of conversation, for family romances of a happier nature had been burgeoning meanwhile. Coincidentally, his sister Mary had also formed an attachment for a Presbyterian, a young man of Scottish parentage named James Ebenezer Davidson. Born and educated in Adelaide, he had joined the Adelaide Steamship Company and had first met the family when he came to Wyndham as purser on the *Junee* in the previous year. The Durack brothers, who maintained a final say in their sisters' affairs, had no objection to an engagement, for Jim Davidson was not only amenable on the religious issue but was personable, intelligent, and an amusing companion. He had, moreover, an astute head for figures and the shrewd eye for business of his Scottish lineage—faculties he had recently agreed to put to the service of the company as accountant/bookkeeper.

M.P. took part as best he could in the happy family chatter concerning P.B.'s impending marriage. Eva, his sisters declared, had many times avowed that she would never marry a man on the land, and there she was preparing a trousseau to wed one in the remotest wilderness imaginable. They put it down to the eloquence of Pat's persuasion and his remarkable staying power. Perhaps, M.P. mused, he had himself given in too easily to a decision in which his beloved had been obviously directed against her own inclinations.

Before embarking on the *Tangier*'s return trip to Wyndham he made a last visit to Lytton in the desperate hope that Meg might again exercise the prerogative of her variable sex. He was unable to see her alone, though whether at her own request or on her mother's insistence, he was not to know.

> 20.7.99: I will refrain from saying anything further with regard to our meeting and parting. I will scarcely need being reminded of it by my diary for its memory must remain buried forever in the depths of my heart. What changes time may work with regards to our feelings is difficult to predict but certainly the thought that we may never meet again as before is no happy one to carry on my way.

Waving back to the Dohertys and his sisters as his ship drew out, he tried not to think of the girl in blue with a white parasol who had stood there beside them ten months before. It was fortunate that in his dejected frame of mind he had the cheerful company of J. D. Moss whose firm acted as solicitors for C.D. & D., and who was curious to see something of the vast domain over which the partners held their somewhat precarious control. Moss, an agreeable and versatile young man, did much to entertain his travelling companions. He provided violin accompaniment to the pleasing soprano of two lady passengers, told droll stories and initiated stimulating conversation:

> 26.7.99: Tonight discussion veers to the equality of man and woman. Captain Neate has no time for women who assume to positions in life hitherto exclusive to the male. Moss and I would not deny women's being on equal terms with men but would regret such being the case for their own sakes . . . The Captain becomes rather abusive in some of his assertions re the fair sex . . .

The subject was fittingly topical, as the extension of the franchise to women, frequently raised in the colony but resisted by the Forrest Government, had become again a lively issue. Within that year (1899) the Government's stand was to be reversed, probably in view of there being many more women in electorates other than the goldfields where most of the Premier's opponents were centred.

Moss revelled in his few weeks in the north. Having pictured it as a monotonous and forbidding country, he found it a land of exciting colour, of endless variety and surprise. The mid-year weather was benign and bright; the grass shone gold in the sun, and the flat-topped ranges were draped in misty curtains of delicate hue. The rivers and creeks, their wet season passion spent, had withdrawn into quiet palm-fringed pools with a covering of pale blue lilies and scalloped leaves on which spry, stick-legged little jacandas darted and preened. He found it a land of birds, from great, flightless emus to soaring eagle hawks with seven-foot wing spans, from stately jabirus and dancing brolga to twittering myriads of painted finches and screeching hordes of parrots and cockatoos.

M.P. and his brothers, warming to their guest's enthusiasm, organized crocodile- and duck-shooting expeditions and initiated him into local methods of rounding up cattle and mustering brumby horses. Moss, his imagination stimulated by world travel, conjured up for his hosts a picture of Kimberley as an international holiday resort—station homesteads equipped with modern tourist amenities; rodeos such as he had witnessed in the

United States; sightseeing and shooting safaris led by Aborigines of the calibre of Pumpkin, Boxer and Ulysses, colourfully dressed for the part; exhibitions of tribal dancing and singing with charming youngsters like Deology well to the fore.

> 15.8.99: Moss enjoying himself enormously [M.P. records]. He appears to have the impression that our lives in this country consist of carefree, holiday activities in happy contrast to the drab existences of hard working city dwellers like himself. I tell him that he might change his mind once the novelty wears off and the wet sets in with its attendant discomforts.

He was cheered, nonetheless, by the exuberance of his young friend for he liked to share with appreciative visitors the compelling beauty of the northern landscape and the fascination of its wildlife. It was with some regret that he left Moss at Argyle with P.B. while he rode off with Boxer to pursue the interests of his company in the Territory. Boxer was now his usual travelling companion on such trips because, unlike the Kimberley-born Aborigines, he did not mind how far afield he rode or among what potentially hostile tribespeople. It could hardly be said that he was without fear, or had no reason for it, but he prided himself on being alert to every native wile and strategy, sleeping at all times 'with one eye open' and a hand on the revolver in his belt.

At the company's Newry Station homestead, about forty-five miles on their way, the travellers spent the night with the manager Jim Patterson, a braw Scot who was later to become part-manager of Ord River Station, and with Jerry Skeahan, his head stockman, youngest of the four sons of M.P.'s Aunt Mary and her inebriate husband Dinny Skeahan. Jerry had come over from Queensland to join his brother Jack on Auvergne but was then helping out on Newry where there was a shortage of men. A quick-moving, slow-speaking youth of the 'wire and whipcord' variety, he was somewhat in awe of his elder cousin and anxious to impress him with his toughness. Both he and Patterson expressed themselves forthrightly on the subject of 'the tick fiasco' and assured M.P. of their wholehearted co-operation on the company's border conspiracy. In fact it would seem that whatever differences M.P. might have had with his men on other scores, he had no need to doubt their loyalty on this issue. If the law insisted on being an ass, it deserved, by local standards, to be taken for a ride.

It was another two days' hard travelling to the homestead at Auvergne, the firm's unwieldy property that covered more than 3,000,000 acres from the Newry border to the Victoria River and sprawled south to embrace the

Baines and its numerous tributaries. In M.P.'s opinion it was a run that, except as a convenient area for the filtering through of Territory cattle, the company would have done better without. There was good country and fine pasture within its boundaries, but there were also vast stretches of inferior, rugged terrain where the cattle tended to drift and run wild. It was a hard place to muster, dangerous going for horsemen, and well nigh impossible to control.

The men were branding at the homestead yard when he arrived, 'the three big Jacks' (Skeahan the manager, Villiers, and Frayne), plus Teddy O'Neill, 'Fat Dan', 'Thin Mick', and a contingent of black off-siders. Jack Skeahan had been in the country since 1886 when he had stowed away as a boy of fifteen on the same ship that brought M.P. and his brother J.W. to Kimberley. His anxiety to escape what he had seen as a dull, dead-end existence in Queensland had rendered him a good and reliable servant to the company, though apart from his job and certain family affiliations he had little in common with M.P. Having run away from college in Goulburn after only a few months, his formal education was limited, but he was a tough and competent stockman and had no complaints to make about the Spartan conditions and stark isolation of Auvergne.

> 21.8.99: What a contrast! [M.P. writes of his night with this rugged company]. Three weeks ago entertained with classical songs rendered by the gentle Miss Healy and Mrs Neate, now by the rollicking rhythm of bush camp songs, colloquial jingles rendered with a strong indigenous twang and some of Irish origin which bring poor old Father vividly to mind.

The eighty miles from Auvergne to Victoria River Station, a brisk two days' ride for these seasoned travellers, was not without its incidents.

> 24.8.99: Camped at the entrance to Jasper's Gorge we are awakened to the alarm call of niggers close by. We pack up warily but they do not appear. A ride of about five miles through the gorge with precipitous overhanging cliffs on both sides, from the top of which, were the natives maliciously disposed, they could have rained down rocks on our heads.

On the next day's stage he met an intrepid character named Arthur Richardson who had travelled from Perth on a bicycle hoping to complete a circuit of Australia within five months. He informed M.P. that three others, Donald MacKay and the brothers Alec and Frank White, had started off from Melbourne at the same time, travelling in the opposite direction, their mutual aim being, 'to draw a bond of unity around the colonies in the interests of Federation'. M.P. records that:

> 25.8.99: Richardson has only a piece of calico for cover and carries not more than 25 lbs. of luggage. His pedometer registers 2,587 ⅜ miles—a worthy performance indeed! He is now headed for the Katherine.

Further news of the stout-hearted cyclists was to catch up with M.P. over the months to come. One of the White brothers was forced to retire from the venture after an accident to his cycle at Pine Creek, but Alex White and MacKay pushed on, surviving an attack by Aborigines shortly before arriving at Newry Station. They completed their journey in eight months and eleven days, taking just twelve days more than Arthur Richardson[1].

Donald MacKay, at that time thirty years old, was to continue his adventurous career and to make his name as one of the last 'space-fillers' of the Australian map. On several aerial surveys between 1931 and 1937 he discovered and charted large areas of desert country in Central and Western Australia, gifting copies of all his maps and reports to the Commonwealth Government and the Mitchell Library. Lake MacKay, north-west of Alice Springs, is named after him. He figures in Frank Clune's *Last of the Australian Explorers* (Sydney, 1942). He and M.P. were to meet up more than thirty years later, though at this time their tracks did not converge.

On arrival at his destination M.P. got down to business with Bob Watson[2], the manager. As no other arrangements had been made for the sale of Victoria Downs cattle, a deal was quickly clinched and a muster organized. M.P. had been on friendly terms with Watson for a number of years and decided that it was no use beating around the bush with him regarding his company's tentative interest in the property. Watson confirmed that Goldsbrough Mort were interested in negotiating a sale, and said that Forrest, Emanuel talked of taking up an option pending inspection. So far no one from that company had turned up, and there was nothing to prevent him showing M.P. anything he wanted to see.

They spent the next four days riding around together, talking country, seasons, stock, blacks, cattle-thieves, cattle-tick, and other hazards of the area. It was none of Watson's business—perhaps not even in his own interests, since he might lose his job in the event of sale—to present a rosy picture of the property. Tick-fever, he said, had a firm hold of certain areas and was causing heavy losses, though not as many as the blacks who were still every bit as formidable in those parts as in the first years of pastoral occupation. There was an estimated 27,000 head of branded cattle on the run, a decrease of 7,000 in five years owing to the effects of tick and Aboriginal spears. There was no denying, however, that the place had potential if some company was prepared to put money into its development—and could afford to risk losing it!

The idea of the original owner, C.B. Fisher, of its becoming a horse-breeding centre had never been properly developed, while the abandonment of the sheep-raising project successfully started in 1890 had been a sad mistake. On this subject, M.P. heard further from his drover, Morch—how he had, in that year, brought 1,005 breeding ewes from Darwin to the Victoria Station and how, despite a phenomenal increase in two or three years, the flock had been sold on someone's foolish impulse to Joe Bradshaw for his Fitzmaurice run. Bradshaw had done no good with them, for what the blacks did not account for had died as a result of the many other hazards of that wild environment.

M.P. wrote his partners in Fremantle a full account of his findings and left it to them to decide whether they would try to forestall Forrest, Emanuel in making an approach to the owners.

From Victoria Station to Newcastle Waters, where he hoped to purchase more cattle, his way lay south down the Victoria to the Armstrong River and on to the station via the Murranji track. This stage of his journey brought memories of his old friend Nat Buchanan who had pioneered the route as a means of cutting off about a thousand miles when bringing cattle west to Wave Hill in 1883. Travelling in melancholy mood, he thought of all those who had given their lives, many with the zeal of men dying in a holy cause, to the opening up of this unpromised land. He was jolted out of his introspection by the welcome of Harry Lewis, part-owner of Newcastle Station with his brother Steve, who was handling their business in Adelaide. Lewis was glad enough to sign over their cattle for the coming year which, seeing that Morch was there to meet M.P. on his arrival, seems to have been a foregone conclusion. Over the next week they mustered 1,000 head, from which M.P. cut out the poorer, or tick-infested, beasts, sending Morch on his way with a mob of 672 head.

Before rejoining the droving party, M.P. put in a fretful week sending wires from a nearby telegraph camp, awaiting replies, and observing, without the objective insight of which he was capable, the process of adaptation to circumstances at work among the displaced tribespeople. The traditional use of women as tokens of trade or friendship did not necessarily indicate a lack of concern for their welfare within the concepts of tribal practice. This, however, M.P. did not appear to concede:

> Came this morning on a camp of niggers among whom sits a hoary-headed old devil with three lubras whom he uses as chattels. I am told he does a lucrative business with the Chinese and others here in the telegraph department camp. From the leg of one young gin I observed him drawing blood which I hear is prescribed to dispel an evil charm worked on her by one of his enemies.

He caught up with Morch on the Armstrong and accompanied him to Victoria Station where he was to pick up another lot and take the combined mob through to Auvergne. On this journey M.P. realised that, despite Morch's own capacity as a contract drover, he had made the mistake, no doubt in the interest of his own pocket, of employing a majority of Aboriginal assistants. With few exceptions natives were not, in M.P.'s experience, suited to long droving-treks, as they tended either to relax too readily into an Aboriginal dream or to startle a mob by some foolish manoeuvre. As a result of one or other such failing, the cattle had rushed on the Murranji track, causing the loss of nearly 100 head, some missing, others trampled to death. Morch, feeling his reputation at stake, was as downcast as a military leader caught out in some fatal error of judgement. M.P., respecting his feelings, refrained from making the obvious caustic comments, and in a letter written to await Morch's arrival at Auvergne used a milder approach than in many of his communications to men found wanting:

> We presume you are still prepared to continue with us as we to employ you ... As mentioned before, however, there is one condition we request—that is the employment of white labour as far as possible, with not more than say, two native boys, in the service of droving ...

By the beginning of November M.P. was back in Fremantle to present a detailed report on his inspection of Victoria River. He found his partners in even more optimistic vein than when he had left them last at the end of July. The war in South Africa, threatening for some time, had at last broken out, and an unprecedented wave of loyalty to the British Empire—less expected in the west than in the eastern colonies—had swept the continent. The first overseas contingent of Western Australian recruits had just sailed from Albany in the south of the State, and further volunteers were rallying to the cause. This unfortunate turn of history promised a lively trade for Australian stockbreeders which C.D. & D. had every intention of exploiting.

John Moss, who had returned to Perth full of enthusiasm for the potential of the north, had expressed interest in his own company's going into partnership with C.D. & D. in the purchase of Victoria River Station. It was a prospect that pleased Connor and Doherty more than it did M.P., who was doubtful of the wisdom of further complicating their affairs, but he agreed that it might be necessary from a financial point of view if their negotiations with Goldsbrough Mort were to take place. Since the manager of this company, J. M. Niall, was based in Melbourne, M.P., accompanied by his sister Mary, set off at once to interview him on behalf of his firm.

He was informed on arrival that the bedrock price for the property was £25,000. He offered £22,000 to which figure Niall at last agreed on a basis of £10,000 cash down and the balance payable in six to nine months. M.P. believed that his partners would be eager to close on these terms since they had been from the beginning keener on the acquisition than himself. In the meantime, however, Moss and his colleagues had received such off-putting information about Victoria River that they had withdrawn from the proposition. The intelligence, from wherever it came, must have been fairly convincing as Connor and Doherty now also showed signs of waning confidence. They wired M.P., proposing payment in four more widely-spaced instalments, the offer to be placed under option for two weeks. Niall agreed to the option but on the former terms. At the end of the stipulated time Connor and Doherty would not agree to Niall's terms nor he to theirs, and the matter was closed. For a few weeks, however, the course of North Australian history had hung in the balance over so small a matter as the timing of instalments. It is interesting to speculate what might have been the future of C.D. & D., had they added this enormous area to the immense estate they already held. A few weeks later the property was purchased for £27,500 by a syndicate including Forrest, Emanuel, Sidney Kidman and G. S. Yuill. The same group then bought Carlton Station on the lower Ord from the Hart brothers as a depot for stock being brought from the Territory for shipment from Wyndham.

M.P., while waiting for the outcome of his negotiations, had set out for a visit to Tasmania with his sister and his brother Jerry who had joined them from Sydney. They found the island disappointing.

> 2.1.1900: Have come to the conclusion that Tasmania is much behind the times, its general atmosphere one of lethargy. We find even the museum closed . . . At Port Arthur we visit the island's principal claim to fame and are shown round the convict quarters by an old man boasting having served a 24 year sentence—3 in

> irons—and of bearing the scars of many a lash . . . Later we see pictures of the original, now extinct, Tasmanian Aborigines. What a mild and docile cast of countenance compared with the sable tribesmen of our northern areas!

Jerry was in excellent spirits, having recently attained his science degree and with it a research scholarship to Cambridge University. He had not abandoned the idea of joining the company some day, but for the time being the die had been cast for him in a more exciting direction. The youngest in the family, he was after all to be the first to venture into the great world 'overseas'. The three saw in the New Year together in Melbourne, making bright plans for a family meeting in London, a visit to Ireland, and a grand tour of the Continent.

During this time M.P. had been in correspondence with W. S. Osmond, owner of Ord River Station, with a view to persuading him to sell his cattle. Osmond having at last consented to see him for a brief interview, he set out for Stawell where the old man was reputed to be living as a recluse at his residence, The Sycamores. This proved to be an imposing mansion, set in spacious gardens but transmitting to the visitor an atmosphere of profound gloom. M.P. devoted more than usual space to his comments on this encounter.

> 22.12.99: The old gentleman's greeting was reticent to say the least. He cast furtive glances in my direction from underneath bleary eyes and my first attempt to engage his attention re purchase of his bullocks for the coming year was brusquely repulsed. He thereupon began questioning me on political issues of the day as though to test my stability—the war in South Africa—W.A.'s stand re Federation. He declares himself as Federalist and hopes to see the Commonwealth a *fait accompli* within his lifetime. However, he thinks W.A. right in not entering too impulsively. He asks about the possible development of mining in East Kimberley, a proper examination of auriferous country and how to induce further population? The problems of communication which are one of the district's main drawbacks also come under review. He moots the running of a small mail service between Darwin and Derby, calling at Wyndham en route . . . I made to leave at 12.30 p.m., but he asked me to stay for lunch. The meal was followed by whisky soda and Ceylon cigars. We talked until tea time, then strolled through the gardens where he showed me a wide variety of exotic trees. Stopping beside one recently planted he said a

friend had asked why he bothered to put it in, seeing he would not live to see it grown. 'I'll live to see it large enough to make my coffin,' he replied.

It was 10 p.m. before we got down to the business I had come to talk about. After haggling for a while over a few shillings he capitulated, submitting all his cattle to us for the coming season at £5 a head. He then most cordially invited me to call again at any time . . .

When M.P. called once more on his return journey from Melbourne, the old man had taken to his bed and could receive no visitors. He died within the next few weeks, long before his young tree had reached maturity, but at least within the year of Australia's achieving her national unity[3].

7
Turn of the Century

January 1900–May 1901

By mid-January, M.P. was back with his partners and their families at Fremantle, all expressing appropriate sentiments on the dawning of a new century. None had any doubt whatever that the prosperity to which they drank was a foregone conclusion, though still tantalizingly just out of reach. It seemed to M.P. that his immediate future was to be 'the same old round' of long, lonely rides arranging the purchase and disposal of cattle, with occasional trips to the south on the monotonous coastal run. For a number of his relatives, however, the year was to mark a turning-point in their lives of a sort he wished most earnestly for himself.

Mary's marriage to Jim Davidson, the first of these happy events, took place at Fremantle early in March. M.P. records it as a congenial gathering of close friends and relatives, though he regretted the unavoidable absence of all the bride's brothers except himself—J.W. being in Wyndham, P.B. at Argyle, and Jerry on his way to England.

The young couple were to have a home in Fremantle but Jim, as the company's accountant, would be required to move about, not only from the head office in Fremantle to Kimberley, but to the Kalgoorlie goldfields where the firm had recently purchased a butchery business. Since fares were of no account on the company's chartered runs (a factor which no doubt explains the alacrity with which they all moved up and down the coast), Mary would be able to accompany her husband to the north—at least while she remained 'free from encumbrances'.

At much the same time Black Pat Durack had been married in Melbourne to Susan Downes, and his brother Long Michael (M.J.) to Bertha Levinson, daughter of a well-known Jewish family of Anglican persuasion who had a prosperous jewellery business in Perth. Bertha, anxious to share as many facets of married life as possible, had become a convert to Catholicism. M.J. had made it clear from the beginning that he would never take her to Kimberley: in Long Michael's opinion the Almighty had never intended the north for white women and children, as evidenced by the way He visited His wrath on those who refused to face this fact. For his part, he had set up a home base in Cottesloe where his wife would remain, during his comings and goings, to rear a healthy family. He had no patience with his brother Black Pat's taking an innocent city girl to a shack on the bend of the Ord. M.P. had listened to many similar tirades from his father's cousin, and could not but agree that, since M.J.'s alternative was the depressing bachelor establishment at Lissadell, it was just as well that he could afford a home in the south.

Musing on these two hard-bitten brothers of the overland tracks, M.P. hoped that marriage would prove the mellowing influence that already seemed promising. Not since 1886, when the first goldminers had come surging into Black Pat's store on Cambridge Gulf, did M.P. remember him in such good spirits as when going north on the *Tangier* with his lively and attractive bride. M.P. was intrigued to know what Susie had found in common with a man who was not only twice her age but as withdrawn as she was outgoing. The girl herself had no hesitation in explaining that he had at first been courting her elder sister, to whom the very thought of life in the bush was anathema. Susan, on the other hand, was fascinated by what she had heard of the Kimberleys, and their attachment had grown through her lively interest in the area. She was looking forward eagerly to her new life and declared herself fully prepared to take the rough with the smooth.

Passengers on the same voyage north were Galway Jerry and his wife, who had come south together for the first time in many years to be present at the Davidson wedding. With them were their youngest son Neal and little Mollie, last remaining of their five daughters. They had left their second son, Jack, at school in Perth and were anxious to return to the Dunham, where young Patsy had been carrying on in their absence with the help of several trusted Aborigines.

Before long M.P. was back in the routine of station life—up and down the road between Wyndham and Argyle, over the border to Newry and Auvergne, organizing mobs, interviewing men, overseeing the building of fences, yards, and mills. With the termination of his correspondence with Meg Wilson, his enthusiasm for photography had suffered a temporary decline but he now had a new interest to which he devoted considerable time. He had brought with him from Perth a dozen pedigree carrier pigeons which he hoped would save many miles of hard riding by conveying simple messages between Argyle and outlying stations. Now, wherever he and P.B. travelled they had pigeons in small cages strapped to their saddles, and the diary entries are enlivened with encouraging reports:

> The pigeon P.B. took to Newry yesterday returned with message in less than an hour after despatch . . .

> Sent a pigeon to Octo yard with Ambrose. It returned with a letter bearing news of rain in that vicinity.

Such references continued for over a year, after which no more was recorded of the experiment. Some of the older Aborigines however recall having heard that these obedient winged messengers were one by one attacked and killed by disapproving eagle hawks. It would be more than thirty years before the advent of transceiver radios, installed by the Royal Flying Doctor Service, would overcome the vital communication problem of Australia's isolated areas.

An interesting variety of black and white inhabitants are woven into the pattern of M.P.'s bustling days. His first cousin, Ambrose (eldest son of Stumpy Michael), who had been head stockman at Argyle for the past two years, figures largely in the diary from this time on. Then twenty-five years old, Ambrose was an efficient stockman of quiet disposition and a power of tough common sense. As time went on the Aborigines, who referred to him among themselves as *Lagaga* ('tall one, skinny one'), came to regard his methods and precepts with the awe accorded in other cultures to the law laid down by Moses. Afflicted, like so many of his fellow bushmen, with a skin totally unsuited to Australia's fierce ultra-violet rays, he rode at all times with a handkerchief tied across the bridge of his nose and another worn under his hat covering the back of his neck. He and M.P. were as closely attached as brothers, and there is no hint of rancour between them in the many years of their association.

A married couple named Robert and Ellen Bell-Blay were then employed at Argyle, the wife taking charge of the household management while her husband attended to a miscellany of odd jobs, from mending gates to planting vegetables in the kitchen garden and lucerne and oats in the horse paddock. Robert, slim and spry as a sparrow, had won some renown as a jockey in the Portland areas from whence he hailed. He claimed to have known Adam Lindsay Gordon and to have witnessed the intrepid poet's taking a horse over a fence a few feet from the edge of the precipice above Mt Gambier's Blue Lake. This story was one of the many that would hold his Kimberley associates entranced to the end of his long life.

Another newcomer to Argyle that year was a young Miriwung woman named Mingeet, otherwise Dinah, who, herself childless, was destined to become one of the much-loved, universal 'mothers' of East Kimberley. A good-natured, handsome girl, she had been claimed by Boxer as his rightful reward for having led a police party on to a camp of cattle-spearers hiding out in the Ord River gorge. There was apparently no tribal objection raised to this union, and M.P. was pleased to add the match to his list of marriages for the year. Boxer, he remarked, was to be congratulated on his good taste, for Dinah soon proved to be not only comely but intelligent and eager to learn. What was his consternation therefore, before many months had passed, to hear that she had moved to Ulysses' camp; and, fearing trouble between the two firm friends, M.P. summoned them to a conference. Both insisted that there was no trouble between them. It was simply 'an arrangement', for Boxer had soon decided that married bliss was not for him. At such times as he was not working in the stock camp, or travelling as companion to one or other of the Durack family, he preferred to move about alone and unencumbered, and no questions asked. It had pleased him therefore, in a single gesture, to restore his personal freedom and bestow a valuable present on his closest friend. Whether or not Dinah had been consulted in the matter, she was seen to be going about her household tasks with her customary contented smile.

Others to enter the scene at this time, and destined for a lifetime of association with the family, were Alf and Jack Martin. Then figuring as stockmen on the C.D. & D. books, they and their three younger brothers, who joined them somewhat later, were to leave their mark on the country in various capacities: Alf, having proved his worth in lesser roles, as manager of Victoria River Downs from 1926 to 1945[1].

Working at that time as a stockman on Newry and Auvergne was Harry Peckham who was later to become known as a reliable and intrepid packhorse mailman. Drowned in the Victoria River in the wet of 1911, his last words to his Aboriginal attendant being 'save the mail', he was immortalized as 'the Fizzer' in Mrs Æneas Gunn's *We of the Never-Never*. A monument now stands to his memory near Elsey Station on the Stuart Highway.

Also striding into the picture in 1900, and to remain a controversial figure for over half a century, was Charles Edward Flinders, son of a London stockbroker and grand-nephew of the renowned navigator. Many were to wonder why a man of his education and apparent potential should have chosen a life in this remote backwater, the only explanation we are likely to get being a brief comment in his own unpublished memoirs:

> It was expected by my family that I should follow in my father's footsteps, cooped up in an office on the London Stock Exchange, but the free and easy life in Australia appealed to me much more. I embarked on the S.S. *Bengal* which left Tilbury Docks [for Fremantle] on the 3rd of December 1886 . . .[2]

After some time as police trooper in the Cossack area, he went to Derby as Customs Officer and Clerk of Courts. Bored with this job, he went 'cattle punching' at Sturt Creek, and after that took on a mail contract between Derby and Fitzroy Crossing. In 1900 he drifted to the Wyndham area and from this time on is frequently, if seldom favourably, noted in M.P.'s journals. Flinders never kept a diary but he too had plenty to say, sometimes through the press under various pseudonyms, in disparagement of C.D. & D. in general and M.P. in particular. As the years went by, however, and they found themselves among the few remaining old-timers of the area, they came to appreciate each other's company. It was to M.P. that Flinders turned to provide a foreword to his reminiscences, in the writing of which, no doubt in deference to the law of libel, Flinders' aptitude for lively and vitriolic comment was disappointingly subdued. M.P. rose graciously to the occasion:

> I find myself as I read these memoirs, forgetful of my immediate surroundings, seated with my old friend at his residence, Goose Hill, listening to his stories of the past, exchanging anecdote for anecdote. He and I have been left, with the passing of so many old associates, almost alone with our reminiscences. The years of our acquaintance have been long, and I am proud to say that whatever our differences of view on passing problems of the day (and they have been many), our friendship has survived them unimpaired . . .

Considering all that was to pass between them in the intervening years, of which more anon, it is interesting to know that their relationship should have ended on such a congenial note[3].

As the year went by, news seeped through from the outside world of fighting in the Transvaal and the relief of Mafeking, of war between Russia and China, and in September—closer to home—of the results of the Federal referendum. M.P.'s comments on this last issue are typical of the rhetoric which would reach its full flowering during his political career of a later date.

> News from south. Much excitement on Federation day in Perth and Fremantle. The press calls attention to the big majority voting for Federation in the north[4] and seems to attribute this to a fear of 'the yellow peril' among workers in the area. No! I venture to assert it was their broad view of nationality—their wider and more expansive vision, which is a feature of men living outside the metropolis where

> people are too often influenced by their leaders without bothering to think for themselves. In general men in the far outback are without prejudice or parochialism, their views being directed towards the expansion and development of Australia as a whole.

Perhaps in extolling the broader view of men of the outback he was thinking of the support he had received from his stockmen on circumventing the 'narrow' government policy relating to the tick barrier. The following entry of about the same time indicates that he was still much preoccupied with this issue:

> Those who live directly on the border line see exactly the many harassing conditions imposed by the border restrictions—also the anomalies arising from the line of division. They see how self interest and blatant prejudice are totally opposed to local conditions and geography.

Some members of C.D. & D. apparently still felt that acquiring further property might somehow work to their advantage in this matter. The suggestion that Long Michael might, in view of his marriage, be considering the sale of Lissadell had so far proved to be without foundation, but M.P. had long had it in mind to look at some unoccupied country between the Durack range and the Bow River which the surveyor Billy O'Donnell had reported as promising for pastoral purposes.

He set out in this direction towards the end of September with Jim Patterson from Newry, two Aborigines, Pumpkin and Tommy, and nine horses. Young Tommy, a recent addition to the Argyle stock camp, was a member of the Djaru tribe that inhabited the area under inspection, and it was thought he might be useful as an interpreter.

Riding south from Turkey Creek, they followed up the Ord as it turned west and, skirting the range, made back from the headwaters of the Bow—country long since occupied, but then, except for a few salient features, quite unmapped. M.P. and most of his bushmen associates, no matter how new to them the area traversed, were never in any danger of being lost. They always knew, at least roughly, where they were and in which direction they were heading, though they sometimes ran the risk of finding themselves in waterless country. As long as they could see signs of blacks' camps they knew they had nothing to fear on this score, but the Aborigines for their part were anything but reassured by the sight of them.

> Open looking country. Fires away to the westward . . . Saw some blacks in the creek but they screamed at sight of us and made for

> their lives . . . Pumpkin and I decide to go ahead and look at the country out east. We ride over basalt downs—good black soil but no water—no sign of blacks. We dig but with poor result . . . Proceed east and down another fall where we capture a nigger at a spring. He has with him two roasted puppies which he was evidently preparing for his morning's meal. Other puppies he carries alive, perhaps to serve up later on. The sable buck is very much alarmed to find himself at our mercy and talks vociferously in his own tongue, calling in alarm to his brethren who do not appear in his defence. We escort him back to our camp where we get him in conversation with our interpreter, Tommy. He has brought all the puppies, roasted and alive, along with him—a distance of six or seven miles, keeping pace with our horses through the spinifex with less concern for it than shown by the horses. We start on at 3 p.m., taking the nigger as our guide to water. He leads us on about eight miles where we come upon a spring. Here we let him go and take the horses in to water.

The expedition, during which they named a number of landmarks for the maps of later years, continued for another week, the general impression gained being that although there were stretches of good country there was nothing comparable to the best areas on Newry and Argyle. M.P. could see no advantage in adding it to their estate.

Embarking for Fremantle, with his brother P.B. and the last shipment of cattle for the year, M.P. was pleased to find among his fellow passengers two friends from Victoria River Station, Bob Watson and Justin Curr. Since the sale of the property early in the year, Watson had been replaced by D. J. Ronan[5] who had been cattle-buyer for Sidney Kidman, a shareholder in 'the big run' with Forrest, Emanuel. Watson, now in search of another job, hoped that the next place he landed would be a more manageable proposition, and said he did not think M.P. and his partners would regret having turned down this deal. There is nothing to suggest that they ever did, even though the purchasers were to sell out only nine years later to Bovril Australian Estates Limited for £180,000, a price that included Carlton Station, near Wyndham, which was valued at about £15,000. Justin Curr, whose company M.P. had enjoyed on several occasions while he was book-keeper and horsebreaker on Victoria River, was going south to try his luck as a horsetrainer in the racing world, where he was to make his name.

M.P. had brought along with him the boy Deology whose attractive looks and manners had made him such a general favourite. Together with a pony brought for their children from Argyle, the boy was taken home by the Dohertys and plunged into a whirl of urban excitement.

P.B., whose marriage was soon to be celebrated in Brisbane, set off thither with his sister Bird, while M.P., after three short weeks of business and social activities, returned to Argyle with the wide-eyed Deology whose accounts of his city experiences were to entertain his tribespeople for the rest of his short but eventful life.

The year drew to an end on a convivial note, with a Christmas gathering at Argyle which included five family members. With M.P. there were his cousin Ambrose and his second cousin Jerry Brice, then employed by his brother M.J. at Lissadell. Also in the party were his Uncle Galway Jerry and his son Patsy, Mrs Jerry (pregnant with her ninth child) having gone south with her younger children. Besides the family, there were Robert Bell and his wife (the only white woman present), the Martin brothers, Alf and Jack, a store- and book-keeper named Durkan, and Sir Alec Cockburn-Campell who, having bidden a final good-bye to the country at the end of '99, was back again in the Argyle stock camp within three months.

The Argyle Aboriginals so far numbered only fourteen, most of them, as time went by, to become part of the folklore of the land. There was Pumpkin, head of the community, with his wife Valley (since recovered from her wound), faithful old Patrick and his Violet, Charlie and Nelly, Ulysses and Dinah (their names now linked as they were to remain to the end of their lives), Boxer, Nipper, Tommy, Billy Barlow (a recent arrival from Wave Hill), and the two youngsters, Deology and Joe.

M.P., in a New Year letter to his brother Jerry, then experiencing the cold shock of his first English winter, gave a brief description of the occasion.

> Christmas was sweltering hot as usual and the flies and mosquitoes in festive mood. There was the customary seasonal doling out of gifts to the blacks—new dresses for the women, shirts and tobacco for the men, boiled sweets and jam for the kids. All then competed in running and jumping contests such as you will remember from the old days on *Thylungra*, the phonograph meanwhile grinding out some well worn popular songs . . . Poor old Uncle Jerry [then 49 years old] returned to the Dunham with young Patsy a couple of days ago. I tried to persuade him to stay a while as he is not looking the best. He had a heavy fall from his horse a few weeks ago and apart from that has had more than his share of hardships

and sorrows over the years. I don't think they will do much good at the Dunham—too cut off and quality of the country patchy—all right for a subsidiary or outstation but not much of a livelihood otherwise. We are thinking of making him an offer for it and if he accepts he would be well advised to get a nice little place in the South to tide them over for a few years . . .

Business was not as good as anticipated last year owing to a breakdown of the *Tangier* which threw her back three months leaving all our cattle for shipment late in the year and the season not too good. They were in poor shape on arrival at Fremantle. At present we have 3000 head on hand for the next year's shipment. Our drover, Hardcastle, completed a most successful trip delivering 600 out of 615 from Newcastle in the Territory. All augurs well for a good year . . .

But in that unpredictable land no one could safely forecast an untroubled interval. Hazards lay not only in the state of the market, the nature of season, in shipping schedules and political manoeuvres, but also in a miscellany of human factors, including the performance of station workers and the often capricious behaviour of the Aborigines.

M.P., in Wyndham a few weeks later, one night received an urgent summons to the Ascot outstation. There he found his cousin Patsy in an exhausted condition, having ridden bareback from the Dunham—a distance of about seventy miles—with a bullet wound in his forehead and the news that his father had been killed. Asleep on the verandah of the homestead, Patsy had woken about 3 a.m. with a burning sensation above his left eye. He called to his father, but receiving no answer had got up and found him lying dead with a bullet through his head. He had run for help to the natives' camp but finding it deserted had walked two miles to catch a horse, and had ridden to Ascot. He found it hard to believe that the culprits had been the station blacks, of whom there were only five: a man named Roger, young Banjo Aramanga who had been reared on the Dunham and had been Patsy's constant companion; a twelve-year-old boy named Monday; and two women, Daisy and Alice. Banjo had been trusted to carry a Winchester for the past two years, and the day before, in a camp across the river, had been helping Patsy clean two rifles which they had left behind when they returned to the homestead at nightfall.

M.P. set out at once in company with Durkan the Argyle book-keeper, his cousins Long Michael and Jerry Brice, and their stockman Jim Dillon who had been camped nearby with a mob of cattle.

A youth named Charlie Good, who had come north earlier in the year to work for Tom Kilfoyle, also joined the party. He and several native assistants had been assigned the task of getting rations from Wyndham to Rosewood with a team of about forty packhorses. Hearing that the Ord was in full flood at the Ivanhoe crossing, he had decided, on experienced advice, to take the other track via the Dunham, and to try crossing the river at Lissadell. Writing many years later of his adventures in Kimberley, he recalled meeting Patsy (a mate of his Christian Brothers' College days in Perth) on his way to Wyndham.

> It was about 11 a.m. when a chap galloped up, riding bareback, his shirt wrapped around his head. It was Patsy Durack. He told us the niggers had shot his father and blown his own eyebrow off. He implored us to push on to the Dunham as fast as we could while he rode on to Wyndham, another 60 miles, his legs red raw. I gave him my blanket and a surcingle—he wouldn't take my saddle. We pushed the heavy laden pack horses to their limit and just after noon the following day, about 3 miles from the Dunham homestead, your father rode up. As a J.P. for the district he decided to hold an inquest, and although under age I was sworn in to act as a juryman.[6]

M.P. now takes up the tale:

> 25.2.01: We arrive on the scene of this terrible tragedy at 2.45 p.m. Lifting the rug from my uncle's face I find this gaping wound in his forehead—his face much discoloured and the body swollen a good deal. Death appears to have been instantaneous . . . We hold an inquest—M.J., J. B. Durack, Durkan, Jas. Dillon, C. Good jurors—self coroner. Verdict: wilful murder at hands of some person or persons unknown . . . Start to dig a grave alongside the two little girls, Vera and Annie, recently deceased. The police arrive this morning at 6 a.m., being 15 hours behind the rest of us from Wyndham. They take a cursory view of the wound, and all that is mortal of my poor uncle—Father's last brother—is underneath the cold clay at 7 a.m. We read a few prayers over the grave and leave him there with his two departed little girls. It is certainly poor reward for so many years of weary toil to be finally shot in cold blood by the blacks. The boys belonging to the place are all fled. As Patsy has no recollection of hearing a gun report it is presumed that he was shot first and stunned, that his father then

> sat up and was shot through the forehead, though whether by the same person or another is as yet unknown. We are strongly of the opinion that the boy Banjo is party to this crime.

The police party following the tracks of the station natives came upon them at last in a bush camp and brought them in to Wyndham. Banjo was charged with the murder of Jerry Durack and Roger with the wounding of Patsy, though the latter seems to have been acquitted of the charge as he was not sent to Perth with Banjo, Monday, and the two women.

The fact that the case was to be tried in the south was no doubt a concession to the public opinion that the accused were unlikely to receive a fair trial in Kimberley. That suspicion was not unjustified, but M.P.'s description of 'unpleasant remarks' expressed in the *Western Mail* as 'utterly fallacious' was also valid enough.

A correspondent signing herself 'A Woman' (Perth, 22 March 1901), writes as follows:

> . . . A West Australian pioneer once told me that in almost every case he had heard of in which the blacks had attacked the whites, outrages on their women had been the original cause of it. These poor blacks, though hardly allowed the name of men, yet share the feelings of men and deeply resent such cruel wrongs as these . . .
>
> It is earnestly to be hoped that the proceedings about to take place in the North with regard to the Durack murder will be fully reported to the country at large. Justice and humanity demand that public opinion shall be thoroughly aware of them . . .

Whoever the writer's informant may have been, he did not apparently have first-hand knowledge of the situation between black and white in Kimberley. In a fairly close investigation of all the killings of white men by Aborigines in this area, I have found very few cases in which the appropriation of a woman could have been responsible. A wife in Aboriginal society was an asset to be shared for gain or good relations, and Aborigines on the whole were not slow to see advantages accruing from making their women available to the white settlers. With only a few exceptions a white man's taking an Aboriginal woman uninvited appears to have raised less resentment than a black man's doing so. The latter case was a breaking of tribal law and involved a loss of the husband's prestige, whereas the former not only involved some material reward but was evidence of a shared humanity with men whose behaviour was in many respects so alien and so puzzling.

The trial, as reported in the *Western Mail* of 11 May 1901, reflects something of the contemptuous attitude of the southern public to the northern landholders, recalling that of a large section of the English public when the early Swan River settlers were faced with the same direct confrontation with Aboriginal tribespeople.

The case does not appear to have been taken very seriously. Banjo is described as 'a slim youth of about sixteen years old with a profusion of glossy, black hair'. We are told that entering the dock 'in what had probably been used by a white man as an under shirt, an ill-fitting pair of trousers and without boots, he looked anything but a desperado'. The charge against him that he did 'feloniously, knowingly, and with malice aforethought kill and murder Jeremiah Durack' was interpreted by Constable Freeman of Wyndham as follows: 'Aramanga, policeman been tell 'em big fella Gov'ment you been shoot 'em old man Jerry Durack, and kill him altogether.'

The case was tried by Acting Justice Pennefather, with R. B. Burnside as prosecutor and R. S. Haynes acting in defence of the prisoner. Banjo pleaded 'not guilty', though he had told Constable Freeman that Roger had persuaded him to kill one of the men while he dispatched the other. Roger, he said, 'been all day sool 'em me on, sool 'em me on.' Although given every opportunity to do so, he gave no evidence of having been ill treated, as was suggested in a number of indignant letters to the paper of that time. The motive would seem to have been to make off with the station stores, though in a state of panic following the deed they got off with nothing more than some matches and tobacco and the two rifles.

After Patsy Durack had given his brief evidence, Constable Freeman stated that there were no other natives in the immediate vicinity of the Dunham. The nearest tribal groups were many miles away.

> Mr. Haynes: What do they do—spear cattle?
> Witness: Yes, if they get the chance.
> Mr. Haynes: And dodge bullets, eh? What do they do for a living?
> Mr. Burnside: Perhaps they're politicians. (Laughter)
> Mr. Haynes: I thought they might be civil servants. (Renewed laughter)
> The witness said the natives were nomadic people.
> Mr. Haynes: They are 'moved on'.

Young Monday's evidence was also the cause of some amusement:

> The boy stated that 'old man Durack' was dead.
> Mr. Burnside: How do you know?

Monday: 'Dem two boys shoot 'im.
Mr. Burnside: How do you know?
Witness: I know.
Mr. Haynes: *That's* conclusive!
Mr. Burnside: Where were you?
Witness: Asleep. (Laughter)
Mr. Burnside: How do you know him shot?
Witness: I hear 'em shot—two. (Laughter)
His Honour: I shall take that down. 'I was asleep and heard a shot.'

The witness, continuing, stated that after he heard two shots he saw Aramanga and Roger running back, the former having a rifle. Aramanga hid in a large hole, where the goats camped. The witness hid there also. Banjo said: 'Two men shot.' Witness and Banjo remained in the hole until daylight when they went to the house and got some matches and tobacco and the party of five then set out into the bush. The two big 'boys' had rifles.

Rosie and Alice gave evidence of a corroborative nature . . . They left the station because they feared that when Patsy Durack came back he would shoot them.

Following addresses by counsel and the summing up, the jury retired. After an absence of a quarter of an hour they returned a verdict of 'not guilty'. The prisoner was discharged.

The verdict might well have been more welcome to the southern public than to Banjo himself, now perilously released from the protection of the law. It is generally supposed that he was returned to Wyndham where he soon succumbed to the rough justice of a tough country. On the other hand Gordon Buchanan in his *Packhorse and Waterhole* (Sydney, 1933) quotes an unidentified informant as saying that he saw Banjo in Perth some years later. According to this source, the authorities, deciding that he stood little chance of survival in East Kimberley, had enlisted him as a police tracker.

The affair was not without its repercussions in Kimberley, where hostile utterances in the south had roused the settlers to similar unfair generalizations regarding the behaviour of the Aborigines. Connor, as spokesman for the district, informed the Premier that pastoralists would soon be forced to abandon their properties if firm steps were not taken against black murderers and marauders. Settlers declared that Aborigines were a treacherous breed and even the supposedly 'civilized' were not to be trusted. The trend towards employing more Aboriginal labour was halted and firearms were removed from a number of natives who had been formerly trusted to carry them. Pumpkin, Ulysses, and Boxer, whose loyalty was never in question, voluntarily handed over their weapons, thus saving M.P. the embarrassment of having to confiscate them under pressure of current opinion.

In all fairness to the Aborigines, treachery to their white employers was not characteristic. Much was made of the three cases in which native workers turned on their white associates, but how many more were those in which white men owed their lives to the sometimes unmerited loyalty of their Aboriginal helpers?

The trial over, young Patsy returned to the north with his mother, only sister and three younger brothers, the last born in Fremantle soon after his father's death. M.P., reporting on their arrival in Wyndham, makes the following observation:

> Thinking of my poor Aunt Fan and the baby Frank who was not destined to know his father reminds me of a curious quirk of fate, for Uncle Jerry himself was born after his own father's untimely death near Goulburn in 1853. Strange also that my father was left at a tender age to carry on as head of the family, whereas it is his namesake and nephew, young Patsy, who must now take over in the same way. Fortunately he is a wiry, intelligent boy, a good stockman and a devoted son.

8
A Bride in Kimberley

May–December 1901

The 8th of May was always observed by M.P. and J.W. as an important anniversary, for it was on that day in the year 1886 that the brothers had camped for the first time on the banks of the Behn River and established the site of the Argyle Station homestead. M.P. seldom failed to note this occasion in his diary and in 1901 he dwelt upon it at some length. At that stage of his life fifteen years seemed a long time, and he and his relatives already referred to their first years in Kimberley as 'the early days'. Looking back on the 'sorrows, trials and disappointments' they had since experienced, he was confident that he and his associates were facing a bright new era of opportunity. Everything pointed to a turn of the tide to accompany the new century—a new monarch on the throne of England, and a new outlook for Australia with the opening, that same month, of the first Federal Parliament, an occasion for which the Commonwealth had been honoured by a visit from the Duke and Duchess of York.

A census taken in that year listed the population of the Kimberley district as 510 (excluding Aborigines)—an increase of only eleven on the census of ten years before. If this seemed a poor indication of progress, the fact remained that for the Kimberley pastoral industry, with lately consolidated metropolitan and goldfields markets, the outlook had never been more promising. In the past five years the number of cattle in East Kimberley had almost doubled to an estimated 112,551 head, about 50,900 of them on properties owned by C.D. & D., which company had already secured contracts for the shipment of over 10,000 head in the current year. The partners had also recently increased their assets by the acquisition of the butchery in Kalgoorlie which, like the Wyndham Hotel and the smaller Three Mile enterprises, was already bringing in a steady return.

Cattle-tick was a continuing problem, but where border restrictions were concerned the producers would seem to have won the day. It was by this time officially allowed that the western part of the Territory should be included in the Wyndham hinterland which meant, in effect, that quarantine restrictions were defunct.

The prospect of a meatworks in the port was being kept well to the fore by Connor and Doherty from their vantage point in the south, while the firm had recently placed negotiations for a market in South Africa in the hands of two reputedly live-wire agents named Fell and McInnes, who were then in Durban.

To be sure, the directors of C.D. & D. were not yet in a position to declare the long-hoped-for dividends, but they had been able at least to increase their salaries and to agree upon reasonable individual expense accounts. Another new phase, where their personal lives were concerned, was the impending arrival of P.B. with his bride Eva, and, somewhat apprehensive of her reactions to the Argyle homestead, M.P. embarked, with the help of Mrs Bell and the Aboriginal women, on an energetic spring-clean. In the process of going through his papers he came upon a neatly tied bundle of thirty-five letters and telegrams from Meg Wilson, whose rejection of their attachment he still found hard to understand or to forgive.

> I started to read the letters over but threw them aside with feelings of regret and disgust that one who could write so feelingly of constancy should have proved herself so false to this boasted attribute. All this correspondence consigned to the fire.

Frank Connor had that year been opposed for the first time in an election for the East Kimberley seat, by William Stretch[1] of Denison Downs, a respected resident and a formidable rival whom Connor succeeded in defeating by a single vote. While fighting his campaign in East Kimberley he had seen a good deal of M.P., though it is doubtful that they had much enjoyed each other's company. As is suggested in their later correspondence, Connor found M.P. tediously cautious and conformist, lacking in the bold and imaginative drive required of the successful empire-builder. Even as a drinking companion he was disappointing and refused to go to the extent of letting down his guards and revealing himself as a common and fallible mortal. M.P. found Connor inconsistent in argument, emotionally unstable, and politically short-sighted. There was little doubt that Connor's was the single anti-Federation vote registered in the East Kimberley district, which, whatever it might have said for his independence, did nothing to convince M.P. of his judgement. Admittedly he had soon seen the light on the tick question, but he had lately taken to advocating the spending of more government money on sinking artesian bores, with a view to splitting the country into smaller holdings. This proposition, however impractical (as evidenced by the fate of many smaller landholders of a somewhat later date), might be seen to indicate that Connor was capable of divorcing his interests as a landholder from his role as a former of government policy. To M.P., however, the proposal suggested 'pandering to the popular vote' rather than following the dictates of common sense, for, as anyone with experience of the area knew, the Kimberley district was not of almost limitless carrying capacity, as Connor averred. Man could provide artesian bores to water any number of stock, but he could not, by so doing, supply the animals with sustaining pasture. Nor should it be forgotten that over half the acreage of the big pastoral estates referred to was waste country, much of it tea-tree scrub, jagged limestone, and inaccessible range.

The partners succeeded, however, in maintaining a co-operative public front. Connor's victory coincided with the return of P.B. and his young wife, so that the banquet at the Wyndham Hotel for the re-elected member served also as a congratulatory function for the newlyweds. Eva, tall, slim and elegantly dressed, moved graciously in the mixed gathering of local business people and bush workers, though her first impression of Wyndham hardly tallied with Pat's description of a brisk and progressive outback trading-post. Fortunately, however, the weather was pleasantly cool, the welcome of the people warm, and the banquet a pleasant surprise. Connor made a witty and stimulating speech on the future of the East Kimberley district and its cattle trade. He also proposed a flattering toast to the bride and groom, and complimented Eva on the generous spirit in which she had agreed to share her cultural gifts and womanly charms with this isolated community. Pat, aglow with pride and optimism, responded in kind and M.P. took the opportunity of toasting 'The Commonwealth of Australia'.

If Eva had any complaints to make during her first weeks in Kimberley, they could not have been about the lack of company that had soon defeated the brave intentions of Black Pat's amiable bride. Prepared to face any hardship, lack of amenities, rough work, or wet weather temperatures, Susie had not foreseen being left in the minimal accommodation of the Mantinea run with two or three aged Aborigines who shepherded the milking goats, while her husband and his half-dozen younger native assistants, male and female, rode off for weeks on end, mustering, droving, or helping out on Lissadell. She was found, in a state of near dementia, trying to walk to Wyndham in the cruel heat and quagmire of the wet. Whether under pressure from his wife, his family, or his own better judgement, Black Pat decided that the time had come for him to get out of Kimberley. He and Susie had gone south not long afterwards to take up a property called Arrino near the wheat-belt township of Three Springs. The Mantinea run thereafter came within the estate of C.D. & D., giving them an uninterrupted fifty-mile stretch of country from Ivanhoe to Wyndham.

P.B. needed no such example to persuade him to treat his wife with more consideration. Come what would, Eva would be the central concern of his life, for better or worse, for richer for poorer, in sickness and in health. With them on their first trip to Argyle together went M.P., Frank Connor, and Father O'Brien who was visiting the scattered Catholic flock of East Kimberley. Shouts of Aboriginal welcome greeted them on arrival at Argyle, Pumpkin eager to be presented to the bride as a fellow Queenslander and an adopted relative. Ambrose and his four white stockmen were in from the cattle camp, and the Bell couple had prepared a superb meal, complete with a variety of home-grown vegetables, bread warm from the oven, cakes, tarts and scones.

Anxious to introduce Eva and Father O'Brien to the bush community, P.B. took them by buggy on a round of the neighbouring properties. Together they jogged over the rough tracks to Newry and Auvergne, called at Rosewood to see the Kilfoyles and at the Dunham to offer their condolences to Aunt Fan Durack and her children. It was Eva's first meeting with this unfortunate branch of the family and one she would never forget. She failed to understand how a woman, after the loss of no less than four children, two in Western Queensland and two here, followed by the death of her husband at the hands of a treacherous Aboriginal, should have been prepared to return with her remaining family to this desolate wilderness. To her horrified query Pat replied that he supposed she had had no option—an answer that did nothing to reassure the bride of her own future prospects in Kimberley. For P.B., always deeply concerned for others in their times of trial and loss, their short sojourn at the Dunham was indeed a sad one. Nonetheless the journey itself, with his beloved at his side, was one of which he had often dreamed. Regaling Eva and the genial priest with his colourful repertoire of local anecdotes. and serving devoutly at daily Mass, P.B.'s cup of happiness was full to overflowing.

Within a month of their arrival at Argyle they were back in Wyndham to bid farewell to their visitor at his ship and to attend the annual race-meeting. All the bush people had come in; those who could not afford hotel accommodation camped on the marsh or dossed down with friends in town.

Many years later I was to hear an account from my Aunt Eva, a lively and amusing raconteur, of this gala occasion. As a stage presentation it would, she declared, have been dismissed as far-fetched, the cast for the most part being a tragi-comic mixture of bush types, diminutive to outsized, with revolvers stuck in their cartridge-studded belts, in most cases the worse for drink and either over-gallant or spoiling for a fight. The handful of bush women, entering the town by buggy or wagon, looked faded and drab, though P.B. assured his wife that they all dressed to kill for the big day. Asked what he advised she wear herself, he insisted it should be her best, including a white hat with osprey feathers and pink flowers. Eva complied, to her unforgettable embarrassment. 'The course' was a glaring stretch of white salt marsh, the only shade cast by a spindly stand where the two judges, M. P. and C. E. Flinders, argued over the results of almost every race. An east wind blew up to welcome the racegoers and sprayed them with a generous coating of dust throughout the day. Alas for Eva's fashionable hairstyle and feathered hat! Only the experienced bush women, wearing dust-coats over their simple frocks, their bonnets tied firmly under their chins, were at all suitably attired. But what was to Eva a matter of greater mortification was to have created the impression of playing the *grande dame!*

The race ball was another ordeal, but one from which the discovery of her skill as a pianist allowed her a welcome respite. It also won her the reputation of providing an unselfish service to the community, and she was released after midnight with a hearty vote of thanks.

As the year progressed and the temperature began to pledge its ardent promise for the coming wet, Eva continued to accompany her husband on his between-station trips, but with decreasing enthusiasm. Towards the end of November they set out together for Newry, M.P. recording that the horses 'caved in' halfway and they were forced to camp for the night. With great difficulty they got through to the station by noon of the following day. Met by Jerry Skeahan and Sir Alec Campbell with the Auvergne bullocks, they lunched on salt beef and dry bread at the bachelor establishment and struggled back to their previous night's camp. 'Next morning,' M.P. writes, 'we nursed the horses back to Argyle through driving rain, all hands wet through and exhausted by the heat.'

Of next day (20.10.01) he reports:

> Eva in very odd spirits this morning, expressing herself eloquently on the subject of picnics in general. It appears she never cared overmuch for this form of entertainment at the best of times and finds it extremely difficult to appreciate as a way of life!

There were many aspects of life in the north that, too commonplace to merit a mention from older hands, had come as a shock to the gently reared city girl. Most of the men working at lonely outcamps on the big runs had native women as companions, and sometimes a half-caste child or two in testimony of the relationship. When P.B. praised the staunch dependability and good character of the German contractor, Louis Dagenhardt, Eva had been decidedly unimpressed. What she had seen was a distasteful individual, face and hands encrusted with the grime of years, sharing his camp with an Aboriginal couple and a half-caste boy. P.B. could not forbear to enlighten her: the child could of course well have belonged to Dagenhardt, but in fact was the offspring of their own first cousin, Jack Skeahan, whose name he bore. Linda, the child's mother, and her husband Paddy had been with Dagenhardt fencing and yard-building on Auvergne for over a year. The child had been born there, and when Dagenhardt moved on to the next job, had been brought along with him by his mother and her Aboriginal spouse.

Eva was predictably scandalized but the half-caste Jack Skeahan would have reflected no discredit on the family had they chosen to acknowledge him. He was to become one of the finest stockmen and all-round handymen in the Kimberleys, and eventually the owner of Sophie Downs Station near Hall's Creek[2]

M.P. continued meanwhile on his vigorous rounds, securing contracts with station managers, interviewing stockmen, drovers, fencing and well-sinking contractors. Though his overall optimism never flagged, he complained of the monotony of the bush life, accentuated perhaps by P.B.'s fulfilment in contrast to his own personal loneliness. His diary notes sometimes peter out to the merest jottings or snatches of Shakespearean soliloquy:

> Tomorrow and tomorrow and tomorrow
> Creeps in this petty pace from day to day . . .

The irksome border restriction no longer worried them, but the tick problem refused to go away:

> 22.9.01: Four beasts dead in Dakan's mob. Others very sick.
> 12.10.01: Alf Martin reports 32 dead in Sturt Creek mob.

Fever was rife on stations and outcamps, and in Wyndham. Indeed it was taken so much as a part of everyday life that M.P. was surprised when the doctor informed him that J.W., as a result of repeated attacks, was in a seriously low state of health. Never a malingerer, always more concerned for others than himself, J.W. had obviously pushed himself beyond the limits of normal endurance. He had no wish to leave Kimberley, where he had earned himself an important place in the community, but was at last persuaded that the Kalgoorlie business was in urgent need of his experience.

He left in September on what was intended as a temporary move, though his headquarters were in the south from this time on. As M.P.'s only close confidant he was surely missed, for although M.P. got on well—as who didn't?—with his brother P.B., this relationship had always operated on another level. Not for Pat those long, philosophical discussions that had whiled away the lonely bush nights of his elder brothers' earlier years in Kimberley and had continued growing in depth and interest with the extension of their considerable reading and experience. Pat's conversation ran on practical, homely lines. He was a stockman and a family man with a warm heart and a simple faith. As far as he was concerned, the riddle of the universe had been adequately answered for mankind by the good Lord through his prophets and saints.

M.P.'s logical and methodical mind, always anxiously seeking an acceptable and continuing pattern of life for himself and his family, could now see new problems on the horizon. If Pat had not yet accepted the fact, it was clear to himself that Eva was not cut out for life in Kimberley but was unlikely to accept a compromise whereby, like M.J.'s wife, she would keep house in the south during the six to eight months her husband was in Kimberley. It seemed to M.P. that his brother, like their cousin Black Pat, would eventually have to opt for a property in the south. This, if J.W. was not to return, would leave only himself of the Durack members of the firm in control of the situation in the north. For years he had cherished the hope of going abroad, and his brother Jerry's letters had further served to unsettle him. Early in the year Jerry had written from Paris (where he had gone to attend a conference of physicists at the Sorbonne), tossing off tantalizing references to attending theatres and concerts, visiting museums, palaces, art galleries. 'Believe me old chap in matters of taste and art we are barbarians ... My stay has been all too short. I come again during vacation.' But for all the writer's excited discovery of the cultural centres of the old world, it was obvious that he often yearned for contact with his family. He frequently urged his brothers to join him, if necessary one at a time, and for even a few weeks; 'and bring poor old Bird. There are more eligibles this side of the equator than that!' It was absurd, he declared, to say that they could not afford a trip. In fact from the firm's point of view he believed they could hardly afford not to know more of the outside world and the possibilities of expanding their markets.

The reasoning appealed to M.P. By the year's end he had decided that if he were to make the break he must leave while the going was good.

9

SOUTH AFRICAN SOJOURN

January–August 1902

Soon after his arrival in Fremantle, M.P. waited on Sir John Forrest, now a member of the first Federal cabinet, to whom he had written on receiving news of his brother Alexander's death in June 1901. In this letter he had expressed his sincere regret at the passing of a truly great Australian for, despite the fact of their business rivalry and difference of opinion on the federal issue, he had admired Alexander Forrest and trusted his integrity in the face of the bitter criticism with which he was assailed from certain quarters[1]. For many years Alexander Forrest had been accused of using his political influence to maintain a stock-tax to keep out 'healthy competition' from the eastern colonies, and of being the chief beneficiary of the resulting monopoly. If the two companies agreed on little else, they were staunchly allied in denying that charge, and in producing figures to show that the disparity in prices was largely owing to the cost of transport[2].

M.P. informed Forrest of his intended trip abroad and his hopes of negotiating a South African market that he believed could be big enough to involve growers from all over the State. Forrest gave practical evidence of his interest by providing the traveller with letters of introduction to Sir Gordon Sprigg, Prime Minister of the Cape Colony, Sir John Robinson, lately Prime Minister of Natal and still a powerful influence in the spheres of politics and the press, and (most important of all in M.P.'s eyes) to the great Cecil Rhodes. On parting, Forrest expressed a hope that he and M.P. would meet in London in June, as both planned to be there for the coronation of King Edward VII.

At this time C.D. & D. had in mind not only the proposed trade investigation in Durban but a scheme to be discussed in London for the floatation of their business with a company including outside shareholders, to enable them to develop the East Kimberley cattle trade on a scale broader than their own finances allowed.

The travellers sailed from Albany on the S.S. *Ninevah*, M.P. in high spirits, noting that this was his first departure for foreign shores. The trip was lively and interesting—the company varied and congenial.

> It has taken us but a few days to throw off our guise of conventional aloofness and reveal to each other the purport of our visit to African shores ... I talk to a Captain Dufrayer of his exploits in South Africa—hot engagements in the Boer War that earned him the Queen's sash.

It transpired that Dufrayer represented a Victorian company that was hoping to place a big contract for Australian cattle in South Africa. On this basis he and M.P. at once got down to business, discussing the commission to be paid by C.D. & D. on Dufrayer's securing contract of 50,000 at £20 a head. At the time it seemed that all should be fairly plain sailing where this deal was concerned, since Dufrayer, as well as M.P., had official letters to Cecil Rhodes and other influential South Africans. There were also stimulating contacts of another kind.

> Promenading the deck with Bird we meet several charming young ladies bound for South Africa ... We indulge in games of whist and nap. I learn piquet, play cricket, enjoy concerts in the music room and conversations with the lovely Miss Gill about our existence in the realms beyond. Her theories are quite in unison with my own. Reading Laing's 'Problems of the Future ... '

Before the sixteen-day voyage had come to an end it was obvious, despite the characteristic restraint of his observations, that M.P. was much attracted by the charming Miss Gill.

> Pairing off with the partners whom we find most congenial to our tastes and modes of thinking I find myself with a certain beguiling fellow passenger. We discuss the much talked of issue of women's equality, calling up names of many illustrious women whose greatness was writ large on the scroll of fame and thence to the many exemplary women who show as resplendent stars in the firmament of their own time.

But alas—Miss Gill was on her way to meet her betrothed, a young man from Victoria who had gone into business in Durban. A number of *Ninevah* passengers, including M.P. and his sister, were invited to the wedding a few days later. M.P. recorded that the bridegroom paid him a special, if quite unnecessary, tribute for the kind attention to his fiancée on the way over, while he himself responded on behalf of the passengers.

If M.P. experienced any regret at parting in this way with his delightful companion, he was soon enough caught up in the excitement of his new surroundings. Greeted in Durban by a competitive host of Zulu rickshaw men nimbly prancing under extravagant headgears of polished horns and flamboyant feathers, he set out with fellow passengers on a tour of discovery. M.P. was vastly impressed with the museum, with its display of exciting wild life and geological exhibits including specimens from the Kimberley diamond mines which reminded him of rock formations he had seen around the Ord River. It is strange therefore that in his continual search for minerals in that other Kimberley he seems never to have considered the possibility of finding diamonds. Not until the late 1970s would world attention be drawn to the Argyle Station area (by that time under the waters of a vast man-made lake), as perhaps containing the richest diamond potential in the world. Following this discovery it was often assumed that the Kimberley in North Australia had been named for the resemblance it bore to Kimberley in South Africa. In fact the former was named after Lord Kimberley who was Secretary of State for the Colonies from 1870 to 1874.

When seeing over the Transvaal cold-storage premises, M.P. was pleased to note that all the meat on display was from Australia, but was informed by the manager that their next supply would be coming from America as Australian prices were too high. Attending the stock sales he found the situation more encouraging, for here he learned that up to 12,000 horses a year were being shipped from Australia and sold at high prices on a ready market. Captain Dufrayer, an interested member of the party, assured M.P. that he was optimistic for the future of both Australian cattle and horses on the South African market. He arranged to meet M.P. on his return from Cape Town, where he hoped to interview Cecil Rhodes.

At the Durban Club M.P. met a friend of Rider Haggard who invited him to inspect his incredible collection of ivory and feathers procured when trekking wagons through the interior twenty-five years earlier. M.P. listened spellbound to tales of early days in Natal, of the amazing exploits of Chief Cetewayo, of the customs and practices of the many African tribes.

> To see the pure, manly, unsophisticated Zulu I am told one must go to Zululand. Here they are fast becoming arrogant and degenerate. Everyone unanimous that missionaries are spoiling the native people.

It is not long before an element of doubt appears regarding South Africa's interest in Australian cattle. A week after his arrival in Durban we find the visitor writing to his home base:

> It seems there is a slight prejudice against our cattle here, owing to heavy losses from shipments after arrival, particularly the last lot coming from Brisbane and supposed to be immune. There were 500 landed here last December for one of the big farmers. Soon after their arrival up country at the property of Mr. Baynes, M.L.A., whom I will try to see shortly in Maritzburg, these cattle contracted what they here call 'lung sickness'—to us 'pleuro'—and lost heavily. I have no doubt this can be got over. We must use every means to have stock inoculated before leaving. Along with the 500 mentioned came 100 odd heifers from around Rockhampton. They all contracted lung sickness soon after landing, were inoculated and are doing fairly well but a scraggy lot and do little credit to Australia. They are valued here at £15–£20 a head, which indicates that there should be a big thing in this business . . .
>
> I hear that Cecil Rhodes's brother has acquired big possessions in Rhodesia and is calling for 20,000 head for stocking purposes. They say South America can knock us out in this respect. Assuming that we did undertake a big contract of 40/50,000 breeders, 2 to 3 year olds, what do you consider the lowest we could land for Durban or Capetown? . . .
>
> Fell & McInnes[3] who are supposed to be operating here on our behalf I met briefly. I made an appointment to talk with them at length but they did not turn up and I hear that McInnes has since left for Australia. He had a great old spree here—was going around, I am told, with £2000 in notes in his pocket telling everyone he has entered into a big contract for shipment of 6000 head of heifers but he has not apparently disclosed our name in connection with the affair. It was obvious he resented my coming over—said my being here would militate against their efforts but would or could not say how . . .

A postscript to this letter reads:

> Bird made love to all the officers coming over and has now quite forgotten that such a man as Stuart existed! [M.P.D., Durban, to J.W.D., Fremantle, 7.2.02]

At that time twenty-eight years old, Bird had by no means lost the bloom of youth. She dressed with quiet good taste and her appealing personality, and mixture of friendly warmth and gentle reserve, always helpful and accommodating, rendered her an ideal travelling companion. To M.P. her company was an asset. A fellow travelling on his own might be any sort of a confidence man, but in company with a sister like Bird there could be no doubt whatever of the respectable and genuine nature of his background. He knew, moreover, that anything she might say of him behind his back could do nothing but enhance his image. Truth to tell, Bird was not as close to her brother Miguel as to other members of her family. Since childhood days she had stood rather in awe of him as being, next to her father, head of the family by some sort of divine right. It would never have occurred to her to dispute his decisions, whether they suited her or not. It was Miguel who decided that it would be good for her to accompany him, Miguel who determined the itinerary and date of departure and told her how much she might spend on equipment for the journey. If she met someone she considered 'the right man' in their travels, it would be Miguel who would have the last word.

Intent on following up the report of the Queensland cattle dying after arrival, M.P. went with his sister to Pietermaritzburg where he met Mr Joseph Baynes for whose property the stock had been purchased. Baynes, a sturdy Yorkshireman, was famous in South Africa on many counts. He had established a dairy industry on modern lines, introduced the first cattle-dipping procedure in Natal, and was now in an influential position in the local Parliament. His opinion, not therefore to be lightly dismssed, gave little hope of further cattle being imported trom Australia. The story of the losses he had sustained was all too true. 'This', M.P. admitted, 'does not sound very encouraging but am hopeful nonetheless of Dufrayer's interview with Rhodes whom I should also be meeting soon.'

The result of the Boer War was by that time a foregone conclusion, though the treaty was not to be signed for several months. M.P. and his sister, on the train from Pietermaritzburg to Ladysmith, noted in passing a few Boers camped with their wagons by the wayside in dejected family groups, the women looking 'browbeaten and forlorn', the men casting furtive glances from under their wide-brimmed hats. Everywhere was sad evidence of the long-drawn-out siege: graves and monuments to the fallen or victims of typhoid, and shell-shattered buildings. At Ladysmith M.P. procured a horse and with a bushman guide rode over the site of the recent battlefield, with sad thoughts for the sufferings of soldiers and civilians.

Back in Durban they took ship for Port Elizabeth, meeting on board two military agents who were confident that the demand for Australian horses must continue for at least two to three years. They accompanied the visitors to watch the unloading of horses from Russia and New Orleans, and together visited a Boer encampment where a number of women and young people were being looked after by the British government.

> All seem well cared for and the children bright and cheerful. Everything, including teaching, provided and the women paid for work done. Some of the young fellows, however, actually refuse to go out and work in town, choosing rather to loiter idly about their tents.[4]

In Cape Town at last, M.P. wrote at once to Cecil Rhodes, enclosing the letter of introduction from his State Premier, Sir John Forrest, and stating that his company was in a position to supply the South African market with up to 100,000 head of cattle. While hopefully awaiting a reply from the great man, M.P. interviewed such important personages as Sir Gordon Sprigg and the principals of the big stock-dealing firms of De Beers and Mitchell, Cotts & Co. He was diligent in stressing the geographical advantages of North Australia over other parts of the Commonwealth, and the excellent shipping facilities available in Wyndham, while carefully pointing out that the herds of North Australia, after long exposure to the problem, had become immune to tick or Texas fever. He was listened to with polite but non-committal attention. It was the forthright Mr Graaf, manager of the South African Cold Storage Co, who finally told him that he was wasting his time: 'If South Africa wants cattle she will turn to the Argentine. We've had too much trouble already with Australian stock.'

M.P. wrote appreciatively enough, though without his usual verve, of the surrounding sights—the bright shops and colourful crowds, the towering majesty of Table Mountain, the beautiful gardens established by the Dutch settlers of two centuries before.

When the day for their scheduled departure arrived, he had had no word from Rhodes, to whom he had since written yet again. It is unlikely that Dufrayer's request for an interview met with any more success, for Rhodes was at that time struggling for breath in his residence at Groote Schuur, his great life-force almost spent.

The travellers boarded the *Kildaran Castle* for London without regrets. They had not warmed to Cape Town, partly no doubt because Cape Town had warmed too excessively that summer even for visitors inured to a torrid clime. Their hotel had provided poor service and indifferent food, and to make matters worse M.P. was suffering from an attack of the debilitating tropical fever that beset him periodically, however far he was from its place of origin. Nonetheless, as the ship sailed his spirits rose in expectation of his first encounter with the city of London:

> One of the fondest dreams of my life, now, Deo Volente, about to be realised.

10

The Distressful Country

March–June 1902

It was unfortunate for such an enthusiastic traveller as M.P. that, as well as being a poor sailor, he was haunted by these attacks of fever on sea-voyages. The combined effect is reflected during his passage to England by an uncharacteristic lack of interest in his fellow passengers.

> I spend most of my time reading, Bird meanwhile enjoying gramophone recitals and amiable chit-chat with Lady Ruthven and young Carmichael. Lord Ruthven, an affable looking old gentleman who, like myself, is most of the time buried in a book.

On 17 March, when the band struck up 'The Wearing of the Green', he was reminded suddenly that this was the day on which his father had always elected to celebrate his birthday.

> What memories flood upon me, reaching back to childhood days on Thylungra, Western Queensland. It might be said that we have gone far since then though we have never since succeeded in recapturing the happiness that we then knew.

When his fever receded he played piquet with Mr Richards, a Member of Parliament from Cape Town.

> This gentleman declares that Britain's past actions in South Africa have given the Boers reason for their attitude. Of the Kimberley diamond mines he states that for £90,000,000 we paid the Free States a paltry day's earnings of £90,000. He considers Chamberlain far more capable of holding the reins than Salisbury.

Madeira was a welcome break from monotony, leaving a happy impression of houses dotting a verdant mountain side, of abundant fruit and flowers and the pervading scent of roses, of fine food and Madeira wine in a luxury hotel 2,000 feet above the smiling bay—'all, for a party of three, at the cost of 32/6!'

Southampton greeted the travellers on 29 March with a chill blast and mizzling rain, but there, aglow with excited welcome, was brother Jerry with tickets for Waterloo Station and bookings made at Morley's Hotel. He declared that the anticipation of their arrival had kept him awake for two nights, but he begged that their grand tour of London and its environs should be deferred to his impending vacation. He had, in fact, tentatively arranged with the families of Connor and Doherty that they should go first to Ireland, returning for King Edward's coronation and the sightseeing festival of their lives. Soon after their arrival therefore, M.P. and his sister embarked at Holyhead for the fair shores of County Meath.

M.P. had now, by sheer force of will and his naturally robust constitution, thrown off his malaise, and presented to a welcoming assembly the expected picture of virile Australian manhood. Here on the wharf was Denis Doherty's father, 'a charming man with a benign face and a ready and cultivated wit', and his younger son, two unmarried daughters, and sundry grandchildren; together with Connor's animated sister, Mrs O'Leary, whom they were later to visit in her fine home at Rossmoyne. Bird had known and loved the Doherty family in Ireland since she had visited them with Mrs Denis Doherty and her children in 1897. Jerry, too, had been a fairly frequent visitor since entering Cambridge University two years earlier. The Dohertys' home was at Warrenpoint, across the bay, 'where all repaired to discourse at lively leisure before a crackling fire'.

Over the next five weeks M.P. became immersed in the land of his forefathers, though with apparently little sense of identification. He had in fact come to share with other members and branches of his family a belief that their roots lay not in Ireland but in France. Evidently the notion had arisen from the similarity of the name to the French Du Roc, members of which clan took refuge in Ireland after the Revocation of the Edict of Nantes in 1685. From supposition the idea had become 'established fact', and it was not until the 1930s, when statements of the family's being of French origin reached Ireland from Australia, that the fallacy was exposed. Authorities on Irish history attested vehemently to the name's derivation from O'Dubraic of the ancient Gael, and to the O'Duracks' having pastured stock on the banks of the Shannon at Ogonelloe for over a thousand years.

> I had not fully realised [M.P. writes] the extent to which the Irish are a distinct race and people from the English. I am constantly surprised by their brightness of intellect, their originality of thought and speech, their wit and humour and excellent physique and am perplexed that a people so blessed with unique talent should have come to accept the poverty that prevails throughout their land. With so much liveliness and independence there is at the same

> time so much apparent apathy. Many live in houses needing but little to repair and throw their kitchen refuse into the street before their very doors.

He was shocked and oppressed by the poverty he encountered on his excursions with the Dohertys and their friends. The ragged clothing of the vendors at the village fairs, the mendicants in the street and at church doors, set him wondering at the affluence of the churches that towered above all other buildings in every town and village.

> As I contemplate this magnificent marble, these altar rails of solid silver, I wonder to what extent the struggling community is taxed for the erection and upkeep of such a splendid edifice. They tell me that England is to blame for everything but can the clergy, of whom there is certainly no shortage in this 'Isle of Saints and Scholars' do nothing to brighten the existence of their faithful flocks—or at least show by example how they might better help themselves? I do not, however, test the sensitivities of my companions by voicing such sentiments.

He was shocked, too, by the vehemence of anti-English feeling of which no amount of forewarning had fully prepared him.

> I had no conception of how deep this feeling went. I heard only today of how a man named Lynch was returned for Galway, not because he was a better man than his able opponent, Plunkett, but because he knew how to hate England more.

Nor was it only amongst the poor that he encountered this bitter antagonism. The guest in Belfast of an affluent and charming family named Donnelly, he was surprised how the customary fun and laughter could give way, at a mention of England's name, to sudden and eloquent vituperation. Attending the police court in Belfast, he was again distressed to encounter a band of poor boys known as 'the Bogey Clan' being sentenced for all but killing a boy in a riot triggered off by religious antagonism. Saddened, he writes:

> If this outlook pertains in all strata of the community one wonders what will be the end of it.

But if often puzzled or repelled, he was also charmed and beguiled. Used all his life to the Irish in Australia, that environment must, he decided, have subdued much of their natural spontaneity. On their native soil rich and poor alike had an ease of approach, a gift for instant communication, that made it impossible, even for one as reserved as himself, to feel a stranger in their midst.

> Everywhere I encounter instances of this happy lack of self consciousness. Today in Dublin a fashionable lady dropped her flowers while hurrying from the Gresham Hotel to attend a marriage ceremony. She turned to Miss Doherty to pin them to her corsage, but Miss D., in her kid gloves, did not succeed. The woman thereupon appealed to me, gracefully bowed her thanks and sped to join her party.

The Dohertys escorted M.P. to places often referred to nostalgically by his two Irish partners. In Newry he was shown the houses in which they were born, the place where Denis Doherty had come a cropper from his pony, the ditch into which Frank Connor had stumbled as a small boy in his new velvet suit. Mr Doherty senior, well versed in the history of his country, enjoyed accompanying the visitor to the sites and shrines of Ireland's storied past. In Sligo they visited the Holy Well, 'the Lourdes of Ireland', and the temples of ancient pagan worship where, in later days, hunted priests with a price upon their heads had celebrated Mass. They stood together on the Hill of Kings, burial place of the last of Ireland's pagan queens, while Doherty, his face aglow and silver locks blowing in the wind, recreated for his fascinated listener the tragic pageant of the centuries. M.P. was moved to ask of his diary:

> Did ever any country experience so unfortunate a history? And what wonder her population continues to drift to other lands! We witnessed even today such heart rending scenes as I will never forget—sorrowing parents bidding farewell to sons and daughters leaving evidently for America, as I see their trunks labelled for the Dominion Line. At worst what lies ahead of them can hardly equal the privation they have known in their home land.

Did he recall that it was little more than fifty years since his own family had suffered just such a leave-taking, but from far greater privations, their baggage more humble, their chances of survival, on that much longer journey to a land still largely unexplored, considerably more frail? Yet, here he was, a son of the next generation, returning as a sightseer first class on luxurious ocean liners, putting up at the best hotels—and with a pastoral heritage at his back bigger than half the counties of the Emerald Isle!

Bird taken charge of by her doting Irish friends, M.P. set off alone from Sligo on a round tour of the south. Curiously, although he went to Galway,

Limerick, Killarney, and Cork, he did not visit Loch Derg or the district of Ogoneloe where his father had been reared, nor does he mention enquiring for people of his own name, as was his brother J.W.'s first thought on making the same journey at a later date. To M.P. it was an intriguing, beautiful, but decidedly foreign, land which he travelled at the mercy of a series of guides who stopped, obviously by prearrangement, at wayside cottages and little hostelries.

> What am I to do with so much Limerick lace? But at least I have been sent on my way with the blessings of the vendors ringing in my ears. Who are these lovely Irish girls, their humble cottage hung with devotional pictures, who press me to drink their brew and warm myself at their fire? Not far along we stop yet again—another cottage, more young women of sprightly grace. It's no use. You can't get past their blandishments and their blarney, repeated all the way along with beguiling appeals to buy their wares.
>
> 'Musha, and a good morning to yere honour, and won't ye be having a drop o' the mountain dew? A blessin' on ye of the Holy Virgin and all the saints in heaven. And where would ye be coming from? Australia is it? And where is that atall could ye be telling us?'

One of the hostelries was run by a Mrs O'Grady whose story was celebrated through several counties:

> Evicted from her house by a government caretaker after keeping seven policemen at bay for a week or more, a subscription was raised for her which enabled her to set up in her hotel premises. The caretaker has since been boycotted, and no one has spoken to him for over two years. Under threat of similar treatment no one has yet dared take over the place from which she was evicted. Such is the loyalty of the Irish to their own!

Back at Warrenpoint at the end of May, M.P. was pleased to read the glad tidings of peace in the Transvaal. Few flags were flown in the Irish towns and villages, some of the friends on whom he called to bid good-bye being more than doubtful that a victory for England against the people of any nation was a matter of rejoicing.

The Donnellys, who saw them off from Belfast, made no bones whatever about where their sympathies lay. 'Miss Daisy', whom Jerry had apparently been courting, bade M.P. somewhat sarcastically to wish 'Dermot'[1] a capital time at the coronation of Britain's exemplary new monarch. M.P., though he no doubt smiled politely, did not think that for all her cleverness and good looks she was really a suitable match for a young man with his eyes on an academic post within the British tradition of Empire. In his view, strong political opinions, unless reflecting those of her husband (and even then preferably voiced with becoming moderation), ill became a member of the fair sex.

11

A Traveller's Tales

June–August 1902

London on 23 June 1902 was a city of carnival excitement. Patriotic streamers of red, white, and blue fluttered from posts, roofs, and balconies. Fresh paint glowed on signboards over taverns and shops, and tiers of seats lined the route where the royal procession was to pass. Every colony and outpost of empire had been allotted its separate stand each appropriately and competitively decorated; that of Western Australia, where Jerry had booked seats for his brother and sister well in advance, flaunted banners resplendent with black swans and golden nuggets.

The State of Western Australia was so well represented in London at that time that M.P., walking the Strand on his return from Ireland, recorded having seen as many familiar faces as he might have expected to encounter in St George's Terrace, Perth. Most of them were present that night, along with M.P. and his brother, at the State's coronation dinner, a grand occasion at which the Hon. Henry Lefroy, then Agent General for Western Australia, was seated between Sir John Forrest and the Anglican Bishop C. O. L. Riley who played a leading part in the affairs of the young State. M.P. found himself seated beside Winthrop Hackett, M.L.C. who since 1887 had been the able and influential editor of the *West Australian*, and Sir Edward Wittenoom[1] with both of whom he engaged in a spirited conversation about the future of the goldfields.

Riding next day atop a bus to the city, the brothers remarked on excited crowds gathered around billboards and scrambling for papers at the news-stands, while paper boys shrilled from every corner: 'Celebrations put off!' 'Coronation postponed!'

People gazed at each other in amazement, some shrugging it off as 'a hoax, a stunt to sell the papers'. Further bills and special editions, however, revealed that the King had been taken ill and was to undergo surgery. An official publication of the *St James Gazette* dispelled any lingering doubts. The royal show was off until further notice. Seat-holders began scrambling for a return of their money, and the crowds that had thronged the festival city drifted despondently away.

But for M.P. the coronation had been no more than an item on his considerable itinerary. Much as he had enjoyed his sojourn in Ireland, it is clear that he found England more stimulating. He thrilled to the sights and sounds of London, to its shops, theatres, and clubs, its countless centres of fame and fable, its cathedrals, museums, galleries: to the Crystal Palace, the Hippodrome, Earl's Court in Kensington, to Buckingham Palace, Whitechapel, Petticoat Lane, the Tower, Big Ben, and the Houses of Parliament; to its toffs, its cockneys and its street vendors. Calculating that this might possibly be his only trip abroad (though certainly not if he could help it), he was determined to fit in as much as possible. Almost every night he attended concerts and theatres. He saw Forbes Robertson and Gertrude Elliot in *Hamlet*, Sir Henry Irving and Ellen Terry in *The Merchant of Venice*, Seymour Hicks and Ellaline Terris in *Blue Bell*, Mary Moore and Sir Charles Wyndham at the Garrick, and Nellie Melba at Covent Garden.

> Often as I watch, [he records] my thoughts wander back to East Kimberley where, in the solitude of the bush, I have so often longed for the chance to see these great figures of the stage.

At Brompton Oratory he was much moved by a sermon exhorting the people to pray for and stand by the King of England and forthrightly rebutting accusations of Catholic disloyalty. The preacher impressed upon his congregation that out of 22,000 soldiers in the Boer War, over 6,000 had been Catholic. His final words M.P. found particularly memorable:

> May Queen Alexandra continue to shed the lustre of her noble traits and may the Wisdom that sitteth at the side of God continue to direct Edward VII, Emperor, in the Government of his people. I have done. God save the King!

At Cambridge with his brother, he records having walked in awe the same flagstones as had John Milton, Francis Bacon, Isaac Newton, Oliver Cromwell, the two Pitts, Lord Alfred Tennyson, Lord Byron, Harvey, Macaulay, John Fisher, and a host of others.

> One is reminded as one's footsteps echo from the adjacent walls that it is here Newton was said to have measured the velocity of sound.

Jerry, enjoying his life at Cambridge where he had rooms at Bradwell's Court, revelled in providing his elder brother and sister with inside information about historical sites and personalities, and introducing them to a host of interesting contemporaries. The two brothers appear to have been in close harmony as they moved about together and discussed their prospects, including the chance of their C.D. & D. shares soon paying dividends or being translated into a lump sum by an outright sale of the properties.

They had had good news from Fremantle office that the South African Government had, after all, agreed to take a trial draft of 3,612 heifers, which were to be shipped immediately. This was somewhat puzzling to M.P. in view of what had seemed so firm a rebuttal of his negotiations. He was soon to learn that the deal was a result not of his own but of Connor's representations, for, impatient at what appeared to him to be M.P.'s inept handling of the situation, this partner had decided to sail for Cape Town himself. Rhodes had died just before his arrival, but Connor had lost no time in meeting the people most important to his ends and proceeding, not to sell stock, but with practised subtlety to sell himself. The difference between Connor and a confidence man was that everything he claimed for himself was true, and he saw to it that his *bona fides* were clearly established in personal encounters and press interviews. He stressed his longstanding admiration for South Africa and his desire to make an assessment, on behalf of the State of Western Australia (where he represented a vast pastoral electorate), of property management and stock-breeding methods in the province.

Not for Connor M.P.'s careful documentation of daily expenses with self-congratulatory comments on little economies. The worldly-wise Irishman took care to stay at hotels where the right contacts were to be made, and rather than waiting to be entertained he issued dinner invitations with the casual aplomb of one accustomed to moving in affluent circles. Nor did Connor wait for his guests to raise the subject of tick-infestation in Australian cattle. Instead he raised it himself in such a manner as to leave no doubt of his being not only an authority on the problem but also conscientiously—and so far successfully—concerned with the enforcement of tick precautions in his electorate. The idea of supplying Kimberley beef to South African markets appeared thereafter to evolve as a result of his appreciation of their needs and his having warmed to the concept of establishing amiable trade relations between the respective countries.

Although M.P. was curious to know by what tactics Connor had succeeded where he had failed, he found the news nonetheless welcome, and the possibility it indicated of a lively overseas trade did no harm to the various negotiations he had on hand. The Durack brothers evidently made a good impression on their London business contacts. Interviewed for the *St James Gazette*, a paper circulating among people of wealth and influence, they explained their interest in North Australian pastoral properties covering over 12,000 square miles, and extolled the prospects of the cattle industry in that area. The resulting article aroused considerable interest, and the brothers soon found themselves in consultation with some of the biggest financiers and stock-breeders in England.

While the prospect of an outright sale of the properties for £300,000 was being discussed with one group of London investors, the brothers were more seriously negotiating with Dalgetys and the big shipping company of Angier Brothers for the flotation of a shareholding company, also with a capital of £300,000, to control, develop and possibly enlarge the area of the C.D. & D. estates. Meanwhile the Angier family extended the Australians their friendliest hospitality, including them in theatre parties, dinners at the Bath Club, the Kingston Regatta, a reception for Lord Kitchener and weekends at their house in Brighton, this association providing M.P. and Jerry with a fascinating insight into the lives of affluent Edwardians. They went hunting over the downs, played tennis, billiards, snooker, and cards, and were 'charmingly entertained with edifying conversation and musical recitals'.

It was with friends of the Angiers that M.P. attended the Carlisle stock show. This resulted in his being invited to the property of a stock-breeder named Woods, about seven miles from Wickham Market, which had been formerly owned by the Marquis of Hereford.

> The shooting here [M.P. reports] is said to be the finest in England, the bag for the last year having been 30,000 odd. There are no less than thirty game keepers and many other servants, including liveried footmen who stand about motionless as statues.

He was much attracted by the Suffolk stock on the property, and was offered 'the bargain deal' of a bull named Sadborne Sheriff and two fine brood mares for £600. He left England still giving thought to the proposition, but there is no evidence of his having finally accepted it.

Bird, meanwhile, had been eagerly entertained by a variety of escorts, and, unaware of a rumour that she was heiress to a private fortune, she took the attentions showered on her in good faith. One of her most ardent admirers was a young man of aristocratic connections named Cusack who outraged M.P. and his brother by approaching them to discuss a financial settlement in anticipation of her accepting his proposal. He expected, he informed them, to inherit a title from an elderly relative and would be in a position, in this event, to put them in the way of valuable business connections. It was necessary, however, that he be guaranteed finance to assist in keeping up his elevated station. It must have come as a surprise to the young man to discover that the two mild-mannered Australians, apparently so respectful of the English upper class and their time-honoured tradition, could display such an unfortunate streak of churlish arrogance. The romance, if such it could be termed, was firmly nipped in the bud.

The irons of sundry business propositions were still hot in their respective fires when M.P. and his sister bade farewell to Jerry and their English friends, and set sail for France. M.P. opens this stage of his travelogue on a romantic note: 'I step onto French soil for the first time in my life with a throb of emotion for what was originally the home of my forebears.'

This fond illusion added to the excitement and delight with which both he and Bird set forth on an orgy of sightseeing. M.P. waxed eloquent on the visual splendours and historic details that were unfolded as they moved on foot, by carriage, and by train from Calais to Paris and thence, by thrill-packed stages, to the Swiss frontier. Of his visit to the tomb of Napoleon, the indefatigable chronicler records:

> It is with some feeling of emotion that I look on the tomb of Napoleon's great Marshal Duroc, in whose veins flowed the blood of our family. I am the first member from Australia to gaze on this memorial since our exodus at the time of the French Revolution in 1792[2].

In evidence of his identification with the French psyche, M.P. resolved at this stage to embark on a study of the language, of which he remembered no more than a few phrases acquired at school. On his return he purchased several French texbooks which he carried around with him for some years, making occasional mention of having put in a few quiet hours on the study of the verbs. That would seem to have been as far as the intention carried him. He delighted, however, in translations of French literature and studying French history, with particular emphasis on Napoleon and his favourite Marshal who was not, he was disappointed to find, of the unassailable integrity he had attributed to this 'ancestor'.

At the Swiss border Bird complained that, having seen so many sights, she had 'everything jumbled up' and would be glad to get home. Not so M.P., who tackled Switzerland with a fresh burst of 'veneration and awe', making detailed notes on Byron's *Prisoner of Chillon* and his escape therefrom, on Julius Caesar's welcome, 2,000 years before, to the city of Genoa 'where came Rousseau and Voltaire, Mesdames de Maintenon and de Stäel and where Calvin preached his doctrine of Reformation in 1536 . . .'

On 8 August he records:

We board the S.S. *Austral* at Marseilles, myself at least with feelings of deep regret that our tour is virtually at an end. Truly it can be said that I have never in my life lived as fully as in these past five months. I wonder indeed how I can ever settle down to the humdrum monotony of station life in Kimberley.

12

The Traveller Back to Base

October 1902–December 1903

M.P., boarding the *Tangier* for Wyndham a few weeks after his return from abroad, was 'restless and upset'. The day before embarking he had met again, apparently by chance, with Meg Wilson from whom he had parted so abruptly two years before. What passed between them we can only surmise from the brief comment in his diary:

> I thought that I could now have looked upon that face without the slightest stirring of emotion, but it was not so. Why must a man be so prone to sentimental idiocy, allowing his heart to overrule his judgement or his head? It must not be. I cannot meet this girl again.

Whether he did or not, his journal contains no further mention of her name.

He approached Wyndham with a heavy heart.

> Dead, dreary, wretched old Wyndham, sleeping under the foot of the hill, the sight of which sends a pang of regret to one's heart—not because I hate Kimberley—rather otherwise—but because the sight recalls the past fifteen years with their joys and sorrows, meetings and partings, and after my recent adventures abroad, further impresses the harshness and isolation of this little known terrain. When will this district shake off its mantle of sleep?

Wyndham seems nonetheless to have been comparatively lively at the time of his arrival. Among a number of residents in town to catch the southbound *Tangier* were his brother P.B. and his wife Eva, agog to hear of M.P.'s recent travels and eager to discuss personal and company problems. While others caroused noisily in the bar, they sat in their private hotel quarters above, talking of that other wider world of cultural antiquity and intellectual advancement in which their younger brother seemed now well launched on his way.

From the traveller's tales, conversation inevitably returned home to company affairs. If C.D. & D. could be said to have had any policy over the five years of its existence, it was that it should remain at all times flexible, keeping open every possible option. The partners, even to each other, represented their northern holdings as an asset of inestimable potential, while privately fearing that it might prove a cumbersome white elephant, better unloaded, if and when the going was good, on some other keeper.

At the end of 1902 the firm was tentatively negotiating on at least four fronts: (a) the outright sale of the northern properties, walk in; walk out, at £300,000; (b) the flotation of a bigger company with outside investors; (c) the purchase of small adjoining properties that would at once give them direct access to more cattle, get rid of the neighbouring poddy-dodgers, and present a more impressive-looking proposition to potential buyers; (d) the acquisition of property in the south of the State, thereby keeping their irons in two fires and providing an alternative area of family activity in the event of sale—or, in P.B.'s case, a strong-minded spouse.

It was not a state of mind conducive to preoccupation with land-husbandry or long-term projects for the improvement of pasture and stock. The very thought of necessary facilities, such as cattle-dips and the tapping of artesian water supplies, set them organizing committees to besiege appropriate government departments. After all, the land was not freehold and although the pastoral leases had been extended in 1898 for the next thirty years, the tenure thereafter could not be guaranteed.

When M.P. returned from abroad, Frank Connor was still in Durban awaiting the arrival of the trial consignment of C.D. & D. cattle and hoping to negotiate a regular South African trade. He had cabled the Fremantle office that of the 3,612 animals shipped, only 108 had died on the voyage. This was considered 'very satisfactory', and all were poised for lucrative developments when a further message wrote 'finis' to all hopes of trade in that direction.

> Our cattle held in quarantine. Government Gazette notice stipulates no more Australian cattle allowed to enter Natal.

The disappointment on this score was somewhat offset by brighter prospects in the metropolitan and goldfields markets. The landing of cattle at Fremantle, hitherto a crude process by which the animals were driven down a gangway to swim ashore, had now been facilitated by the provision of a jetty for the unloading of the stock. This overcame considerable loss and saved time and effort in railing the stock to slaughter yards at Guildford and Kalgoorlie.

J.W., in Fremantle to meet the returning travellers, had been able to report with genuine enthusiasm on prospects for the goldfields trade. The population of that area had doubled over the past three or four years, and with recent amenities, including electric light, tramways, and a water supply to be opened early in the New Year, the increase seemed likely to continue.

News of the firm's prospects in the south was of more than usual interest to P.B., for Eva, having recently suffered a miscarriage at Argyle, had given an ultimatum about their remaining in Kimberley. If Pat wanted a family, as he so ardently declared he did, he must, she insisted, find a less remote and outlandish place of residence. She had rejected the compromise of setting up a domicile in Fremantle to which her husband would commute at convenient intervals. In fact she firmly refused to be the full-time mother of a family without the support of a full-time father.

M.P. had seen this situation arising for some time, and had already given thought to an alternative. He informed his brother that there was recent talk of a great future for stud stock in southern agricultural districts that would soon share the benefits of the almost completed goldfields water scheme. Were P.B. prepared to take over the management of a property in this area, M.P. had little doubt of his having the support of his partners.

P.B.'s immediate plans were to accompany his wife on a visit to her people in Brisbane. Eva would then set up a temporary base in Fremantle while he returned to wind up his affairs in Kimberley.

Members of the family when going south often took one or another of their Aboriginal employees to see the sights of the metropolis, and this time it was Boxer's turn. Expected to stay with the Dohertys until after Christmas, he was, to M.P.'s surprise, back on the *Tangier's* return trip, having apparently seen enough of the 'big smoke' in a single week. The version, as given to his white friends, was that he had been generously fed and entertained. He had ridden in a train, travelled by ferry to the zoo, and enjoyed the bright lights and shops of the city, but the mid-November weather, which the inhabitants insisted was summer time, had seemed bitterly cold to him, and walking on the pavements in new boots had given him sore feet and stiff shins. His swift return may also have been influenced by urgent tribal concerns, for Boxer had already learned to tread carefully in his two worlds, balancing his roles as trusted servant of the white man with that of Aboriginal 'dreamer' and 'doctor man'.

Travelling with Boxer on his return trip was a married couple engaged to replace Bob Bell-Blay and his wife Ellen, who had left Argyle some months before. M.P. had been sorry to lose this cheerful and capable pair but was pleased, as always, when people in his employ took sensible steps to better themselves. They had saved while at Argyle and hoped in time to take up a small sheep property in West Kimberley. M.P. had seen them off in their buggy, headed in that direction and provided with good references and introductions. He was to hear from them some years later that after working on various properties they had purchased a block of land from Mr Gus Pegler, with money borrowed at a high rate of interest from the astute Ben Copley. Ellendale, originally a smallholding, was gradually extended to a sizable and well-developed sheep property[1].

The new recruits for Argyle were Charlie Eich, a young Belgian migrant, and his wife Maud (*née* Coberoft) who claimed to be a descendant of Australia's first free settlers. They, too, were to stay only a year or so, but they kept in touch with M.P. and his family thereafter and from all accounts enjoyed their short experience of the north and its inhabitants.

All C.D. & D. station hands were busy mustering for the December shipment, a number of men later to figure prominently in local history having turned up in the area during M.P.'s absence. Among them was Rudolph Philchowski[2], one of the most mysterious of the district's considerable miscellany of mystery men.

M.P. describes him as:

> A fine upstanding stamp of a fellow who springs to attention when addressed with a smart click of the heels. Speaks good English with marked German accent and would appear to be a man of considerable education. Why he should be prepared to work as a stockman in a Kimberley cattle camp is beyond me, but he rides well and makes no complaints, so no questions asked.

Philchowski would continue to puzzle, and often to annoy, M.P. until their association was abruptly terminated ten years later.

Another to enter the company chronicle at this time was Bill (W.J.C.) Jones. A young man of New South Wales station background, his reasons for abandoning a secure and comfortable living for the harsh conditions of the north were never clear, as his story was inclined to vary with the telling. The most feasible version was that his decision to leave home followed a dispute over the terms of a will, during which he told his brothers they could keep the lot as he was getting out for good. Whether he meant it or not, having come to Kimberley the country took over, as it was prone to do, and assured that he maintained his promise.

An experienced cattleman with enough education to keep reliable records, Bill Jones[3] soon became M.P.'s right-hand man in the inspection and purchase of stock from surrounding properties. He was stubborn, proud, and often argumentative, but a shrewd judge of stock and a good friend to his fellow workers including the Aborigines. He was also loyal to the interests of the company, whose members soon came to regard him as indispensable.

Soon after his return to Argyle, M.P., obviously missing his brothers, wrote to J.W. in somewhat nostalgic strain:

> Here I am again back in the scenes of our earlier days which were brought vividly before me yesterday as I went through piles of old letters, papers and scraps of diaries reminding me of when we were battling about together. I read of a day when you and I started over for Kilfoyle's from M.J.'s, made three attempts to cross the river and you got badly sunburned. Another day we were mustering bullocks for Will Byrne and you shot a huge barramundi . . . Some of the letters dated away back to 1874 at Thylungra. Remember Mr. Healy's[4] old boco mare? Well I came upon the receipt for her amongst the papers . . . I made pretty well a clean sweep of the lot . . . Blatchford & Black [of the Kalgoorlie firm of Black, Blatchford and Grut, mining engineers and metallurgical assayers] who came up on the boat with me gave a favourable report of making a reservoir at the Three Mile Gorge. I fitted them out with horses from Wyndham for Hall's Creek. They appear both good, practical fellows and may do something for us with the Ruby Queen. [M.P.D., Argyle, to J.W.D., Kalgoorlie, 20.11.02]

The New Year opened with a fine display of sheet lighning and a dramatic roll of thunder—a good omen, M.P. was confident. He doled out a couple of bottles of whisky to his men but partook of none himself, having made a pact with Doherty that if the latter would give up tobacco for the coming year he himself would give up alcohol. The resolution was evidently harder for Doherty, who was an inveterate smoker, than for M.P., whose drinking habits were moderate.

Another of his New Year resolutions was to shorten the track between Ivanhoe and Argyle, a project that his father had investigated with Duncan McCaully some seven years earlier. The brothers had then been too preoccupied with other concerns to take much notice of Grandfather's claim of having found a possible short cut through the range near Granite Creek, but M.P. now decided to act on his advice. He and McCaully spent some days looking for an easier site than the one previously suggested, which, at a casual glance appeared quite improbable. Finding that it was the only place remotely possible, they decided that a pass could be made by cutting into the hill on the steep side of the range, the slope on the northern side being gradual and presenting no problem.

M.P. engaged an Irishman named Tom Scanlan, presumably a family connection through his late Aunt Bridget's husband, to undertake the task with two assistants. Scanlan had been a stockman in Queensland before coming to Kimberley, where he took over the mail run between Wyndham and Hall's Creek. Hearing of M.P.'s scheme to make a road up a precipitous mountain face, he had taken a bet that it was not 'crazy' as so many averred. To prove it he had applied for the job, and set to with cheerful confidence.

In November M.P. was in Fremantle, having travelled down with a number of witnesses for a legal battle that had been building up throughout the year. It was a tangled issue, ostensibly to do with a breach of contract but emerging from a morass of personal conflicts and rivalries so complex that when the case came to be heard it was hard to predict on whose side the various witnesses would come out. Prominent among the *dramatis personae* was Jim Patterson, who had been managing Newry Station for C.D. & D. before going into partnership with the Copley brothers in the purchase of Ord River Station from the estate of W. S. Osmond. The Copleys, Ben and Sam, were migrants from Yorkshire who had made a considerable fortune from real estate investments in Perth suburban areas. Jim Patterson, the practical stockman and working member of the association, had quickly begun to make good with the property that had stagnated under Osmond's parsimonious regime. Before long the partners were following the example of C.D. & D. in chartering their own ships and disposing of some 4,500 head of cattle a year, but the fact that the Copleys held the pursestrings did not mean that Patterson, the burly Scot, accepted their orders without question. When C.D. & D.'s drovers had turned up at Ord River to take delivery of 2,000 head for which a contract had been signed by the Copley brothers in Perth, Patterson firmly refused to cooperate. He declared that he had not been informed of the deal, and that at the end of the unusually long dry season he had turned all the stock horses out to spell, and that in any case there was insufficient time to organize a muster.

M.P. had filled the gap as far as possible by hurrying to Wave Hill and contracting for 500 head, which were quickly mustered and sent on their way with the redoubtable Hasty Byrnes. Renowned for being as quick off the mark as he was impatient with others who were not, Byrnes got the cattle down in time, through wet weather quagmire and over flooded waterways.

Meanwhile, C.D. & D., operating through solicitor John Moss, had issued a writ against the Ord River partners for breach of contract and subsequent damages. The case was scheduled to be held in Perth at the end of the year, and most of the witnesses called for both sides went south on the same ship. By the time they arrived at their destination, the matter had been thoroughly discussed, the main point at issue being whether or not it had been impossible in the circumstances and the time allowed to muster the contracted numbers. As experienced stockmen with their reputations at stake, it was hard for Copleys' witnesses to maintain that they could not have carried out a job in which those of the rival contingent saw no real difficulty.

When the case opened on 1 December, the list of witnesses for and against read like a *Who's Who* of the Kimberley and Territory camps. Among those called for Copley and Patterson was the ace drover Jim ('Silver King') Dillon, who, probably unknown to the defendants, was one of those ubiquitous Durack family connections so liberally scattered through the stock camps of Australia. Another was Dick Townsend, Wyndham agent for Forrest, Emanuel, soon to take over the management of Victoria River Downs from Jim Ronan, who was also a witness for the defence. There was also Arthur Young, still officially manager of Ord River and an old friend of M.P., whose employment with Copley & Co would seem to have terminated with his evidence. Jack Kelly, one of Ord River's battling border raiders, had also, for some misguided reason, been summoned for the defence.

Looking them over, M.P. could see only one witness likely to prove reliable to the Copley cause. This was Stephens, the Wyndham stock inspector who had been a thorn in the flesh of C.D. & D. for a number of years. M.P.'s assessment proved correct. On 9 December, after all evidence had been taken, he reports:

> Although the result is set down by the public as a foregone conclusion in our favour, yet the nervous tension on my part and with other members of our firm is very high . . .
>
> The opening words of the judge are encouraging: 'Although the amount involved is considerable the issues are very simple.' When he dwells on the words 'reasonable time' my apprehension of some legal hocus-pocus begins to rise but it is finally ruled that Copley accepting the approved bills on 27th November last was acknowledgement that the time was reasonable. The fact of their letting men and horses go in November (as was falsely alleged) was no

excuse for having entered into this contract. They were supposed to keep men and horses to carry it out.

The Judge summed up that, taking everything into consideration . . . the defendants are liable for damages to the extent of £6,500, with costs.

Thus a great victory!

13
Propitious Stars

December 1903–April 1905

For all their problems and complexities, these were good times for the firm. The State's population had doubled over the past decade, their herds had multiplied to at least the same extent, and cattle in the metropolitan and goldfields markets were bringing a steady price of £6 to £7 a head. The company had not yet been able to pay the anticipated dividend, but the partners' annual salaries had been raised to more than £1,000 each and they had begun to invest in small suburban and country businesses and properties. The Kalgoorlie enterprise, under J.W.'s able direction, was fairly flourishing, as were the incidental Wyndham businesses—hotel, store, and butchery.

From a personal point of view, the partners would also appear to have entered upon a fairly propitious phase. In December 1903 Eva had presented P.B. with a healthy baby daughter whose christening in the name of Sheila, with Mrs Connor and M.P. as godparents, followed the successful termination of the Copley case. Mary and Jim Davidson, who had recently acquired a house in Cottesloe, were present with their two little ones, Kenneth and the baby Douglas. Bird was housekeeping in Claremont for the Dohertys, who were then visiting Ireland. Anxious for their children to receive a broader education than was available in Australia, they were also arranging to board their two eldest daughters at a convent in Brussels that was much in favour with well-to-do English and Irish families.

Connor, at the peak of his parliamentary career, was then wielding considerable influence in the making and breaking of political regimes, his residence a veritable lobby for politicians and those who sought to sway them. He had moved with his growing family from their original house in High Street, Fremantle, to a place named Clanrye that they had had built for themselves on the seafront at Cottesloe. It was a spacious home with a number of spare rooms, one of which was kept for J.W. on his frequent visits from Kalgoorlie. In Doherty's absence M.P., too, spent a good deal of time there, catching up on the political front.

He found Connor bitterly opposed to the Walter James government on the grounds of its total indifference to the needs and problems of the Kimberley pastoralists. He had been more than ever disgusted by the amalgamation that year of the East and West Kimberley electorates, leaving as representative of the interests of the entire district a member of the Broome pearling fraternity[1] with its iniquitous 'black labour' policy. When M.P. remarked that the pastoralists, with their Chinese cooks and Aboriginal employees, would be hard put to sustain a case against coloured labour, Connor replied that they were merely making limited use of an existing labour pool, not clamouring for the wholesale introduction of a potential 'yellow peril'. It was certainly hard to refute his statement that if all the Asians and Aborigines were to disappear from the scene overnight there would be more than enough white workers available to meet the needs of the pastoral industry.

M.P., whose politics were predictably cautious, found Connor's decidedly uneven platforms somewhat disconcerting. He was no sooner in agreement with him on some issue than his partner would come up with an addendum that he found quite unacceptable. Certainly M.P. thought the government should be pressured in every way possible to assist in the provision of artesian water—but definitely not for the purpose of encouraging smaller holdings. Assuredly the James ministry should be censured for its neglect of Kimberley pastoral interests—but it should not be opposed to the extent of forming an Independent Party to support the rise of a Labor movement whose members were continually reviling C.D. & D. as organizers of the so-called 'meat ring'. This, however, was no idle threat on Connor's part, for it was the backing of his Independent Party that was soon to raise Henry Daglish to the position of the State's first Labor Premier[2].

At most meetings in the company's Fremantle office or at Connor's house was his loyal friend and supporter Charlie Moran, son of an early pioneer of the Darling Downs district in Queensland. A classical scholar of pastoral background, Moran found himself more at home in politics than the various other vocations he had assayed. Attracted to the goldfields in the early '90s, he had brought all the fire and eloquence of his Irish ancestry to winning and holding the Yilgarn-Coolgardie seat. By this time he had established a headquarters in Perth, but he kept in almost daily touch with Connor, as did their mutual friend, J. J. Holmes, the down-to-earth head of a wholesale butchery and part owner of Rosewood Station with Tom Kilfoyle. Holmes had entered Parliament as member for East Fremantle in 1897 and was at that time Commissioner for Railways. Hammered out at all their sessions were the latest developments on the tick front, the immediate need for dipping facilities, and—at longer range the solution, as they saw it, to all their problems—the formation of a freezing and chilling works at Wyndham.

Business was, of course, interspersed with a good deal of social diversion. They attended the races and treated each other and their womenfolk to luncheons, dinners, and entertainments, including regular musical evenings at which Connor and Moran enchanted their audience with renderings of songs in the ancient Gael. The Connors had invested in a pianola which encouraged the company to brush up on a comprehensive repertoire of popular ditties and operatic excerpts.

A young woman named Elodie Pombard, who had migrated from the Seychelle Islands with an elder brother and two sisters some years before, attended all their gatherings. They were the orphaned childen of a French judge and his Creole wife, and the reason for their coming to Australia is long since forgotten. Soon after their arrival the girls had been taken in charge by the Oblate Fathers in Fremantle, and two of them eventually joined the Sisters of Mercy in that port. Elodie, while toying with the idea of following their example, was persuaded by Mrs Connor to join her household instead and to assist with the raising of her family. The relationship between the two women—never that of mistress and servant—was to develop into one of a curious complexity from which neither was ever to escape. At this time Elodie, in her early twenties, was a pretty and accomplished girl speaking excellent English and the purest French, was a good pianist, a witty conversationalist, and had a flair for the training of children with emphasis on the tenets and traditions of the Catholic Church. Already courted by several eligibles, she had eyes for no one but J.W. who accorded her the gallantry that he extended more or less impartially to a considerable circle of lady friends, both married and single. This fact had not escaped Elodie who, noting the rapt attention with which he listened to the spirited opinions and sophisticated sallies of the elegant Alicia Connor, endeavoured, not without some success, to emulate her. As time went on her innocent utterances took on something of the worldly-wise cynicism of the older woman, whom she would never cease to blame for obstructing her romance. At this time, however, M.P. thought it not unlikely or unsuitable that his brother and the personable little Frenchwoman should make a match of it.

M.P. kept a horse for his use when in Fremantle, where he missed the constant exercise of his life in Kimberley. Mounted on Guardsman, he cantered along the seafront from the port to Cottesloe, where he would call on his sister Mary and her family, and on his cousin M.J. and wife Bertha who was suffering a slow recovery from the birth of a still-born baby.

> Poor Bertha [M.P. writes] finds it hard to accept the doctor's verdict that she cannot bear another child. She appears to wander somewhat in conversation.

It was a blow from which neither M.J. nor his wife would ever fully recover. How different might their lives have been if with their consistent rise of fortune they could also have raised a family to share and inherit it!

Inevitably, M.P.'s activities included an excursion to Mundaring Weir where streams from the Darling Range near Perth had recently been dammed to supply water to the goldfields. M.P. was excited by the wonder and significance of this engineering feat, built at a cost of £2,700,000, by which 5,000,000 gallons of water a day were pumped by steam engines through 351 miles of piping. J.W., who accompanied him on the expedition, had been present when Sir John Forrest, amid festival excitement and much speechifying, had turned on the water at the reservoir near Kalgoorlie in January 1903.

M.P. listened enthralled to his brother's lively tales of life on the goldfields and of the personalities, politics, and prospects of the area. There had lately been some indication of a slump in the mining industry. Investors had been more cautious and a few mines had closed down, with resultant unemployment, but J.W. was confident that it was no more than a temporary recession. Mining, he believed, would continue to grow in importance to the State revenue and to the prospects of C.D. & D. His predictions came true only in part, for although mining would continue to be of major importance to the State, the boom days were already in decline and a steady drift that had begun from the fields to the coastal areas was not to be stemmed. The voice of the miners demanding prior rights to State resources would never again ring out with such authority.

Fortunately the government, despite their protests, had been mindful of the importance of primary production and had encouraged the opening up of southern agricultural areas by a steadily growing network of communications.

P.B., from a home base in Fremantle, had meanwhile procured 10,000 acres (soon to be extended to 20,000) in the Wagin district, about 143 miles south-east of Perth, and was enthusiastic about its prospects as a stud sheep and general farming property. Keen to show his brother the new company acquisition of which he was to be manager, he set out with M.P. by train early in the new year. On horseback and by buggy they traversed the selected area and adjoining properties, where they yarned at length with pioneer settlers, most of whom had come to the district as sandalwood cutters and had stayed on in high hopes of its future as a farming area. They one and all dismissed as minor problems such hostile factors as dingoes and poison weed. In bringing the virgin land to productivity there was, they agreed, much to be done, and at considerable cost. Admittedly the natural pasture was scant and coarse, but there was a ready pool of labour available for ring-barking the trees, a process guaranteed to sweeten the soil, improve the quality and quantity of natural grasses, and build up the soaks and springs that were a feature of the area. P.B. also planned to embark at once on a programme of stock- and dog-proof fencing at £54 a mile (including fence clearance to a chain on either side, against bush fires) and the division of the property into fourteen paddocks with a dam in each, to be sunk at an average cost of a shilling a yard.

Prepared to throw himself heart and soul into the new venture and to make the environment his own, he expounded on the project with typical enthusiasm: 'Just look at old Craddock's vegetable patch! Did you ever see such cabbages?' 'Old Spanwick put in those 200 acres of crop on his own—at 87 mind you! He says it's the healthiest district in the world!'

If P.B. expressed any further regrets about leaving Kimberley, they were never recorded, but in sentimental token of the country to which he had given his youthful energies, he named the new property Behn Ord[3]. M.P. entered encouragingly into the spirit of the enterprise, though he doubted whether any woman would talk *him* into exchanging the savage magnificence of his northern horizons for a pocket-handkerchief of jam tree and mallee scrub. Much as he enjoyed his sojourn in the south, the lively exchange of ideas with men of affairs, and the refining influence of their womenfolk, it was never more than a few weeks before the urban life began to pall for him. After all, in the city he felt himself to be of little importance in the scheme of things, while in the north his comings and goings were of paramount interest to the scattered inhabitants, his opinions eagerly sought, and his instructions attended to.

Returning after three months' absence, it would seem that he had been genuinely missed by the crowd of station hands, in town on one pretext or another, who were at the ship to welcome him. Among them were Alec Campbell, Bill Jones, Charlie Good, Ted Wormall, Duncan McCaully, Jim Crisp, and his cousins Jack and Jerry Skeahan—to be greeted one by one with his firm handshake and usual enquiries, perfunctory about their personal welfare, specific about that of the stations and the stock.

Several men who had come in with cattle for the February shipment returned with him to Argyle, taking the track over Granite Creek to see how Scanlan was progressing with the new road. To M.P's satisfaction work on this project was almost completed, despite the fact that Scanlan's helpers had walked off the job because of wet weather conditions that they declared to be 'inhuman'. This was obviously not altogether an exaggeration but Scanlan, although suffering from a severe bout of fever, was determined to carry on. M.P. sent a man from Argyle to assist him and went off on his bustling station round. Two weeks later he was shocked to hear from Bill Jones at Ivanhoe that Scanlan had since died, and had been buried at the foot of the hill on which he had been working.

> 26.3.04: I proceeded thence on horseback [M.P. writes] together with Walsh and boy Frank. Found the grave of Scanlan on the hill, at his head a board with name cut signifying that he died on April 1st. Poor chap—destiny appears to have made a fool of him and what a lonely spot to be buried!

The road was finished within the next few weeks and M.P. had the satisfaction of seeing a carrier make the descent successfully.

> Over the hill and down without the slightest difficulty, this being the first wagon over what a great number of people declared to be an impossibility.

The project had already been dubbed 'Durack's Folly'[4], as it is known to this day, though experts affirm that it was not folly but a remarkable example of bush engineering. It was used for many years by teamsters and travellers with buggies, wagons, or drays as a means of shortening the track between Ivanhoe and Argyle by about twenty miles. It was also used occasionally by drovers, but was abandoned for this purpose in 1907 after a mob panicked on the steep decline and fourteen beasts plunged to their death over the side of the hill. The track fell into disuse when the road was improved after the advent of motor-cars some ten years later. K. J. Kelsall, an engineer connected with the Ord River dam project, discovered the route in later years and wrote of it as follows:

> While it was relatively simple to ford the river in selected places with cattle and drovers' horses, it was not really practical to negotiate the crossing with supply waggons, buggies and pack horses. The original pioneer Patsy Durack and his son M. P. Durack endeavoured to locate an easy passage across the final precipitous ridge. Eventually they selected a route ... and constructed a roadway that was later christened 'Durack's Folly'.

> Perhaps the proposal was unduly ambitious. It would certainly have been a significant project with modern equipment, but with the facilities that were available over 70 years ago, the achievement was quite amazing. The term 'Durack's Folly' is, therefore, not derogatory. Rather does the road now stand as a monument to the indomitable spirit of those early pioneers.

M.P.'s journals make clear that there was no lack of white labour in these years. Some of the men he mentions soon fade from the scene, among them those who succumbed to fever, while others were to remain in the picture for the next thirty to fifty years. None of these station workers and few station owners or managers was then married, and most never would be, as the trend was for fewer rather than more white women to take up residence in East Kimberley. Inevitably there was an increasing number of half-castes, though not as many as might have been expected. In fact there were surprisingly few children, either full black or part white, born in the station camps from this time until the 1950s, when the introduction of child endowment and social services gave sudden impetus to regeneration. As long as they exercised sensible discretion and there were no complaints from the Aborigines themselves, M.P. turned a blind eye to the activities of his men in this respect. If a man's actions challenged the firm's interests, however, it was another matter.

A case in point was his difference with Philchowski who had the effrontery to ask for a rise on the grounds that he was worth at least two of the other employees. M.P., while admitting that the man had style, did not consider that he was as competent in the stock camp as many less pretentious older hands. The request refused, Philchowski took umbrage, gave notice, and set himself up in a wayside store at Carlton Reach on Ivanhoe Station. His establishment, a bough shed and a couple of canvas tents, did not look particularly attractive but many hitherto reliable bush workers, mainly teamsters bringing goods from Wyndham to the outlying station, hung about there until their money had run out. The reason, as M.P. soon discovered, was that 'basic necessities' claimed by Philchowski as being his stock-in-trade included a supply of sly grog and a few Aboriginal women who had been traded by their own men for tobacco, sugar and tea.

Requested to remove himself, Philchowski informed M.P. that he had as much right to deal in merchandise as the firm had to run cattle in the area. With the backing of the police, however, M.P. had the best of the argument, and Philchowski thereafter took over the mail-run from Wyndham to Hall's Creek. He soon afterwards became part-owner of Spring Creek

Station with the astute but illiterate battler, Joe Fegan, with whom he had struck up an incongruous mateship.

Apart from occasional visitors, such as the surveyor Alec Salmond whom M.P. had known twenty years before in Western Queensland, and Arthur Haly, the genial stock inspector who was to become one of his closest friends, there were few men around with whom he could converse on any topic beyond current happenings and station routine. About these, however, there were usually enough to keep a conversation going from the evening meal until time to turn in.

Local gossip flourished through a word-of-mouth medium generally referred to as 'the bushman's mulga wire', described by an anonymous versifier of the time in a rambling jingle of sly digs and 'in' jokes.

When the conversation's weary
And the subject matter's slack,
There's no need for you to worry
Or to curse the dreary track,
For varied news and plenty
Is awaiting your desire
In that latest modern wonder—yes!
The Bushman's Mulga Wire . . .

The reason Charlie Flinders
Has embraced the Faith of Rome
Will be treated as a 'Special'
Or a Hallelujah Pome;
And Mick Rhatigan's opinion
When Bridge snared the altar wine
Shall be represented only
By a dash and single line.
How business on the Ord is brisk
In a certain kind of 'Hey'
That gives entrance to the humpy
Where the gins sleep after tea,
Why Jack Kelly's gone off whisky
And to sanctity aspires
Are a few of many items
In the Bushman's Mulga Wires . . . [5]

More respectable items for the mulga wires of 1904 included the arrival of a flock of angora goats, which were to thrive at Ascot, Ivanhoe, and Argyle for many years. Then there was C.D. & D.'s new chartered ship, *Moira*, the smartest vessel on the coastal run; and in the middle of the year came a narrow victory for Connor over Sydney Piggott in the Kimberley election.

In September terrible bush fires devastated hundreds of square miles of country, destroyed fences and yards, and had all hands out fighting the flames for several weeks. Mobs coming into Wyndham had to be rerouted to provide feed on the way down, and shipping dates altered on account of the delay.

Another happening of the year was the mysterious disappearance of Constable Henry Parker, last seen strolling down the Wyndham jetty to visit a friend on the S.S. *New Guinea*. The puzzle was solved a few weeks later when Jacob Kuhl[6] made the following deposition:

> Yesterday I caught an alligator[7] in a trap I had set up on the gulf. I shot him and took him down to the jetty and skinned him. Then I opened him up and found some clothing like portions of a uniform ... and some human bones. I put them all into a bucket and took them up to the Police Station ...

Like the tick question, another subject of never-ending conversation was the possible cause of 'walk-about' disease that accounted, in some areas, for 50 per cent of the stock horses. Theories abounded, and continued to do so until 1952 when the problem was finally traced to its source[8].

Yet another well-worn topic was the denuding of pasture on the river frontages, necessitating the constant shifting of stock to better-grassed areas. This highlighted the need for artesian waters, and also indicates the rapid increase in the number of cattle, which was by then in excess of both the southern market and the shipping space available.

Early in 1905, M.J. and his partner Lumley Hill of Lissadell Station embarked on the ambitious project of overlanding 4,000 head of cattle to an alternative market on the eastern coast. For this job they employed the well-known contract drover, Walter Rose, who set out in April with a plant of seventeen men and eighty horses.

> It will be interesting [M.P. remarks] to watch the outcome of this new movement. It appears that they intend taking the Murranji track through Newcastle Waters and across the Barkly Tableland.

As it happened, this expedition was to be hailed as one of the greatest feats in Australian droving history.

Owing to severe drought conditions in the Territory and Queensland, the party had to take a zigzag route in the wake of scattered storms and in search of pasture. They had several times to turn back on their tracks and camp for long periods. Pleuro-pneumonia broke out in the mob, but was controlled by inoculation. Five hundred died from redwater or tick-fever, and another 300, along with eleven head of horses, from other causes. One of the men died from beri-beri and before the end of the trek all but two of the seventeen assistants had deserted. Nonetheless, Rose made the 2,200-mile journey to Richmond in seventeen months, and sold the remaining 3,200 head of cattle at a higher price than that offering on the West Australian market[9].

Before long Gordon Buchanan and his relatives, the Gordon brothers of Flora Valley, began overlanding stock to Narrabri in New South Wales, while the Copleys, in partnership with Sam Muggleton of Frog Hollow, started big mobs on the route to Queensland.

All but forgotten today, these great movements of cattle were to proceed successfully for a number of years, prices on eastern markets being sometimes almost double those in the west. This was no doubt the reasons why M.J.'s financial graph maintained a steady incline while that of his cousins, with their more diversified policy, continued to fluctuate precariously.

14

A Girl in a Man's World

May–December 1905

There can have been few girls in Australia at that time with as long a chain of admirers as M.P.'s first cousin Catherine Durack, more generally known as Kathleen, or Kit. The fifth of his uncle Stumpy Michael's family of seven girls and three boys, she came to Kimberley in May 1905 on an extended visit to her brother Ambrose at Argyle. An attractive young woman, bravely unorthodox for her time, with a lively disposition, a keen sense of fun and adventure, and a warm heart, it is little wonder that she should have become the romantic dream of so many lonely bushmen. Few of them ever declared their devotion, for apart from the characteristic shyness of their kind in the company of white women, it was obvious from the time of her arrival that it would have been a bold and confident man indeed who ventured to break the guard of her possessive male relatives.

She had no sooner set foot in Wyndham than young Patsy, eldest son of poor widowed Aunt Fan, in from the Dunham to meet the ship, had staked a claim to her attention. The two had been briefly associated as children in Queensland and they immediately established a warm rapport. Among much they held in common was the belief that their fathers had been shabbily treated by their respective partners. In the case of Kit's father, the partners had been M.J. and Lumley Hill; in that of young Patsy, Tom Hayes and Tom Kilfoyle were held responsible for their financial situation. Kit, then twenty-four years of age, had since leaving school earned her living in a Brisbane shoe-store, a mundane occupation that she had gladly abandoned on the invitation of her Kimberley relatives, despite sundry dire warnings. Patsy had been doing a man's work as long as he could remember and had experienced more than his share of hardship and heartbreaks, but Kit found him, at twenty-three, to be mentally astute and refreshingly exuberant. He had inherited, along with his father's dancing feet and singing heart, a sense of showmanship and a reckless gambling streak that had caused Galway Jerry's fond but often exasperated eldest brother Patsy to label him a 'kippen-head'. M.P., though fond of his young cousin, was embarrassed by show-off tendencies typified by the usual manner of his entry into Wyndham—'a circus performance', balancing on the backs of his galloping buggy horses, often with his mother and her younger children bouncing about in the vehicle behind. Fortunately, Patsy's mother, Aunt Fan, enjoyed the performance. 'When M.P. and his lot come to town no one knows the difference,' she used to say. 'When my Patsy arrives the whole place wakes up.'

Aunt Fan, as she was widely known, was by this time herself regarded as one of the great characters of the district: generous, hospitable, quick of tongue and of temper, she had risen above her sorrows and vicissitudes and tried to make life as bright as possible for her remaining family. Visitors were always welcome at her humble homestead, and she was traditionally a key figure at bush race-meetings and social gatherings. She took her younger children south over the summer months, boarded in rented premises and trailed them about on an endless round of visits to friends and relatives. Tolerant enough of human weaknesses, she refused to condone anything that savoured of 'sitting down on the job'. She was remembered as having once broken a wharfies' strike in Wyndham by rallying the women of the town to unload a shipload of desperately needed supplies. She was also once brought before a magistrate in Wyndham on a charge of having dealt harshly with an Aboriginal woman who had dared to go 'walkabout' on washing-day.

Kit won M.P.'s unqualified approval on their first journey from Wyndham to Argyle when she insisted on remaining with him in the buggy on its perilous descent of Durack's Folly, with a log hitched on behind by way of a brake. Others who had accompanied him on this route had chosen to alight at the top of the hill and make their own way down on foot.

With a woman about the place again, Argyle soon took on a more homely and cheerful aspect, and everyone, including the Aborigines, looked happier. Ambrose, who spent most of his time mustering on the run, was delighted that his sister would often join him for a few days in his bush camp. She enjoyed the novelty and adventure of riding round the cattle, eating salt beef and damper, drinking tea black from the billy around the open fire, and sleeping under a net on the hard ground.

Not long after her arrival, M.P. took her across the river to Lissadell, a place with sad associations for Kit whose father, Stumpy Michael, had taken it up on his return from an exploration of the Kimberley district which he had led in 1881. The repercussions of a court case following his death in 1895, and ending with the estate's being adjudged the sole property of his cousin M.J. and partner Lumley Hill, had continued over the most impressionable years of the girl's life; and it is perhaps surprising that she consented to visit the disputed property. Long Michael was not indifferent to the bitterness felt towards him by his late cousin's wife and family, and took every opportunity of justifying his position to his other relatives. Having accepted the fact that he and his wife could have no children of their own, he had written to Stumpy Michael's widow asking whether they might adopt a member of her family. Kate Durack had been at that time teaching music and running a boarding-house in Brisbane, the elder daughters helping to provide for the education of the younger girls and their brothers, Clare and Fergus. Despite her struggle to make ends meet, Kate's answer to M.J.'s proposal had been predictably and emphatically in the negative. Brave, unforgiving, and independent to the end, she had died three years before her daughter came to Argyle.

As it happened, M.J. was not in the district at this time and his brother J.B., then in charge of the station, was out in the cattle camp. The only ones to greet the daughter of the property's first owner were a few aged Aborigines and a fever-stricken Chinese cook, the book-keeper whom M.P. had hoped to see having recently died of fever at Turkey Creek on his way to the doctor in Wyndham.

M.P., as on all occasions when he had reason to visit this station, remarked on the stark desolation of the homestead where it was all too obvious that no white woman had ever been in residence. This time, when the sun went down they could find no light whatever—not even a candle—to show them to their uncomfortable rawhide beds.

From the time of Kit's arrival, young Patsy found an unusual number of pretexts to bring him to Argyle. The mooted purchase of Dunham cattle by C.D. & D. and of horses by Ambrose required considerable negotiation and not, as previously, by medium of an Aboriginal courier. Before three months were out he and Kit, in defiance of contemporary social and religious taboos regarding the marriage of first cousins, had announced their engagement. M.P., writing to J.W. in September, makes an unexpectedly casual reference to the matter:

> Kit . . . appears to adapt to this kind of life admirably. She is never down in the dumps . . . always as jolly as a sandboy, is a keen sportswoman, a good shot and has now adopted, under my persuasion, the more rational 'cavalier' style in the saddle and wearing a divided skirt. I suppose you heard that she and Patsy are engaged. They are pretty 'bad cases' on each other.

M.P. himself, though obviously enjoying the companionship of his agreeable cousin, gives no indication of being romantically attracted to her. In any case the principles of eugenics, strongly engendered by his stockbreeding experience, would never have permitted his thoughts to stray in that direction. Since his visit to England three years before he had corresponded with Miss Vera Angier, niece of the shipping magnate Sir Theodore Angier; and his journal indicates that his romantic musings at that time were otherwise engaged. He records his great pleasure on receiving a photograph of the charming young lady in presentation finery, a gesture that set him wondering how soon he could visit England again. Writing his chronicle of that day, he allowed himself a wistful comment: 'One wonders will the original ever see Argyle. Perhaps—maybe—who knows? One can at least hope so.' Whether or not the young lady in question entertained thoughts of visiting that antipodean backwater, the two were to meet again sooner than M.P. then foresaw.

There was as usual plenty of movement at Argyle, with the coming and going of employees, business associates, travellers, and relatives. Jim Davidson had come to Wyndham on the firm's business, bringing his wife Mary and their three children, and they were occupying the cottage adjoining C.D. & D.'s store. Denis Doherty had travelled north with them and joined M.P. on his station rounds, regaling him with a fascinating account of the adventures and contacts of his recent trip abroad. This had convinced Doherty that the firm should have a London-based agent, since only with an interested party in the commercial centre of Empire could they keep abreast of market opportunities. The other members of the company had already agreed with him on this score and were of the opinion that Doherty himself would be the ideal man for the job. Needless to say, the position would also suit Doherty very well personally, as he was anxious that his third daughter and only son should share the educational opportunities he and his wife had already opened up to their two elder girls. In fact Mrs Doherty had elected to remain in London with her younger children, no doubt in anticipation of her husband's speedy return as the company's representative.

M.P. could see the logic of Doherty's proposals for an overseas agent, but had certain reservations regarding the forthright policy of expansion urged by his two Irish partners. He had been inclined to accept an offer made to Doherty in London of £25,000 for the Auvergne run, and to concentrate on improvements to Newry, Argyle, and Ivanhoe. Connor and Doherty, on the other hand, still maintained that Auvergne Station was a far more valuable asset than the original Durack holdings on the western side of the border, and that the firm should aim to extend rather than reduce their vast leaseholdings. Doherty claimed to have gathered, from wide-ranging and impressive-sounding contacts, the fact that investors had sharp eyes open for North Australian properties, the larger the better, overseas investors being tremendously impressed by the extent of these potentially rich cattle kingdoms in the southern hemisphere. The only factor which inhibited competitive bidding from various magnates was the distance from markets—otherwise the lack of processing works anywhere on the coast for 2,000 miles northwards between Perth in Western Australia and Townsville in Queensland. With the inside knowledge available to the firm, however, it seemed obvious that this disability would soon be rectified. The company would then be in a strong bargaining position and would be able practically to command its own price.

M.P., though always more cautious and sceptical than his partners, was infected by Doherty's enthusiasm to the extent of considering every direction in which they could logically enlarge their boundaries. It was during Doherty's visit that they reopened discussions with young Patsy and Aunt Fan concerning C.D. & D.'s purchase of the Dunham lease and a percentage of its estimated cattle. As usual in such negotiations, this estimate was a fairly hypothetical figure, agreed upon only after considerable argument, at about half Patsy's original reckoning and twice that of Doherty and M.P. The agreement stipulated that Aunt Fan and her family should carry on there as before, but that in the event of a sale the property and half the cattle would be reckoned as part of the C.D. & D. estate. The ready cash paid in consideration of the lease and portion of the stock was no doubt sorely needed at that time to help with the education of Aunt Fan's three younger boys and their only remaining sister. This proposal seems to have fallen through or else to have been valid only for an interim period, as the matter of C.D. & D.'s purchasing the Dunham was still being discussed in 1910.

Doherty's enthusiasm for expansion probably explains M.P.'s further expedition of this time around the Bow and Wilson rivers, where they had taken up an option lease which they had not so far stocked. He returned to Argyle to report to Doherty that he thought they might as well sell the rights to this chunk of country to Jack Kelly of Texas Downs. It would be largely stocked, no doubt, from C.D. & D. cleanskins, but this occupation would probably deter the cattle-spearing and -chasing activities of the Aborigines, of whom he had encountered big groups encamped around the wild gorges and water-holes. It would be more to the point, they decided, to begin stocking the 2,353 square miles of country to the south and east of Auvergne, for part of which the firm had been paying option rates over a number of years.

The Skeahan brothers had also taken up part of this area, which they already referred to as Bullita Station[1]. The amenities on this property consisted of no more than a couple of rough yards and a bough shack, but the country was carrying a considerable number of cattle and horses bearing the Skeahan 557 brand. These were stock that had wandered into the area from Auvergne to run wild, producing cleanskin progeny that the Duracks would not have begrudged their battling cousins. The situation, however, gave them access to a limitless number of C.D. & D. calves, and no amount of family feeling could blind the partners to the fact that the Skeahans were unlikely to have more scruples than any of the marauding smallholders already on their borders.

With this in mind, M.P. set out with Ambrose and Ulysses (naming a creek after the latter along the way) to explore the country in question. As a result C.D. & D. came to an arrangement with Ambrose Durack[2] and the Skeahan brothers, by which the latter parties put in between them 1,785 head of cattle and seventy-six horses in exchange for 1,248 shares each to an association known as the Bullita Pastoral Co, in which C.D. & D. held 2,497 shares. In this way the firm gave the Skeahans an incentive to co-operate in their new venture, and left them nothing to gain by branding Auvergne cattle.

On this same expedition M.P. found himself retracing a route he had frequently taken when droving cattle to the Territory in the 1890s, and which also came within the unstocked C.D. & D. leaseholdings.

> Camped at the big permanent spring where in the early days Tom Kilfoyle and self used to water our bullocks bound for the Darwin market. Decided to name this creek 'Kildurk', a combination of our two names, in memory of former days.

The half-million acre Kildurk block was to be of more significance to his family in later years than he could then have imagined.

The idea of stocking these remote leases was not, M.P. realised, as simple as it sounded, for it raised at once the problem of boundaries, particularly those dividing the Kildurk/Bullita blocks from Kilfoyle's Rosewood and Deacon's Waterloo. The approximate nature of early surveys rendered it almost impossible for the various parties to agree where these boundaries lay, each naturally claiming rights to a line embracing the best permanent watering-sites.

While in the area, M.P. called at Waterloo to discuss the matter with Mrs Tom Deacon, whose husband had died at Ivanhoe in June of that year and at whose burial, close to the homestead, M.P. had officiated. Deacon's death at forty-five years old had made a greater impression on the community than the demise, mostly from fever, of a number of younger men within the same year[3]. He had been in the country almost from the beginning of white settlement and was a familiar figure on the drovers' route to Wyndham, shadowed at all times by the Aborginal Jimmy Deacon whom he had reared from his earliest years. It was Jimmy who had galloped up the road to meet M.P., then on his way to Wyndham, to inform him that his master was on his deathbed at Ivanhoe. Those who had known Tom Deacon declared that he would never be truly dead while Jimmy was alive, for the Aboriginal had modelled himself on his boss in every way possible—his walk, his seat in the saddle, the angle of his hat, even his forthright and often colourful manner of speech. He was now back at Waterloo, assisting the widow to carry on the property.

M.P., as an old friend of Tom, was welcomed at the station and pressed by Mrs Deacon to stay at least long enough to have his laundry attended to. They came to an agreement about the boundary which would no doubt have taken much longer had Tom been still in control. M.P., always appreciative of a woman's influence, remarked on the general cleanliness and homely atmosphere of this remote outpost and expressed admiration of the widow, who was a member of the Darcy family that was to play such a big part in the Kimberley stock camps from about that time on.

His return via Rosewood caused him to reflect upon how soon after a woman's departure a station homestead could revert to an uninviting bachelor camp. He found Tom Kilfoyle in lower spirits than in all the long years of their association, moving restlessly about among a litter of old newspapers and dusty household effects. His wife had gone south a year or so before, taking their son Jack, then twelve years old, to attend the Christian Brothers' College in Perth. Both had been too worried about the boy's health to consider sending him to boarding-school at that stage, for not only had he lost an eye as the result of an infected insect bite but he was in poor health owing to recurrent attacks of fever. Kilfoyle feared that his boy would have neither the constitution nor necessary eyesight to take over management of the property that would one day be his own, but he hoped that he might graduate in some lucrative profession and be able to afford to employ a manager. In voicing these doubts, however, Kilfoyle had underestimated the magnetism of the country that had already shaped the destiny of his only son[4].

M.P. returned to Argyle, pondering somewhat gloomily on the nature of a region that, for all its potential and scenic grandeur, remained seemingly so resistant to the forces of change and progress. For all his natural optimism and determination to 'travel hopefully', his journals are still to a great extent chronicles of hardship and misfortune. While every year brought its considerable roll-call of deaths, the births he had so far recorded had been negligible. Few married couples in the country had locally born children. The McCaullys at Ivanhoe and the Deacons of Waterloo, having no children of their own, had each adopted a baby girl, while the Kilfoyles, who had hoped for a large family, had produced only the one rather delicate son. Even the station Aborigines, who might have been expected to produce a generation of trusty workers, had so far proved unaccountably infertile, and this despite its being made known that bonus rations, including a tin of jam, would accrue to any C.D. & D. couple on the birth of a child.

Never lacking in a conscience towards the Aboriginal people, M.P. had been roused that year to more comment than usual on the situation. The reason for this was the result of a commission undertaken by Dr W. E. Roth, surgeon, anthropologist and Chief Protector of Aborigines in Queensland, to investigate the Aboriginal situation in North Western Australia. Extracts from the report appearing in the press early in 1905 had called forth a spate of letters and articles with hit-or-miss assessments and suggestions as to how the problem should be handled. M.P., writing to his brother J.W., early in the year remarks:

> I read the article you referred me to in the 'Nineteenth Century'. I agree with the writer that the natives are not so low in the scale of intelligence as most people have regarded them. Our own experience certainly tells us that in many instances they exhibit a good deal of intelligence and common sense. I could myself give many instances of intelligence and observation displayed by our boys and since I have had a little to do with teaching them along with white youngsters we have had on the stations at various times I have often known them to be more apt pupils than the white. How far they could carry on beyond the rudimentary stage is rather questionable . . .[5] [M.P.D., Fremantle, to J.W.D., Kalgoorlie, 13.2.05]

He wrote again a little later:

> Oh yes, the papers are still going strong on the native question . . . There is too much sentimental bosh in 'The Morning Herald' articles but there is a lot of truth in Dr. Roth's report . . . The pearlers, however, may be justified in their indignation. I was speaking to one of them recently—a man named

> Blackman who said Dr. Roth had a good deal of personal feud with pearlers and settlers on the eastern side and introduced personal bias in his findings. Blackman says that when he was pearling around Thursday Island Dr. Roth referred to them all as 'the amphibious scum and riff-raff of Queensland'.[6] [M.P.D., Fremantle, to J.W.D., Kalgoorlie, 15.2.05]

M.P. makes no comment on Roth's statement that:

> The pastoralists have taken most of the native boys from the tribes; the blacks come in from the bush and get tobacco and food from the boys working on the stations; this leads to a lot of immorality with the women. There is no power to stop squatters, drovers and teamsters taking their women and boys away. Women are seen on the road dressed up as men. 'Kombo-ism' is rife . . .[7]
>
> Carrying the present practice of Might against Right to a logical conclusion it would simply mean that were all the land in the northern areas to be leased all the blacks would be hunted into the sea . . .

The main weight of Roth's criticism fell on the police, for most of whom M.P. himself had little time, though probably for different reasons. He would no doubt have agreed with the finding that little, if any, of the money provided to feed Aboriginal prisoners on their way to trial in Wyndham was used for this purpose. Not all the squatters in the Kimberley district, however, were as restrained in their reactions—particularly those who had been named as begetters of neglected half-caste children.

The report resulted in the passing of the Aborigines Act, which introduced the issue of permits for employers of Aboriginal labour, and empowered the government to create native reserves and to appoint a Protector of Aborigines to each magisterial district. This Act caused general rumblings of irritation throughout the Kimberleys, but the settlers knew well enough that it would make little difference to the pattern of life in their isolated communities. The police would continue to ride out, arrest as many cattle-spearing suspects and witnesses as possible, and bring them in on the same neck chains as condemned by the Commissioner[8]. The cohabitation of white men and black women would continue regardless, as often as not with the connivance of the tribal men. Wages and education for Aboriginal workers would remain 'impractical ideals' and reserves a good intention. White men beyond the reach of the law would continue to take it into their own hands if the Aborigines provoked them. No one was likely to report their actions, though the occasional spearing of a white man never failed to resound loudly through the countryside.

The spearing of a stockman named Hugh McKenna, whose body was found near Wild Dog by the teamsters Cleary and Philchowski in September 1905, had the local police force and a special contingent of bush workers out in pursuit of the culprit. At much the same time a report reached Argyle that four white men sailing from Auvergne to Darwin in the launch *Wunwalla* had been killed by blacks while at anchor off Port Keats. The victims were Fred Bradshaw, brother of 'Captain Joe', founder of Bradshaws' run, a stockman named Ernest Dannock, a Russian named Ivan Egeroff (sometimes spelt Egoriffe), and young Jerry Skeahan.

M.P. set off in haste to Auvergne to investigate what he thought possibly 'a wild rumour'. He found Jack Skeahan quite distraught and blaming himself bitterly for his brother's having embarked on the ill-fated journey. It seemed that Jerry had broken his arm in the stock camp, sustaining a complicated injury that left the bone protruding, and he had set out with an Aboriginal companion on a 200-mile ride to the doctor in Wyndham. On the same day Bradshaw's launch called at Auvergne to pick up mail and messages for Darwin, and Jack Skeahan, anxious to save his brother a long, painful ride, sent a messenger off, full gallop, to bring him back so he could sail to Wyndham instead[9].

Several months elapsed before the story of the massacre, or as much as could be pieced together from a garbled mass of evidence, came to light. The four white men had evidently gone ashore at Port Keats to interview members of a geological party who were drilling for coal thereabouts. Finding, on their return to the launch, that the Aboriginal crew had deserted, Bradshaw and Egeroff had gone in search of them. As they were, expectedly, nowhere to be found, their pursuers rounded up a substitute crew at gunpoint and secured them to the vessel with leg irons. While the launch lay at anchor for the night, some twenty Murambata tribesmen swam out and climbed aboard. The sleeping white men were battered to death with stone axes and clubs, and their bodies thrown overboard. The fettered Aborigines were then released from their chains and the launch scuttled. Before long there had begun one of the biggest man-hunts in Northern Territory history, and eight suspects were eventually arrested. When six of these escaped and two were shot in the attempt, others were rounded up as suspects and witnesses and were brought to Darwin. Evidence brought forward at the trial, of Ivan Egeroff's brutal treatment of Aborigines over a number of years, resulted in the sentences of the condemned being commuted from death to life imprisonment, a side-effect perhaps of the recent Roth report.

The remains of the murdered men, washed up at last on the beach, were gathered up by Joe Bradshaw and buried on the summit of a flat-topped mountain near the mouth of the Victoria. It was here that old Bradshaw himself was to be buried when he died of fever in 1915, the hitherto unnamed landmark being known from that time as Bradshaw's Tomb[10].

15

More Traveller's Tales

December 1905–October 1906

A gap of several months in the record of our usually indefatigable chronicler results in a sudden transition from a wet-weather Christmas at Argyle ('Alas! all the ducks shot yesterday gone bad by this morning in the intense heat—so mundane salt beef a prelude to the festive plum pudding') to a crisp May morning in London where he writes from 184 St James' Court.

It is clear from references in his subsequent correspondence that he had travelled there from Fremantle with Denis Doherty, who was rejoining his family in London although his position as agent for C.D. & D. in that city had not yet been confirmed. M.P., welcomed by Sir Theodore and Lady Angier, had been staying with them at Brighton but there is no specific mention of the lovely Vera. Could the unaccountably missing few months have been deliberately deleted by M.P. to bury forever another unfulfilled romantic dream? Whatever the reason or accident behind this broken thread in his narrative, we lose the pretext for this journey. Business considerations would, of course, have been part of it—investigation of markets, establishing or renewing potentially valuable contacts. But, however well justified from that point of view, a dominant factor in the journey was no doubt M.P.'s insatiable hunger for travel. In other circumstances he could well have found his milieu as a travel writer or foreign correspondent, for he had all the necessary energy, enthusiasm, capacity for objective observation and powers of communication.

When his diary was resumed he had been to Ireland and stayed a few days in Belfast with the Donnellys, of whom he wrote to his brother Jerry, by that time Professor of Science and Mathematics at the University in Allahabad:

> They made earnest enquiries about you and as for Daisy—she is quite ratty over you. You must have enticed her, but she doesn't quite like you in those Regimentals! . . . Lady Angier told me she has a brother in Allahabad—something in the army. Have you

> met him? ... They all asked after you most kindly. [M.P.D., London, to J.J.D., Allahabad, 8.6.06]

On 29 May M.P. wrote to J.W. in the early hours of the morning, eager to convey to him the details of a truly memorable occasion. This was the annual Western Australian dinner, where 260 guests included a number of distinguished political figures from Great Britain and the colonies. The main speaker of the evening was Winston Churchill who had recently been appointed Under Secretary of State for the Colonies. This was a controversial choice, as Churchill's attacks on Joseph Chamberlain's preferential trade policy had rendered him unpopular with many Australians at that time in London. He was coldly received when he rose to speak, but it did not take him long to win round his audience completely. In M.P.'s own words:

> He declared it his belief that we (Great Britain and the colonies) were beginning to understand one another better and were being brought together by the fact that this great globe of ours is visibly shrinking, as it were, due to the many scientific elements contributing to the annihilation of space. He could only trust that the Liberal Party to which he now belonged would guide the destiny of our great Empire illuminated by the true light of justice and peace. It was Britain's policy to give her colonies freedom to go their own way in all matters including trade and policy. He believed that this was the only way in which true unity could be achieved within the Empire.
>
> The wild applause that followed this speech was interrupted when some fellow whom Kirwan declares slept through the address and was thus uninfluenced by it, stood up and proposed the toast of Chamberlain. Walter James rose and made some scathing remark and the chap walked out amid a chorus of boos and hisses.
>
> Altogether it was quite an intellectual feast ... There were many other fine speakers ... yet after Churchill they were quite flat. James[1] and John Kirwan both spoke briefly to toasts. A flattering tribute was paid to James's contribution to the prosperity of our State, the speaker remarking that he was shortly leaving this 'land of fogs and functions' and going to one where there was 'more sun and less ceremony' and wished him every success and prosperity in the 'land of the Black Swan and the white man'.

M.P. was up again at seven that same morning to assure himself of a good position at the Derby, an exercise that entailed a three-hour drive in a four-in-hand.

> Doherty and I had a good look at the horses in the saddling paddock—admired Spearming, the Carbine colt but others more ... The English race horse is generally bigger than ours but seems to lack the polish or finish that Australian trainers give their horses. (This may be due to the climate.) They struck me as being pretty tight boned ...
>
> Such a dense mass of people I never saw—a seething throng—all intent on enjoying themselves and prepared to laugh at everything and anybody, whether a coster with his little donkey cart or a Duke in his carriage, I could hear the banter as they passed. There were coster women singing and dancing with arms joined around motor buses; gipsy fortune tellers, nigger minstrels, concertina and bagpipe players ... [M.P.D., London, to J.W.D., Fremantle, 1.6.06]

The next day he is off with Doherty and the local manager for G. S. Yuill[2] to the Smithfield market, intent on gathering all possible data regarding the chilling and freezing of beef from the Argentine. At the Australian Club and other happy hunting-grounds of business magnates, the partners talked of forming syndicates for a chilling and beef-extract works in Wyndham, and discussed 'the recent meat scandal in Chicago' and its possible effects on the industry in Australia. With Kirwan and the Doherty family M.P. also attended Sunday Mass at Farm Street Church, to be warned, in the golden diction and discerning phraseology of Father Bernard Vaughan, of the dangers and evils of materialism. Whether or not M.P. and his friends applied the orator's penetrating comments to themselves, they noted with some amusement the rich and fashionable apparel of the congregation, whose carriages and liveried servants waited without.

At the end of June M.P. set sail from Liverpool for Canada and the United States, in the *Empress of Ireland*.

> One hundred 1st class passengers, 350 2nd and 750 3rd class. Most of the emigrants appear to be fine, youthful types—crowded out of their own country, many declare, by Jews, Russians, Scandinavians invading English cities ... There are pathetic scenes and many tears as the band strikes up 'Auld Lang Syne' and we set sail with the green flag of Ireland fluttering from the bow ...
>
> What a dream of luxury and comfort this ship is! ... But none

> of the supercilious attitude sometimes encountered on English lines . . .

Taken in hand by fellow passengers returning to Quebec, he enjoyed the sights of this city, absorbed its history, and commented on the inhabitants:

> So many speaking French but with names like Macgregor, Jones, Flaherty, and with much of the unselfconsciousness of the Irish. A perfect stranger stopped me in the hotel lobby today, asking me how to spell 'souvenir!' The people generally are well dressed but many, particularly the women, appear somewhat stunted physically . . .

On board the express train for Montreal and thence for Toronto, he writes of his enchantment with the scenery, the pine-tree forests—so different from the Australian eucalypts—the tidy farms of mixed cattle, the timber being floated down the big rivers, the wonder of Niagara Falls and a hotel of 600 rooms each with its own bathroom and telephone, no less!

All the things he had heard and read of America, and much besides, were here unfolded before his eyes. He warmed to the friendliness of the people so eager to demonstrate why theirs was indeed 'God's own country'; but beneath their almost gentle courtesy he was aware of an immense vigour and drive.

On the train to Chicago the spell was broken when an officious conductor asked 'a devil of a lot of unnecessary questions' and demanded that he pay an 'alien's Poll Tax' for entering the USA for two days. He had never thought of himself as an alien anywhere before, and resented it strongly. Chicago itself had a nightmare quality, and for the first time he felt 'a stranger in a strange land'.

> On Michigan Avenue my head begins to swim and I feel actually faint—cars rushing, horns blowing, people hurrying, omnibuses, express waggons and cabs, trains alongside, bells ringing, whistles blowing, and over all a slow, grinding noise of some factory or dynamo. To make matters worse I arrive in the midst of a heat wave and I am aware of the awfulness, that so many have experienced under far worse circumstances, of being alone and unknown.
>
> I remember being told that a member of the family migrated to Chicago some time after our branch came to Australia. I look up the telephone book and there, sure enough, is the name of Durack. On ringing the number I am cordially invited to the home of

> Denis Francis Durack who would appear to have been Father's first cousin[3]. He is about 30 years old and left Ireland at 15. He manages a big express and storage business for the firm of Werner Bros., and is also an insurance agent and money lender. He lives at 435 Bildar Avenue and is married to a charming young Swedish woman who speaks good English and several other languages. They have two delightful little girls.

More than sixty years later one of these 'little girls', Marie Durack Judsen, with her rubber-planter husband, Karl, was to travel from Florida to Western Australia to meet her long-lost relatives. Correspondence between her branch of the family and ours had begun, as with many other far-flung branches, after the publication of *Kings in Grass Castles*, and has continued ever since.

Next day, fully recovered from the dismay of his arrival, M.P. called to protest 'on principle' against the $2 alien poll tax, first at the Customs House, whence he was referred to the Alien Immigration Department, which passed him on to the Manager of the Central Pacific Railway, who admitted that 'Britishers' were officially aliens in the United States. What appears to have upset M.P. was that Australians but not Canadians should have been put in their place in this way. The Central Pacific Railway Chief, obviously a man of tact, eventually smoothed things over by agreeing that the tax was unfortunate and by enumerating the many fine things he had heard about Australia—its excellent government, its lack of civic corruption, conspiracies, murders or suicides.

Mollified, M.P. made his way to the Chicago Union Stock Yards, founded in 1865, occupying an area of 640 acres, and employing 600 workers. He lists here, and later on at Armour's stockyards, the number of beasts killed per day, the methods employed and prices averaged—all obviously with a view to his company's dream of a meat-processing establishment in their own area. 'The cattle just like Argyle stock—a lot of crossbreeds mostly from red poll shorthorns.' For all his enthusiasm, however, two days of watching stock go down under the killer's hammer, the warm stench of blood, and the sight of so many girls obviously overworked in the canning and labelling sections, with hundreds waiting to fill their jobs if they dropped out, were more than enough for him. This was, after all, a sordid aspect of the industry that, as co-ordinator of mustering and shipping programmes in the clear unpolluted air of the Australian bush, he had so far escaped. He had been influenced also by his recent reading of *The Jungle* by Upton Sinclair, revealing the scandalous conditions for employees in the Chicago Meat Works. 'I came away quite sick,' he writes, 'and grateful for the continued hospitality of these kindly Chicago relatives.'

'Glad to escape from this modern Gomorrah of the West', he took the train for Minneapolis, the beauty and architecture of which he eulogized at considerable length.

> They say 'see Naples and die', but I say 'see the new Capitol of St. Paul and you have realised the brightest imaginative dream of a lifetime' . . . Could hardly tear myself away from the four large paintings in the rotunda representing the civilization of the North West. The first depicts the American genius leaving home, the Goddess of Fear holding him back. In the second he is led by the Goddess of Wisdom and Hope and moves on, driving savagery from the country. In the third, again led by Wisdom and Hope, he breaks the soil and is rewarded with an abundant yield. In the fourth panel the American genius, seated on his throne, distributes the products of Minnesota to the four corners of the earth . . . Other paintings in the Senate Chamber depict explorations to the source of the Mississippi and symbolic compositions portray Courage, Equality, Freedom and Justice . . .
>
> One beautiful painting was 'The Progress of Flame'—the transmission of knowledge through the ages with a Goddess passing a torch from one to another . . . No aspect in the history of this great country has been omitted. Here we see the pioneer sowing, reaping, logging, milling, stone-cutting. We see Commerce, Mining, Navigation . . . and around the walls quotations from great men down the ages. I jotted down a few of them . . .
>
> 'Let us develop the resources of our land, call forth its powers, build up its institutions, provide all its great interests and see if we in our day and generation may not do something to be remembered.' . . .
>
> 'Votes should be weighed not counted.' . . .
>
> 'Education's a better safeguard of liberty than a standing army.' . . .
>
> 'Let us remember that our interests's in concord, not conflict, and that our real eminence rests in the victories of peace not those of war.' . . .
>
> '. . . To be prepared for war is the most effectual means of preserving peace.' . . .

> With regret I leave this great building to catch my train to Winnipeg.

From his railway carriage he writes J.W. a detailed description of the passing landscape:

> As I feast my eyes on the prodigal bounties of nature I see why this part of the State is known as 'The Pride of the West ...' I have no doubt many an inhabitant blesses the day that brought him to this fruitful haven from the smoke-laden, congested cities of older lands. It is hard indeed to reconcile the peace of this rural scene with what I read on taking up a New York paper this evening. What a record of civic eruptions, murders, conspiracies, hold-ups, divorces, suicides and earthquakes! ...

In Winnipeg he presented a letter of introduction to the President of the Central Pacific Railway and, after an edifying conversation on the remarkable development of railways throughout Canada and the States, was given letters to ranchers in Calgary.

He resumes his detailed description of the passing scene from the Imperial Limited train through Brandon and the ranching centre of Medicine Hat, where he is intrigued by the supply of natural gas serving the community.

> I have with me the book 'Le Chien D'or,' telling of the early romances of Quebec but here before me is the panoramic book of nature unfolding romances more thrilling and enrapturing than events of the days of Louis Quebec. The book remains shut all morning as we speed over the broad plains past miniature lakes covered with wild fowl, prairie dogs surrounding a carcase, coyotes, herds of horses and now, away in the distance, the pitched tents of the cowboys on the bleak plains.

In Calgary he was kindly received by the local representative of the Central Pacific Railway and the Secretary of the Board of Trade, who had actually heard of Australia and its cattle industry, and put him up as a member of the Ranchers' Club. Here he was delighted to meet Mr J. Kirkewood Lee whom he had met in Kalgoorlie some six years before and who was now in the land business thereabouts. This encounter led to many contacts and discussions, recounted in some detail, concerning land values, leaseholds, and the price of handling and marketing of stock. Driving behind a pair of beautiful black horses priced at $1000 each, he inspected a number of ranches and abattoirs, and was surprised to find that hides (inferior to the

Australian product because of their being marred by such a multiplicity of brands) were bringing up to $8 each in Chicago. This market he intended inquiring into for C.D. & D.

A few days later he writes to his brother from the Bald Headed Prairie where he is camped with the cowboys of Western Canada, 'learning of Cayuses and Mavericks, Alcades and Bronco Twisters'. He had gone out there 'to see some steers belonging to Messrs. Burns & Co.', and also to get a first-hand glimpse of the running of a cattle property in that locality, though it is doubtful whether the most efficient manager or cowboy would have had much to teach M.P. that could be used to his advantage. Nonetheless, his few days hereabouts were to remain a highlight in his memories, to be looked back upon from the 'prairies' of a far stranger and more remote region which was as full of exciting colour and romance.

> This 'outfit', as they call it, consists of 15 men, 2 wagonettes and 50 horses. They have here 3000 bullocks of all ages from 18 months upward which they hold day and night, putting them together about 9 p.m. wherever they happen to meet up. Two men watch until 4 a.m. when they are relieved.
>
> There are some great names amongst these fellows and it's interesting to hear their tales. 'Slippery Bill', the head serang, got his name from his ability with the bow knife when living down in Mexico. Then there is 'Ba Ba Jimmy', 'Mopoke Tom', 'Deadly Dick' from Wyoming, 'Slim' from 'way down Montana', 'Sloppy' the cook from East Ontario . . . and 'Barb Wire Johnnie' who is credited with being the best Bronco buster on the Prairies of Western Canada.
>
> I slept with them in their tent under six blankets, a huge beaver coat and canvas covering similar to what our chaps use for their swags. They were keen to hear about Australia but I kept them going with questions about their lives out here in the West.
>
> As I turned in, one of the boys slipped me a six chambered Colt's revolver, telling me that I may not need it but it's a useful toy to have in case of some reprisal on the camp. They are mostly wild, reckless young chaps scarcely recognising the existence of God, Heaven or Hell and their language scarcely fit for publication in a lady's journal. They hail from many countries—a number originally from England.
>
> Their horses are herded night and day by men called 'Wranglers'. Every man carries a rope on his saddle and lassoes his horses each

> morning—this process being a popular pastime. They are all out by 4 in the morning, the cook, who carries coal and wood, having the stove alight in his tent.

Why going to bed with a revolver in the American West would have impressed M.P. it is hard to say, since he had never camped in the bush without a firearm in his life. Nor were the nicknames and exploits of the cowboys any more colourful than those of his daily associates in Kimberley and the Territory.

At Banff he was impressed with the standard of the Central Pacific Railway Hotel, and the good looks and fashionable dressing of the women. He revelled in the animal life of the Buffalo Park and admitted to being 'somewhat done up' after walking six miles to the Observatory, 7,380 feet up Sulphur Mountain. As the train sped him to Vancouver he was almost lost for words: 'The Blue Mountains in New South Wales, which I had thought impressive, here shrink to comparative insignificance.' He met an Australian friend in Vancouver, embarked with him on a sightseeing expedition, and booked his passage for Yokohama on the *Empress of Japan*.

This marked the beginning of his love affair with Japan and the Japanese people, from which he was never fully to recover even when confronted with horror stories of the Burma railway and the prison camps of the Second World War. The impression he gained had much to do with his having secured the services of a guide named Sansho Nishaguri, a charming and erudite man with whom he corresponded for many years. It was no doubt also influenced by the Anglo-Japanese Alliance of 1902, which had improved the image each land had of the other and brought about a stimulating increase in trade.

M.P.'s progress from Yokohama through Kamakura and Nikko to Tokyo, Najayo, Kyoto, Osaka, Kobe, and Nagasaki reads like an enchanted dream. It is possible that the Japanese themselves may have reciprocated something of the fascination felt for them by this tall, broad-shouldered, trim-bearded, and courteous stranger whose keen blue eyes regarded them and their country with such admiring interest.

> In all other places I have visited I have been among people of like or similar genus. Here I might have set foot upon another planet. It comes as something of a shock to find among the followers of so called 'pagan doctrines' so much that is lacking in our Christian communities. My philosophic Buddhist guide assures me that in their economy money has never been an asset equivalent to courage, knowledge and art—hence they have despised money.

> The merchant, trader and shopkeeper ranks below the artisan and the peasant farmer; which may well account for the want of commercial integrity, of which the Japanese are often accused. This has its counterpart in the fact that people were lifted out of the rut of sordid greed and made a nation of honour, high principled and indomitably devoted to their country . . .
>
> Sometimes, on the tiny trains, among the tiny, hurrying people, I feel like Gulliver in Lilliput but then I encounter students of the new Japanese Army and Navy—many of quite magnificent physique, strength and stamina. I gather there is a growing tendency to include meat in the Japanese diet, thereby increasing their general shape, which may augur well for the Australian cattle industry . . .
>
> I find no beggars in the streets, gambling and the sale of indecent pictures is prohibited. No one demands a tip. Everywhere I encounter politeness, courtesy and discipline . . . The children as one passes hail one with a happy 'Ohayo', and the politeness with which they greet the stranger is extended to friends and acquaintances who bow and smile to each other when they meet. This natural gentleness appears to include even the horses and oxen seen carting timber and other supplies, and all in good condition. I am reminded of the words of St. Francis Xavier: 'Truly I cannot cease from praising these people. Verily, they are the delight of my heart.'

China and the Chinese, as encountered on the next stage of his journey, M.P. found less to his liking. His first impressions of Shanghai and Hong Kong were of 'crowded, rubbish-littered streets, foul smells, people covered with abominable sores, much evidence of poverty and beggars everywhere'. In contrast to the Japanese, the Chinese had no smiles for the foreigner and few enough, as far as he could see, for each other. The only one from whom he received a truly courteous greeting was a young Australian-born Chinese whose father was a Wesleyan minister in Ballarat. He was on a visit to relatives in Canton but was soon to return to Australia to study Engineering Survey.

M.P. seems, however, to have established some rapport with his Chinese guide to whom he refers as 'my attendant spirit'.

> He is not loath to tell me that there is a general feeling against the foreigner here. The Americans and Germans are bidding strong for Chinese trade and I notice that the army rifles are of German manufacture. My guide tells me that they are cheaper than the

> English, but he assures me that England is the most accredited nation in the Chinese trade.

He visited temples, palaces, theatres, factories—but his enjoyment of the colour and antiquity of the scene was generally spoiled for him by the prevailing poverty. While appreciating the magnificence of stage decor and dressing, he was revolted by the bound feet and tottering gait of the actresses. Enchanted by the beauty of locally manufactured silks, he visited a silk factory and was sickened by the cramped and inhuman conditions philosophically accepted by the 600 women workers.

The oppressive heat that had accompanied his arrival in Hong Kong climaxed in a devastating typhoon causing the loss of millions of dollars to shipping and an estimated 10,000 lives.

> I emerge from my hotel to a scene of destruction and desolation—houses left roofless with shattered windows, telegraph poles and uprooted trees blocking the streets, ships sunk, sampans and junks capsized, the sea shore strewn with the bodies of men, women and children, dogs and cats, pigs and poultry ... the greatest disaster since 1874.

In Canton he found the City of the Dead more edifying than cities of the living.

> The Chinese are very particular about the conditions in which they bury their dead. I gather that it is a bad omen for the prosperity of successors if a coffin is destroyed by damp and mould.

Prisoners sat miserably in stocks in the side streets and trials were conducted in a ramshackle building.

> The magistrate sits at a high table with attendant interpreters, the prisoner on his bended knees receiving a blow from a baton with every question asked. One I saw was accused of kidnapping—a common practice my guide informs me. Children whose parents cannot pay the ransom are sent away to be sold to wealthy merchants who are seeking heirs. If such is the case many poor children might be considered fortunate ... Burglary and pick-pocketing is also very rife, as who would wonder in this land of so much wealth and want?

Executions by beheading or garrotting were carried out almost casually in the public gaze. He witnessed two or three of them and came away with a set of photographs sold in a nearby shop that were found years later with shrieks of fascinated horror by his growing family. 'Tomorrow I board *The Australian* for my homeward voyage and glad I will be to get away from this place.'

On 10 October M.P. writes that he 'took his hat off' to his native land after an absence of eight months abroad, and that on the night of his arrival in Darwin he saw more hard drinking than anywhere else on his travels. He had never liked this sweltering shanty port that was to be known in years to come as 'Australia's Front Door', but it was, after all, Australian soil and he had a few old friends there whom he looked forward to seeing. Among them was George Washington Mayhew, part owner and editor of that most individual and lively chronicle, the *Northern Territory Times*. Since Mayhew had married Mrs Tom Kilfoyle's sister, Mary Byrne, M.P. was always received at their home as a member of the family; and Mayhew being at that time laid up with a severe tropical skin complaint he was a captive audience for the traveller's tales. M.P. reminded Mayhew of the prophecy of an early Government-Resident that Darwin was destined to become 'an Australian Chicago', and assured him that he need have no regret of its not having been fulfilled. It needed more than this, however, to cheer Mayhew at that time, for the future of the Territory was looking decidedly gloomy. The Immigration Restriction Act (generally referred to as 'The White Australia Policy'), passed at the time of Federation, may indeed have been good news for Victoria and New South Wales where the Chinese population drawn to the goldfields was flocking to the cities in disturbing numbers, but for the Territory it was just another disaster. Within five years the Chinese population had fallen from over 7,000 to well under 2,000, and gone was the cheap, uncomplaining labour on which had depended the future of mining and agriculture. The only Orientals now left were the few, some of them mining independently, who had chosen naturalization at ten shillings a head in place of a sentimental wish to die in their homeland.

While awaiting transport to Wyndham, M.P. set off by launch with Sandy Grant to visit the Union Reef at West Arm. This was a tin mine which Grant had taken up with those two dogged prospectors, Phil Saunders and Adam Johns, whose reports on the possibilities of gold in the Kimberley district had led to the Hall's Creek rush of 1886. As always where mineral discovery and development were concerned, M.P.'s spirits rose. He records with some enthusiasm the lode of free-showing tin both here and at Hang Gon's Wheel of Fortune mine where the Chinese were reputed to have taken £28,000 in the past three years. There was much animated talk of the Territory's potential mining wealth—immense lodes of tin and silver lead, vast deposits of coal not only at West Arm but at Mount Wells, Finnis River, Bynoe Harbour, MacKinlay Range and Port Keats.

With still some days before his ship sailed, M.P. then visited Will Byrne, brother of Mrs Kilfoyle and Mrs Mayhew, at his Brock's Creek property and rode off with him to inspect some country Byrne had taken up on the site of the abandoned Daly River Mission. M.P. thought the country and its possible mineral potential good enough to justify his putting in an application, on behalf of his company, for 500 square miles. Since there is no further reference to this matter, we can only conclude that he had second thoughts about it on hearing soon afterwards that (typical of the Territory's bright dreams) most of its mining projects had faded out.

M.P.'s old friend Dr Maurice Holtz, whose successful botanical experiments and dream of establishing an immense food bowl in the Territory had done so much to boost local morale, had recently left Darwin to become Director of the Botanical Gardens in Adelaide. His son Nicholas, however, was carrying on the tradition of distributing plants and advice to would-be growers, and was at that time enthusiastic about the production of sisal hemp. Time was when M.P. had come away laden from Holtz's little Eden, but the only specimens he had so far succeeded in coaxing to maturity at Argyle were a few poincianas that continued to give colour to the wet-weather garden until they were discovered by the white ants when his own life was drawing to an end. This time, leaving for Wyndham on the *Wai-Hoi*, he made no mention of ambitious plans for planting fodder crops, or for improving the aspect from the house on the Behn that was then still the nearest place to a home that he knew.

16

A STOCKMAN'S STORY

March 1906–January 1907

Life at Argyle during M.P.'s absence was described by a twenty-two-year-old stockman named Frank Eipper in letters to his family in New South Wales. The grandson of a German-born Presbyterian minister who came to Australia in 1838 and set up a mission to the Aborigines at Moreton Bay, Eipper had been gently reared and educated in the Scone district of the Upper Hunter Valley, where his father earned a somewhat precarious living as a horse-dealer. In his decision to strike out for himself in East Kimberley the young man had no doubt been influenced by a friend named Cliff Johnson, who had returned to Scone after working for some years in Wyndham with C.D. & D. It was early in March 1906 that Eipper, then twenty-one years old, presented Johnson's letter of introduction to J.W. in his firm's Fremantle office. He evidently made a good impression on J.W., who soon afterwards saw him off on one of the firm's chartered ships with a letter requesting Jim Davidson in Wyndham to do what he could for him. Eipper wrote his father from Wyndham two weeks later[1]:

> He [J.W.] is a real 'white man'. He shook me by the hand and wished me all luck in the Nor' West and told me to look after myself. I was the only passenger on the way up and lived like a fighting cock. It took nine days to get here and on arrival I interviewed Mr Davidson (who is married to a Miss Durack) and he is waiting for word [about a job] to come back from the stations now . . .
>
> The firm, C.D. & D., run the show here. They have the hotel, store, butcher's shop etc., and own some thousands of square miles comprising several stations, and charter three boats which take away about 20,000 bullocks each season. The cattle that come in here do not come up to the Belltrees and Scone bullocks. They have to travel too far and the country around the coast is not much good. The shores all round Cambridge Gulf are low-lying mangrove swamps where alligators abound to catch every stray nigger.

There are thousands and thousands of blacks up here and over one hundred in prison in Wyndham where they work in chain gangs on the roads and are filling up the swamp around the town. On the day we landed two blacks were tried and sentenced to death for the murder of a couple of white men a few miles out. The two murdered men had taken the gins away from the blacks and so caused the trouble. I reckon it is good enough for them though I am told that the blacks will spear a man for a bag of flour or stick of tobacco.

The temperature here goes to over 120° at times but does not knock you out like Scone heat. The men here get around in shirts or singlets, hats, trousers and boots—no socks.

I am marking time doing any work I can get and have just done two hours lumping on the wharf for half a crown per hour. It's a pity this work is not more regular as the pay is so good.

I felt the parting with you all very much and have spent many a miserable hour over it but I have plucked up courage and not looked back. Father you have nothing at all to reproach yourself with. I can see now that I have not been a son worthy of such parents so far but I hope to retrieve my shortcomings in the future. It will not be for want of trying, anyhow. It would have been far better for me if you had made me steer out for myself a few years ago. I just hope Mother has ceased fretting.

I hope you do well out of your horses at the sale. The horses here are nearly all Queenslanders . . .

Eipper's next letter home was written from Argyle to his sister Emmie some three months later.

I am writing this as we are camped for dinner on the banks of the Ord River with 1100 head of cattle. There is a lovely view in front of me—the long, clear course of the big river, its banks fringed with trees, bamboos and pandanas palms, with lofty red, granite mountains in the background. It is pretty dry on parts of Argyle this year and we have to remove a lot of cattle to what is called 'The Stud Station' [Ivanhoe] where grass and water are plentiful . . . There are nine of us with the cattle this time—four whites and five blacks . . . The head stockman is Charlie Good[2] who has been in Kimberley for the last six years and now has a pretty good 'stocking' (savings). His father is a civil engineer in Perth, ex India. He built the Bombay gaol and the Wollongong,

Warrnambool and Fremantle breakwaters. Charlie, a few months younger than I am, was born in Ceylon. He and I are great mates, but he is leaving before Christmas as he and his father are buying a small sheep station down South and I'll be sorry to see him go. He is violently in love with Miss Durack, sister of Ambrose D. the Argyle Manager.

The other stockman in our party is Paddy Boyle who was at school with Ambrose in Brisbane. He's a very good all round fellow and knows our part of the world having spent eight months at Segenhoe, Scone. He holds the belt of champion lightweight of Queensland and is showing us how to use the gloves . . . He is a fine gentlemanly fellow who has travelled a lot and upsets one's idea of a pug being necessarily a rough customer.

The camp cook is about twenty years of age and knows nothing much about anything, least of all preparing food. This is a pity as Argyle is the best station for tucker in Kimberley. We have any quantity of rice and dried fruit allowed us, also currants, pickles, sauces, jam, honey, treacle, syrup and coffee. The cook can have anything he wants. There is any amount of game here—wild geese, ducks and turkeys galore but we do not bother them much. We often have fish, though. The blacks are adept at spearing Barramundi which are delicious eating and weigh anything up to 50 pounds. The country here also swarms with emus, pelicans and dingo and we sometimes spot a few wild buffaloes.

C.D. & D.'s property extends all the way from Wyndham to Argyle—about 100 miles—and then out to two other big places in the Northern Territory. Argyle is the head station and the others are looked after by sub-managers under the Argyle manager. There are about 25,000 cattle on Argyle—all Durham shorthorns. They mostly roam about on what they call an 'open-range', but there is one very big fattening paddock, about 100,000 acres. It won't hold them if they want to get away but we usually know where to pick them up. There is also a four square mile horse paddock around the station and each stallion has its own enclosure.

We sometimes muster for four or five days at a tailing yard, then bring the cleanskins to one of the four big branding yards. We brand 50 to 250 a day and about 5000 were branded here last year. I generally have three horses—sometimes more—for mustering and camp work. I've had some pretty rough horses to mount since

I started. I was thrown twice, quick and lively, by the first horse I mounted here but have sat all comers since.

Ambrose is a very nice man and a good boss. He is a splendid chap on a stock camp and a keen sport and is very devoted to his sister.

Whenever Charlie and I get into the station we make the most of our opportunities. When last in about a month ago Miss Durack and her friend Miss Woodland asked us to take them kangaroo hunting, so we caught the horses, strapped on our rifles and started off with three staghounds at foot. The ladies ride astride in divided skirts and look splendid. We had a most enjoyable day. We also have a very good time when we spend an evening at the homestead. Miss Durack has a nice postcard album and was delighted when I gave her half a dozen beauties of my own. When out riding on her own she always has one of the gins in attendance. They look so natty in their white moleskins, white shirts and turbaned felt hats. I will greatly miss Miss Durack when she goes away on her holiday.

The ignorance of some of the men here is appalling. One chap on hearing that I come from Sydney asked whether I knew a mate of his over there called Skinner who had once explained to him how they work elevators in the big smoke. A lift, he was told, consisted of a small board with a rope through a hole in the centre. You clutch this in your hands and stand with a foot on each side while you are hauled up with a steam windlass. In this joker's language treacle is known as 'flybog'.

Nine-tenths of these Kimberley men are real hard drinkers and can't make a living anywhere else. Luckily, however, we have a pretty steady lot on Argyle.

I will save a lot of money over here Emmie. I started on £1 a week but after about a fortnight Ambrose gave me a 10/- rise and from the first of August my pay went up to £2 a week, With board and keep provided, living costs very little here and clothes £15 a year at the outside.

I will make out my will and send it over to you to look after as soon as I get back to the station. One never knows when one might get a spear in the back or snuff out with malaria which no one escapes up here, so better be on the safe side. By the way, I came across a skeleton a few days back—a white man I think. There are a good few such, of both blacks and whites, around

> here. I will send a good skull to Jack Crothers when I get time. He asked me to procure him one . . .

When Eipper wrote again to his sister soon after his return from Ivanhoe he was warding off a bout of fever with liberal doses of quinine and would also seem to have been trying to ward off a bout of the blues. Camped out on the run his thoughts, no less than those of his love-sick mate, Charlie Good, were obviously much with the two girls at the house.

> Charlie and I went in for a change of horses the other day. We had to come back that night but sent the packs and men on ahead and took Miss Durack and Miss Woodland for a moonlight ride. We went about fifteen miles and got back about ten o'clock then set out again for this camp. It was a perfect night and we all enjoyed the ride tremendously. Miss Durack wants to go home to Brisbane in October and come back in April or May. It will be pretty deadly in the interval with no ladies in the place at all. I feel somewhat down in the dumps here at times, thinking of home and familiar faces, but pluck up courage somehow. A few years will soon pass and then I hope to see you all again with a few pounds in my pocket.

Eipper wrote soon afterwards to his father from another stock camp on the Argyle run.

> We've just had a couple of days going after cleanskins. They take catching as they are on part of the run where the blacks come in and are very wild. I've had plenty practice pulling them over by the tail. I generally do the ear-marking and the head stockman does the castrating. We've also speyed about 500 heifers this year.
>
> There are twelve of us in this camp—Charlie Good, Paddy Boyle and myself the only white stockmen—the rest blacks. Boxer, our oldest boy, is about 30 years old. He came from Queensland and has been with the Duracks for over 20 years. He is a fine all-round fellow, a bit of a Sandow, very strong and efficient but also sweet-tempered and generally acknowledged to be the best all-round boy in W.A. I cannot fault him in any way. The other stock boys are also good sorts, pretty good horsemen and generally a big help to the pastoralists. The same cannot be said of the outside blacks who are a constant menace to both cattle and horses. They are most troublesome in the wet season when they know we cannot get about. It is then they come down from the

mountains and get into the stock. They kill a lot of cattle and even when they fail to kill a beast their spearheads often make lumps in the hides which spoil them for market. They speared a thoroughbred stallion and some blood mares last wet season. We're not throwing away any chances this year but we can't hope to keep them out of the cattle.

It's not only the blacks that they have to contend with either. It's also the small holders. The worst place off in this regard is Ord River Station which carries between 80,000 and 100,000 head. There's a ring of small places around this run and they've all built up their herds by duffing from the Ord.

I've learned to plait since I came over here and can make whips, belts and hatbands pretty well. A bit more practice and I'll be a second George Eland. I can make a bit of money out of my whips as soon as I can get some kangaroo hides. That old greenhide whip I bought for 6/6 in 1903 I sold recently for 22/6! I'll have quite a respectable cheque by Xmas time and will be able to let you have enough to get the house painted and make any needed repairs. I suppose £15 ought to square it but have it done thoroughly whatever the cost. If you sell the sulky and want to spend it on the house have palisading put up in front . . .

Our cook has just been sacked. I'm not fretting over it either. I've never suffered from indigestion in my life before . . .

The next letter, this time to his sister, was written from Lissadell in mid-October.

I was suddenly sent over here to attend a muster and get back any of our cattle that had strayed this way. There are no fences between the runs here as you know. Stock gets out of bound at times. After being here for nearly two weeks I'll be returning to Argyle tomorrow and hope to have a few days at the station in the young ladies' company. Good news! The girls are not going away for the wet after all. Ambrose has persuaded them to wait 'til next year when he had promised to take them to the Melbourne Cup. That means I'll be able to enjoy their society from time to time for another year or so.

Charlie Good has gone, I'm sad to say. I sold all my good clothes to him before he went as, what with the moths and the mould, they don't keep up here for many months. They ruined both the suits Charlie brought up a couple of years ago. Mine just fitted him and I got more back than I gave for them.

Lissadell Station belongs to Hill and Durack, and Hill's nephew is a stockman here. He was born and educated in England and is a very nice fellow. I also get on well with the two Duracks on the place. They are very hospitable. It is a nice little homestead with good outbuildings, a Chinese cook and six lubras to wait on us, so what more could a mortal want? Time does tend to stand still here though. I am writing this in the office and on glancing up the calendar displayed tells me it is February 1893. Which reminds me—please send me a 1907 calendar and with luck it will reach me before January. I'd also appreciate some more copies of *The Advocate* for Scone news and Christmas Numbers of *The Strand* and *Pearsons*. I've pretty well exhausted the Argyle library.

There is to be a big race meeting on the Behn River about 30 miles from here on the 9th of November and we're expecting a good crowd at Argyle for Christmas. There's to be races and a day's pigsticking as well. There are plenty of wild pigs around here. One way and another we expect to have some good fun.

He was back at Argyle and obviously in good spirits when he wrote to his mother on 23 December 1906.

Our Head Manager, Mr. M. P. Durack, is going South from Wyndham just after Christmas and will take this letter to post for me. He arrived about a month ago, just back from a world tour and soon after his cousin, Ambrose, went off on a holiday across the border with a string of racehorses. M.P.D. has been in charge here since and I like him very well.

Since Charlie Good left I have been doing most of the stock work here, with a plant of blacks to help me. I know the run of the country here pretty well now and how to work the stock. Paddy Boyle has been promoted to carpenter, a craft at which he excels.

Since the beginning of October we've had about 20" of rain and the grass is everywhere 18 ins. high. We're hoping it will hold off for a while now as we've planned a shooting picnic for tomorrow at the Big Lagoon about eight miles out where there are swarms of water fowl. On Christmas Day we're to have a day's sport which all are looking forward to, although the temperature is at present touching 120°.

I put in most of my spare time plaiting and made one of the young ladies a belt the other day—a small return for the sewing and other little things they do for me.

> I hope there will be a big batch of mail for me by next boat. I'm longing for news! . . .

M.P., back in Wyndham on 16 November, had ridden at once to Argyle where he took over from Ambrose who was bent on attending the Christmas race-meeting at Victoria River Depot. He received a cheerful welcome from the two girls, the station hands, and a succession of visitors who, on their various pretexts, were negotiating the seasonably boggy plains and flooded rivers. Everyone was in good spirits. A fencer named Jack Russell claimed to have found traces of copper near the junction of the Ord and the Behn. It was the sort of news that never failed to arouse M.P.'s interest. He lent Russell five horses and an offsider to continue the search, and over a drink to the success of the venture they signed an agreement that C.D. & D. should hold one-third share in anything found—'be it gold, silver, lead, tin, copper or other minerals'.

Boxer reported a group of Aborigines up to their usual wet-weather cattle-chasing tactics, but somehow managed to convey to M.P. that some at least may have had a reasonable point of view. There were certain parts of the run where they had always hunted kangaroo at this time of year, but now if they were discovered by the police in even such an innocent pursuit they were liable to be arrested on cattle-spearing charges. On 23 December M.P. reports:

> With Boxer to interview some bush blacks at Hick's Creek. They ask permission to hunt kangaroo thereabouts. I agree and promise they will not be interfered with providing they leave the cattle alone.

Much as these people must have resented asking permission to hunt on their own tribal territory, it would seem that they had come to the conclusion, or perhaps been persuaded by Pumpkin and Boxer, that negotiation with the white boss was now their only means of protection.

By Christmas Eve the festive spirit was as high as the thermometer. Kit Durack, accompanied by Frank Eipper, Paddy Boyle, Norman Wellman and several Aborigines, had gone off for a day's duck-shooting at the Big Lagoon, while Emily Woodland[3] had ridden off along the track to meet Jack Skeahan and Fred Hill who were due in from Auvergne. Guarded references in M.P.'s diaries had already indicated the blossoming of a romance between his cousin Jack and Kit's young friend Emily, who had been eagerly anticipating Jack's Christmas visit. M.P. tells us that:

> The travellers, Hill and Skeahan, had just swum the Stockade when met by Jones and his fair companion. The Behn which they had crossed without much trouble was also a swim when they got back to it but they contrived a boat out of three packsaddles covered with a fly on which the young lady gracefully floated across with the exuberant Skeahan in command. Next boatload they got the gear across and so to the homestead amid much merriment. Joyous laughter and convivial exchange continued throughout the evening. Plans for tomorrow—a variety of sporting events—well in hand.

But M.P.'s entry for 25 December was on a very different note, the Christmas spirit extinguished by the sudden intervention of fate.

> Poor young Eipper was drowned this morning in front of the house after plunging in for a swim before the day's events. The boys, Boxer and William (from Port Darwin) and Norman Wellman who were with him at the time, tried very bravely to save his life. William even managed to get hold of him and to push him on to a tree but he made no apparent effort to hold on and after this he sank altogether. It is believed he was already dead, for he made no sound nor any attempt to save himself after throwing up his hands—just glided down with eyes set and head thrown back. He had already swum the river to the other side where he had indicated the rapid beating of his heart before diving in again to return. Hence he probably suffered heart failure whilst in the water. This sad event put an end to the day's programme. All hands in search of the body. So far to no avail.

Five days later Eipper's body was found eight miles downstream and was buried close by on the riverbank, the funeral attended by all the men who had gathered for the Christmas festivities that had ended so tragically. Eipper had been well liked by his workmates and by the two girls whose company had meant so much to him. Kit's warm letter of sympathy brought great comfort to his relatives and resulted in a lifelong friendship with the Eipper family, whom she was later to meet in New South Wales.

17

Allied Interests

January–April 1907

M.P. returned to Fremantle early in the New Year to find that the anticipated interest in his recent travels was overshadowed by business and family problems requiring urgent conferences. The development of the beef industry in the north-western Murchison, Gascoyne and Irwin districts, so much closer to the market, had caused a severe drop in the price of Kimberley cattle, and C.D. & D., though always confident of good times ahead, were forced to admit that there was more money going out than coming in. In fact this had been brought to their attention by the West Australian Bank which, despite the firm's long and loyal patronage, had recently been discourteous enough to point out that their overdraft of £33,948 was £948 in excess of the limit.

There were worries, too, of a more personal nature. Though informed while abroad that J.W. was indisposed, it was only on his return that M.P. learned how a severe attack of double pneumonia had brought his brother close to death's door. On asking why he had not been better advised, he was told that the family had acted on J.W.'s own earnest instructions. 'By the time he gets the news I'll be either dead or better,' he had insisted, 'so why spoil his trip?'

J.W.'s general health had improved since his timely removal from Wyndham to Kalgoorlie five years before, but fever had undermined his constitution and left him with little resistance to other ills. With M.P. and Doherty overseas, and Connor much involved in political affairs, he had, in the previous year, taken over the firm's main office at Fremantle and with it a considerable load of work and worry. He and his sister Bird had thereupon set up house together in a pleasant residential quarter of the port, and here he had been devotedly tended throughout his illness by a young South Australian nurse named Gertrude Johnstone. Attractive and accomplished, Johnnie (as she was generally known) was being courted by several men in the Perth/Fremantle social orbit, but it did not take M.P. long to realise that she had eyes only for his brother. J.W., though of homely enough features and of less imposing physique than his brothers, had a 'way with women' that had been a byword in the family since his boyhood days. His kindly courtesy, incorrigible generosity, keen sense of humour, and multiplicity of interests endeared him to a wide circle of friends and had long since established his reputation as one of the State's most eligible young men. Only Mrs Connor voiced worldly-wise doubts on this score, laughingly assuring the love-lorn Elodie Pombard that she need have no fears of his making off with the pretty nurse—or, for that matter, with anyone else. It was her opinion that, like many another man of Irish Catholic upbringing, he was frightened of any physical relationship with women. 'Mark my words,' she declared, 'he'll go on playing the field indefinitely and end up a wise old bachelor.'

Elodie, not convinced, continued to light candles to the Blessed Virgin for the protection of her beloved from the wiles of an Anglican fortune-hunter. She was disturbed, nonetheless, for Alicia Connor's prophecies often proved correct and she was no doubt right when she claimed to know J.W. better than his closest relatives. For years, until he and Bird set up their ménage together, there had always been a room at his disposal in Alicia's household and a warm welcome at the family board. J.W. addressed Alicia respectfully as 'Mother', and during his illness she had been a regular bedside visitor. Her husband had also been deeply concerned, for, truth to tell, the good relations he maintained with the Durack brothers were largely due to J.W.'s understanding and tact. J.W. was genuinely fond of Connor, appreciative of his political zest and entrepreneurial gifts, and had been a strong source of encouragement when Connor suffered his first electoral defeat at the end of 1905. Then outvoted by Arthur Male of Broome, he was back in 1906 as M.L.C. for the North Province, a seat he was to hold for the next ten years.

At the time of M.P.'s return from the North, Connor and his wife, for reasons discussed over many inter-company and private sessions, were organizing a trip to England. After all, who better than Connor to follow up the propositions investigated by Doherty and M.P. while in England together the previous year? Among these had been Richard Tilden Smith's scheme for establishing a floating abattoir for the northern cattle-growers. Such a device might well, it was agreed, serve as a temporary substitute for, or even a workable alternative to, the long-hoped-for local meatworks. No one seemed then aware of, or concerned by, the fact that the plausible promoter had launched a number of dubious Kalgoorlie mining companies in London in the 1890s and had since been involved in the disposal, for £50,000 each, of northern Kimberley pastoral leases that were soon afterwards abandoned, sight unseen.

Another proposition to be examined was the sale of, or amalgamation with London investors in, the Kimberley properties; and yet another the floating of a substantial loan to assist the company to carry on until the establishment of one or another method of modern meat-processing.

Apart from business considerations, Connor saw the trip as a much-needed holiday for his wife who was worn out by child-bearing and -raising, and with the social activities that were important to her husband's interests and her own self-fulfilment. That Elodie Pombard would care for their household at Fremantle in the interim was taken as read.

J.W., too, had been strongly advised of the need for a break and, with the approval of all concerned, had accepted the Connors' suggestion that he accompany them, leaving Denis Doherty as business manager in his absence. Doherty had only recently returned from England, where he had left his family, hoping to finalize the establishment of the London branch that for some reason—probably the current price of cattle—continued to hang fire.

When the S.S. *Scharnhorst* sailed in mid-February, the Connors and J.W. were waved good-bye cheerfully enough by Doherty, M.P., and Bird, and no doubt less happily by Johnnie and Elodie.

The firm's interests, once centred in the port, now called for ready access to the heads of government and public services, business associates and the daily press, which were mostly based in the capital. The office in Fremantle had been therefore duplicated by one in St George's Terrace, Perth, the Esplanade Hotel being M.P.'s Perth place of residence and the family home his headquarters in Fremantle.

Whereas previously they had travelled the twelve miles to and fro by train, they had recently acquired a company car in which, from this time on, they commuted daily between the capital and the port. There were few traffic hazards in those days, but punctures and mechanical problems, accepted as part of the inevitable price of this modern amenity, were frequent and time-consuming. M.P. never failed to record his surprised delight on completing a trouble-free journey.

> 7.3.07: Doherty, Bird and self to Robbs jetty. No hold-ups whatever. Time occupied on way back from yards to the hotel, 36 minutes. One of the fastest and pleasantest runs I have yet experienced. A few dead chickens left in our tracks.

Doherty, in the absence of his family, had taken up residence at Surrey Chambers near the Terrace place of business, where he and M.P. held daily conference. What they now saw as their main worry was not only competition from other parts of the State but from a powerful stock dealer in New South Wales. This was none other than G. S. Yuill, a director of the Adelaide Steamship Company, representative of the Orient Line, and a shareholder in the Victoria River Downs Pastoral Syndicate. Yuill had offices in Sydney, Melbourne, and Adelaide, and an agency in London, the representative of which M.P. had met the previous year. Whatever Yuill's actual intentions regarding competitive activities in the west, he was seen by local growers as an insidious octopus and his shadow on the horizon was sufficient at this time to bring about an apparently unlikely détente between C.D. & D. and their business rivals in the Kimberley cattle-trade. These were the companies of Forrest, Emanuel and Copley Brothers who, together with C.D. & D., had been sometimes referred to disparagingly as 'the meat ring', the term implying a state of concord that had not existed up to this time.

The men involved were of very different backgrounds—the Copley brothers, Sam and Ben, hard-dealing businessmen from the north of England; Isadore and Sydney Emanuel, sons of Solomon, the shrewd Jewish banker, storekeeper and pastoralist of Goulburn; Denis Doherty, the genial Irishman; and the bush-reared Durack brothers. In view of their mutual problems, however, the group had a great deal in common at this time. M.P. and P.B. (who was frequently in Perth from the firm's Wagin estate) found themselves for the first time enjoying reminiscences with the Emanuels and remarking on the coincidence by which their respective fathers, always firm friends, had died at much the same time eight years before. They talked, too, of the expedition of '82, financed by these two men and led by Patsy's brother Michael Durack, which explored the then unmapped Kimberley district—an adventure shared by Sydney Emanuel, at that time twenty-one years old, and his tutor, John Pentacost. Sydney vividly recalled every member of the party and was interested in news of Tom Kilfoyle, to whose tough resourcefulness he and his companions had owed so much.

Meetings in their various places of business became warmly cooperative. They now saw East and West Kimberley not as the dichotomous provinces usually represented, but as a potentially rich, though deprived, area struggling for existence against an indifferent government and the selfish interests of more fortunately situated districts. The tick question, once the source of bitter inter-company and political manoeuvring, had become a matter of mutual irritation against 'so-called government controls'; and where once they had bickered over shipping arrangements they now discussed the advisability of sharing transport facilities.

Together they waited on the Premier, the Governor, and the Minister for Agriculture; and expressed their united views to 'Agricola' for his columns in the *West Australian*. Isadore Emanuel, quoted at length in that paper on 16 February 1907, put forward a strong case for 'those with a finger on the pulse of the far northern cattle industry'. It was clear to such men, Emanuel declared, that the time had come for the erection of a cold-storage works at Wyndham—the natural marketing point, though the need for a similar plant at Derby should soon become apparent. In brief, the Kimberley pasturelands were by this time producing more cattle than the people of the State could consume, and to prevent a glut ships were urgently needed to open up an export trade. As it was, no alternative presented itself other than (as two major companies were already doing) sending cattle nearly 2,000 miles overland to Queensland, where the necessary facilities were available. There should be no difficulty in persuading the northern cattlemen to establish the necessary meatworks if the government would agree to carry the venture over the first ten years, during which time it would probably be worked at a loss.

It was soon afterwards announced that James Mitchell, the Minister for Agriculture, had promised to provide two-thirds of the cost of erecting a freezing-works in Wyndham—a sum of £40–50,000—interest free for the first five years, and thereafter on guarantee of 5%. There were the inevitable few disgruntled comments in the press, one writer likening the action to 'greasing the fat pig'.

> Why should rich firms like these [he asked] get large sums of government money free of interest whilst a struggling farmer can get no more than £500 and pay 6% for it? [R.W.W., *West Australian*, 22.2.07]

The majority opinion, however, was congratulatory, everyone taking the long-awaited meat-processing facility to be almost a *fait accompli*. The bank was reassured and the company overdraft continued to rise, apparently without causing much worry to anyone concerned.

But in the running of a State-wide business entailing the raising, buying, selling, and shipment of stock, there were problems enough to keep them all fully occupied. Jim Davidson, Mary's husband, was expected from Wyndham in mid-March on the S.S. *Mildura* which was transporting 700 head of C.D. & D. cattle to Fremantle. The scheduled date of arrival slipped by with no sign of the ship, and wires confirmed that it had not yet touched at Geraldton. Two days later a message from Onslow announced that the vessel had run aground at the North-West Cape and was a total wreck. Anxious hours followed before it was known that all hands were safe and were to be picked up by the S.S. *Burrumbeet*. The cattle, however, had perished to a beast. This meant organizing another mob to replace the lost consignment and another ship to transport it.

M.P.'s congenial spell in the city drew to a worried close, his short excursions on made roads giving place once more to long weary journeys over rough bush tracks. His next few months in the north were enlivened by the discovery of deposits of copper and coal in the vicinity of Wyndham. Needless to say, he lost no time in visiting the various sites and in taking up mineral leases covering a total of 1,280 acres. The excitement waxed and waned and finally faded, but it provided a lively talking point for some months at least, as did his idea for the manufacture of furniture, suitcases, satchels, and handbags from crocodile skins which he collected and salted down to take with him to Perth. For company on various shooting expeditions he had his cousin Kit and her younger brother Fergus, who had that year come from Queensland to join his relatives at Argyle. Fergus, a sprightly eighteen-year-old, found life in the north a grand adventure and provided cheerful company for Ambrose in his lonely mustering camps, and sometimes for M.P. on his long trips between stations.

Owing to the absence of both Connor and J.W., M.P. returned south earlier than usual that year. Kit accompanied him to Fremantle where she was received into Bird's affectionate embrace and introduced to the gentle round of Perth society. The big event of the moment was the annual Royal Agricultural Show at which Bird toiled in the tea-rooms to assist some local charity. M.P.'s contribution lay in judging shorthorn cattle and stock horses, and in driving a four-in-hand around the exhibition ring. People's Day on 30 October he reported as having drawn a crowd of over 35,000, 'taken all in all a prosperous and well-dressed assembly'.

For some years now Bird had been active, if so far unsuccessful, in the role of matchmaker for both M.P. and J.W. In this she had the constant encouragement of P.B., who was genuinely worried about the protracted bachelorhood of his two brothers. In Pat's eyes a man without a wife and family, worries and all, was condemned to a life of loneliness and unfulfilment, and he not only wished but prayed fervently that his dear ones should be spared this fate. A number of close friends and relatives believed that Bird herself would not marry before J.W., to whose welfare she was devoted. J.W., on the other hand, was said by some to have vowed not to marry before his sister, whose several frustrated love affairs he had taken much to heart. Evidently Elodie and Johnnie, though always in the offing, were understood to be out of the running for M.P. Others frequently mentioned as being included in the family's social activities at this time were Miss Ethel Butcher, the Misses Patterson of Pinjarra, the Misses

Quinlan, Leake, and Mannsell. With none of these, however, is there any indication that M.P. got beyond making polite conversation over luncheons, teas and after-theatre suppers. In fact the only one for whom he gives written evidence of infatuation over this period was the actress Grace Palotta[1] who, playing in *The Man from Mexico*, had Perth at her pretty feet. A guest at the Esplanade Hotel, she shared a breakfast table, and exchanged lively travel anecdotes, with M.P. and his sister. Having seen her off on the *Britannia* with a farewell champagne toast, he asks of his diary: 'Why must my life be this endless succession of meetings and partings? I wonder will it be my lot ever to meet the divine Grace again. In any case she will ever remain a sweet memory in my soul.'

Dame Clara Butt and her husband Kennerley Rumford were also delighting Perth audiences at the end of 1907. While performing at His Majesty's Theatre they too stayed at the Esplanade, and had happy memories of their meeting with J.W. and Frank Connor in London earlier in the year. They were interested to hear of J.W.'s further adventures in Ireland and the United States, as related in the following chapter.

Despite apprehensions and uncertainties regarding the future of the firm, M.P.'s journal indicates a balanced enough mingling of business and social activities over this period. Personalities from all walks of life called at the office or were met at the club and hotel for leisurely chats. Family members visited or were visited. P.B. moved buoyantly between Behn Ord and the Brighton Hotel, Cottesloe, where Eva and their two children were spending the summer months. Jerry Durack's widow, Aunt Fan, had come south with her younger children and was renting a place in Guildford. Cousin M.J. (Long Michael) and his wife Bertha had occasional family tea-parties at their Cottesloe residence, where Duracks and Levinsons met compatibly. Their relatives still felt deeply for the couple's misfortune in the loss of their only child, and Mary Davidson, down from Wyndham over the summer months, was sensitive about visiting them with her healthy little family of two sons and a daughter. On 'Bertha's afternoons' she took turn about with Bird, or left her brood with Elodie and the Connor children at Clonrye.

M.J.'s brother, Mantinea (otherwise Black Pat Durack), called at the office to report from his Arrino property near Three Springs. He and Susie now had two sons and were making out well enough despite the poor price of sheep.

This branch of the family had that year suffered a bereavement, in the death of their forty-four-year-old brother James Matthew. Tenth of the thirteen children of Darby Durack and his wife Margaret (*nee* Kilfoyle),

Jim had followed his elder brothers to Kimberley in the 1880s and had accompanied M.P. on a number of droving-treks to the Territory in the early nineties. A skilled stockman and congenial companion, with a flair for ballad verse, he had later gone prospecting in the Murchison goldfields and had since roved the outback as miner and stockman. At the time of his death from beriberi he had been droving for Sidney Kidman in the Camooweal district. A long and sentimental tribute to his memory appeared in *The Manly and North Sydney News* on 24 August 1907. Written by an old schoolmate, W. B. Melville, it has much to say of his scholastic and sporting prowess when at school in Molong, and later at St Stanislaus' College, Bathurst.

> Jim Durack carried all before him at College. He captained our cricket team and was the Charles Santley of the singing class. Many of us sheltered our shortcomings under cover of his confident lead ... After leaving College he returned to Molong and put in three months at the C.P.S. office, but no office could hold a spirit like his ... All the boys and girls and half the adults of the town were at the railway station to see him off to wild Westralia. He never revisited Molong or the resorts he loved so well in boyhood days ... A light hearted, handsome and casual Australian, he played well his part in the pathless wilds, served the cause of Australian development and left a memory of cheerful comradeship, of grit and of gentleness.

Copies of the above were handed round to be read and reread, and cherished for posterity in family cutting-books.

Ambrose Durack arrived in Fremantle toward the end of the year and set off with his sister on the S.S. *Grantala* to visit their family in Queensland. For Kit, whose engagement to her cousin Patsy had come adrift in the meantime, that was the fateful journey on which she met her future husband, Daniel Evans, who was an engineer on the ship.

Meanwhile G. S. Yuill's competition was a matter of increasing resentment in the company and must have prompted M.P. to deal with some of the big Murchison growers on their own ground. We find him, at the end of November, visiting stations in the vicinity of Geraldton, Northampton, Moora, and Mingenew, and arranging the purchase of stock with local owners and managers. He also had in mind, in the event of a sale of the firm's northern holdings, the possible purchase of property in the Murchison district. He had heard much talk, among members of the Pastoralists' and Graziers' Association, of fortunes to be made from sheep-, cattle-, and horse-raising in the Irwin and Greenough River areas, but although he was impressed with two or three properties he visited, it is clear that none of them measured up in his estimation to the rich, rolling pastures of the Ord. 'I can't say,' he writes, 'that I would really want to own any of the country traversed this week.'

As the year drew to an end he gave his usual summing up of the immediate situation.

> A pleasant evening at Fremantle seeing the old year out and the new in. Left at 12.30 a.m., and got as far as Cottesloe when the car refused to continue further. Consequently Bird and I obliged to walk, reaching the Esplanade shortly after 3 a.m.
>
> Today to the races with sisters Mary and Bird, D. J. Doherty, John Kirwan and the Misses Quinlan. Kirwan disturbed by the concentration of our population [then approximately 200,000] in or near the capital and vows, if elected to the Legislative Council, to fight the cause of decentralization.
>
> What the future holds for C.D. & D. is difficult to predict. One thing only is clear. We cannot keep going as during the last year or so when the new firm of Yuill & Co. has so cut into our business and prices that we can only carry on at a loss. At our November meeting with Emanuel and Copley we discussed the possibility of a general combine, all buying, selling and killing done here under one head to embrace the new company of Fuller & Naughton as well. Emanuel declares that he and his brother are prepared to fight G. S. Yuill & Co. to the bitter end and are prepared to join any issue that the rest of us might suggest to fight the interlopers for supremacy of trade. The meeting dissolved without any practical result. Connor and wife are recently back from abroad and we are now anxiously awaiting J.W.D.'s return before committing ourselves to any future plans.

18

J.W.'S YEAR ABROAD

February–November 1907

J.W. never ceased to refer back to his 1907 odyssey, but it was only recently, on turning the brittle pages of his letter-diary, that I realised how much it had meant to him. Here he was, off Australian soil for the first time in his thirty-nine years, and all the more excited for having already travelled to most parts of the world through his prolific reading and keen imagination. At the time he saw it as no more than a prelude to the travels he hoped yet to embark upon, though in fact the nearest he would come to going abroad again was via the pages of *The National Geographic Magazine*[1].

He judged it a propitious beginning to his journey that Norddeutscher Lloyds was at that time celebrating its fiftieth anniversary, the occasion being marked on the S. S. *Scharnhorst* by a display of fireworks, a concert, toasts and speeches.

> Our Captain informed us that during 1906 the Company's fleet of 176 ships (56 in the China trade) encircled the globe 276 times, ran 6,000,000 miles and carried 400,000 passengers. In all the time it has been operating it has not lost a single ship. We toasted to another equally successful half century . . .

Alas for the fate of this and all other great German shipping companies within the next decade—let alone fifty years. The *Scharnhorst* was to become the property of the French government after the First World War and was finally scrapped at Genoa in 1934. Her passengers of February 1907, however, sailed on in happy confidence of harmonious international trade relations and an ever more extensive *entente cordiale*.

At Colombo, J.W. disembarked and awaited transport to Calcutta whence he intended travelling to Allahabad to visit his brother Jerry, now generally known as Dermot. His few days in Ceylon served as an introduction to Asian-European relationships which, for all his reading, came as something of a surprise to him. The term 'Boss' as used by Aborigines, though an admission of authority in a European-structured economy, did not carry the same undertones of flattering deference as that of 'Master' in an Asian setting.

> Being addressed in the third person leaves this new chum at something of a loss: 'What time will the Master have tea this morning?' This Master is small fry in his home country but his head now begins to swell and he thinks he must be *Somebody*. He feels inclined to reply: 'The Master will have his tea, by the Grace of God and your presence, between seven and nine a.m. according to how the Master feels when the morning comes.'
>
> If he lived among these people long methinks the Master would do well to remember the oft repeated admonition of the good Dr. Gallagher[2] 'Gnothi Seauton—Man know thyself'.

Visiting a Buddhist temple, he found himself in philosophical conversation with a monk who, hearing that he was in the meat trade, gave gentle warning of the terrible retribution awaiting those who killed creatures of any kind, including fleas and flies. J.W. said he understood that Buddhists ate fish and must therefore be responsible for killing them. 'No Master,' the monk replied, 'we take them from the water and they die of their own accord.'

> This reminds me [J.W. continues] of our old cook, Ah Hooy, who could not understand our renouncing meat on Fridays. 'You won't eat fowl,' he said, 'but you eat egg. Chicken make egg, egg make chicken. What the difference?'

The Lascars who manned the ship *Simla* from Ceylon to Calcutta reminded J.W. of the crew of the *Rajputana* on which he and M.P. sailed from Queensland to Cambridge Gulf in 1886. Their language, he thought, resembled the Aboriginal tongue spoken by the Boontamurra tribe of Cooper's Creek, many words being curiously similar and one at least—namely *galu*, man—actually being identical.

At anchor off Calcutta, awaiting a launch to pick up the *Simla*'s passengers, he spent a sleepless night in oppressive heat and attacked by hordes of mosquitoes.

> As I lay this morning half awake, [he writes] I heard the plaintive semi-whistle of that Ord River bird that calls from the trees at this time of day. I fell into a fevered sleep and dreamed I was camped on the bank waiting for the river to go down. Poor old Uncle Michael was there and Tom Pethic, and when I heard

> Uncle say, as he *did* say, 'We'll tie Pethic to a horse's tail and swim across,' I woke up. Yes, truly, both these good men have since swum the river. What small associations revive memories. That bird call, so unexpected, carried me back to the past in a semi-conscious state. And the present in its turn will be past and we, too, but memories . . .

By the time J.W. boarded the train for Allahabad he was properly rigged out in black singlet, white coat, trousers, and topee, and equipped with a black umbrella. This was on the advice of Richard Wingfield Stuart, one of the many fellow travellers with whom J.W. discovered personal links. Stuart had helped float a syndicate for the takeover of his father's property, Thylungra, in Western Queensland twenty-five years before, and their chance meeting in Calcutta had been one of warm rapport.

Dermot was awaiting his brother at the end of the 500-mile journey, and took him at once to the Allahabad Club. This academic member of the family, now very much the pukka sahib, had never been as expansive a correspondent as his elder brothers. In fact his letters were usually terse and sometimes even irritable.('Of course I can't meet you in Calcutta. You must understand that my time is not my own.') But there was no disguising the eagerness of his welcome and his hunger for news of Australia. He had so far found Allahabad, although the capital of the United Provinces, something of a dead end. J.W. was surprised, as a university post at this meeting-place of the two great, sacred rivers seemed to him romantic and fascinating beyond words. Apart from the interest of his professional and social contacts, Dermot had a vigorous sporting life as well. He owned four good ponies and played polo almost every day; and, enjoying the reputation of being a crack shot, he accompanied the local Maharajah on occasional tiger shoots. It was little wonder that J.W. saw his own life as comparatively restricted and humdrum.

Dermot, always inclined to picture his brothers as living in comparative affluence with time at their own disposal, assured J.W. that the gilt was quick to wear off this exotic gingerbread. For one thing, the salary that had seemed so enticing from afar was quite inadequate for maintaining requisite standards in this snobbish outpost of the Empire. He only hoped his family was not under the illusion that he had no further need for the long-promised company dividends.

J.W. explained that the price of cattle did not as yet warrant such payments and that all members of the firm were living, and travelling when the chance arose, entirely on their modest salaries. The promised erection of a meatworks in Wyndham should, however, soon alter the situation, for this would not only open the door to overseas export but would increase the value of the properties in the eyes of outside investors. In the event of a good offer, the partners would have to decide whether to sell outright or to stay in as members of a syndicate. In any case Dermot would assuredly realise full value on his shares, and his financial problems (like those of all others concerned) would be happily resolved. Meanwhile, a personal loan from J.W. to clear up some immediate debts cheered him considerably, and conversation was allowed to veer to the fairy-tale pageant of India's past and the social and economic realities of her colonial present.

> I have apparently much to learn [J.W. writes, with a hint of gentle cynicism]. It would seem that thanking the servants for their attention and expressing interest in their family lives and problems is detrimental to the prestige of the British Raj.

J.W. was joined in Allahabad by his friend William Moxan, manager of the Adelaide Steamship Company in Fremantle with whom his firm enjoyed a compatible business association. For Moxan this visit was in the nature of a pilgrimage, for his father, although born and raised in Essex, had served for many years in the Indian army. Dermot, warming to their interest and enthusiasm, arranged to accompany them on a sightseeing excursion to Benares and thence to Agra, where they viewed with awe the gleaming magic of the Taj Mahal and the glorious pearl mosque of Akbar's historic fort. Moxan and J.W. then departed for Bombay, every stage of the journey, every mosque, tomb, and shrine, described in loving detail, along with the people encountered. Among these were several followers of Annie Besant[3] who, following an earnest discourse, saw the travellers on their way, wreathed in garlands of roses and weighed down with Theosophical literature.

In Delhi they presented a letter of introduction to a distinguished personage known as the Maulvai Hafir—Learned Man who Knows the Koran by Heart. He generously lent the visitors a carriage and driver, and saw them off at the train for Bombay bearing gifts that J.W. was to treasure for the rest of his life.

In Bombay he and Moxan were taken in hand by a group of Australian horse-dealers who were supplying between them about 5,000 head a year for the Indian market.

> Moxan and I have been shown around Bombay and entertained right royally—out to the races, thence to Fitzgerald's circus and champagne suppers at luxury hotels and restaurants. Our

> conversation has been mainly of horses, station properties, stock prices and markets. What a contrast to that entered into with our Theosophist travelling companions of a week ago or with the gentle Maulvai Hafir who talked of the sacred book of Islam and its immortal revelations! India has surely opened my eyes to the blatant materialism of our Western culture and our pre-occupation with mundane matters of the here and now.

On 1 April J.W. bade good-bye to his Australian friends and sailed from Bombay by S.S. *Africa*. He was intrigued to find among the passengers no less a celebrity than Colonel Francis Edward Younghusband, with whose career he was well acquainted. He had read the Colonel's book, *Heart of a Continent*, and had followed news items about his dramatic opening of Tibet to Western trade some three years before. J.W. would have liked to converse with this intrepid adventurer but was discouraged by the vessel's generally unsociable atmosphere.

> In fact I never did see such a bored, sour-looking lot on a ship. They are mostly military people whose sole purpose in embarking on the voyage is to get home. They don't play cards or deck games or appear to do more than pass the time of day with each other. The only ones I converse with are my table companions, Green, a Bombay banker, Kerr, a Scottish engineer, Laing of Liptons Ltd., and a nice old Presbyterian minister.

He and the congenial Green disembarked at Suez, took a train to Cairo and booked into Shepheard's Hotel. After nine days of non-stop, fascinated sightseeing, they embarked on the *Hohenzollern* at Alexandria.

> Goodbye to Egrpt—her storied past and noisy present—her pestering camel men, donkey boys and dragomen. We have explored her pyramids, her mosques and her museums, her schools and her ostrich farms. We have distributed pocketsful of 'baksheesh'. We have even visited the spot where Pharo's daughter found the baby Moses ('At least that was her yarn,' as my friend Green irreverently remarked.) I intended writing you of it all but feel now that I can't. It has all been marvellous beyond words.
>
> I plan to disembark at Naples and spend about three weeks in Italy.

Green went his own way from Alexandria but J.W. had by this time acquired two other travelling companions—a man named Gibbs and a much travelled young American named Miss Mary Davidson. With these experienced globetrotters he made out an itinerary that leaves the reader almost as breathless as it must have left them. Having 'done' Naples, Venice and Pompeii, they embarked on the tourist circuit of Rome.

> I can't say we have seen all the cathedrals and churches in The Holy City as they have one for every day of the year. Yes—365! And there are Padres everywhere—surely enough to supply the world! Tourists stroll about amongst the congregations attending Mass with their vociferous guides and their Baedekers, maps and books much more in evidence than their Keys of Heaven. It astonishes me why it is allowed.

Florence, Venice, Milan were followed by Switzerland, and the famed scenic wonderland of Lucerne.

> I am so enraptured with it all that I want to think, not write about it. In any case it has been so often described by abler pens than mine. Suffice it to say that my journey so far has filled me with new life and energy. And now there is Paris to look forward to!

As usual he soon found pleasant companions, this time including one Pat Murphy of Kathdrum, County Wicklow.

> Murphy [J.W. writes] took me at first to be an American. Finding I was an Australian he nearly fell on my neck. 'But for Australia I wouldn't be here,' he said. 'My brother made his start on the goldfields in Ballarat, then went tea planting in Ceylon and that's where he died and left me £300,000. I'm now on my way to Rome to have Masses said for him but first I want to see Paris. It's something I've longed to do all my life.'

Here follows a long, amusing story of J.W.'s rescuing Murphy, an innocent abroad indeed, from the clutches of a suave gang of card-sharpers. 'If you really want to see Paris,' J.W. told him, 'you'd better stick with me.'

After a punishing tour of Versailles, the Louvre, the Beaux Arts Gallery, Notre-Dame, and after taking in the races at Longchamps, the Folies Bergères and the Moulin Rouge, Murphy complained of sore feet, and was last seen in company with the seductive female member of the gambling syndicate.

The sideshows at the Moulin Rouge would seem to have been the only attraction of which J.W. did not approve.

> The so-called 'artists' would have been heavily fined, if not imprisoned, in Australia! . . .
>
> Tomorrow [27 May] after these ten exciting days I must say 'Aux Revoir cher Paris' (not 'Adieu' as I will assuredly return to this delightful city). Connor and wife have promised to meet me in London at Charing Cross.

J.W. found that Connor, after several weeks in his home country, had become deeply involved in Irish politics and had addressed several meetings on the subject of Home Rule.

> He has been in close contact with John Redmond[4] and has also conversed with Augustine Birrell[5] the Chief Secretary. 'You know, we Irish totally rejected Birrell's Bill,' Connor tells me, 'we want Home Rule or nothing.' We talked until midnight and almost forgot we had a cent invested in Australia.

If London could be said to have had a hey-day, it must surely have been that glittering Edwardian decade during which she revealed herself to members of my family. In lodgings with the Connors at the Hotel Cecil, and booked into the Australasian Club, J.W.'s daily entries are packed with interesting encounters and stimulating activities. The club was a convenient meeting-place for the many Western Australians then in London for their State's annual dinner at the Trocadero. This year the main speakers were John Winthrop Hackett, editor and part-owner of the *West Australian* newspaper, and C. H. Rason who, having relinquished the Premiership of the young State to Newton Moore the year before, was now Agent-General in London. Also among the guests were J.W.'s Perth friends, Sir Edward Wittenoom, manager of Dalgety & Co, and his wife; surveyor Fred Brockman with his wife and daughter; and a host of other Perth, Fremantle and Kalgoorlie acquaintances. He and Connor were also much in the company of business tycoons and promoters who frequented the 'swagger clubs' to which they were introduced by the shipping magnate Sir Theodore Angier. These included Richard Tilden Smith, whose scheme for a floating abattoir they found of less interest since learning of the promised government finance for a freezing-works at Wyndham.

There was much talk with one and another potential investor of a takeover of the C.D. & D. holdings, Connor waxing eloquent on the boundless carrying capacity and gilt-edged future of the country in question. That the contentious G. S. Yuill was party to some of these discussions aroused no worried comment from J.W.'s pen. It would have been interesting to note the reaction of his partners back in Perth on reading that he and Connor had 'lunched with Yuill at the club and enjoyed an interesting talk on the station and cattle situation in general, and labour problems in particular.'

Mrs Doherty and her family, then living in Slough about eighteen miles from London, figure largely in J.W.'s letters, with requests that his comments be passed on to Denis Doherty in Perth. The elder girls, Kathleen (Katch) and Auvergne (Verne), fluent in French, were now becoming proficient in German as the Doherty household included a cultured Bavarian Fräulein. Byly, the youngest girl, always bubbling over with fun and mischief, and Roy, the adored baby of the family, were not less promising.

> I went with the family to visit Roy at Beaumont [J.W. writes]. He is well grown, athletic and very enthusiastic about his college. He took me to the dormitory and dressed up in his regimentals which suit him admirably. He is beautifully put together as are also the girls. They are all as bright and good as they are beautiful. In fact I have not met a finer family anywhere on my travels. Katch and Vergne sang for us in both French and German, and Fräulein accompanied them. The advantages of their education are only too apparent.

This last comment was no doubt made in answer to those who had criticized the Dohertys for insisting on their children being educated abroad. With such a start in life, J.W. saw brilliant careers in store for each of them, even if the London agency did not eventuate and they were forced to return to Australia.

Whenever possible this little family accompanied J.W. on sightseeing excursions to shows, exhibitions, concerts, and theatrical performances. Together they enjoyed productions of Gilbert and Sullivan and grand opera, and heard Clara Butt and Amy Castles[6] at the Albert Hall. A friendship formed with the Melbourne-born Castles sisters by M.P. when in London the year before was now extended to J.W. and his companions. Clara Butt and her husband Kennerley Ramford also joined the compatible circle, encouraging Frank Connor to sing in his native Gaelic and declaring it a pity that he had not embarked on an operatic career.

The horse show in Dublin at the end of August lured J.W. and his partner from the distractions of London to the different preoccupations of Irish life. For J.W. it was the beginning of an extended sojourn in the land of his forebears, with whom he obviously felt a stronger sense of identification than had M.P. After being warmly received by the Doherty family at

Warrenpoint, and by Connor's people in Newry, he visited Dermot's friends, the Donnellys in Belfast. Of this family he wrote:

> What lovely people these are! I doubt I have ever met a family with such wide interests and varied talents. They are all fine singers and their conversation sparkles like wine. They have no affectations or self-consciousness whatever. Miss Daisy was interested to hear of brother Dermot but there is no prospect of any romance between them now. I cannot imagine this high-spirited Irish girl, with her strong views on British imperialism, hitting it off with those entrenched sahibs and memsahibs of India.

His next objective was his father's birth-place in County Clare, where he was soon engaged with an assortment of Duracks (some spelling the name 'Durick'), Dillons, Scanlans, Brogans, and the rest, in unravelling the tangled chains of kinship and association.

> I was shown today by a Michael Durack the house at Scariff where poor old father was born—now a cart shed—and the farm they had occupied when the family migrated to New South Wales. I also called on members of the Scanlan family—Michael (aged 32) a wealthy merchant—nice chap—and William Scanlan of Scariff, brother of big Uncle Pat and Aunt Mary Gostello[7].
>
> At Banagher I had a marvellous welcome from Harry and Joe Bowles and Mrs. Bowles who is Uncle Pat Tully's[8] sister. I'm sure the King of England was never better treated. We talked until 3 a.m. and I was awakened at daylight by the squealing of pigs in the street. It was market day in Banagher. What memories it revived of stories father told us of his boyhood hereabouts! It could have been yesterday. I milked a cow for them this morning as they were all so busy gathering in the harvest. It's a long time since I last performed this humble but satisfying task.

Except for a short farewell on his return from the United States, J.W.'s first visit to Ireland was to be his last, but the country and its people left an impression that was to remain fresh in his memory. Although he, too, subscribed to the legend of the Duracks' French origins and had obtained while in Paris a document concerning the family Duroc complete with heraldic crest, he was essentially Irish in character and sentiment. The flair for friendly communication and witty repartee that he so much admired in the Irish were no less his own.

Before leaving England he had booked his passage to New York on the

Lusitania, due to leave from Queenstown on 6 October. When the time came, farewelled by the Connors and many other friends, he felt a sense of keen regret, but the ship's orchestra was playing excerpts from musicals he had recently enjoyed and the atmosphere was one of cheerful relaxation.

> All in all the passengers are a jolly lot and when the orchestra strikes up 'Rule Britannia' the corks go 'pop' and everyone drinks to the success of this ship of ships. There are 3000 souls on board and many of them migrants for Canada.
>
> Could I but describe the exquisite beauty of the library and music room with their open fireplaces and costly furnishings! But mind you, the Germans are after her! Mr. Carlyle, Manager of Harland and Wolffs in Belfast, told me they had an offer from Germany for a bigger vessel, though they can't yet make up their minds about *turbines*.
>
> We have sweeps on each day's run. Today we made 617 miles . . .
>
> Our trip from England to America completed in 4 days, 19 hours, 52 minutes. A record!

J.W. was met in New York by a family connection named Michael Dillon, who had been with them in Kimberley ten years before and was now in touch with a number of Duracks who had migrated to the States before J.W.'s branch left Ireland for Australia. Among them was Walter Lysaght Durack of Brooklyn, whose parents had come from Ireland in 1840. Born in Manhattan in 1859, he had been admitted to the bar in 1888 and had specialized in cases concerning real estate. Elected a City Magistrate-at-Large in 1901, he was, according to J.W., a witty conversationalist, vigorous campaigner for the Democratic Party, and a source of lively information about American life, history, and politics[9]. In Chicago J.W. stayed with Denis Francis Durack, his wife and two little girls, whom M.P. had met the previous year. They welcomed him into their household and organized his inspection of the Union stockyards and sundry big canning factories

Back in New York, he found himself plunged into the drama of the bank crash following the collapse of the Knickerbocker Trust.

> 23.10.07: An unforgettable experience—people sleeping on the steps of the bank and queues hundreds of yards long with boys selling their positions to anxious depositors for $10 or more. As a visitor I was able to secure a ticket from a firm of stock brokers to enter a Wall St. exchange. What a spectacle! All those well groomed fellows yelling and charging the money market like

> madmen. The big banks were releasing blocks of millions of dollars to ease the panic but this acted as no more than a feeble spray of water on the flames. It's said to be the greatest financial panic for over forty years.

Three days later he was writing from Washington:

> I am at a most delightful little hotel called 'The Richmond', very convenient, nice people and tariff $3 per day inclusive of three meals—comparatively cheap . . .
>
> Went at once to pay my respects to the Capitol and found it quite awe-inspiring . . . I stood for a while outside the White House, hoping I might catch a glimpse of the great Theodore Roosevelt. He is immensely popular here. All say he is fighting graft and corruption at every level.
>
> I then visited the Navy and Army building especially to see the original Declaration of Independence, but a facsimile transcript only was on view, the original being kept locked away as the light was fast fading it. However a British subject may have felt in 1776, *this* subject found it intensely moving in 1907.

While in Washington, J.W. caught up with his erstwhile travelling companion, Mary Davidson, who introduced him to her distinguished aunt, Mrs Fleming, Curator of Astronomy at Harvard University[10]. Together they visited the Harvard Observatory where J.W. was shown the latest methods of charting the heavens and defining its phenomena.

> Mrs. Fleming [he writes] is the only woman to hold such a position at this University. She is as entertaining as she is erudite and while her mind probes the mysteries of the universe her feet are well and truly on the ground. She tells me that her son was 'in copper' but, to her intense satisfaction, got out of it before the Wall St. crash. She invited me to stay with them for a week during which time she hoped I might meet the illustrious Andrew Carnegie who is a close friend of hers. She tells me that though now about 70 he has the brain of a man in his prime and often locks himself up for a week at a time to work on some project. It takes three secretaries to keep up with him. He has a wife of about 40 and one daughter and Mrs. Fleming stays with them when she visits New York.
>
> You know how I have long admired and quoted Carnegie's 'Gospel of Wealth' in which he asserts that rich men are merely

> the trustees or custodians of their fortunes. I deem it a great privilege to have talked with someone who knows him and would never have presumed to meet him in the flesh. My itinerary, however, did not allow me more than two days to enjoy the company of this remarkable woman and her family. My passage was booked on the *Saxonia* for October 29th.

He continued writing from the ship on 3 November:

> As our Captain and I paced the deck this morning he, hearing I hailed from Australia, casually remarked: 'I believe there is a river in your North West called after an uncle of mine—a surveyor.' It had not occurred to me, so far from home, to link his name with an association of our own. 'Why yes!' I told him. 'My uncle named the Pentacost river in 1882 after the surveyor and geologist who was with him exploring the Kimberley district. John Pentacost was tutor to Mr. Emanuel's sons, one of whom was in that same party.' A long interesting chat ensued. This world of ours is wide indeed, but in some respects how surprisingly small!

It was three months before J.W. returned to Fremantle but his travelogue, or as much of it as is extant, ends on this note.

19

Of Schemes and Dreams

January–May 1908

The early part of 1908 was clearly a time of doubt and indecision for C.D. & D. Even Frank Connor's characteristic optimism had been somewhat subdued since his return from abroad. The financiers, potential partners or purchasers, whom he and J.W. had contacted in England had assuredly expressed keen interest in the firm's vast North Australian pastoral holdings, particularly in view of the imminent erection of a local meatworks as promised by the Western Australian Government. All they needed was proof that this project was under construction before proceeding with any official business agreements.

So confident had the partners been in enlisting their State's co-operation that they were satisfied enough with this response, and thought it more practical than Tilden Smith's proposal for the building of a privately financed floating freezer. Connor, however, was both surprised and disappointed on returning to Perth to find that the all-important meatworks was still no more than a talking-point. The reason given was that the technical adviser of a big freezing company in Sydney, who had been hired to investigate the situation in the Wyndham area, had assessed the cost at a minimum of £100,000 which was £25,000 above that originally estimated. The expert's budget had included the necessary facilities of a jetty on the site and a supply of fresh water to be pumped from twenty miles away. James Mitchell had decided that this was considerably more than the State Treasury could run to at that time. Suggestions that the matter be referred to the Commonwealth Government were soft-pedalled when it was hinted that certain Northern Territory pastoralists who had been talking of the advantages of a meatworks in Darwin were likely to have more influence with the Commonwealth Government than those from far-away Western Australia. A works in Darwin was the last thing any of the Kimberley pastoralists wanted, for where East Kimberley was concerned it would have frustrated their purchase of Territory cattle for shipment from Wyndham, while the droving distance, especially from West Kimberley, would have rendered it impractical as an outlet for themselves.

The idea was then mooted of an amalgamation of Kimberley pastoral interests to finance the immediate construction of a meatworks in Wyndham, and this proposition was discussed animatedly for a few weeks between a number of companies. It was seen by some as a way not only of quickly extending markets to the outside world, but also of out-manoeuvring competitive interests, notably those of the wily G.S. Yuill. Connor and Doherty were confident of a positive reaction from overseas investors when they were informed that a freezing-works was about to be built, but M.P. and his brother P.B. were not so sure. They could not imagine any outside investor buying in before the meatworks was completed. The idea of proceeding on a private basis also worried them, for even with financial assistance from other Kimberley pastoral companies the project would have considerably increased C.D. & D.'s ominously soaring bank overdraft.

Discussion on this important issue was interrupted early in February by the return of J.W. on the *Mooltan*. Partners, relatives, and friends who had gathered to meet him at Fremantle were delighted to see his cheerful countenance beaming from the ship's rails. He was seen to refer to a man at his side whom, after excited greetings on the wharf, he beckoned to join them. 'I must introduce you all,' he said, 'to my good friend and fellow traveller, Mr George Skelton Yuill.'

This could hardly have made a more stunning impact than if J.W. had introduced his welcoming party to the Devil himself, but it seemed that, when met face to face, there was nothing markedly sinister in either his manner or his looks. He and J.W. told how they had become firm friends on the voyage and had discussed the problems of the Australian pastoral industry not as business rivals but as two men faced with mutual industrial problems. J.W. had listened with keen interest to Yuill's life-story, about his boyhood in Aberdeenshire as the son of a minister of the Federated Church of Scotland and his subsequent career beginning in China with the big shipping company, Butterfield and Swire[1]. He had come to Australia in the 1880s and had soon risen to be general manager of the Orient Line. Before long he had become associated with the Adelaide Steamship Company from which C.D. & D. had chartered ships for many years. In the meantime he had become involved in the development of commerce with Britain and the Far East, and pioneered an agency for the export of frozen meat and butter. It was this business, including the wholesale purchase of beef at the lowest possible prices, with which he was now mainly concerned and on which he was only too willing to expound over luncheon with J.W. and his partners. He had, he declared, almost as much W.A. beef as he wanted at that stage, so it was futile their discussing the cut prices which were of such concern to local pastoralists. He was interested, however, in talking about the erection of a Wyndham freezing-works, and was even prepared to help finance the undertaking on a share basis.

After Yuill's departure for Sydney, M.P. and his brothers reported this conversation to the Copleys and Emanuels, who warned that he had been playing a typically shrewd game to catch them off their guard. Whether Connor and Doherty were equally sceptical is nowhere recorded, but J.W.'s return certainly coincided with a new twist to their inter-company discussions. It is obvious that the partners not only talked a great deal with each other but also about each other, and that, although for the most part well disposed, they did not always see eye-to-eye. It would seem that despite having so many interests in common they had in fact rather different ambitions and attitudes to life. Connor and Doherty appear to have seen success as making enough out of their estate, as soon as possible, to live abroad in the higher echelons of society. Doherty, having persuaded his Australian-born wife of the advantages of an English and Continental education for their children, was still waiting, with growing impatience, for his partners to agree to setting him up in a London-based agency. Once free to operate in this way he was confident of soon negotiating a more than satisfactory sale of the company assets. Even if it took three to five years before an established meatworks doubled the value of the Kimberley properties, he could live meanwhile with all the social and cultural advantages of the old world, his holidays divided between relatives and friends in Ireland, friends on English county estates, and at fashionable Continental resorts. He saw his London office as becoming a rendezvous for business tycoons and politicians with their fingers on the pulse of world events and financial trends.

What Connor wanted is not so clear, but correspondence indicates that he saw the Duracks, with their limited bush background, as ingenuous when it came to the subtle use and cultivation of influential people. They were, in his opinion, too prone to be taken in by the plausible go-getter or the hard-luck story. Though Connor confessed to being himself susceptible to the plight of the down-and-out, he declared that he was aware of his weakness, whereas the Duracks, in their naivety, were frequently misled. It did not matter where their private affairs or money were concerned, but it seemed indicative to their partners of a lack of business flair which could result in their failure to seize any opportunities of selling out as soon as possible at a maximum profit. Sometimes Connor wondered whether the Duracks, for all their statements to the contrary, really wanted to sell out at all, or whether they knew what they wanted to do with their lives if they did so. He even detected in the brothers more than a hint of sentimental attachment to that harsh, virgin country they had taken over from the unenterprising blacks. Where M.P. was concerned, it was even possible he might regard a sale as representing not so much a desirable goal as the loss of the kingdom he rode like a monarch with a topee for a crown.

There can be little doubt that all concerned sometimes regretted having formed the association that had once seemed to their mutual advantage, but that the Duracks should have been the first to suggest going their separate ways seems to have come as something of a shock to their partners. At a meeting, soon after J.W.'s return, to discuss the various alternatives ahead of them, M.P. announced that he and his brothers were prepared to accept the sum of £40,000, clear of all liabilities, for their share of the company assets: this would allow the purchasers a free hand to negotiate, without inept encumbrances, for private or government assistance in getting the abattoirs that would at least double their assets. The suggested figure, to cover not only the firm's northern cattle-runs and the Behn Ord estate near Wagin, but the Wyndham and Fremantle businesses and the Guildford slaughter yards, was surely reasonable enough, even by contemporary standards. Connor and Doherty, however, as the brothers no doubt anticipated, nonetheless turned down the offer in a matter of minutes, on the pretext that the price was too high; though in truth their refusal was more likely owing to the sheer problem of management. If the meatworks project were delayed indefinitely and buyers consequently held off, what then? Neither Connor nor Doherty had any desire to take over M.P.'s position as General Manager of the northern properties or P.B.'s in charge of Behn Ord, but where could they find, or how afford to pay, men of equal experience to take their places? For all that Connor might have criticized M.P. on matters of judgement and policy (and sometimes enjoyed mimicking him in his authoritarian role), who after all could approach his knowledge of station management, which included not only his long experience in the breeding and handling of stock but also in dealing with the North's peculiar human problems, including the unpredictable Aboriginals and a curious variety of white employees and bush associates ranging from black-sheep aristocrats to unlettered eccentrics, many of them refugees from justice, conventional society, or unwanted wives? Who else could actually sit in a saddle for so long in that intolerable heat, or negotiate a buggy over those unmade roads and stony, mosquito-infested creek beds? For that matter, which one of them, Connor or Doherty, each with his political, social, and family responsibilities, would be prepared to take over J.W.'s job as Manager of the Perth and Fremantle offices? When, in the event of such a takeover, would Doherty be free to rejoin his wife and children in England? For him it might even mean abandoning the idea of a London agency and getting the family back to Australia—perish the thought!

The refusal accepted, the brothers then asked their partners whether, since they found the price too high, they would be prepared to sell out to the Duracks for the same sum. This proposition broke up the meeting and sent Connor and Doherty away in a state of shocked bewilderment to talk it over.

They returned some days later with the proposition that the Duracks should keep the northern stations and their partners should take the Wagin property with an additional £20,000. M.P. (the chronicler of these negotiations) was surprised when P.B., whose total personal commitment to, and faith in, the Behn Ord estate he had taken for granted, spoke up in favour of this proposition. A proviso, however, was soon added to the effect that it should be applied in the alternative: in effect, that the brothers should keep Behn Ord and let their partners keep the rest of the estate.

This interchange of challenging propositions went on for two weeks, during which time M.P. was also approached by the General Manager of the big merchant firm of Dalgety & Co with the idea of their purchasing the properties for £60,000 as soon as it was officially established that a meatworks was to be opened in Wyndham. None of the partners appears to have been very impressed with this offer as they had better prospects to investigate in this contingency.

All members of the company had now grown tired of the contest and had come to the conclusion that they had best carry on together, for the time being at least. It was agreed that Connor should continue as Chairman of Directors at an annual salary somewhat in excess of those of the other partners, and that Doherty should open an office in London where he would attend to all the firm's business, including the sale of wool and hides, thus saving the commission and charges previously paid to Jowitt and Son. This decision was soon afterwards amended to the effect that, apart from his annual salary of £1,500, Doherty was to receive a commission of not less than £550 per annum.

It was also agreed that M.P., before returning north, should visit the other capitals to investigate every possibility of hastening the erection of a meatworks. He records, with an obvious sigh of relief:

> Everything therefore settled satisfactorily for the time being. We all shake hands and agree to continue to the best of our separate and combined capacities.

It is obvious, nonetheless, that M.P.'s state of mind was still far from settled. A quotation from Byron, scribed in his diary about this time, indicates that business problems were not his only preoccupation:

> Oh that the desert were my dwelling place
> With one fair spirit for my minister,
> That I might all forget the human race,
> And hating no one love but only her.

There can be little doubt that he had longed for years for the ideal marriage partner whose presence would identify some place as his own. So far Argyle was still closer to being his home than anywhere else, but while Ambrose was Manager he was actually in charge. Of recent years it had been he, with the help of his sister Kit, who had been head of the house, who engaged or sacked the cooks and dictated the standards. When M.P. turned up he was welcomed as an honoured guest, and was farewelled in the same spirit as at the other company homesteads of Ivanhoe, Newry, and Auvergne. The house at Fremantle, while convenient and comfortable enough, had never felt much more like home to him than his other place of residence at the Esplanade Hotel in Perth.

Now forty-two, little older in appearance than ten years before and just as vigorous, he was apprehensive of the passing of the years. He had certainly not purposely avoided matrimony, but the several young women to whom he had felt seriously attracted had, for one reason or another, too soon passed out of his life. This consideration depressed him from time to time but he was confident enough that some day, somewhere, he would meet the woman of his heart's desire. Whether this was at the back of his mind when he set off for Adelaide early in March with his sister Bird, he does not say. He merely records his pleasure at finding Sir John Forrest among his fellow passengers on the *Moldavia* and notes that they spent much time discussing the past and future of their State, with emphasis on the problems of the Kimberley district and its pastoral industry. Another subject of special interest was the fact that the Federal Parliament seemed at last disposed to fund a preliminary survey of a railway to link Kalgoorlie with the South Australian rail-terminus at Port Augusta. This, despite attacks against the uselessness of a 'desert railway' from the press in other States, was seen by all with interests in Western Australia as a major step in overcoming their constricting isolation. It was still to be ten years before the completion of that 1,051 miles of rail, but that Forrest hoped to return to Perth with full confirmation of Commonwealth co-operation was a matter of keen satisfaction to all who shared the information.

Forrest obligingly added to M.P.'s list of contacts in the frozen-meat business, and the two parted with warm goodwill at Adelaide, where M.P. disembarked to be greeted by his sister Mary and her husband who had brought their children to visit members of the Davidson family in South Australia. With them at the wharf was Gertrude (Johnnie) Johnstone's younger sister, Bess, who invited them all that evening to the Johnstone home at the Semaphore. It was an enjoyable occasion for M.P., chatting with her father[2] and his plump, amiable wife who had emigrated from England with her parents as a child. The highlight of the visit, however, was obviously a walk along the Semaphore jetty with Bess—'a most attractive and entertaining girl with a lovely figure and no affectations whatever'. He assumed she would have 'a host of followers', but before he had time to investigate this assumption his busy programme had called him in another direction.

Three days later he was in Melbourne, where he and Sydney Emanuel had arranged to confer with William Angliss[3] on questions relating to the frozen-meat trade. Angliss received them cordially and drove them to inspect his extensive meatworks at Footscray. He informed them that, apart from the land on which it stood, the entire establishment, including freezing, chilling, boiling-down and preserving works, had cost him about £50,000, and he recommended them to interview the consultant he had employed. This they did, though realising that the expenses attached to building a works in Footscray were hardly comparable to those that faced them in the remote and undeveloped north.

Emanuel and M.P. continued to Sydney where they made a number of calls together, though Emanuel drew the line at consulting with G. S. Yuill. M.P., on the other hand, found both Yuill and his associate Anderson hospitable and informative.

Otherwise most of his time in Sydney was spent in happy reunion with family and friends. He found his father's cousin Tom Durack at the Newmarket Hotel, of which he was proprietor, and enjoyed a long session of 'lively family chat'. He was also interested in inspecting a display of trophies for swimming won by Tom's daughter Fanny, mostly while she was still at school. The family was proud of her athletic achievements and scornful of the prudish attitude of a section of the public that labelled women who swam in public as 'not only coarse and indecent, but immoral'. At that time Fanny was seventeen years old and her greatest achievement had been winning the 100 yards N.S.W. women's title. Within three years she was to win two major Australian championships and to create a record for the 200 yards Australian title. This marked the beginning of a remarkable career that M.P. and his family were to follow with keen interest[4].

Various members of the family were then staying, along with M.P., at Petty's Hotel. These included his cousin M.J. with his wife Bertha and brother J.B., who soon discovered that their old friends W. F. Buchanan and Tom Cahill were also in Sydney.

Buchanan, like his younger brother Nathaniel who had died in 1901, was among the most outstanding pastoral pioneers in Australia. Then eighty-four years old, his pastoral empire had been built up largely from scratch, with the help of hard, practical experience, natural foresight and keen powers of observation. Born in Dublin in 1824, he had arrived in N.S.W. with his parents and four brothers in 1837. The family took up grazing properties in New England, from where young William Frederick, having served his apprenticeship, soon extended his interests to include goldmining, the breeding of pedigree stock, the export of beef to Britain, and the development of freezing facilities. In the early 1880s he had acquired pastoral leases in the Northern Territory adjoining Wave Hill, which had been taken up by his brother Nat and the latter's relatives by marriage, Hugh and Wattie Gordon. In 1890, in an effort to promote overseas interest in Australia and to encourage exploration, he had written a book entitled *Australia to the Rescue*, which was published in England[5].

Tom Cahill, together with his brothers Paddy and Matt, was also among Australia's most memorable stockmen. Sons of a pioneer of Queensland's Darling Downs, they had joined Nat Buchanan droving cattle to Glencoe Station near Darwin in 1878, and a few years later also brought stock to Wave Hill where Tom Cahill had remained as manager until 1905.

The five men, as pioneers of the overland tracks and early Kimberley and Northern Territory settlement, found much to talk about, and repaired together to the Flemington cattle sales. Despite what M.P. considered absurdly inflated prices for stock in many cases inferior to the Kimberley product, M.J. saw fit to purchase forty head of young Hereford bulls and a stallion, which he intended shipping from Sydney to Wyndham. He had already engaged two young men to look after the stock en route and to continue in his employment on Lissadell Station. One of these, named Gordon Broughton[6], has left us his own account of his interview with M. J. Durack at Petty's Hotel, where he had approached him in search of a job.

> The grim, taciturn cattle man gave me a bare ten minutes, but that was enough. He was a tall, lean man with a large moustache and a fine head of iron-grey hair. His features were fierce and

> aquiline and, sitting very erect, he bored me through and through with piercing eyes, his voice a harsh rasp. I knew he would be a hard boss . . . but when he found that his sister knew my parents, he gave a grim smile and said: 'Right. I'll give you a job as book-keeper on Lissadell cattle station in East Kimberley. You'll get a pound a week and tucker and you'll be kept busy believe me . . .' Then he looked at his watch and said quickly: 'The Burns Philp boat *Airlie* leaves Sydney on the 1st of April. I'll send you a steerage ticket and I'll meet you at Pinkinbah in Queensland. You and Keelar will take the stock round to Wyndham. Later in the year I'll be up to Lissadell.' He got up, gave me a vice-like hand-grip and the hint of a smile and the next moment I was out in the corridor . . . [G. W. Broughton, *Turn Again Home*, Brisbane, 1965]

There was another family gathering to see the ship *Airlie* on its way from Sydney. This was not to farewell M.J.'s stud stock, but because the passengers included M.P.'s sister Mary, husband Jim Davidson and family, who were bound for Wyndham via Brisbane and Darwin rather than returning to Fremantle and plugging on up the monotonous west coast. The Davidsons had with them as companion help a capable and attractive girl referred to as Ethel. She was in fact Ethel Flinders, a daughter of Charles Edward Flinders by his first marriage, who was later to marry W. R. Willesee, agent and cattle-buyer of Wyndham.

Also to see the ship away was M.P.'s cousin Kit, who, having visited her family in Queensland, said she was now returning to her brother Ambrose at Argyle. This surprised M.P., in view of the attentions being pressed upon her by the young engineer, Dan Evans, whose ship was in Sydney Harbour at that time.

It was of course inevitable that M.P. and other relatives from the west should include Brisbane in their itinerary, and with it happy gatherings of the clan who turned up from many parts of Queensland when news of their arrival spread.

The Durack family had now come to include many others by marriage, some of whom were influential in business and political circles. Frank Tully, eldest son of Grandfather Patsy Durack's sister Sarah, had married Anne Leahy, daughter of the then Speaker in the House of Representatives, John Leahy, with whom M.P. had a long conversation which he describes as 'reassuring from a point of view of Queensland co-operation on bringing prices down.'

Less encouraging was his interview with Mr Magee, manager of the Queensland Meat Export Works, who would probably have seen a Wyndham works as being in competition with his own. In any case, he did not think any such enterprise in Wyndham was a good idea at all.

By this time M.P. was anxious to get back to the west and confessed to having 'an attack of the miserables'. This may have been owing, in part at least, to the fact that Bird had announced her intention of remaining in Sydney until the end of the year and then of going to Melbourne for an indefinite period. Why she should wish to take up residence in Melbourne where, although she had a number of good friends, there were few if any relatives, he could not understand. All she would say was that she liked Melbourne and felt it was time she made a change in her life. What she did not tell him was that, in the opinion of several outspoken advisers, she was somehow responsible for her brothers' not yet having 'married and settled down'. Her devoted matchmaking efforts were scorned by these forthright counsellors, who declared that only if she were well out of the way would M.P. and J.W. really begin to look around for the tender care and company which she provided for so little trouble and expense. It was also suggested that while her brothers were around, she stood little chance of making a suitable match herself. Indeed how many times had they not already declared a man she found acceptable to be, for some reason, unsuitable?

Another reason for her decision that Bird had not yet mentioned to her brothers was that a friend, well known in Melbourne's smart set of the time, had suggested their going into partnership in a fashionable beauty business. While staying for some months with various relatives in Sydney she was resolved to make up her mind about this proposition.

So, after all, it was not with his sister but with his cousin Kit and her younger brother Fergus that M.P. returned to Perth and was soon heading northwards on the *Junee*.

20
'Land of Expanse and Romance'

May–October 1908

On arrival in Wyndham early in May 1908, M.P. recorded that after an unusually long time in the crowded cities he was 'back again in the land of expanse and romance'. Of the expanse there could be no doubt, though that he found much romance in his bush life at that time is questionable. It continued to depress him that of all towns he knew, Wyndham had showed the least change over the years. There were the same little white shops and residences shimmering in the same heat-haze on either side of its single street. There were the same faces; the same, mostly drunken, greetings from stockmen in moleskin pants and Crimean shirts; the inevitable gang of Aboriginal prisoners, their chains clanking as they spread broken stones over the tide-eroded thoroughfare; and the same sonic background to it all of bellowing cattle as the mobs stumbled down the rough track over the Bastion Mountain and through the race to the waiting ships. He was down to work at once with Jim Davidson, confirming draft delivery dates from outlying stations and transport from Wyndham to Fremantle.

Ambrose, himself only recently returned from one of his rare holidays and in town to meet the ship, brought with him the sad news of Pumpkin's death while both he and M.P. had been away. They had often referred to Pumpkin as 'the old man', though he could then have been no more than fifty-eight to sixty years old and in physical terms had continued, if not as the most active, at least as the most effective Aboriginal on Argyle. Feeling indisposed from some undiagnosed cause, and with no member of the family at hand to consult, he had wandered off to die alone on the bank of a creek some miles from the homestead.

Pumpkin had been part of M.P.'s life for as long as he could remember. Always at his father's right hand, this remarkable Aboriginal had regarded Patsy Durack as a brother and his sons as nephews, their welfare always foremost in his mind. It was, as my father often reminded us, Pumpkin himself who had insisted on joining J.W. and himself at Argyle more than twenty years earlier, and had Grandfather not arranged for them to travel to Wyndham by ship together, he would probably somehow have made his own way overland. It could not have been an easy thing for an Aboriginal to leave his country and tribal associations, but he had finally won the respect of the local Aborigines and had become as much a part of Argyle as he had been of Thylungra. It was generally ascribed to Pumpkin's influence that the Aboriginal camps at Argyle and Ivanhoe were relatively harmonious and trouble-free. He would even seem to have come to terms with tribal elders who, in earlier years, had failed to 'sing him dead' for his allegiance to the white man, and had speared another woman in mistake for the Mirriwung girl who had consented to marry him. Charlie, the young man deputized to carry out this execution, had long since settled down as one of the most reliable station hands, and was to end up the much loved 'King of Argyle' to whom, together with his family, the place was a haven and a home.

The truth of the matter was that the tribespeople employed at Argyle, as on most other Kimberley properties, were there from choice and had found the station way of life a satisfactory enough substitute for their former hunting and foraging activities. Where the men were concerned, riding horses in pursuit of cattle was a novel and interesting occupation that gave a new sense of purpose and prestige to the long, warm days. The women, too, enjoyed the status accruing from their household roles, especially if there was a white woman at the homestead to chat and laugh with as they worked, to fuss over their little ones and dole out magic nostrums in times of sickness.

In the context of the times, a station where they could enjoy their fill of beef without being hunted down by the police and led away in chains to face the white man's justice was a welcome form of security. Fortunately, too, their employers displayed, if not much interest in, at least a tacit respect for, their tribal customs and beliefs, and did not interfere with the enactment of sacred rites and ceremonies that were now, by mutual agreement, relegated to wet-season holiday time. Such periods were mostly spent on 'walkabout' in the outlying bush, with tucker bags full of the flour, tea, sugar, and tobacco that had become essentials of life. Those who wished to visit friends and relatives on other properties during 'the slack' were mostly provided with a letter or form of passport assuring station managers of the bearers' bona fides and asking that rations provided should be charged to their employers. It was therefore with the assurance of rations and security that the white men had won the labour and loyalty of so many tribespeople, and in this diplomatic game Pumpkin had been associated with the interlopers ever since he offered Patsy Durack a fish from his own tribal waterhole in 1868. He and the Boontamurra group to which he belonged had not seen those first white strangers as a potential threat to their future. Pumpkin's story was that he had recognized Patsy Durack as a brother he had lost years before, who had simply rejoined him as a 'jumped-up white-fellow'.

Ambrose reported that the old man's death had been the occasion of prolonged grief and much wailing at Argyle, for besides Valley, his widow, and Boxer and Ulysses, whom he had reared as his sons, all members of the black community thereabouts had come to regard themselves as tribally related to him in some way. M.P., when expressing his own grief to the people, carefully referred to Pumpkin as 'our dear friend and relative now passed away', knowing that to utter the name of one recently deceased would, in tribal tradition, have disturbed the departed spirit.

Kit Durack's return from Queensland and the arrival of her brother Fergus at the station gave reassurance to the camp people, who had been distressed by the absence of any family members over the past few months. They were not to know that Kit's heart was no longer in Kimberley but somewhere out to sea with the young engineer named Dan Evans, whom she had promised to marry when his ship was in Sydney later that year. In the meantime she soon had the homestead looking spruce again and gave a smiling welcome to all who entered it.

M.P. seems to have been glad of the company of his young cousin Fergus, whom he took with him on his routine station round. What Fergus made of M.P.'s 'land of expanse and romance' is nowhere recorded, but his introduction to the country was by no means devoid of incident. Soon after his arrival M.P. notes:

> From Argyle to Newry with Fergus and Boxer and left yesterday for Auvergne, looking at country and inspecting stock on the way. Did 31 miles. Blacks watching from the hills; their fires ablaze and dogs howling all night. Trouble of some sort afoot I suppose. Came on a foal on the other side of the Baines, badly torn about the jaw and rump. Not far along came on an outsize 'gator. Shot the foal and poisoned it for the predator.

Jack Skeahan at Auvergne was then married to Kit's friend Emily Woodland and the remote homestead was rather more comfortable than it had been in former times, but the station run was still a wild and hazardous tract of country. On his next visit a few weeks later, M.P. learned that the crocodile, all twenty-three feet of it, had been found and skinned on his instructions for his collection. He was already aware of the fact that the days of giant wildlife specimens were drawing to a close. The huge crocodiles, the thirty-foot rock pythons that made wide, curving swathes through the long grass and were held in awe, and sometimes even regarded as sacred, by the blacks, were one by one falling prey to the white man's bullets and baits. For Kit, they provided colourful stories to share with visitors including young Gordon Broughton, who was later, in his book *Turn Again Home*[1], to describe his first visit to Argyle at about this time.

> We had run short of a few essential items at Lissadell and the Manager, Fred Hill, sent me over to Argyle with a black boy and four pack-horses to get flour and sugar and to borrow some quinine and laudanum. The river was low so no trouble to cross and with only 25 miles to ride we reached Argyle before sundown. Here, to my delight, I found a gracious stone house, creeper-covered with flagged path and garden. Presiding over the household was Miss Kathleen Durack, an attractive, bright girl of about twenty-six. Her brother Ambrose managed the property and there at that time was their older cousin, M.P. Durack . . . part owner of Argyle and other stations.

A return of the prevalent fever gave him a good excuse to remain at Argyle for two memorable days.

> On a long ride with Kathleen we found many things about which to talk. In the evenings we sat at a dining room table laid with silver and spread with a snowy cloth. The gins actually wore dresses and it was clear that Kathleen expected her men to spruce themselves up at meal times. The decorum of Argyle . . . was in marked contrast to the pagan ways at Lissadell where the lubra bringing our meal to table was often as not dressed in a shirt so short that there was nothing left unrevealed.
>
> Many books lay about on shelves at Argyle and I quickly found that the tall, bearded M. P. Durack was not only a travelled man but one to whom good books were a condition of life. He was very gracious to me and with that and the brief but gay company of a girl, I returned to Lissadell with considerable reluctance.

So far Broughton's introduction to the north had both fascinated and shocked him. The landscape and its wild life he had found varied and exciting, while the bush workers and their living conditions and mores had at least interested him. His description of the Lissadell homestead would have applied to most of the bachelor establishments in the north at that time.

> The buildings, grouped on a bare patch of red, hard-pan ground near a small creek, reflected the pioneer simplicity of cattle-men's lives. No white woman graced this place ... The Manager and Head Stockman lived in isolated state in 'Government House', a harsh, utilitarian structure of galvanised iron, with four small, bare rooms lacking both lining and ceilings. The furniture consisted of three wire bunks, a small deal table and four kitchen chairs. No creepers softened the hard outline ...
>
> Some distance away stood the small combined office store, a pisé building of compacted earth taken from white ants' nests and mixed with straw. Nearby was the stockman's hut with a dirt floor, two doorways without doors and two window openings without windows. The only furnishings were six crude bunks made from bush timber laced with strips of greenhide ...

Broughton, writing from hindsight, was both understanding and gently critical of many local attitudes.

> The basic philosophy of men living in Kimberley was that the cattlemen had battled their way into the empty land with great hardship and at high cost in lives and money; that they were there to stay, and if the wild blacks got in the way—in other words speared men or killed and harassed cattle—they would relentlessly be shot down. It was as simple and brutal as that.
>
> Trained and valued black stockmen were of course well cared for and protected. Some of them came from Queensland and their gins were taken from the local tribes. Consequently they also became the enemies of the bush blacks. They, or rather the white men who had taken the gins for them, had forcibly broken the tribal marriage laws.
>
> The cattlemen, intent on carving out a living in a primitive and hostile land, paid little heed to the ancient Aboriginal laws. And in this, it must be confessed, they did nothing more than follow the harsh pattern of early colonial pioneering in the rest of Australia and in other lands ...
>
> Coming into this vast land of widely scattered homesteads and lonely white men ... I was at first shocked when I came face to face with the fact of sexual intimacy between white and black.

> But before I left that remote region I was ready to acknowledge that no man or woman living a normal life in the settled areas of Australia had right or knowledge to pass judgment on the men of the North ... For the greater number intercourse with the younger and more comely black women was a purely physical matter, devoid of any emotional involvement. There was, however, a great distinction between casual physical contact and actually living with a native woman. The division ... was then sharp and clear; a man who lived with a gin was known contemptuously as a 'Combo'. On the other hand, occasional association was acknowledged by the bushnen to be a physical necessity. It was rarely discussed, silently condoned, and understood. It was unlikely that a sex-driven man in his outback hut or prospector's camp would pause to consider the half-caste problem he was already aware of growing up around him.[2]

The vigorous young stockman, Alec Keelar, who had accompanied Broughton on the ship with the cattle, had died of fever within a month of his arrival at Lissadell. This was the fate of too many, mostly younger men, who had apparently built up no immunity to this 'mosquito-carried' curse of the Kimberleys. M.P., too, remarks the persistence of the 'fever winds' blowing through the country, which by the latter part of the year had resulted in the deaths of no less than eight, mostly young, white employees in the vicinity.

But fever was not the only killer abroad that year. In July M.P. reports the shooting of a man named Scottie MacDonald on an outstation of Texas Downs, owned by Jack Kelly. This would not have caused such a sensation had the killer not been an Aboriginal named Major who was well known throughout East Kimberley as Kelly's best stockman and trusted courier, as well as being highly esteemed by the police as an expert tracker of white horse-thieves and Aboriginal cattle-spearers. He had been with Kelly from childhood, had accompanied him on several trips to the city, and was said by Kelly himself to have twice saved his life. After the shooting of MacDonald, Major had disappeared from Texas and was reported to be hiding out in the surrounding ranges with a group of outlaws who were said to be intent upon wiping out all the *guddea* (white men) in the country.

There are several versions of why Major turned outlaw, and there is probably some truth in all of them. Jack Kelly and his wife reported that Major's change of heart had been actuated by the jealousy of an older woman named Biddy, to whom he had been married according to tribal law. They declared, with substantial evidence, that he had later become attached to a young woman named Knowla, who was also tribally 'straight' for him as a marriage partner and was therefore tacitly accepted by the Aboriginal community. According to this version, however, Biddy became bitterly jealous and, with revenge in view, left Texas Downs for its outstation, Growler's Gully, where she was given the job of goat shepherd by the overseer, Scottie MacDonald.

At an Aboriginal gathering next wet season, Biddy is said to have confided in Knowla that MacDonald was jealous of Major and was plotting to take his life. Knowla repeated this story to Major, who soon afterwards went to Growler's Gully, lay in wait, and fired on MacDonald when he emerged from his shack at daylight.

The Kellys declared that the wounded man had crawled to the road where he was at last picked up by a traveller and brought by buggy to Texas homestead. Others say that Biddy, who hid until Major had made off, helped MacDonald on to a horse and led him to the station. How ever he may have got there, all agree that he died at Texas next day.

Some time before this, Major had apparently been persuaded to join a police patrol in pursuit of the killers of a young stockman named Hugh McKenna. Two Aborigines, Pompey and Nipper, were charged with this murder. Pompey was convicted and imprisoned, but Nipper, a Lissadell boy, thereafter 'went bush' and joined a group of declared outlaws. On other occasions Major had also been used as a go-between to try and dissuade the hill-dwellers from spearing cattle. He is said by some to have had the restraining influence that Pumpkin and Boxer exercised on Argyle. According to Aboriginal sources, however, he had come back from one of these diplomatic missions shortly before shooting MacDonald, and put forth a strong case in defence of the outlaws, some of whom had been ruthlessly shot down in police raids. Both Kelly and the constable awaiting his return to Texas Station had been shocked and made apprehensive by this view of things, and are said to have decided to teach Major a stern lesson by tying him, blindfolded, to a post and flogging him. He was thereafter taken to Wyndham on a chain and, after serving a short sentence, was asked by the police to join them as a tracker (at which skill he was reputed to have had few equals). Major forthrightly refused, giving as his reason the treatment he had received at the hands of the constable at Texas. He was thereupon assured—or so one Aboriginal version goes—that if it was the flogging he resented, this had been inflicted, not by a member of the police force but by his revered boss Jack Kelly. If this story is correct, it can be understood that Major was already sadly disillusioned by the time he was told that MacDonald, another white man whom he had regarded as his friend, intended killing him. Nor, if this was the case, is it to be wondered at that, having disposed of the threat to his life and got away with all the ammunition at Growler's Gully, he should have joined Nipper and his associates in the outlying ranges.

On 14 August M.P., on a visit to Lissadell, records being greeted by his cousin Long Michael (M.J.) with the news that the two men in charge of his outstation at Blackfellow Creek had been found dead in their beds, one shot, the other battered with the spoke of a wheel. The men, George Fettle and Jim Davis, were well-known local personalities, and the Lissadell stockboys, after some Aboriginal detective work, declared that Major, Nipper and their associate Debbie had been responsible.

Knowla, a witness to the murder, later informed the police that Major had once worked with George Fettle and had held him in high esteem. He had been upset to find that Fettle was one of the two victims, and while Nipper and Debbie were divesting the store of rations, rifles, cartridges, and boots, Major had crouched, convulsed with grief, beside the body of his friend.

Over the following weeks reports reached Argyle of stock-camps having been surrounded and robbed by armed blacks at night, and of travellers having been held up and divested of their belongings. In vain the police from Wyndham, Hall's Creek, Turkey Creek, and Wild Dog scoured the countryside. M.P., then in Wyndham, records on 3 September that there was general excitement in the community over reports that Major was hovering around Cartridge Spring and Turkey Creek, and threatening to wipe out the local citizens.

Further rumours spread that the outlaw gang had made off into the wilds of Auvergne and Bullita to get out of the way of the police. If this put some off the scent, Biddy (who had since returned to work at Texas) was not amongst them. She was certain that the wanted men were still in the vicinity, and one day when looking for some straying goats she came upon convincing evidence—a trail of boughs dragged across a dry creek bed to disguise tracks of which she recognized a few traces. She returned to the homestead to inform Kelly that Major and his gang were nearby. The message was at once conveyed to Turkey Creek, from where four policemen and six trackers, with Constable Fanning in charge, set off with Biddy at daybreak next morning.

There are detailed police reports of the final tracking-down of Major and his companions Nipper, Debbie, and their women. In the shoot-out that followed, Fanning collected a bullet through the shoulder but the police party otherwise came out unscathed. Major, Nipper, and Debbie were shot dead and Knowla was wounded. She is said by some to have died soon afterwards, but by others to have become attached to the police force at Hall's Creek where she died many years later, having given a detailed, but poorly recorded inside account of the story from both the Aboriginal and white points of view. It is, at least, generally agreed that Biddy, her mission accomplished in proving her faithless husband a dangerous man to both white and black, returned to live out the rest of her life at Texas Downs.

As news spread of the outlaws' end, a sigh of relief went up throughout the countryside. M.P. wasted few words in concluding the episode: 'We learn,' he writes, 'that Major, Nipper and Debbie have been brought to their final rest, much to the great relief of all.'

G. W. Broughton concludes his retrospective version of the story rather more reflectively.

> This bloody episode was just one of the many, the outcome of which could often be traced back to some form of harsh treatment of the station Aborigines by the white man. In general the station owners and managers were benign but firm, but there were some rough men who combined contempt with brutality in their handling of these primitive people. Men's actions can only be judged as in and of their time, and life was new and raw in Kimberley in the period of which I write.[4]

21
The Link with London

June–December 1908

It is obvious that M.P. was meanwhile concerned with more than the activities of outlaw Aborigines, the control of cattle and horses and of his wide-ranging and oddly assorted staff. Letters, cables, and telegrams from Connor and J.W., then in charge of the Perth office, from Doherty in London, and from Dermot in India were constantly catching up with him, and provide some clue to the company's current problems and diverse policies. Of these (all carefully filed in date order), Dermot's often irritable communications are the easiest to interpret. He wanted more money to cover his expenses, and was unmoved by the fact of its being a time of slump on the Australian cattle market when the firm was desperately trying to reduce its Western Australian Bank overdraft from £35,000 to an agreed £30,000. He was annoyed with J.W. for failing to send him a pony he wanted for a polo mount because Connor had said it would cost as much to ship to Bombay as it was worth.

> The firm appears to be Connor & Doherty in that they at least get all they want. The age of that pony was exactly right. Nobody here trains them younger than five as their legs are liable to go wrong on hard ground . . .
>
> Re my offer—£6,000 for my shares after paying off obligations and debts. This is of course on condition that the stations are not sold for £150,000 to Dalgety . . . [J.J.D., Allahabad, to J.W.D., Perth, 31.8.08]

Dalgety's was only one of several offers to purchase the C.D. & D. properties, completely or in part, at this time, but for various reasons such negotiations somewhere broke down. Doherty was pulling all the strings possible from the little London office he had hired for £20 a year.

> It is only 12 x 9. Big glass panelling cuts it off from a Thames landing stage and it has plenty of window space for the display of the photos and maps I hope to get of our Territory and W.A. properties, including Behn Ord. At present it bears the simple

inscription: 'D.J. Doherty. Australian Produce Merchant.' [D.J.D., London to C.D. & D., Perth, 16.9.08]

Richard Tilden Smith had offered him the use of a much more impressive office but he had been wary of putting himself under an obligation in this regard. It would seem, however, that he was still hopeful of bringing off some negotiations with this enterprising, if somewhat devious, operator.

Doherty constantly protests the careful attention he pays to the company interests in England, as he had done also in Perth during the previous year while Connor and J.W. were globe-trotting. He expresses himself on this subject in a long letter to J.W.

> I can safely say that from 9 a.m. to 4 p.m. I was at my post watching and scheming to break down the losses caused by the new and unfair competition[1]. Perhaps I don't dot my i's or cross my t's with your mathematical care but I can safely say the business had all the careful handling possible at the time as it is receiving from my London office today . . . I regret writing in this vein but I have the feeling that you thought old Doherty and Miguel let things slide in your absence . . . Perhaps this is a bad way of thanking you for your long and detailed letters but I had it on my chest and it is now removed.
>
> I should very much like to get £100,000 at 5% but cannot yet see an opening. You know what I thought of your refusing the previous loan I could have pulled off . . . Now why not relieve the situation by putting up the Wagin interests and selling in five hundred to one thousand acre blocks . . . We've just got to learn to sell ourselves and secure a more peaceful frame of mind. Moss once said to me 'I value my sleep too much to undertake any financial worries.'
>
> My dear Jack, do not be so d---d downcast. Face the difficulties like the man you are and all will pan out right in the end. At least one of our bank accounts is now within the accepted figure £30,000 . . .
>
> My kiddies like all you brothers but you the best of all and they want to know when you'll be here again to give them the sort of royal good time you manage so well. [D.J.D., London, to J.W.D., Perth, 16.10.08]

Doherty's reference to J.W.'s worried frame of mind was probably a comment on his increasingly urgent wires warning of financial disaster if money could not be raised without delay. The emergency was not so dire, however, as to cause the partners to accept offers which did not happen to suit them all. One of these was for the purchase of the southern property, Behn Ord, for £25,000 together with the Wyndham assets including hotel, store and general agency. This proposition, favoured by their partners, was firmly declined by the Durack brothers who, on the other hand, wholeheartedly approved an offer for the purchase of Auvergne Station in the Northern Territory for the same sum. This property, in their opinion always more of a burden than an asset, had belonged to Connor and Doherty before the partnership was formed, and the latter refused to concede that it was not at least as valuable as the Argyle Station run, let alone Behn Ord and the Wyndham businesses. Both these proposals were therefore declined, and were soon forgotten in the midst of high-pressure meetings in both Perth and London of major Kimberley pastoralists.

Their main concern seems to have stemmed from the prospect of big money moving in to buy huge estates in the Northern Territory and establishing a meatworks in Darwin. This possibility gave fresh impetus to the idea of Western Australian interests investing in floating freezers or a meatworks in Wyndham. Doherty writes despondently, as one proposition after another falls flat or gives way to something else:

> It's such a bally dreary business—one day hope, the next hopelessness. One day encouragement—the next Hades, a frozen Hades, that is.
>
> Tilden Smith has, I think, purchased Victoria River Downs, though he's so far only hinted this. He has given Frank Wittenoom his power of attorney to purchase properties or cattle for floating freezers.
>
> By this time you should have seen Emanuel on his return from London and talked all this business over with him and the Copleys etc. [D.J.D., London, to J.W.D., Perth, 27.11.08]

The partners learned soon afterwards that Victoria River Downs, in the Territory, and Carlton Station, near Wyndham, had been purchased by Bovril Australian Estates for the sum of £180,000. The Chairman of the new owners was Sir Hector Rason, Agent-General for Western Australia, his fellow directors being Sidney Kidman, Lord Brassey, and Sir Edward Wittenoom, who represented the company interests in Perth. Richard Tilden Smith had apparently acted as agent in the negotiation.

During this time there was also much to and fro between the C.D. & D. partners about the export of sheepskins, bales of wool, and opossum skins from Behn Ord, the market for these commodities fluctuating from 'lively and exciting' to 'depressed'. Correspondence from the wool-manufacturing company of Robert Jowitt & Sons of Leeds indicates that the main buyers were spinners and top-makers[2].

> Some top-makers are holding out for more money but spinners are not disposed to follow them. The conditions of trade throughout the country, not only in the textile but in other industries, are such as to check anything in the way of an upward movement ... [R. Jowitt & Sons, Leeds, to C.D. & D., Perth, 16.6.08]

M.P., though naturally concerned with these issues, has little space in his diary for matters other than those in his immediate vicinity. From Wyndham in mid-September he records a sad parting with his cousin Kit as she embarks on the *Junee*.

> She is indeed one of the best dispositioned and most agreeable girls it has been my lot to meet and we will all miss her kindness and her company. We had quite a long heart-to-heart before she sailed.

Kit, herself, told me many years later something of what that heart-to-heart had been. She had grown as fond of her cousin Miguel as she was of her own brothers and was as concerned for his welfare as she was for theirs. She recollected talking to him in this vein:

> You know how the cards lie for me, my dear: I'm going to marry Dan Evans, for better or worse; but what about Ambrose and yourself? I'd feel better going away if you were both planning to marry too. There are several Ambrose might consider back home in Queensland but he's so shy with women I can't see him ever making the first move. It's different with you—a man of the world—but time's getting on you know and you need a life's companion. Why don't you marry Bessie Johnstone? No, it's not nonsense—age difference, religious difference—not important really with such a lovely girl. Not used to the bush life? Neither was I. She'd get on well here as I have done.

Kit was worried, too, about her younger brother Fergus whom she believed could go far as a surveyor, though she saw little scope for his potential, even as a station manager, in Kimberley.

Perhaps M.P.'s farewell conversation with Kit bore some relation to the fact that Fergus soon afterwards returned to Queensland and became articled to his elder brother Clare, who was an authorised surveyor. In the few years left to him before his death at Gallipoli in 1915, he pursued a successful career, and when he volunteered for service with the first Australian Infantry Division, he was working with the survey branch of the Queensland Railways.

After Kit's departure M.P. resumed his station rounds, noting having passed a camel team on its way with stores to Victoria Downs. Though horse, donkey, mule, and bullock teams would continue to be used for station work, camels were by 1908 replacing these animals for the cartage of stores to the outpost homesteads. The reason for their acceptance was not only their sheer pulling capacity and sure tread over hazardous river crossings, but the reliability of their Afghan or Indian drivers who, not to be tempted by sly-grog sellers en route, somehow reached their destinations in half the time taken by their competitors. M.P. was soon to know all the camel-men in the country, permitting them, on arrival at a station, to kill a beast according to the dictates of their Moslem creed, and appreciating their obeisance in the general direction of Mecca at the rising and sinking of the sun.

About this time word reached him of the death in the Darwin hospital of Tom Kilfoyle who, like Pumpkin, had been part of his life from earliest childhood. He was deeply affected, and on the return of Tom's widow to Rosewood (presumably after attending the funeral) went at once to visit her and her sister Maggie Byrne. They spent hours recalling Kilfoyle's life since his leaving Ireland in 1849 as a boy of fourteen with his sister Margaret and brother-in-law Darby Durack for New South Wales. He had gone on to become one of the most remarkable stockmen and bushmen in the country, and had been with Grandfather Patsy Durack and his family in most of their subsequent ventures. M.P. now recalled with his widow and sister-in-law many experiences shared with Kilfoyle when opening up markets for cattle at Pine Creek in the early 1890s. Kilfoyle's only son Jack, then fifteen years old and still at College in Perth, was to inherit the Rosewood property.

M.P. returned sadly to Argyle, where he at once set to work with all hands to fight a fire that had broken out in the back paddock. Along with a number of station hands he was also fighting a bout of fever, which did nothing to help his depressed frame of mind. Nor did a few other problems that were awaiting him, one of these being a visit from 'old Jimmy', the leader of an outlying bush tribe who had established a friendly association with Boxer. He wanted to bring his people, twenty-five to thirty in all, from toddlers to the old and infirm, to camp on the river near the homestead, and promised that in return for regular rations they would refrain from chasing and spearing cattle. 'Not a bad bargain,' M.P. writes, '—if only there wasn't such a mob of them. It would mean at least doubling the station order.'

Boxer came up with the suggestion that they should receive regular rations of beef but that for the rest of their needs they could hunt and fish and forage as before. M.P., to whom the situation was by no means new, foresaw that it would work only until the station Aborigines got tired of sharing their own rations, as they would inevitably do. About to set off for Fremantle, he left the decision to Ambrose who would have to cope with the consequences in any case.

He sailed from Wyndham on the *Bullara* and reached Fremantle early in December, still in the grip of fever, which seems soon to have relaxed in the congenial company of his city associates and a round of seasonal festivities. Of the December race-meeting he records: 'It would seem that women's fashions are going through an interesting transitionary change. The socalled "Empire" or "Directoire" dress is much in evidence.'

He attended a Christmas service with his brother J.W. ('same old sermon with same old disregard of historical facts') and they proceeded to a family dinner at the Esplanade Hotel. This party included their close friend Johnnie (Gertrude) Johnstone, and her sister and brother-in-law, Ede and Charles Smith. Charles, an Englishman who had come to South Australia some eight years before, was associated with the Eastern Extension Telegraph Company. He had had an interesting life and seen a good deal of the world, and he and M.P. were soon deep in talk about current affairs and the eastward extension of the cable system which had done so much to alleviate Australia's hampering isolation. The Smith family had now been transferred to Perth, where their home was already a centre for South Australian friends and members of their own family.

With them on this festive occasion was a cousin of the Johnstone sisters named Fan Cherry, who had come from South Australia to nurse on the goldfields during the typhoid epidemic and had recently been appointed second Silver Chain district nurse in Perth[3]. M.P., little knowing the extent to which they were all to be associated in the years to come, noted with appreciation the good looks and bright conversation of 'the three girls from Adelaide'.

The rest of the day was spent with the Connor family at Cottesloe, where they read a long Christmas epistle from Denis Doherty in which he reminded his partners that this was the first Christmas he had spent with his family in four years. Doherty's general tone was one of optimism for the coming year, despite the fact that at the end of 1908 the firm was showing a loss for the first time. The deficit was, after all, only £1,173 which was not so depressing in view of recent developments. It was now said that Bovril Australian Estates were interested in co-operating with the erection of a meatworks in Wyndham, and, whether this proved true or not, the faith shown in the future of the north by Bovril's recent purchase of Victoria River Downs and Carlton Stations would surely, they all believed, serve to boost the value of C.D. & D.'s holdings.

It was therefore in a spirit of optimism and warm goodwill that partners and their families toasted each other and the success of their joint efforts in the coming year.

22

Of Hopes and Apprehensions

January–August 1909

Convinced of bright prospects for the sale of their northern properties, Connor urged that the partners should now keep their eyes open for good, manageable estates in the accessible and civilized south-west. With this in view, he persuaded M.P. to accompany him and his wife to Busselton's New Year Show, which was a focus for surrounding stud-breeders, farmers, agriculturalists, and orchardists.

The occasion, with its enthusiastic crowd applauding the parade of horses, sheep, and dairy cattle, and a gala ball attended by Premier Sir John Forrest and other political figures, was no doubt successful enough, but Connor's efforts to fire M.P. with enthusiasm for the temperate and progressive south country do not seem to have been of much avail.

> After passing Dardanup the homes bear evidence of neglect and poverty in their dreary settings of scrub and sand. The Show itself was disappointing, too. The best feature was ten or twelve ladies' hacks, all other exhibits, except the potatoes, being limited. At the hotel we were served highly coloured imported butter and tinned meat—truly disgraceful for a so-called farming district.

Had such fare been served at the Wyndham Hotel, the manager would assuredly have been taken to task.

At the beginning of February M.P. set off on the S.S. *China*, ostensibly to renew business contracts in the eastern capitals but obviously also for more personal reasons. He was met in Adelaide by his cousin Kit and her new husband Dan Evans; their recent wedding in Sydney, meticulously organized and financed by Bird, had brought together a flock of friends and relatives from as far afield as Brisbane, Goulburn, and Bathurst. Dan, a qualified engineer, was hoping soon to retire from the sea and set up in business. He and his bride were currently renting a house in Adelaide where Kit, with her sister Jess for company, awaited his intermittent returns to port. They had meanwhile kept in close touch with the Johnstone family, and Kit lost no time in informing her cousin that Bess, though still unattached, was too attractive to remain so for much longer.

M.P. had many business contacts in Adelaide but he needed no prompting to call on the Johnstones, and hardly a day passed during the next two weeks that he did not see something of Bess. In later years, persuaded by her family to put down something of her side of the story, she wrote as follows:

> It was my sister Gert who first made contact with the Durack family . . . Brother Ted used to call her 'the odd one out', because she was so independent . . . After our elder sister Kate married Crawford Horrocks in 1896, Gert decided to follow Kate's example and take up nursing as a career. Dad was much against the idea but Gert went her own way. Later, when I wanted to 'go nursing' too, he really put his foot down pointing out that with three daughters married and Gert in another State it was my bounden duty, as youngest in the family, to keep the home fires burning . . .
>
> The first member of the Durack clan I met was M.P.'s sister, Mary Davidson, when on a visit to her husband's family in Adelaide. Gert had asked her to contact us and this she did. She was friendly and out-going and a great talker so it wasn't long before I knew a lot about her family. She told us they owed her brother Jack's life to Gert who had nursed him when he was desperately ill some time before.
>
> Not long after this M.P. himself turned up with his sister Bird on the way to Sydney and I went to meet them with the Davidsons. Marie had told me that Denis Doherty had long ago changed M.P.'s name from Michael to Miguel, not only because there were so many other Michaels in the family but because he said that with his tall, erect figure, trimly cut beard and moustache and courtly manner he resembled a Spanish don. I thought it most appropriate and at the time of our first meeting was rather in awe of him. He even impressed Dad as a man of sensible, forthright opinions, culture and broad education.
>
> When he came through Adelaide about a year later we met again and as he set off by train for Melbourne I was bold enough to say 'Goodbye Miguel!' Having now heard that my full name was Bessie Ida Muriel he smilingly replied 'Au Revoir, Bim! You will be hearing from me.' From that day on he was always 'Miguel' to me and I was his 'Bim'.

> He was soon back in Adelaide from his business trip to Melbourne and Sydney, and it was at this time that he asked me whether I cared for him as he did for me.
>
> When, some time before this, his cousin Kit Evans had said Miguel and I should make a match of it I had thought she was joking. There is no doubt that I thought him a most likeable and admirable man but as a husband he was surely as out of the question for me as I, as a wife, for him. Not only were there twenty years or so between us but his family was as staunchly Catholic as mine was Anglican. Then suddenly there we were, sitting on the beach at the Semaphore talking of the possibility of our becoming man and wife. ['Memories' B.I.M.D., 1963, unpublished]

M.P. records the fateful day briefly in his diary of 27 March, 1909:

> Lunch with Gordon Buchanan[1]. Later with Mr McCann through the Government Freezing and Abattoir Works which are the finest I have seen in Australia, capable of treating 9,000 lambs a day. Met Sir Jenkin Coles[2] who invited me to lunch tomorrow—indeed a very affable, nice man. Had tea with cousin Kit, then off to see Bess. Found her walking on the Esplanade where we sat together looking out to sea and talking about matters of serious moment to both of us.

He begins his record of the following day with the significant announcement:

> Bess is now to me the dearest girl on earth. Wrote a letter indicating my feelings towards her on awakening this morning . . .

He was nonetheless well aware that the engagement he sought, and to which Bess had admitted herself in favour, was still no *fait accompli*. Everything, or so he thought, now depended on Mr Johnstone's reaction to the proposal. Already Bess had warned M.P. that, for all that her father both liked and admired him, and was well known to be a broad-minded and fair man, if there was one thing to which he showed little or no tolerance it was Roman Catholicism. This Bess attributed to his Calvinistic background, although he had been a practising Anglican from the time of his marriage. A staunch supporter of his self-chosen denomination, he had, however, lately become disturbed by what he feared were signs of encroaching Papist influence, such as the two candles that had recently appeared on the altar in their local place of worship.

M.P. confessed that narrow-minded attitudes were common enough in his own sect, though he believed that these were breaking down with improved education and that he would have little difficulty in obtaining permission for their marriage to be celebrated by a Catholic priest in a private home. The main issue was of course whether Bess would be prepared to have any children of the marriage reared in the Catholic faith. He was, after all, a member of a big family of Irish origin, and to back down on this point would represent to his relatives—and to himself—a betrayal of tradition. 'Look Miguel,' Bess said, 'I see your situation quite clearly. To me the important thing is that we're both Christians. Isn't that what matters most?'

M.P. agreed and he must have put his case well, as on 26 March he writes:

> Feeling very happy within myself this morning. Wrote to P.B. and Bird telling them of my engagement, though shall never forget the courage it required last night to ask for Bess's hand in marriage and my state of mind during her father's oration.
> 29.3.09: With Bess down to Kate [Horrocks] and get congratulatory telegrams from the family . . . Said 'goodbye' to dear Bess at the door of my cabin. We are to be married sometime this year when arrangements have been completed to the satisfaction of all.

M.P. did not then realise that all the hurdles had not been surmounted. He had yet to face the reaction of his own Church, which was to boil up behind him as he set off on 17 April on the S.S. *Moira* for Wyndham.

The news of his engagement had travelled ahead of him and had already, as he soon discovered, seeped through to the outlying stations. If not surprised by the congratulations that greeted him on all sides, he was touched by the apparent sincerity of the good will expressed. 'I gather,' he comments, 'that my northern friends must long since have ruled out my chances in the matrimonial stakes.'

He found the genuine delight of the Aborigines especially heart-warming. Most of them were under the impression that he was already married, and he found himself having carefully to explain that his bride was so far only 'promised' for a later date. This they understood as being in keeping with their own customs. It was then assumed that his intended was still a child who would not leave her people until more mature. They were surprised to learn that she was a fully grown young woman whose picture, in the lid of his gold watch, he produced for their inspection. They pronounced her 'pretty one properly' and clamoured to know when they would be seeing her in the flesh. M.P. explained that he hoped to be married later in the year but that he would not be bringing his beloved immediately to Kimberley. In the meantime they would keep in touch by the white man's method of correspondence. This point was so fully appreciated that letters for M.P. addressed to him at Argyle when he was at Newry, Auvergne, or even further afield, now reached him even quicker than before, a courier sometimes arriving late at night when, having released his horse, he would creep around and deposit the mail where M.P. would see it on waking up.

A few diary entries of this period express his bitter disappointment when such urgently delivered correspondence did not include a letter from Bess. This was obviously no fault of hers, as is indicated by the following excerpt:

> Ulysses with mail from Argyle to Newry late last night. No less than eight letters together from Bess. She is writing me almost daily, her letters the loveliest imaginable and drawing her closer to me every day. I certainly won't be able to stay long away from her! Who could have imagined I could reveal in my diary what I have written her tonight. 'Yes, Bim, my dear girl, you are dearer to me than all and everything on this earth. Goodnight!'

He was nonetheless not without some apprehension about bringing a gently raised city girl to this rough-and-ready land of hazards and contradictions. He remembered having warned his brother Pat about Eva's possible reactions, which had proved very much as he predicted. With this in mind, he even found himself listening to M.J.'s tedious advice about setting up a wife in a home in the south as he had done. What right, his cousin asked, had a man with any option to expect a woman to contemplate rearing a family in a country so lacking in the most fundamental social, educational and medical facilities? What would she think of the crude bush homesteads and the people, black and white, such as she would never have encountered before? How would he introduce men whose names, for reasons best not investigated, kept changing as they moved around Australia, or those known only by such ridiculous nicknames as 'Weary Willy', 'Johnnycake-Jim', 'Storm Bird', 'Stone-the-crows' or 'Jabiroo Jack'? Even the 'gentlemen' of the country, such as Sir Alec Campbell, Frederick Booty, Bill Jones, Charles Edward Flinders, Rudolph Philchowski and Douglas Moore, were hard enough to explain. What strange quirks of fortune had brought educated men here to the tough, knock-about life of the cattle camps and had somehow held them ever since? While Long Michael droned on in this strain, it occurred to M.P. that some of his own relatives might be equally hard to explain. He responded, however, on the optimistic note that his intended was vitally interested in people and was looking forward to meeting a greater variety of characters than came her way in suburban Adelaide. He admitted that, perhaps, as time went on, it would become necessary to set up a home base in the south, but to do so at once would mean his being separated from his beloved for at least half the year, which would at that stage have been quite untenable to both of them.

M.P., bumping along, usually alone, over the rough bush tracks, reflected on certain ironical aspects of the situation where both his family members and partners were concerned. M.J. prided himself on the fact that he had never permitted his wife so much as to set foot on Kimberley soil, despite which she had lost her first baby and had been warned not to set her hopes on giving birth to another.

Then there were letters from Doherty which indicated that the civilized environment in which he had insisted his family should be reared was the happy hunting-ground of at least as many cunning, though no doubt more sophisticated, rogues as haunted the wilds of North Australia. Recent letters to J.W., forwarded to M.P. from the Perth office, had set forth a typical example. This concerned Mr Kim Forrest (eldest son of the late Alexander), who was then in London with his wife. It appeared that Forrest had been phoned at the Hotel Cecil by a man calling himself Durack, whom he had taken to be M.P. and whose invitation to lunch at the Carlton the Forrests had happily accepted. They were surprised on reaching the hotel to find not the bearded countenance of their old friend but a clean-shaven young man of about twenty-eight who claimed to be M.P.'s nephew. He was also in primary production, he said, and had business connections throughout Australia. He introduced the Forrests to an equally stylish-looking friend named Meekin, who, on learning that they had purchased a car in London, offered to secure them superior accommodation at the Royal Automobile Club. Next thing, all four were off together to the races at Salisbury where Durack and Meekin seemed *au fait* with the best tips. Durack courteously offered to put the Forrests' money on for them, and at the end of the day they found themselves down by over £1,000.

In the meantime the Forrests had asked young Durack about a number of their friends in Western Australia, all of whom he claimed to know. Mrs Forrest said they had met Denis Doherty in London recently and would be seeing him again within a few days. To this Durack replied that Doherty had recently left on a business trip to Fremantle, so their time would be wasted trying to contact him. Deciding that it might be time well wasted, Forrest called at once on Doherty, who accompanied him to a banking premises where Durack had promised to meet him that mornng.

A detective, requested to be present at the confrontation, was awaiting them—but of Durack there was no more than a message to say he had been called to Scotland on urgent stock-buying business.

> I will do what I can to chase the fellow up [Doherty concluded] and see what I can find out about him. Detective Fowler says he can't move yet as 'Durack' has not done anything against the law that could be proved. It doesn't seem to matter that he has misrepresented himself. That's only a lie. [D.J.D., London, to J.W.D., Perth, 4.6.09]

Doherty continued his report a week later.

> It transpires that while we were discussing 'Durack' at the Bank his two associates, Meekin and Doyle, were being tried for taking down another W.A. man. 'Durack' has got away and even if they catch up with him there is no case against him as Forrest could not prove, as the other man did, that the money had been said to be put on after the race had been run.
>
> So the entertaining (and to Forrest expensive) episode comes to an end and the culprit gets off. Next time he will no doubt be shrewd enough to choose another name. [D.J.D., London, to J.W.D., Perth, 11.6.09]

Had circumstances led these same young tricksters to North Australia, M.P. mused, they would no doubt soon have excelled in gerrymandering brands and earmarks, or fiddling the station books.

In Wyndham about this time to meet a ship from Darwin, he encountered a young French priest named Francis Xavier Gsell, of whom there had been a good deal of talk since his arrival in the Territory about three years before. He explained, in answer to M.P.'s interested enquiry, that he hailed from Alsace, and that, at the age of twenty he had entered the Sacred Heart Missionary Society in Rome. He had come to New South Wales in 1896 and ten years later had been appointed Apostolic Administrator for the Catholic Church in the Northern Territory. Since that time he had been investigating the possibilities of setting up a central missionary establishment for the Aborigines, from which he hoped that branches would evolve to embrace the tribal people throughout North Australia. Like most pastoralists, M.P. was sceptical of missionary activities of any denomination, at least for full-blood Aborigines. He saw them as doing nothing but further confuse a people beginning to adjust to a system wherein they retained their traditional culture under a European concept of land ownership, usage and improvement. He could see some point in the Pallottine Society's establishment on the Dampierland peninsula north of Broome, especially since the arrival of teaching and nursing sisters to care for the many children of mixed Asian, Pacific Islands, European, and Aboriginal background. Where the full-blood tribal people were concerned, however, he was of a different mind.

But although dubious of Father Gsell's missionary aspirations, M.P. appreciated the young priest's sincerity and consented to help him make an investigative tour of the East Kimberley district. They set off together from Wyndham to Argyle, inspecting the inevitable mobs of cattle and meeting local characters. On the track between Newry and Auvergne they came close to disaster when one of the horses shied and bolted along the edge of a steep creek bed. Suddenly the pole broke and the buggy capsized. When Father Gsell claimed that they had been appropriately saved from certain death on the Feast of Our Lady of Miracles, M.P. irreverently observed that the miracle would have been more effective had it either left the pole intact or made available an implement with which to mend it. Faced with a twenty-mile walk to the nearest station homestead, he was gathering wood to boil a strengthening billy of tea when his hand alighted on a file, providentially left behind by some previous camper. They were soon on their way again.

M.P. often smilingly recalled this incident, and from that time on followed Father Gsell's career with keen if sometimes rather puzzled interest[3].

M.P. had brought with him (along with Father Gsell) from Wyndham to Argyle an entertaining young South Australian named Paxton, who was to take over as book-keeper at Lissadell after the departure of Gordon Broughton to join a young friend in China. This was an adventure that Broughton had been warned by his Kimberley friends he would be lucky to survive. His survival in Kimberley would, however, have been considerably more doubtful, as he was of the age group to which the local fever so frequently proved fatal.

When M.P. visited Lissadell a few weeks later he found Paxton laid low on his bunk.

> The poor young fellow did not recognise me. He was staring and apparently unconscious but this morning when I went in to him to say 'goodbye' he caught my hand with both of his and said, 'Oh, goodbye and thank you very much.' He said he knew me but could not recall my name.

Soon after his return to Argyle M.P. received news from M.J. that young

Paxton had died. His cousin's letter, also reminding him of the death from fever of the Durack children at the Dunham and of his own beloved mother at Argyle, did nothing to lift his spirits as he moved anxiously around the homestead to which he hoped soon to bring his bride.

23

A Dream Come True

August–December 1909

By the end of August M.P. was back in Fremantle and soon on his way to Adelaide on the *Mooltan*. The Johnstone family had preparations for the wedding well in hand. According to the bride's own memoirs:

> Mother was still making my trousseau when Miguel arrived. She was a wonderful needlewoman and when we were young made all our clothes—from undies to top coats. There were no press-studs or zip fasteners—only buttonholes by the dozen.
>
> As for the other girls she insisted that my trousseau must include three of everything. The garments were mainly of nainsook and torchon lace, all beautifully finished, the wrong sides as neat as the right. Knowing I was to live on the Kimberley stations she made me six pretty cotton frocks and a simple evening dress, a black voile skirt to the ankles and some pretty blouses for either day or evening wear. My 'going away' outfit was a coat and skirt of brown tweed flecked with blue, a brown velvet hat with a blue bow, brown shoes, brown cashmere stockings and kid gloves.

Everyone looked serene and happy, though Bess confided in M.P. that some of her friends were predicting trouble ahead of them. They warned her that she would be besieged by wily priests and nuns intent on her conversion, and that if she yielded to their diabolical persuasions she would not only grieve and scandalize her relatives but would lose all her former friends. Neither of them took these predictions very seriously, and M.P. called with happy confidence on Archbishop Riley to explain that although his intended was Anglican, her family was satisfied that a Catholic priest should officiate at the marriage ceremony. To his hurt astonishment the Archbishop declared, kindly but firmly, that he could not consent to such a mixed marriage and that without his approval no priest in South Australia could co-operate.

Determined that reason must prevail, M.P. said nothing of this setback to the Johnstone family but proceeded to pull strings among his Catholic friends and relatives. Apparently as a result of these activities, he received a telegram from the Archbishop two days later asking him to call again. He records this interview in a single sentence: 'His Grace now says he is prepared to grant my request on certain conditions though one of these is certainly unreasonable.'

The clause to which he referred seems to have been that relating to the word 'promise' regarding the religious upbringing of the children. Mr Johnstone was reluctantly prepared to accept the fact that his daughter would 'allow' her offspring to be christened in the Catholic Church, but had long since made it clear that a formal promise was another matter. Somehow, with additional persuasion from J.W. and Bird, who had by this time joined M.P. in Adelaide, the problem was resolved, as we learn from M.P.'s brief entry for 9 September:

> The good old Archbishop is now pleased to interpret the word 'promise' to mean that the non-Catholic party will 'allow' any issue to be brought up in the R.C. faith. Thus far dear Bess is happy to agree.

In reaching this solution M.P. would appear, from Bess's account, to have had the tactful support of the priest who was soon to marry them:

> I can never forget that afternoon when Miguel, Bird and I went to the monastery at Glen Osmond and met The Rev. Father Francis Kelly. He was not only handsome and charming but a wonderful talker and I came away feeling quite content with the decision I had made. It was he who married us in the bay window of my brother Ted's[1] house, 'Annandale', on Cross Roads, Unley. He and his wife, Nell, had been living there about two years at this time and, knowing that Dad had put his foot down about our being married in a Catholic Church, they had offered their lovely home for both wedding and reception. They had festooned the place with flowers and hung a large wedding bell from the middle of the arch. There were just members of our two families and a few old friends present, the breakfast being beautifully served in the big dining room. Sister Gert, in a lovely lace gown and big picture hat was my bridesmaid. J.W.D., who was by this time the friend to me he was to remain for life, was best man. It was he who had arranged for a car to take Miguel and myself to Aldgate in the hills—the beginning of a six months wonderful honeymoon. Except for a couple of trips to Melbourne and occasional jaunts into the country with Dad I had had no experience of travel and

the fascinating contacts it involves. I remember making people laugh by saying I felt like a silkworm emerging from its chrysalis into a new world.

I had, of course, had qualms about how Mother and Dad would get on without me but Gert had comforted me by saying she had decided to relax from nursing for a while and to return to live at home in Winchester Street. Worried that Gert would be tied down to chores I had broken in a very good maid to know how our parents liked their meals cooked and served and the home kept. I was surprised to learn how quickly things settled down . . . So I realised that there are few of us who can't be replaced and that life must go on . . .

For the bride and groom it certainly did. M.P., in his limited diary space, records the occasion more succinctly:

Married today at 'Annandale'. Everything went off splendidly in beautiful bright weather and now I have the dearest little wife in the whole wide world.

After the ceremony toasts were drunk and brother Jack spoke most feelingly. Photos were taken before we left for Aldgate Hotel.

M.P. had already realised, at least to some extent, that his own widely spread family was now almost doubled, with members of 'the Johnstone clan scattered not only throughout South Australia, but Western Australia and Victoria. There were welcoming arms, both Durack and Johnstone, when, after two days at Aldgate, the honeymoon couple arrived in Melbourne.

Bird had by that time returned to the Collins Street address from where she and her friend were conducting their fashionable beauty business, which, as she confided in Bess, attracted 'everyone who was anyone' in that fair city. M.P.'s diary gives a brief impression of their round of social and public events, business meetings, shopping sprees and theatrical entertainnents.

29.9.09: Bess and I with Foster to look at the motor buggy agency—the International Harvester Company. Took a trial run in one of the buggies but its performance not very satisfactory in sand. Fancy we get on better with the horse-drawn variety.

Attended Parliamentary Lawn Garden Party . . . After dinner to the Mayoral Ball at the Town Hall in honour of visiting British delegates . . .

> 4.10.09: Called on Angliss, just returned from England where he saw the Bovril people. He thinks that floating abattoirs are practicable ... Called with Bess on Lady Forrest and Morton Craig[2], both in Melbourne. John Kirwan also here. He lunched with us and we later visited Parliament House ... Bess and self for a ride together to St Kilda in an electric car.
> 9.10.09: With Bess to the races at Caulfield, the horses in good form and the women in lovely frocks. Later on board the *Grantala* to see Dan Evans. Kit is staying at the Federal where we called on her and brought a silver rattle for her baby, Barbara ...

Bess's account of this period is rather livelier than M.P.'s.

> In Melbourne we stayed at Menzies Hotel where to me everything was exciting and new. On the night of our arrival we dined there with Bird, my sister Nell and her husband, Bert Davey, whose home was in Melbourne.
>
> How I enjoyed watching all those smart people coming in and out! A number of them with most high-sounding names were known to Miguel who had business appointments with them the next day. Realizing how busy he was, Nell and I arranged to do a round of the shops and Bird insisted that we should have a free beauty treatment at her Collins Street premises. We did and it was sheer bliss.
>
> Not only the days were exciting, but the nights when we all dressed up for the theatre. 'The Country Girl', starring Fanny Dango was then charming audiences at The Princess Theatre so we all went along to be in the swim. Miguel noticed an old friend sitting in front of us—a tall, bluff man named Sam Mackay who owned sheep stations in the North West. When Miguel hailed him he seemed very pleased and insisted that after the performance we have supper with him and meet 'the most beautiful woman in the world'. We later learned that he went every night to see Fanny go through her act and realised that he was quite infatuated with her. Miguel was somewhat taken aback by this as he also knew Sam's very nice wife and their two children, Keith and Elsie. I could not blame Sam, however, as Fanny was certainly delightful and the friendship we made that night was to last through many years ahead[3].

After a blissful week touring Tasmania the honeymooners returned to a round of lively farewells in Melbourne, and set off by train to Adelaide. A week here catching up with family and friends, and they were off on the S.S. *China* for Fremantle. The traditional welcoming group was bigger than usual on this occasion, J.W. having intrigued friends and family with his account of the beauty and charm of his brother's bride. The Connors had organized a special dinner at their home, and Bess was captivated by their wit, vivacity and hospitality.

> Although we had many interesting friends in Adelaide [she tells us], I had never met anyone quite like the Connors or the little Frenchwoman, Elodie, who was their companion-help (and obviously in love with J.W.). After dinner Mrs. Connor went to the piano and joined by other guests she and her husband treated us to a programme of romantic songs. Mary Davidson was there, also Miguel's brother Pat and his wife Eva, who had captured my affection from our meeting at the ship that day and were to hold it to the end of their lives. What a family—all so united but so different as my sister Gert had tried to explain to me.
>
> We had arrived just in time for the annual Agricultural Show. That, too, was quite an experience. Of course I had been to shows before in South Australia but never to anything like this that had drawn people from all over the State, most of them known to Miguel and most welcoming to me. Up to that time I knew very little about cattle, horses and sheep, but I now realised that stock was to be so much part of my life that I had, at least, to try and look intelligent about such things despite my ignorance. Fortunately both family and friends had many other interests and topics of conversation and all seemed most touchingly eager to make me feel at home—as indeed I did.
>
> I was relieved to find that the Duracks had as many Protestant friends as Catholic and that none of them discussed religion except in the broadest of Christian terms. The only priests I met I would like to have seen more of, as they were educated and interesting men and mostly musical.
>
> After the Show Miguel and I, with P.B. and family, caught the train for Wagin and the outlying company property, Behn Ord. How exciting it seemed to me, travelling to farming areas where one not only had relatives but actual business interests!
>
> Pat (P.B.) had recently bought stud rams from the famous Haddon Rig estate in N.S.W. This was regarded as a very important step in the development of Behn Ord and Pat talked of the animals

> as though they were members of the royal family. He and Miguel thought it would be a pleasant experience for me to see the property from horse-back and so it was. I had never ridden before but with the encouragement of my two escorts did a ten-to-twelve-mile circuit quite easily. Pat said it was just as well to get used to this means of transport in the South where the horses were quieter than the mounts I would be expected to handle up North.
>
> 'Take no notice of him,' Eva told me when we got back, 'you won't have to do anything of the sort, unless you happen to like riding for the fun of it.'
>
> I was rather relieved to hear this as by that time I was trying to conceal how stiff I was.

M.P.'s hurried diary entry on their return to Perth indicates that what Eva said was true, as he obviously had grander ideas for the transport of his beloved.

> Arranged with Dan White & Sons for a buggy to be ready by March 15th—patent axle, specially strong brake, improved pole fittings, silver mountings, spring seat with brown leather fittings and special duck cover . . .

It was some three months before he would take delivery of this chariot, within which time he and his bride were to embark on an enchanted journey that was to linger in romantic memory for the remainder of their lives. To this, M.P.'s diary of 7.12.09 provides at least an introduction:

> Dinner at the Esplanade and train to Fremantle with J.W., Connor and wife, Chas. Smith and wife Ede, sister Marie Davidson and a few others. They saw us aboard the *Königin Luise*[4]. We lie for some time alongside the wharf and set off at last to the delightful strains of the ship's band . . . We have a beautiful cabin with attached sitting room. I keep imagining that this—accentuated by the presence of a dear and loving wife—is a luxurious dream.

24

New Horizons

December 1909–May 1910

For Bess the memory of this honeymoon journey was to live on through life as her introduction to an exotic world of wonder and excitement beyond her brightest dreams. She had never been to sea before, though having lived at Port Adelaide she was familiar enough with ships. As she tells us in her memoirs:

> Before the Outer Harbour was built all the ships anchored in front of our home, close to the lighthouse. The sailing vessels coming up the gulf in full sail were a joy to behold and sometimes my friend Alice Beeton and I would go out to meet them in a little steam launch with the doctor and customs men. There were no gangways on the sailing ships but we became quite used to climbing the rope ladders. We were always most graciously received and entertained with tea served in thick cups with ship's biscuits. There were usually a number of fine young men on board training for positions in the navy or on commercial lines. Some on the German ships that often came to Port Adelaide at that time, were of aristocratic families and very charming indeed. We were allowed to invite them home but we received a stern warning from Dad not to lose our hearts to any of them. Sailors, he said, were notoriously fickle and most of them had wives in every port. We took his advice but enjoyed their company very much and I even prided myself on being able, at that time, to speak and understand a little German.

This experience no doubt served her well on the *Königin Luise*, which she explored from stem to stern, chatting with the captain and his officers, exchanging recipes with the chief chef and household tips with the stewards. M.P. found time, meanwhile, to converse with fellow passengers about world affairs and to read the books presented him by J.W. on his departure. These included Carnegie's *Problems of Today*, Searey's *In the Australian Tropics*, and Mrs Aeneas Gunn's *We of the Never-Never* that had been published not long before. From the critical viewpoint of an insider this last book struck him as:

> much overdrawn and over-romanticised, not a faithful depiction of conditions in the North, as I see them anyway. This is not to underestimate the energy and pluck of a woman placed in such circumstances.

From Colombo they took ship for Bombay, and were soon on a train to Allahabad.

> Bess is fascinated [M.P. reports] by one of our fellow passengers, a Calcutta barrister and follower of Madame Blavatsky, founder of The Theosophical Society. He waxes eloquent on the mysteries of the occult and claims to have the power of discerning the human aura.

Having read what he found fairly convincing evidence that Blavatsky's miracles and demonstrations of psychic phenomena were frauds, M.P. was sceptical of this mystical discourse but admitted that it 'helped nonetheless to pass the time'.

Dermot conducted them from the train to his comfortable bungalow which was to be their headquarters during a memorable few weeks of sightseeing and social activities. M.P.'s copious diary entries of the period include a list of the household staff of fourteen men, with their various duties, designations, and rates of pay. Of them all he makes special note of the Chaw Kidar, or watchman, traditionally selected from a class of thieves and supposed, with his inside knowledge, to be properly equipped for his task.

Dermot, by this time well entrenched in the local community, had a wide and varied circle of friends and acquaintances. There was scarcely a day or night when the visitors were not involved with representatives of the academic, military, political, business, and sporting circles. M.P. joined his brother on the polo field and accompanied him on crocodile-shooting expeditions, catching up between times with matters of mutual family and business interest.

Although Dermot's Australian-based brothers wrote to him regularly, he felt that he was being kept in the dark about many of the firm's activities. M.P. protested that if they were to provide a detailed account of their day-to-day negotiations and ever-changing policies, the partners would spend their entire time writing letters and Dermot reading them.

> I explain that the present situation, although still fraught with problems and hazards, is more encouraging than for a considerable time past. Bovril's recent purchase of Victoria River in the Northern Territory and Carlton near Wyndham, and nearly 1,000,000 acres in the hitherto undeveloped North Kimberley area, gives reason to anticipate the accelerated interest of buyers in our Connor, Doherty & Durack holdings.

He added that Bovril Estates, whose members had been interested for some time in establishing a meatworks in Wyndham, were now said to be considering the purchase of a steamer to be converted into the sort of floating abattoir that Tilden Smith (now a member of the Bovril Company) had been advocating for some time. In order to reduce the cost of slaughtering, butchering and freezing operations, they had approached the Commonwealth Government for a permit to employ Asian labour, their contention being that since the work was to be carried out in Cambridge Gulf rather than on Australian soil, this should not infringe on the White Australia Policy. If Bovril was successful in obtaining permission for this project, Connor, Doherty & Durack could either use the same abattoir or consider obtaining another for their own use. The scheme should lead to a wider market than was obtainable by the expensive shipment of live cattle to Fremantle.

It was true that the government had, of recent years, in an effort to provide an alternative to the sea voyage, subsidized the survey and equipment of the 900-mile Canning Stock Route from Hall's Creek to the railhead at Wiluna in the southern goldfields. Owing to the shortage of feed and water, and to possible interference from the desert tribespeople, M.P. could not, however, see its being of much future advantage to the industry[1].

In the meantime the Kimberley companies of Connor, Doherty & Durack, Forrest, Emanuel and Copley Brothers continued to be attacked as 'the meat ring' bent on exploiting the struggling consumer population of the south. In fact, M.P. declared, if there was such a thing as 'a meat ring' it existed among the 'middle men' or wholesale butchers of the south. Producers closer to the main markets could probably sell at cheaper rates than the far northern growers, for whom export markets elsewhere would become increasingly necessary. If a good buyer for their holdings should come forward, C.D. & D. would have no further worry on this score, but their chances of success in either case would be much enhanced by the establishment of a local killing- and freezing-works.

This information would seem to have left Dermot in some doubt about the wisdom of his having recently drawn up a deed of sale with his three brothers for his 7,000 shares in the company at £6,000, payable in ten years time at 4 per cent interest.

Their discussions had not been long in progress when M.P. received, via his West Australian office, a letter from the South Australian Government asking him to accept authority to enquire on their behalf into the possibilities of opening up a market for primary products from South Australia and its Northern Territory. On his previous trips abroad he had enquired into possible markets, and he had travelled in 1902 with letters of introduction from the Premier of Western Australia, but this request gave added stimulus to his investigations and the official document that accompanied it lent his efforts some helpful authority. He realised that there was no prospect of a market for Australian beef in India but was determined to make all possible enquiries on the various stages of his return journey.

After seeing the New Year in at a congenial party he made his first diary entry for 1910.

> With the opening of this New Year I embark, as it were, upon a new phase of life. We have been married now for over two months with so far no evidence of the slightest cloud to dim our happiness. Everyone, including brother Dermot, appears to succumb to the charm of my dear wife who assures me that I have no reason for concern on this score. On the contrary, I am delighted, and I might say, proud.

Indeed, Dermot and Bess do seem to have established the instant happy rapport that followed her meeting with M.P.'s two other brothers, J.W. and P.B., not to mention his sisters, Mary and Bird. While M.P. dealt with his copious correspondence, his wife listened with rapt attention to Dermot's discourses on Indian history and accounts of his own life, from his earliest memories of family and associates in Western Queensland to the chain of circumstances that had led him from there to Sydney University, and thence to Cambridge and to Allahabad. Together they interviewed the vendors who, for reasons no doubt agreed upon between Dermot and his staff, were permitted to present their wares on his verandah. M.P.'s diary lists the articles purchased, with most of which his children were to become so familiar over the years—those serpentine brass candlesticks, that brass tray and matching bowls, those boxes of carved sandalwood, that model of the Taj Mahal (to which noble monument they of course paid due homage during their sightseeing programme).

M.P. records the regret with which they parted from his youngest brother, of whose achievements he was so proud but with whom he did not always agree. From Allahabad they took the train to the holy city of Benares on the Ganges river, where they witnessed the ritual burning of those whose salvation, by having died there, was assured.

At their next stop, Calcutta, Bess insisted on visiting the cemetery to place flowers on the grave of a recently deceased member of the Horrocks family, into which her sister Kate had married in 1896. This caused them both to ponder the complexities of human fate, not only such as had brought them together from their different backgrounds, but had brought to India members of their respective families and so many other mutual associates.

Next stop was Darjeeling, from where they set off on ponies at three in the morning for Tiger Hill to witness the unforgettable sight of the day breaking over Kanchenjunga.

> If the Taj was worthy of a page to itself [M.P. enthuses], much more so is the experience of watching the sun rise from the third highest mountain in the world . . . Looming up, away to the left, is Mt. Everest in all its majesty and mystery, indeed an awe-inspiring spectacle.

On the way back Bess's pony stumbled and threw her, an experience to which she was to attribute the aches and pains of her old age. According to M.P.'s diary, however, the incident caused her little trouble at the time. She remounted her pony and, despite 'a rather sore foot' for the next day or so, is reported as having continued her sightseeing at the usual pace. The fact that there is no record of her ever again having mounted a horse indicates that this was probably the only lasting effect of the incident.

At the end of February M.P. writes that, although having had a very pleasant seven weeks in India, the only place he would really like to see again was Darjeeling, where he witnessed the break of dawn over the roof of the world. He indicates that the human reality of India's supplicating hands and emaciated bodies disturbed and challenged him. A number of his travelling companions over the past weeks had been Americans who were critical of British rule in India. M.P. had argued that Britain's takeover of that country was surely much the same as America's usurpation of the Philippines at a later date. One well-informed traveller, while admitting that the United States had signed a treaty with Spain for the purchase of the Islands, declared that they had at least been 'colonists with a conscience'. The battleship they had dispatched there soon afterwards had been manned, not with armed troops, but with teachers pledged to help the Islanders in their confrontation with the modern world. Moreover, whereas Britain had destroyed the indigenous industries of India, the U.S. had provided a flourishing export market for agricultural products of the Philippines, which had also become an important trading centre for American merchants.

Burma, M.P. found more to his liking than India. In Rangoon there were practically no beggars and the people looked generally better dressed and better fed. The streets were wide and comparatively clean, the buildings impressive and equipped with electric light.

> The place has a more pleasant atmosphere than India and impresses me as being considerably more prosperous. I called on Mr Cohen in Moghul Street to discuss prospects of Australian imports. I gather that although the population is estimated at 300,000 the consumption is limited and would not permit business on a large scale. With improved or direct service however there would seem to be a good prospect of doing something with frozen meat, butter and fruit from South Australia.
>
> A considerable amount of development has taken place in Burma within the last five years ... the citizens speak of the country as 'Golden Burma', the richest possession that Great Britain holds.

M.P. made similar enquiries in Singapore but saw little prospect opening for Australia's trade in that area. From his contacts, however, he received hints of better possibilities in the Philippines where a recent act had established the right to free trade. He was also given introductions to key personalities, with whom he made contact on arrival in Manila at the beginning of March.

The travellers' three weeks in Manila, 'Pearl of the Orient', were an exciting round of business and social engagements, during which they gained an insight into the varied local scene and diverse ways of life. With new-found American friends they toured the city, sailed the Pasig River, attended cock-fights, visited museums and historic shrines, and dined with local tycoons and bureaucrats. These included the Director of Agriculture, Dr Nesom, who escorted M.P. to meet the Vice-Governor-General, Commodore Gilbert. This interview was both affable and fruitful, and he came away with the assurance that the United States Government would favour the introduction of Australian cattle and do everything possible to facilitate the trade. The majority of Islanders, being Christianized, were without religious taboos where meat-eating was concerned, and the Philippines at that time were importing cattle from Hong Kong and French

Indo-China. Authorities were disturbed, however, by the spread of rinderpest and other stock diseases that were decimating the local herds. Every effort was now being made to control the problem, and the cancellation of supplies from Asian centres in favour of imports from Australia, where cattle were said to be immune to tick-fever, was seen as a strong step in this campaign[2].

M.P.'s most significant encounter was, however, with Faustino Lichauco[3], the so-called 'Cattle King of Manila', who was at that time importing 30,000 head of cattle a year, mostly from Saigon. He, too, was worried about the incidence of disease, especially in the context of increasing government measures to control the problem. The advantage of dealing in Australian supplies was therefore as quickly evident to him as to the government authorities. A swift exchange of cables between M.P. and his company's Perth office authorized the striking of a deal for an initial shipment of 350 head from Wyndham as soon as possible, this arrangement subject only to the cattle being inspected by Lichauco's agents, who would travel from Manila to Wyndham on the freighter chartered to transport the stock if passed as satisfactory.

By the end of March M.P. recorded their 'sailing for Singapore on the calm and placid bosom of the South China Sea', Bess happily entertained by her fellow passengers while he applied himself to a study of D. P. Barrow's *History of the Philippines*.

A few days of sightseeing and business contacts, and the travellers were at sea again on a ship bound for Fremantle. No luxury liner the S.S. *Paros*, which having been recently fumigated, is reported to have reeked of dead rats. Her passengers were tedious and her library 'a collection of outdated trivia'. When the ship called briefly at Wyndham, M.P., perhaps fearing that a glimpse of the place at that time of year might discourage Bess from ever wanting to return, went ashore alone.

At Derby, the next port of call, he had no option but to introduce his bride to a northern township, as they were met by Aubrey McGlew and his young wife and escorted to their home for lunch. M.P. was already well acquainted with McGlew, who had entered commercial life in the shipping office of the contentious G. S. Yuill in Sydney. Later he had come to Western Australia, where he joined the firm of Forrest, Emanuel, gained pastoral experience on their Kimberley properties, and then operated their agency in Derby. McGlew had recently taken over, on his own account, the Derby agency for West Kimberley pastoral stations and a number of shipping companies.

Bess, while not much attracted by Derby, was charmed by the McGlews who were from this time on to be counted among her cherished friends.

As they proceeded south she expressed surprise at what she saw as an incredibly long stretch of uninhabited coast. Constable Fletcher, who had joined the ship at Broome, observed that it was in fact occupied by formidable inhabitants of whom he could speak from personal experience. He then proceeded to hold a fascinated audience with the story of his four months' search in the wilds of the Prince Regent River and Admiralty Gulf for a group of Aborigines responsible for the killing of one John Pritchard Jones. It appeared that Jones and his partner, Massin, described as beachcombers and prospectors, had set out by lugger from Broome with an Aboriginal crew early that year. While anchored in Yampi Sound, Jones had been 'lured ashore' by an Aboriginal. He had not been long gone when Massin was attacked by one of the crew, whom he quickly disarmed and shot dead. When Jones failed to return to the lugger, Massin made back to Derby and reported to the police. Constable Fletcher set out with a search party which, after many hazardous adventures, found the body of the missing man, arrested six Aborigines and brought them to stand trial in Broome before Magistrate Wood. Although one of the men admitted to the killing of Jones, all six were sentenced to death.

When Bess observed that these coastal tribesmen were apparently very different from the faithful Aborigines of East Kimberley, Fletcher had smiled indulgently and returned with a shrug to his deck quoits.

News of the prospect of a Manila trade had penetrated to Perth and Fremantle well ahead of the travellers. This lent added excitement to their welcome and was the subject of animated conversation between the partners and their business associates. It was not, however, the only topic of major importance at that time, for May 1910 was the month of Halley's comet, and also the month when every town and city in the British Empire was draped with the black and purple of royal mourning. King Edward was dead, and his son George was proclaimed in his place. Would he prove strong enough for the task ahead of him? M.P., who had in common with the new monarch the year of his birth, sincerely believed he would—'But what does lie ahead of him, or for that matter, of any of us, in the decade to come?'

Michael (M.P.) Durack, 1908

Grandfather Patsy Durack

M.P. aged sixteen, then at St Patrick's College, Goulburn.

The Cobb & Co coach, circa 1920.

J.J. Durack (later known as Dermot) after
taking his science degree in Sydney, 1899.

The Three Mile Hotel, Wyndham, 1899. Rocks held the roof down against the wind.

M.J. Durack (Long Michael) with two of his sisters.

Tom Kilfoyle, related to the Duracks by marrige
and one of the great pioneer bushmen of Australia.

Aboriginal prisoners, mostly arrested on cattle-spearing charges, Wyndham, 1901.

Breaking camp on Argyle Station: M.P. Durack with an Aboriginal stockman.

Cattle being driven down to Wyndham for shipment to market.

The wedding of Mary Durack and Jim Davidson. Seated in front at left are Francis Connor and Galway Jerry Durack; seated at right are Bird Durack (bridesmaid) and (extreme right) Denis Doherty. M.P. Durack is standing, extreme left; Mrs Connor is seated next to the bridegroom. Standing behind the bride is Mrs Jerry Durack (Aunt Fan).

Galway Jerry Durack, killed on the Dunham Station, 1901.

P.B. Durack and his bride Eva, married in Brisbane, 1901.

W.J.C. (Bill) Jones, an indispensable member of the company team.

Aunt Fan, widow of Galway Jerry Durack.

Kit Evans (*nee* Durack)

Mrs Tom Kilfoyle (seated) with her son Jack and sister Josephine.

A gathering of East Kimberley bushmen
under a big boab tree on Argyle Station.

Boxer, by Beatrice Darbyshire–Argyle, 1933.

Francis Connor

Denis Doherty

Aborigines on Argyle Station in the early 1900s. In the front row, left to right, are Pumpkin, Ulysses and Boxer.

Loading a camel train bound for an inland station, Wyndham.

Bess I.M. Johnstone, 1909.

The wedding of Bess Johnstone and M.P. Durack, 22 September 1909. With them are Gertrude (Johnnie) Johnstone, the bride's sister and J.W. Durack, the bridegroom's younger brother.

Bess Durack on her first journey from Wyndham to Argyle, 1910.

Argyle Station homestead, from a painting by R.H. Shardlow.

Patsy, son of Galway Jerry, with his wife Lillas and children Neal and Patricia.

Cattle from East Kimberley being swum ashore at Manila.

Ambrose Durack (left), manager of Argyle Station, with M.P., about 1916.

The children of Grandfather Patsy at a family reunion, June 1912. Back Row, left to right: J.W., M.P., Mary. Front row: P.B., Bird, Dermot.

Ivanhoe Station homestead

One of the hazards of outback motoring: crossing the Ord River near Ivanhoe.

Fergus, younger brother of Ambrose
and Kit, killed at Gallipoli, 1915.

Neal Durack (left) and Leslie Drake-Brockman (later to become his brother-in-law) before leaving with the 10th Light Horse Regiment, 1915.

Ulysses, by Beatrice Darbyshire—Argyle, 1933.

Mr and Mrs P.B. Durack (left) with Sir John (later Lord) and Lady Forrest, and Lady Forrest's nephew, in Perth, 1901.

Bess Durack on the road between Ivanhoe and Argyle.

Ship at anchor, Wyndham jetty.

Reginald (5) and Mary (3)

Roy Phillips, a major in the
Royal Flying Corps, 1918.

M.P. at the wheel of a Dodge that later replaced the 'Khaki Cloud'.

Major Norman Brearley, a pioneer of air travel, 1919.

Rear view of the house at 263 Adelaide Terrace, Perth.

M.P.'s children: (left to right) Reg, Mary, Elizabeth, Kim and Bill.
Missing is David, then one year old.

25

CAT AMONG THE PIGEONS

April–July 1910

The prospect of a Manila trade acted like a cat among the pigeons in the cattle-growing circles of Western Australia. Nothing as exciting had happened since the discovery of gold in the south of the colony which had so dramatically increased its population and hence its demand for pastoral produce. It had seemed at this time that prospects for northern beef producers must continue to escalate indefinitely, but this had not been the case. After the first magnetic decade of prospecting, the goldfields' population began to drift away, many taking up farming or pastoral properties and thereby competing for the market they had formerly helped to swell.

The cost and inevitable losses incurred in shipping livestock from Wyndham and Derby to Fremantle increased the retailers' demand for beef from centres closer to their market. This had forced a reduction in the price of Kimberley cattle from £5 to £3 per head, and had encouraged the overlanding of Kimberley stock purchased by outside dealers to Queensland, where better prices were offered. The possibility of an additional market such as the Philippines was therefore of exciting significance to northern producers. Furthermore, the fact that this new demand was likely to be for lightweight rather than prime fat cattle meant that the better stock could be sold on the home market, and stock of lesser quality could go for as good or better prices abroad.

M.P., on his return from overseas, was everywhere cordially greeted by his fellow pastoralists or their representatives, but despite an apparent eagerness to discuss the Manila prospects, it was obvious that they were all holding their cards close to their chests.

A lively exchange of letters and cables between C.D. & D. in Perth and their agent in England gives some idea of the involved negotiations afoot. Denis Doherty wrote from London that he had discussed the situation with the volatile Richard Tilden Smith who had 'more irons in the fire than ever', among them his association with the Bovril group, on whose behalf he was presumably speaking in this reported interview:

Smith really opened out to me today. He said, 'You know I've always been straight with you old man. I want your properties. I can buy Lissadell from Hill and Durack at £2 a head but this is no good if I can't get your places as well.'

I took a bit of a header here. I told him that now the W.A. Government had decided to put a meat works in Wyndham, it put an extra £1 per head on our properties and I felt sure you would not now listen to a mere £150,000.

'Well Doherty,' he said, 'I'll go into it, again with you and your solicitor friend, Moss.'

Moss is here as you know, also Paterson, Copley's partner, and Arthur Male, M.L.A. for Kimberley. They all have plenty to say on the buying and selling of North Australian properties in the present circumstances ... [D.J.D., London, to C.D. & D., Perth, 22.4.10]

A follow-up cable from Doherty urged his partners to give every assistance possible to two men who were being sent out by Bovril to inspect and report on the C.D. & D. properties. This message concluded with the advice that the firm should contact Frank Wittenoom.

J.W.'s reply reveals the element of doubt that had intervened in previously straightforward relationships. Frank Wittenoom[1], a friend of long standing, had made no secret of being a representative of the Bovril Company, but J.W. was clearly nonplussed about the game he was now playing.

... I see Wittenoom frequently. The other day he asked us to put our interests under offer to them. I said Bovril had all the particulars of our estate through you, via Tilden Smith and although not prepared to make offers we were willing to receive them.

You would seem to suggest that we offer commission to Wittenoom of £10,000 at this end but you also speak of commission to your friend Tilden Smith at the other.

If Wittenoom is acting for Bovril it is no doubt his policy to get the properties as cheaply as he can. If he wants to sell them for a commission on sales, why would he want to get the price down? He has been trying to strike a hard bargain with Hill and Durack for Lissadell. M.J. told him he would give him £5000 commission if he could get him £55,000, walk in walk out. Wittenoom told him that they would do no business other than on a basis of bang-tail muster[2]. Lissadell is now under offer to Bovril on the latter basis.

> Copley tells me that Bovril offered 30/- a head for Ord River. Copley refused but now says that Bovril has approached him again, through Wittenoom. Copley replied that he could do nothing without advice from Paterson now in England (where he is probably, himself, negotiating for sale of the Ord).
>
> If Wittenoom's object is commission rather than making a good bargain for Bovril, we would be prepared to offer him £10,000 commission if he can get us £150,000 for our interests ... It is rather a ticklish question to approach him about but we will do so in a general way when he returns from Moora in a few days ... [J.W.D., Perth, to D.J.D., London, 27.4.10]

Doherty replied, suggesting that the best policy would be to offer commission only to Tilden Smith who was frankly 'dead keen' to get the C.D. & D. properties, knowing what a hold they would represent on the northern cattle trade.

> At present, however [the writer adds], Smith is so full of rubber companies that it's hard to get a word in edgeways. Much will depend on the report put in by the Bovril inspectors, now on their way out.

This letter concluded with a plea for a more adequate expense allowance:

> Don't forget, London is the dearest place to live in the world. I try to skimp but all this negotiation business has put me out of pocket. Smith is such a generous fellow one cannot allow him to do all the entertaining. It costs me a lot to keep pace with him—in the company's interest.

A few weeks after their return, M.P. and his wife sailed for Wyndham on the *Junee*. The *Frithoff* was already on its way from Manila and 350 head of cattle were awaiting inspection by Lichauco's agents at the company's holding depot near the port. M.P. had been given to understand that, subject to their acceptance (of which there was little doubt), the agents would require his guarantee of a further 3,000 head in the near future. This would have presented little difficulty, but the partners now suspected that rival interests might be rallying to buy up as much Kimberley cattle as possible for the same market. It was also on the cards that the Manila agents might attempt to cut up the trade by buying from one and another station holder. M.P. therefore planned to present them with the signed assurances of as many owners as possible that they intended selling their cattle through C.D. & D. This, he reasoned, should be convincing evidence of his company's being in control of the buying situation, or, in his own words, 'of the local growers being secured under one head'.

His new buggy was awaiting him at the Wyndham hotel, and he and Bess were soon on their way. It was as well, with so many other problems on his mind, that his bride's reaction to the bush life and the bush people was not, after all, as he had feared. Her first journey to Argyle is recalled thus in her latter-day memoirs:

> It was a very different life for me that I embarked upon that day. Coming as I did from a close family circle and a sheltered and rather confined home life Miguel feared that it might be a shock to me. But how I enjoyed it! . . .
>
> We set off at daybreak for Ivanhoe, which they used then to call 'the Stud'. It was an exciting journey for me. We stopped for lunch at the Bend of the Ord where Miguel took a ride round a big mob of Argyle cattle on its way to Wyndham. It was there I saw my first goanna—standing high on the river bank with its tongue jutting cheekily in and out. I never thought a lizard could be so huge. We also saw literally hundreds of wallabies and great flocks of birds such as I had never seen before. The scenery and vegetation was also exotic and wonderful to me.
>
> We reached Ivanhoè Station in the late afternoon and were greeted by the manager and his wife, Mr. and Mrs. Duncan McCaully. Duncan was six foot tall or more and must have weighed at least 15 stone. Miguel said he was a fine stockman but it was not always easy to find a horse strong enough to carry him. His wife was tiny beside him—about 5 ft. tall, very slight and dark. She had lost an eye but had a very good matching one that, as far as I could make out, never missed a thing. She had a habit of holding her head on one side like a bird and I never met anyone, before or since, who asked so many questions in such rapid succession. Duncan had met her at Rosewood Station where she had been governess to the family of Mr. and Mrs. Jerry Durack who then lived on that property . . .
>
> Getting over the Ord River next morning was an exciting experience, what with the steep banks and the rocky river bed, but Miguel was used to it and assured me it was quite safe.
>
> And so on we went over 50 miles of mostly sandy bush track to Argyle. It felt like home from the moment I stepped inside but

looked more like it when I had been busy for a week or two. There had been no white woman there since Ambrose Durack's sister Kit left to get married two or three years before. There was, however, a happy group of Aboriginal women who welcomed me like a member of their family and were only too eager to help set the place to rights. We had a lot of fun together and they brought their babies for me to admire and some to be named. An Indian called Ali Bey (we called him Ali Boy) was in charge of the kitchen at that time. He was a good cook, always friendly and amiable, and devoted to Ambrose with whom he had been working for some time[3].

Ambrose was manager of Argyle but was mostly out in the cattle camps at that time of year. He was a quiet, gentle man with a good sense of humour and great love and loyalty for his family. Miguel told me I'd have to do something about finding a wife for him. I was not to know at the time but that was just what I would succeed in doing—even if more or less by happy accident . . .

One aspect of life in Kimberley that especially intrigued Bess was that, as she often said, one never knew what type of person was going to turn up next. Prepared as she had been for the rough-and-ready characters of the bush environment, what surprised her was the number of well-read and widely travelled men of the Kimberley stations and stock camps.

One of these was Frederick Booty who had come to Australia in 1894 to visit his uncle, the wealthy W. S. Osmond[4], in Victoria. Booty, then in his early twenties, had asked to be allowed to visit Osmond's Ord River Station and get a taste of colonial experience before returning to his studies at Oxford. His uncle agreed that he might spend a short time in the north under the supervision of the station manager, Bob Button, but as time went by with no word of his return, Osmond had written demanding of Button that he send young Frederick on his way. Instead Button left the Ord and, in company with Booty and his fellow overlander, Tom Cahill, took up a property which he called Ruby Plains, south of Hall's Creek. Not long afterwards Nat Buchanan asked Booty and Sam Muggleton to come in with him on an outstation of Flora Valley. This they did, and the name of the property—Coojabring—is said to have derived from their frequent requests to passers by to bring them back goods from town.

The friendship between these two men had always seemed to M.P. amusingly incongruous. For himself he found little in common with 'the rough-neck Muggleton', whereas he enjoyed Booty's occasional company and appreciated his knowledge of history, world affairs, and the arts in general. As in the case of Sir Alec Campbell, however, he was concerned that a man of such background, with the alternatives it indicated, should have become for some reason captive of this back-of-beyond environment. From time to time Booty would talk of selling out and going 'home' when the market reached a satisfactory peak. That he was never to do so, except for a short visit in his later life, may have had much to do with the part-Aboriginal family for which he was not lacking in affection or a sense of responsibility. This aspect of his life he seems never to have discussed with M.P. It is remembered of him, however, that when asked on one occasion in the city how northern graziers obtained their labour he replied nonchalantly, 'We breed our own.'[5]

After a short time together at Coojabring, Booty and Muggleton had taken up separate properties, Muggleton a place he called Frog Hollow near Turkey Creek, and Booty Lambo Station adjoining Flora Valley. But arriving at Argyle at this time, Booty had the sad tale to tell of Muggleton's death not long before. He had been taken seriously ill in his stock camp and carried to the homestead on a stretcher, his camp cook, Jack McKenzie, hurrying ahead to render what assistance he could. While he was hastily unpacking, McKenzie's revolver had somehow slipped and shot him dead. Muggleton had also died that night, and the two were buried side by side. Booty was thereafter moved to find that Muggleton[6] had willed Frog Hollow to both his brother Arthur and himself.

In a remarkably short time M.P., with the help of his firm's stock inspector, Bill Jones, and a few hard-riding Aboriginal messengers, had the following signed statement from all smaller holders in the vicinity:

> I hereby agree to sell to Connor, Doherty & Durack Ltd., all my available bullocks for the twelve months following at £2 per head . . .
>
> This offer subject to inspection and approval on station or delivery in Wyndham . . .

Signatures to this agreement included P. M. Durack of the Dunham, Jack Kelly of Texas, Joseph Fegan of Spring Creek, Charles Whittaker of the Wickham, Joe Bridge of Mable Downs, Amos Skuthorpe of Waterloo, James Wickham of Nyerdoyle and Arthur Muggleton of Frog Hollow.

Obviously heartened by this response M.P. reported to his partners:

> The encouragement I have so far received in support of our endeavours to get on to this Manila market has been beyond my anticipation . . .

There should be a big thing in this for us all and if we do make a satisfactory contract with Manila I feel we are morally bound to extend more favourable terms to those who have so far generously given their support.

Anyhow this is a matter which can only be gauged by the trend of events. [M.P.D., Wyndham, to C.D. & D., Perth, 18.6.10]

By this time he was busily engaged between Wyndham and Ascot getting cattle away to Fremantle before the imminent arrival of the *Frithoff*. Bess had accompanied him from Argyle and here takes up the tale:

> Miguel had to camp at Ascot for a few days so Dr. & Mrs. Parer suggested that rather than stay at the noisy hotel I should move into a comfortable cottage at the back of their house. They also kindly invited me to have meals with them so I was free of cooking and housekeeping. Their home, close to the hospital, was a little oasis enclosed in a hedge of oleanders, which I called 'Wyndham roses'—a name that stuck! The house like most in the town was a few feet off the ground with a verandah on all sides and a big central room with comfortable furniture from Singapore, bright cushions and bead screens in the doorways. To step inside from the glare of Wyndham's only street was sheer delight. Their Chinese cook and house boy, Ah Ling, was a treasure indeed, an amiable master of all trades. The dinner he served that night would have done credit to any hotel chef. At about ten o'clock they saw me to my cottage, lit the lamp and impressed upon me that if I was in any way nervous I had only to 'cooee' and they would be with me in a flash.
>
> Alone at last I looked out into the moonlit night and up to the Bastion—that steep, stony hill that appears to be trying to push Wyndham into Cambridge Gulf. In the distance I could hear singing and a clicking of sticks which I had been told came from a native encampment at the back of the town. It was a sound with which I was to become familiar and even to enjoy, but which sounded strange and eerie to me then. I got into bed and was soon asleep. Some time later I was awakened by the patter of rain on the iron roof and an ominous knocking and deep breathing from under the house. For a while, picturing the cottage surrounded by wild natives, I was too terrified to move but at last I made a supreme effort, crept over to the verandah lattice and peered through. Before long I discerned some moving shapes and then

> what seemed like the entire goat population of the town jostling each other in search of shelter. Much relieved, and thankful that I had not disturbed the Parers, I was soon asleep again.
>
> When I told them of my experience next morning they apologised for not having warned me of what to expect if it happened to rain.
>
> I was to have many experiences during my years in the North but somehow that one remains most vividly in my memory[7].

M.P. was back in time to meet Lichauco's agents when they disembarked. He was not clear which of the two, if either, was the senior in authority. Marti, the elder, was a Spaniard, 'past middle age and of shrewd appearance', with less command of English but more to say than his Filipino companion, Dionisio. M.P. drove them at once to Ascot to inspect the cattle in hand. These were approved on condition that the mob was put on board without delay as the *Frithoff* was running to a tight schedule.

M.P. needed no urging where quick action was concerned but his earnest efforts were frustrated, as explained in an exasperated letter to Perth office:

> We had the mob over the hill and into the shipping yards by sundown. We were just about to get them down the race when your urgent telegram arrived stating that the cattle must not be shipped before the Union Bank, Perth, had advised of payment from the Chartered Bank in Manila. I advised Dionisio to cable Lichauco to authorize his bank to pay immediately for the 350 head.
>
> We couldn't, however, hold the cattle any longer, what with the *Moira* waiting to load another mob for Fremantle and the *Junee* chugging up the Gulf. I therefore took the responsibility of going ahead.
>
> We started loading at 7.30 p.m. and all went well until 1 a.m. when friction arose between the Captain of the *Frithoff* and Inspector Marti. For the next three to four hours the ship was the scene of a heated wrangle in a confusion of languages. From what I could make out the Captain refused to put the race into position before receiving his payment of £23.0.0 in cash for pilotage of the vessel. After considerable difficulty and amid general confusion we got the last beast on before 7 a.m. The Captain then moved away from the jetty declaring he would not now accept the fee for pilotage—but would insist upon the charterers finding a pilot for him. At the present moment—9.30 a.m.—the *Frithoff* lies just

> behind the *Moira.* It is already very hot, the cattle are just huddled on board anyhow and there's not a soul on the ship, as far as I can make out, who understands a thing about the handling of stock. I cannot see but that this shipment must be a heavy loss.

M.P. watched the *Frithoff* sail that afternoon with a sigh of relief but Marti and Dionisio remained to keep him guessing.

> 18.6.10: Mr. Marti [he reported] had now discussed business with nearly all the settlers who have come in as also with M.J.D. of Lissadell. I told him of our written agreement with most of these and gave him every opportunity of discussing business but he has so far evaded the question altogether. He has made it clear, at least as far as I can make out, that he does not care to discuss the Manila trade with me. Despite this apparent unwillingness, or pretended ignorance, I think he is quite in touch with all that is going on in respect to our negotiations and is probably getting all the information he can from outside sources . . . All the same their approach is so evasive and their English so poor that I begin to think I'd rather go up to Manila and deal with Lichauco direct . . .

The Manila agents were not the only enigmatic strangers to cross M.P.'s path at this time, for the Bovril representatives Marshall, an American, and Bourdette, an Argentinian, had now arrived to complicate the situation further. M.P., in view of Doherty's earnest plea that they be given every assistance possible, had been awaiting news of their arrival and was surprised when they turned up unannounced at Ivanhoe homestead. Their horses had been supplied from Carlton Station which was a Bovril property. These mounts had, however, soon proved inadequate and it is little wonder that M.P. found the new arrivals in a 'highly disgruntled frame of mind and obviously at loggerheads with each other'. The purpose of their visit, they explained, was not only to assess the value of East Kimberley and adjacent Northern Territory properties for Bovril Estates, but to investigate the feasibility of the company's setting up a meatworks in the vicinity. They had so far inspected a number of sites, including Wyndham itself, but had been everywhere put off by the inadequate supply of fresh water. They were now making for Bovril's Victoria River Station, via Newry and Auvergne which they had been informed by Denis Doherty in London were the best properties in the district.

M.P. and his wife, capably backed by Duncan and Mrs McCaully, received them hospitably and sent them on their way with fresh mounts and an

Aboriginal escort to act as guide and tailer for the horse changes. They were also furnished with letters to the C.D. & D. managers, Tom Woodland at Newry and Jack Skeahan at Auvergne, instructing them to extend every courtesy and assistance to the travellers.

Their activities and comments, as noted in M.P.'s letters and journals for some time to come, gave him little cause for confidence that they would encourage Bovril to bid favourably for the C.D. & D. properties or to proceed with the erection of a local meatworks. He continued politely to facilitate their investigations while at the same time actively seeking to acquire further properties for C.D. & D.

The logic of this policy lay in the fact that whether or not a suitable bidder should turn up, there was nothing to be lost, in view of the Manila trade, by obtaining the grazing rights to as much country as possible, together with the cattle it sustained. He knew that his cousin M.J. of Lissadell was keen to sell to Bovril. He also knew, from the advice given to Doherty by Tilden Smith, that he was unlikely to succeed unless Bovril were to purchase the C.D. & D. estate as well. M.J.'s wish to sell was not hard to understand, for it was known to the family that his wife, Bertha, whom he had never permitted to set foot in Kimberley, complained bitterly of being assigned the role of 'grass widow' for more than half the year. It was not, she argued, as though they had, or could now expect, a son and heir to inherit the far-away property which, as things stood, she saw as a wedge between them that could only grow more formidable with the years. Apart from this, M.J. had developed a taste for city life and cherished the dream of travelling with his wife to the far and fascinating places of which his more fortunate relatives had so much to say.

It was with some confidence, therefore, that M.P. approached his cousin with an offer for Lissadell of £30,000 'walk in, walk out', which, he suggested, was probably more than he would get from Bovril on a 'bang-tail muster' basis of £2 per head. M.J. said he would consider sale at £40,000, but refused to put anything in writing as he expected the Bovril agents to make the better offer before they left the Kimberleys.

Marshall departed a few weeks later without having approached M.J. M.P. therefore again raised the subject with him, only to find that his cousin was now pinning his hopes on being made a suitable offer after the Bovril agents had put in their report. M.P. told him that he was indulging in a pipe-dream but M.J. was prepared to dream on, realising, no doubt, that his ambition to travel, maintaining meanwhile a reasonably elegant headquarters in Perth, needed considerably more than a half-share with his partner, Lumley Hill, of the price so far offered for Lissadell.

During the same few weeks M.P. had been negotiating with his Uncle Jerry's widow, Aunt Fan, and her eldest son, Patsy, for the purchase of the Dunham Station, which, like Lissadell, adjoined the C.D. & D. holdings. He found these relatives by no means as difficult to deal with as M.J. Aunt Fan, who had been vacillating about the sale of the Dunham to C.D. & D. since her husband's death nearly ten years before, was now in no two minds about wanting to dispose of the property. Of a naturally buoyant and optimistic nature, she had now come to admit that the place had brought her little more than unrewarding toil and heartbreak, of which the graves of her dear ones, clearly visible from the mudbrick homestead, were a constant reminder. Two of her four sons were then in Perth, Jack (J.P.) studying for the law and Neal in his last year at college. Her household, when M.P. arrived to discuss the matter of sale, consisted of her sons, Patsy aged twenty-eight and Frank aged ten, her daughter Mollie aged sixteen, and a seventeen-year-old girl named Lillas Mulligan.

Lillas was the daughter of a government accountant known to the Duracks in their Queensland days. When his wife died, leaving him with two young daughters, he had come to Perth where he boarded the girls at the Sacred Heart Convent. A year or so earlier, Aunt Fan had persuaded him to allow Lillas to come to the Dunham as a companion for her daughter Mollie.

Aunt Fan responded eagerly to M.P.'s expression of interest in the property, and said she would be glad to get out if offered no more than 2s 6d per head! The Dunham Station comprised approximately 307,000 acres but the terms of settlement, as with all leaseheld properties, were fixed according to the agreed price per head for the stock it carried. In this case the number of cattle was estimated at 3,500, for which Patsy and his mother accepted £1 7s 6d a head, the final price including payment for twenty-five head of horses, together with all station gear and plant, fifteen saddles, five pack-saddles, one dray, one buggy, harness, etc., and also right and title to the brands 3DI and L3L.

M.P. at once reported on this negotiation to the Perth office.

> I have purchased the Dunham subject to your approval and enclose copy of conditions of sale. I believe it is in our interests, in view of the Manila trade, to get this property. If you agree I intend having about 1,500 head of Dunham cattle brought to Ascot as am sure they will do as well as the cows we brought here from Auvergne. [M.P.D., Wyndham, to C.D. & D., Perth, 21.6.10]

A reply to this communication came with all possible speed, warmly approving the purchase, and so the deed of sale was duly signed. M.P. assured his aunt that she could regard the Dunham as her home as long as she liked, and offered Patsy the position of manager at £3 a week which was the usual wage at that time.

Modest as the terms may appear by present-day standards, they were accepted with considerable relief for they made it possible for Aunt Fan to purchase a home in the south for herself and the younger members of her family. Where Patsy was concerned, it freed him from the responsibility of trying to make the station pay which it had somehow never done. It had moreover put him in a position to propose to the gentle Lillas Mulligan.

The next move in the firm's new policy of expansion came from the Perth office, and was something of a surprise to M.P. According to a wire received on 15 July, C.D. & D., this time subject to *his* approval, had purchased Fossil Downs in West Kimberley for the sum of £25,000.

Will MacDonald had apparently come to Perth a short time before and offered them the property, to which he had driven cattle from New South Wales in the 1880s. His reason for wanting to get out could probably have been summed up in the single word 'loneliness'. He had brought his bride from Goulburn to Kimberley in 1902, and their only son, Kimberley, had been born in Derby the following year. The boy had developed a crippling form of rheumatoid arthritis in his early years and it was obvious that he would never be fit for station life. Concerned for his welfare, Mrs MacDonald had returned with him to New South Wales some time before and her husband, not now in good health himself, was anxious to join them.

M.P. hastened to congratulate his partners on the 'remarkably good deal' they had struck, thus securing for the company a strategic base in West Kimberley where the ruling interests had so often been in conflict with their own. The general state of satisfaction was, however, short-lived, for a few days later a further communication advised M.P. that MacDonald had died in Perth on 16 July and that his brothers, Duncan and Donald, then in Goulburn, disputed Will's power to sell without their consent. As indicated in a letter from Doherty, the question this raised had become a legal one.

> If the MacDonald brothers cannot produce a deed of partnership setting forth Will MacDonald's limitations, I should think they were bound to carry out his contract as he had full power of management to sell stock and buy for the property. I shall have a yarn about it with John Moss and get a lawyer's point of view

> when he returns from grouse shooting in Scotland. [D.J.D., London, to C.D. & D., Perth, 2.9.10]

In the meantime P.B. had written from Wagin to his brother, J.W.:

> Jack, old man, if they—the MacDonald family—don't want us to have the place, then let them keep it. I don't feel like fighting over it, do you? Haven't we got enough problems on our plates already? [P.B.D., Wagin, to J.W.D., Perth, 26.7.10]

This line of thought must, after all, have prevailed as there is no further reference to the matter in the company records. Nor is there anything in M.P.'s diary or more voluminous letters to indicate whether he was disappointed or relieved that the purchase of Fossil Downs had fallen through. It must, however, have occurred to him to wonder whether, in the event of purchase, he would have been expected to extend his activities from the vast area he already covered to include journeys to supervise the firm's new acquisition[8]. In any case, he would have had little time to brood on this question for Marti and Dionisio, having evidently decided that C.D. & D. had control of the local market, were at his elbow arranging for the shipment of a further 3,000 head of cattle at £3 10s per head. The first few hundred of these were on their way to Manila when a telegram from Perth advised that the Washington Government was threatening to prohibit the import of cattle from Wyndham on the grounds of reported disease in the first shipment. M.P. confided to his diary that he attached little importance to this report, which would no doubt soon be found incorrect.

Nonetheless the news came at the same time that signs of pleuro were detected in a mob coming in to Wyndham from Victoria River Downs. There was consternation on all sides, Marti and Dionisio wringing their hands, M.P. organizing immediate inoculation measures for all incoming stock and wiring Sir Edward Wittenoom (Dalgety's agent) in Perth, and all others in the area who had pinned their hopes to the development of a Manila trade waiting anxiously in the wings.

26

Propositions and Promises

July 1910–January 1911

The shock wave caused by this quarantine restriction vibrated not only through the Kimberley district but through the Perth and London offices of C.D. & D., and Bovril Estates. Marti and Dionisio, seemingly as concerned as anyone, set sail for Manila after assuring M.P. that the ban was, after all, only a ninety-day quarantine during which time the stock would no doubt be kept under surveillance and finally declared clean.

Theories abounded regarding the true cause of the restriction. M.P. was inclined to suspect the dealers from Saigon and Singapore whose trade had been cancelled because of the prevalence of rinderpest. Others blamed rival Western Australian pastoral interests. P.B., writing from Wagin, expressed a widely held opinion in simple terms:

> It is only jealousy. We can get enough cattle to keep the price down and there's some of them this doesn't suit. They don't want to see us make a go of it. It's rotten luck, though, just as we were steaming so nicely ahead. [P.B.D., Wagin, to J.W.D., Perth, 27.7.10]

Doherty wrote sadly from London that whatever the cause of the contretemps, he feared it would greatly prejudice their chances of making a good deal with Bovril for the sale of the properties. Apart from the Manila hold-up, there was also the news, conveyed by Tilden Smith, that at least one of Bovril's inspectors had reported unfavourably on the Kimberley district. Marshall had even declared that the owners, when estimating the numbers of cattle on their properties, appeared to be afflicted with double vision. He also considered that at least half the beasts being shipped away were unfit for freezing. If the Bovril Company was still interested in setting up a chilling- and extract-works, the only site Marshall was prepared to recommend was not on either of their own places, Victoria River or Carlton, as Smith had hoped, but on C.D. & D.'s property, Auvergne.

None of this came as a surprise to M.P., who was aware of the fact that Marshall had sailed from Wyndham with no better impression of the country than he had had at the time of their first meeting.

> This country had nothing to say to Marshall. He was at loggerheads from the beginning with the climate, the vegetation, the animal and human population and his fellow inspector Bourdette, from whom he parted company at Victoria River. I have some sympathy for him, however, as he was too old for the job and was for much of his time here in poor health.
>
> I know the place he thought suitable for a processing site. It is on the Big Lagoon, on the West side of, and quite close to, the West Baines River ... [M.P.D., Wyndham, to J.W.D., Perth, 26.10.10]

Meanwhile M.P. had written to Sir Edward Wittenoom, the influential squatter-politician in Perth, stressing the importance to the State, and to the mutual interests of Bovril and C.D. & D., of somehow reasoning with the Philippine Government. He had made arrangements for the meticulous dipping of all stock being held on arriving at Ascot, and had conferred with M.J. on the disposal of over 3,000 head of Argyle and Lissadell cattle that had been awaiting shipment to Manila. The cousins who, although in frequent communication and on tolerably good terms in a family sense, had seldom seen eye-to-eye at a business level, would seem on this occasion to have been exceptionally co-operative. Having together organized the droving plant and estimated the date of its arrival on the Queensland coast, M.J. undertook to supervise the delivery and payment of the stock. It would, he said, be a good excuse for Bertha and himself to visit relatives 'on the other side'.

In the midst of these negotiations Frank Connor turned up, having taken time off from his parliamentary duties to confer with M.P. about their current problems. It may not have been entirely accidental that his visit coincided with that of Government Surveyor Sanderson and party, who were to advise on the feasibility of the long-talked-of meatworks.

Having inspected sundry possible sites, Sanderson indicated his intention of recommending Wyndham as the most suitable location and of having water pumped in from one of several outlying sources. He did not see the project as an alternative to the Manila trade, but stressed the advantage to growers of being able to ship frozen beef rather than livestock to overseas markets. This would overcome the risk of stock being quarantined on one pretext or another, and would allow for the sale of better quality livestock in the south of the State.

Connor was still in the north when word came through that the government had approved Sanderson's advice that a meatworks be erected at Wyndham in the near future. This news was received with considerable elation but Connor, viewing the matter from his parliamentary vantage point, warned M.P. not to put too much store by it. From what he knew of current issues and public opinion, he thought that a Labor government was likely to win by a landslide in the forthcoming election and that in this case an expensive project to benefit the northern 'beef barons' would not make the priority list.

Over this period the partners also discussed a recent interesting communication from Doherty, whose letters for some time past had been far from cheerful. A long-suffered affliction of the leg had at last necessitated a costly operation and extensive hospital treatment. The walking stick he had previously used for sartorial effect had now become a necessity and he feared that, what with the expense involved in maintaining his home in Slough and educating his four children, he would soon have to move into 'cheap diggings for distressed Australian pastoralists down Whitechapel way'. He missed his stimulating friend, Tilden Smith, who had taken off on some new venture, and now, with the collapse of the Manila trade, his horizon was gloomy indeed. His latest letter, however, had been in decidedly more cheerful vein.

> Smith is back at last and has just rung me up. He now has a freezing-plant to deal with cattle at Madagascar and will probably get the market for the French army . . .
>
> He has asked me to form a syndicate on behalf of our company for Youings Timber at Wyndham. He said you might as well join in and get the agency there . . .
>
> The biggest timber men in the world are in this venture and if it can be done they will make it go . . . Smith has 500 shares. They will want you to do the carting if possible. There should be a good profit in this and it will bring trade to Wyndham. The Syndicate is to be called:
>
> *Cypress Pine Syndicate.*
>
> The Manager, Mr. J. Boxall, to whom I gave a letter of introduction to your good selves, should arrive soon in Fremantle. He will go to Wyndham and report on the possibilities . . . [D.J.D., London, to C.D. & D., Perth, 12.8.10]

Connor and M.P. discussed this proposal with the Commissioner for Tropical Agriculture, Adrian Despeissis, who was also in East Kimberley at that time. Despeissis agreed to give the matter his attention but was then mainly concerned with diagnosing the cause of, and finding a cure for, the prevalent Kimberley horse disease, and was urging the introduction of tick-resistant Zebu cattle to be crossed with Shorthorns. The partners were interested but were too preoccupied with matters of greater urgency to give the idea more than passing attention.

The timber expert of whom Doherty had written did in fact turn up at about that time, and apparently put in a favourable report on the potential of a cypress timber industry in the area. Despeissis, too, was as good as his word and included information on the subject in his *Handbook of Tropical Agriculture:*

> *Callitris Verrucosa,* Cypress Pine, sometimes called 'Camphor wood' . . .
>
> The wood is dark, fragrant, friable and suitable for cabinet making . . .
>
> These forests will form an asset of no mean value in Northern Kimberley whenever some means are provided for getting the timber from the forests to shipside. The continuous fringe of swamp country thickly lined with mangroves and the swift tides rising and falling 22 to 32 feet up and down the long inlets will make transport a difficult and onerous undertaking.
>
> The largest forest yet reported is near Elephant Hill, some 40 miles north-east of Wyndham . . .
>
> Should it be found practicable to open up and exploit these cypress pine forests, the erection of saw mills would not only prove a source of wealth to the State but would offer one of the best means of gaining a better idea of the coast-line of Kimberley and of pushing settlement into the heart of a rich country, now occupied by some thousands of treacherous blacks. [*Handbook of Tropical Agriculture*, A. Despeissis, Government Printer, Perth, 1913]

Whether because of those crocodile-infested tides, the hypothetical numbers of wild inhabitants, or the sheer inaccessibility of the cypress forests, the subject quickly faded from the company files. In any case, the partners in Australia were no doubt too preoccupied with the disposal of their livestock to have welcomed involvement in retail problems of another kind.

Connor, when taking leave of M.P., declared that if the Manila market had not reopened by the end of the year he would go himself to the Philippines and exercise his powers of persuasion on the misguided authorities.

During this time, M.P. when travelling by buggy was usually accompanied by his wife, whose unfailing good spirits and lively interest helped him maintain an image of cheerful confidence. He knew, however, as the year progressed, that the happy, honeymoon phase of their lives was drawing to a close, for he had promised that Bess would be returned to her parents in Adelaide in good time for the birth of her child in the New Year. He accompanied her to Fremantle on the *Junee* early in October but was obliged to return immediately to the north. Of their parting he wrote in his diary: 'Slowly the image of my own dearest girl fades from my view and I am left on deck to my reveries.' One wonders whether these included his leave-taking, from the same wharf, of another girl dear to his heart twelve eventful years before.

A surprise awaited on his return to Wyndham, where he found his Aunt Fan ready, with her daughter Mollie and her youngest son Frank, for departure to Fremantle. Patsy was to be married the following day to Lillas Mulligan, who had been recently joined by her elder sister Nellie. M.P. had previously heard nothing of the young people's intentions and his record of the happy event reads somewhat tersely:

> 27.10.10: P. M. Durack married to Annie Lillas Mulligan at 11 a.m., Sgt. Buckland performing the ceremony. Present, Nellie Mulligan and Neal Durack. Witnesses, Mr. and Mrs. C. McManus and self. Afterwards to Dr. Parer's House. Patsy appeared somewhat nervous, Lillas sad and demure—unconscious, as it were, of what it all meant.

From Lillas's own story, recounted to me in later years, it would seem that she had been anything but unconscious of what she had taken on. The acceptance of her lot in a world of tough men and bellowing cattle had not been a simple matter of falling in love. Nearer the truth was the fact that, through some quirk of fate, Patsy had become her responsibility and his life her destiny. She was grateful to his mother for having taken her into the family and understood her wish to escape from the north. Knowing, however, that she would not leave Patsy at the Dunham without a woman's influence, what else could Lillas do but accept the boy's proposal and carry on as best she could? Her sister went back with them to the Dunham, intending to return to Perth, but her meeting with Jack Martin, then in charge of Ascot for C.D. & D., was soon to lead to another Wyndham wedding.

One reason for the urgency of M.P.'s return had been his promise to Ambrose of a few months' leave of absence, and since there was no one else immediately available he had to take charge at Argyle himself. As General Manager for the company he was used to being constantly on the move, and although always carrying a heavy administrative burden, he had not previously been tied down to the day-to-day frets and emergencies of a station manager's life.

He found things at the Argyle homestead in a state of unusual disorganization. Repairs to the roof had been interrupted by the effects of fever on the two itinerant carpenters, and to complicate matters further the wet season had set in rather earlier than usual. M.P.'s diary gives some idea of the general situation.

> 5.11.10: The joys of station managing! Unroofing the house has disclosed how efficiently the white ants have carried out their job. When it rains it's hard to find a corner to shelter in.
>
> Old Borthwick here from Wyndham having had to walk from Slatey Creek where his packhorse died. He's too old, at 75, to be knocking about the country looking for work. Put him on to the roofing job as the other two men still down with fever.
>
> Prosser, 'the Storm Bird', in, full of ailments and complaints as usual. Next, Bill Nottman, with a genuine case of eye trouble. Dealt out the usual nostrums.
>
> The cook, Willie Let, gives notice—wants to go to China to see his mother.
>
> The men who went off to Tanami diggings with such high hopes—or those of them who have survived—are drifting back. McLaughlin and Murphy propose giving me equal shares with them in any alluvial gold they might find on Argyle. Lent them three horses.
>
> Billy Barlow up from the Stud—says 'too much Duncan McCaully all day growl'—wants to join the Argyle stock camp. Ulysses warns of 'woman trouble' at the back of it.
>
> Boxer and Deology report the two English bulls badly infected with tick—looking very poorly.
>
> Afghan with 11 camels here on way to Ord. Told him he can't camp in home paddock near the blacks' camp. He leaves reluctantly.
>
> So much for today! What tomorrow?

A few weeks later Bill Jones arrived to report that he and Patsy had finished shifting the requisite number of cattle from the Dunham to Ascot and Ivanhoe. What was the next job required of him? The reply came with no hesitation whatever: Bill could now take charge at Argyle until Ambrose returned in the New Year. Having been on C.D. & D.'s books since 1903, and in this time having filled many roles besides that of company stock inspector, Jones was quite undaunted by this assignment. He had always made a hobby of encouraging confidences and probably knew more about the bush people of that time, black and white, than anyone else. The petty complaints, ailments, intrigues, and squabbles that were inclined to irritate M.P. were a source of keen interest to Jones, from whom I was later to hear much that did not find its way into family journals or company correspondence.

M.P. was back in Perth in time for Christmas and immediately afterwards on board the S.S. *Osterly* for Adelaide.

> Met by Mr. Johnstone and son Ted and home to my sweetheart after a separation of 15 weeks for which she looks none the worse.

Seeing the New Year in with the conventionally bright and hospitable Johnstone family was a refreshing change from his rough-and-ready bush life, but there was little escape from the affairs it involved. Letters and cables from Wyndham, Darwin, or Perth reached him almost every day.

The two Poll Shorthorn bulls, imported from England, that had been his pride and joy, had died at Argyle[1] ... Could he buy two Jack donkeys, up for sale in Adelaide, for Will Byrne who could pick them up when delivering draught horses to Argyle later in the year? ... Would he make a point of seeing Sidney Kidman in Adelaide and getting his views on their mutual problem of the Manila hold-up? ...

But these were small issues compared with those raised in a letter from the London office which was forwarded to M.P. from Perth. Doherty had been once again in consultation with Tilden Smith, who had little faith in the Western Australian Government's promise to erect a meatworks in Wyndham. If this project did not begin to materialize early in the New Year, Smith declared himself willing to take on the task at an estimated cost of £25,000. This did not include the provision of an adequate water supply, which was surely little enough to expect of the State Government, whichever party was in power! The letter continued:

> I will give it to you as far as possible in his own words. This is what Smith says:
>
> 'My proposition to you is this. If your firm will join me and take half interest, which would mean a risk of only ... £12,500, I will send my men from Madagascar to duplicate the freezing plant they have set up there. This could be ready to work about next June. I would give your people full management and control of Victoria River Station, the buying of all cattle in East Kimberley

and The Territory for these works ... and feel sure you can work this business on sound commercial lines ...

The running of the works themselves must of course be supervised by experts but they will be subject to your absolute control.

Your markets for the chilled beef would be in Western Australia, Manila and perhaps Singapore, Japan and Vladivostok. Then there are the by-products to be considered. Hides alone should show a substantial profit ...

It is necessary of course that your people should treat the matter under discussion as strictly *private* and *confidential*. I am generally dissatisfied with the management of Victoria River from a commercial point of view and want to put an end to it. I do not therefore wish other parties butting in to complicate the issue. It could be detrimental to the project if Sir Edward Wittenoom, Messrs. Emanuel and others out there should become cognizant of any negotiations between us at this stage.

I want you to give full power of attorney to one of your directors and get him to England as soon as possible so that we can devise a co-operative scheme. We might decide the best course to be amalgamation of our properties giving your firm full control and management. A tentative value on Victoria River might be £180,000 and C.D. & D. properties at £150,000 ...' [D.J.D., London, to C.D. & D., Perth, 25.11.10]

Doherty would seem to have been disappointed in the response to this communication. There were no excited cables, and having allowed reasonable time for the arrival of ship's mail he began his next, uncharacteristically brief, letter rather testily: 'I am without any of your esteemed favours ...'

M.P.'s reply to J.W., written on receipt of Doherty's letter, probably indicates how the proposal was viewed by the various company members in Australia:

There is one thing Doherty appears to forget in his various propositions and that is our financial position. He seems to take it for granted that we have unlimited capital to call upon. The estimated price given by Tilden Smith for the erection of a freezing works is quite absurd. It would be at least three times that amount ...

Smith's proposition when sifted out is no proposition at all. Its essence, or so it appears to me, is that he now finds himself in a most embarrassing position re Victoria River Downs and is asking

> us to help him out . . . His estimates of V.R.D. at £180,000 and our properties at £150,000 are unacceptable. Our properties are worth at least as much . . .

M.P. proceeded at some length, asking what right Tilden Smith had, as one member of the Bovril Syndicate, to negotiate a deal without the knowledge of the others concerned. Personally, he was disinclined to consider the proposition unless everything was 'open and above board'.

> Before any one of us went home to discuss this business with Smith we would surely need to have the support of Sidney Kidman and other members of the Bovril group. It is as though Smith were using us as detectives since our position enables us to know the conditions under which Bovril is being managed.
>
> I am seeing Kidman at the South Australian Hotel in the next day or so and mean to raise with him a possible co-operation in tackling this Manila business. I will not of course make any reference to the Tilden Smith affair. [M.P.D., Adelaide, to J.W.D., Perth, 14.1.11]

This time of waiting was full of social and business activities for M.P. He attended the stock sales with Kidman, purchased stud bulls to replace the lost sires from overseas, visited the Port Adelaide freezing works, and consulted with numerous representatives of the pastoral industry.

Much discussion centred upon the recent takeover of the Northern Territory, hitherto a dependency of South Australia, by the Commonwealth Government. An Administrator had been appointed who was said to espouse an enterprising new policy of diverse industrial development which should soon increase the value of Territory properties. M.P., though somewhat doubtful of the area's potential for the schemes envisaged, could not but entertain day-dreams of selling Auvergne at a handsome price and being rid of the problems with which it assailed him.

Bess, as her time drew near, entered a fashionable Adelaide nursing home, known as Quambi, the owner of which was Mrs Bartel, sister of the landscape artist, Hans Heysen.

On 28 January, when paying his customary morning visit, M.P. was delighted to find himself the father of 'a bright little cherub ushered into this world at 5.45 a.m.'. His diary notes continue:

> I am met as usual by the smiling face of my dear wife. It is only after greeting her that I observe the baby lying on her arm. It took me a few seconds to realise the fact of the little mite's arrival in

Australia. I am much gratified to find Bess so bright and well whilst her eyes glowed lovingly on our little son.

The first man to offer congratulations was the Rev. Father Francis Kelly who officiated at our marriage in September '09. Dispatched telegrams to relatives near and far . . .

The naming of the child represented something of a problem. As the eldest son in a long line of eldest sons, it had seemed fitting to the Durack family that he be named according to tradition either Michael, Patrick, John, or Jeremiah, but this had already led to such confusion that the Johnstone clan favoured a radical change. Why not William after his maternal grandfather? But there was already a William Durack, brother of Long Michael and Black Pat, who was then medical officer in the Port Hedland area[2]. Of the many names put forward Bess favoured Reginald, after Reg Cannaway, a Johnstone family connection who was later to marry her sister Gert. And, lest the Duracks appeared to be overlooked, why not also the name of the port with which they had been so closely associated since 1886? So Reginald Wyndham it was.

27

Full Steam Ahead

February 1911–January 1912

The New Year had so far disclosed the answer to only one of the many questions that had preoccupied the C.D. & D. partners in 1910. To M.P.'s obvious joy and satisfaction the expected child had proved to be a healthy son and heir, and the phase of his personal life which he referred to as his 'Bim-era' was proceeding happily.

On the business front, however, nothing had been satisfactorily resolved. Was the State Government to proceed with the erection of a meatworks in Wyndham? If not, could the Commonwealth be persuaded to allow Asian labour to kill on board Lichauco's refrigerated steamer?

While in Adelaide M.P. had interviewed both the South Australian Premier and the Minister for External Affairs, pointing out the anomaly by which Asian workers, on three-year terms of indenture, were allowed in for the Broome pearling industry but were denied admission to Wyndham for a few days at a time. The South Australians admitted the contradiction and professed to see the advantages of Lichauco's proposal. They were nonetheless doubtful of the Commonwealth's relaxing its White Australia Policy to provide a new outlet for cattle from Wyndham. The argument would seem to have been that there were enough markets in Australia, and that if the northern growers wished to export frozen beef they could continue droving their bullocks to meatworks on the Queensland coast. The main point at issue, as seen by all concerned, was how to persuade the respective governments of Australia and the Philippines to cease obstructing a mutually beneficial trade.

M.P. had received several cables from Lichauco urging that a member of the company should go up and discuss the impasse with local officials. Connor, still Independent Member for North Province, agreed to undertake this mission while Parliament was in recess. He was already on his way when M.P. embarked from Adelaide on the R.M.S. *Orsova* with his wife, infant son and a nurse named Nance Tiddy who had agreed to go north with them for a few months. Nance, the daughter of an accountant who had migrated from Cornwall, was born in Maitland, South Australia and when sixteen years of age had gone off to visit her relatives in England.

While there she had trained as a nurse and on her return had been employed at the Quambi private hospital in Adelaide. It was there that she met Bess Durack, through whom she was to form a lifelong association with the family.

To M.P.'s pleased surprise their fellow passengers included several old friends. One of these was Dr, now Bishop, Gallagher, the revered headmaster of his schooldays at St Patrick's College, Goulburn. Another was Father P. J. Clune, born in County Clare and ordained at All Hallows, Dublin, in 1886, whose impending consecration as Bishop of the Perth diocese was the reason for a gathering of prelates to the Western State. His first appointment had been as a teacher under Dr Gallagher at St Patrick's College, by which time M.P. and J.W. were far away in the wilds of Kimberley. Their mutual association in both Ireland and Australia had however forged a bond between them since their first meeting in 1898, when Father Clune had arrived in Perth as one of a pioneer band of Redemptorists. That M.P., whose comments on Sunday sermons were inclined to be caustic, was at once impressed by those of Father Clune, foreshadowed the reputation he was to win as one of the State's most outstanding orators.

Many members of the Durack family attended the consecration ceremony at St Mary's Cathedral and participated in a dinner organized by M.P. and J.W. to welcome their old teacher and to congratulate the new Bishop. It was a happy occasion, on which M.P. was complimented, with Irish eloquence and tactful avoidance of the sectarian issue, on his choice of a life's partner and the birth of a son. Conversation ranged widely from the past students and teachers at the Goulburn College to the recent address delivered by Cardinal Moran, who was also in Perth for the consecration, deploring what he saw as a modern tendency in education to encourage sport at the expense of intellectual activities.

M.P. had much to occupy him during his two weeks in Perth. There was shopping with Bess for items of furniture required at the Argyle homestead, and at another level, interviews with governmental officials relating to the sadly obstructed meat trade. Premier Wilson informed him that a team of experts was then on the way to Wyndham to advise on the site for a meatworks, but in view of a site having been selected and officially approved in the previous year, M.P. could see this as nothing more than a political tactic to further evade the undertaking. This suspicion he kept to himself, while urging the Premier to support the use of a refrigerated steamer with Asian labour for a trial period of twelve months. He was assured that a telegram to this effect would be dispatched at once to the

Federal Government, but if this promise was honoured he heard nothing of any reply. Despite these frustrating encounters, a cable received just before his return to Wyndham sent him hopefully on his way. This message was from Frank Connor, advising that prospects for the reopening of the market from the Manila end now seemed promising and that the firm should tie up options for the purchase of cattle from as many sources as possible.

The population of Wyndham turned out early in April with more than ordinary enthusiasm to welcome M.P. and his family. A young man named Roy Phillipps, who had come up not long before as assistant to Jim Davidson in C.D. & D.'s Wyndham office, wrote of the occasion in a letter to his mother[1] in Perth.

> Champagne flows like water up here whenever anything happens, such as the arrival of M.P., who turned up the other day. We got it for dinner at the pub ... Mrs M.P. is just the thing. I think she is the most beautiful woman I have ever seen. Her baby and nurse were also in the party and we had an altogether really good time ...
>
> A scientific expedition came up by the same boat. It is headed by Price Connigrave, the chap who married Viotti Pearce ... They are off into the never-never, not a man of them ever been in the bush before—supposed to be taking photographs and collecting insects ...

The writer seems to have been under the impression that the party was more likely to collect a few well-aimed Aboriginal spears, but although new-chums in the Kimberley area they were not totally lacking in experience of bush conditions. Price Connigrave, a South Australian, had joined the staff of the W.A. museum in 1896. Here he became a senior geological assistant and had been involved in numerous field trips. He had left the museum to organize this expedition now to explore the country and wild life between Cambridge Gulf and the Drysdale River. Other members of his party were Lachlan Burns, W. T. Collison, J. Wilson, J. Murray Prior and two Aborigines[2].

M.P. saw his return to Argyle at this time as being of special significance for, apart from introducing a son to his heritage, he was travelling in a convoy of three buggies with not only four men but four women. He went ahead with Bess and the baby. Next came Ambrose with Nance Tiddy and Aunt Fan's third son, Neal Durack, who was then in some form of partnership with Bob Sexton of Bedford Downs. Then came the Ord River bookkeeper, Doug Moore, with his mother and sister who had recently arrived from England. Described by Bess as being of genteel breeding and very pleasant company, they had come out to see in what antipodean backwater their boy was hiding himself. Doug, in his latter-day memoirs, indicates that they found it unique and interesting if, in some respects, disconcerting.

> It didn't take long to show them Wyndham's places of interest. The tide in those days used to come right up the main and only street. I took them for a walk accompanied by my cattle dog, Bluey. My sister threw a stick into the water for him to fetch but he had no sooner jumped in than he was clamped in the hungry jaws of a crocodile and that was the end of him . . .
>
> We set out from Wyndham with the Duracks, we three Moores bringing up the rear—two mules in the pole and two horses in the lead, the Aboriginal boys following with our extra horses. M.P.D. and Ambrose would have the billy boiling by the time we reached our various stopping stages . . .

On the four-day journey to Argyle, they stopped off at Ascot and Ivanhoe, where M.P. rode around several mobs of Wyndham-bound cattle. He devoted much of his diary space to his son's progress and behaviour:

> 29.4.11: The young man has been very contented all day and in fact appears to be interested in the means of transmission. He likes to watch the horses as we go along and enjoys the motion of the buggy. He put in his first night camped out in the wilds of Australia under the Boab tree where, some 25 years previously, his father camped, about August 1886 when our teams first made the track from Argyle to Wyndham[3].

As usual M.P. expressed relief when they were safely 'over the hill', which meant that they had negotiated the precipitous descent of Durack's Folly. On this occasion Bess, who had previously ridden beside him all the way, insisted on descending by foot, carrying the baby. 'Before,' she later explained to us, 'there were just the two of us and if anything had happened we might as well have gone together. Now we were responsible for another life and I was not prepared to risk it.'

M.P. was shocked, on arrival at Argyle, to find work on the house not yet completed and everything 'in a state of disorder', but he now knew that household contingencies could daunt his Bess no more than they had his mother and other female relatives. Whether it was organizing meals and beds for unexpected visitors so that they would feel welcome and relaxed, or making semi-literate bushmen feel as at home as those of obviously superior education, she took it all in her cheerful stride. On this occasion, with Nance Tiddy's capable assistance, it was a simple and happy exercise.

Among the many callers at that time, besides the Moore family who stayed for several days, was Frederick Booty of Lambo, recently returned from a visit to his relatives in Melbourne. While there he had called on M.P.'s sister Bird, whose beauty-parlour activities should, he thought, be extremely lucrative if they were as effective with her clients as they were with herself. Also staying at Argyle during that month was Will Byrne of Brock's Creek, with 290 head of draught horses for C.D. & D. and the present of a pedigree mare and foal for Reginald Wyndham. M.P. saw him away, accompanied by his five Aboriginal stockmen and Boxer, of Argyle, who said he needed a holiday and would rather spend it with his old mate Byrne than anyone else.

Among passers-by of whom one would like to have heard more was an unnamed wayfarer described as 'a footman who had jumped the ship *Viking* and turned up with an Aboriginal woman who had followed him from Cockatoo Spring'.

By this time a cable from Connor had advised that the port of Manila was again open to North Australian cattle and that Lichauco was anxious for shipments to begin as soon as possible. This meant a lot of hard riding for M.P. and his staff, and the daily diary entries fairly vibrate with their excited activity. C.D. & D. would seem, as before, to have had the wholehearted co-operation of the surrounding landholders, with whom M.P. began briskly negotiating numbers, prices, and delivery dates.

Much of their buoyant spirit rubbed off on the station Aborigines as they rode around the cattle and to and fro with urgent messages. The fact that 'Umpy', otherwise *Ngirragull* or *Goorung* ('Big fella boss belong allabout') had now not only acquired a wife but a son was apparently a matter of genuine significance to them. It was no doubt seen as indicating that the people who had taken over their tribal lands and disrupted their way of life were, after all, to have descendants to whom they could relate and in whom they could continue to find security in their changed world.

M.P. had been saddened to learn in May that year of the death of his old friend W. F. Buchanan, brother of the legendary Nat, otherwise 'Old Bluey', who had died ten years before[4]. It came as a pleasant surprise, however, to find that the executors of Buchanan's estate had given C.D. & D. the option of 2,500 bullocks from Wave Hill Station, with the promise of a further option for the following year.

Young Patsy Durack's situation at the Dunham had developed complications during M.P.'s absence. Most of the cattle that had been shifted to better pastures nearer the market had quietly moved back to their familiar haunts during the wet season. The job of mustering them up again, which Patsy would normally have taken in his stride, had been interrupted by an unexpected turn of events.

Early in January a worried Aboriginal had arrived at the Dunham to report that John Winn, owner of the neighbouring property (known sometimes as Ellen Vale and at others as Liahwan or simply Old Hessian Station) had been laid low by a sickness that looked somewhat worse than the familiar Kimberley fever. Winn was an Irishman who had run his property with the help of a few Aborigines and who had been on friendly terms with his Dunham neighbour.

Patsy had set out at once in the station dray and brought the sick man back with him. Nursed by Lillas and her sister, he lingered for a few weeks, asking repeatedly that they sing him 'The Dear Little Shamrock'. He died, as it happened, on the birthday of M.P.'s son and heir, an event of which the old man had hoped to hear. That he willed his property to Patsy and Lillas proved a somewhat mixed blessing, as part of the legacy was a debt of £800 for goods purchased at C.D. & D.'s Wyndham store. It also meant that Patsy would have either to employ a manager to run the place or somehow look after it and the Dunham himself.

He circulated the information that this 'excellent' property was up for sale, but when no bidders came forward despite his 'bargain price', he arranged with M.P. for C.D. & D. to take over a half-share of Ellen Vale as payment for the debt. Having agreed to manage this property instead of the Dunham for £250 a year, he proceeded to pack up and move out with what he called (in a letter to M.P.) his 'fowls, donkeys, ducks, dogs, cats, goats, poddy calves and other things too numerous to mention, including wife, sister-in-law and a few Aboriginal retainers'. The Dunham was left to look after itself, except for being mustered at intervals of its persistently returning stock.

The *Junee* had been chartered for the first shipment to Manila of that year and M.P. reports being in Wyndham to see the cattle away.

> 20.7.11: Lichauco's inspector, Dionisio, is on the scene again, this time operating with an associate named—appropriately in the circumstances—Resurecion!
>
> Started shipping about 11 last night. Six head of horses, 569 bullocks—a good lot mostly from Rosewood and Lissadell. Finished

up 2 a.m., after which the Captain lets go and they are on their way.

And so begins another attempt at the Manila trade to be hoped this time luckier than the last.

On board the *Junee* is young Frank Connor from Fremantle, to join his parents in Manila.

It was not, of course, to be plain sailing, for no sooner had one difficulty been resolved than another arose. When the reopening of the Manila trade had been confirmed, Connor decided to establish a base in the Philippines, commuting south occasionally to maintain his parliamentary position. He had now been joined by his two elder sons and his wife, who had left the younger children in charge of Elodie Pombard at their Fremantle home.

Connor had written enthusiastically on arrival of the July shipment saying that the quality of the cattle had made such a good impression that Lichauco had had no hesitation in doubling the numbers required. He had therefore arranged for two ships to run continuously throughout the year, including the wet season. M.P.'s reaction to this information was conveyed in a letter to Perth office.

> I received notification by special messenger that Lichauco had chartered the *Germanica* and I must arrange to load her at once. When endeavouring to meet this contingency I get another message stating that Lichauco won't send the *Germanica* after all as it is going to Saigon. I might say I received this second cable with considerable relief as M.J. has now reneged on the numbers guaranteed earlier in the year being under the impression that the price will soon be raised and that it would be wise to hold off.
>
> Apart from this, to keep two ships going from November to March was outside all consideration under conditions that prevail at that time of year. I cannot understand how any member of our firm could entertain the idea. It could only have ended in dissatisfaction to both parties—if not disaster.
>
> It is only by keeping a certain number of cattle in reserve at Mantinea and Ascot that I see any prospect of keeping the *Macduff* going through the wet . . . [M.P.D., Wyndham, to J.W.D., Perth, 22.8.11]

Correspondence at this stage indicates something of a breakdown in communication between Connor and his partners. There is, in fact, more than a hint of acrimony in their exchange. Connor complained of a failure to co-operate with his proposals and a lack of appreciation of the successful efforts he had made on behalf of the company. In reply to J.W.'s request that he take a more realistic view of the difficulties arising from contradictory cables and contracts to ship cattle throughout the wet season, he wrote somewhat sarcastically:

> I hope your own intelligence has grasped the situation before now and that you will understand they were *not* silly cables. I just happened to know why I sent them and you did not. I am not so ignorant of the seasons as you would imply. I know when it's summer or winter both climatically and financially . . .
>
> I am trying to follow your letter but there are so many big words . . .
>
> I formally accept your protest and I am not in the least bit annoyed. But when you say you are disgusted to find how frail a thing human friendship can be I begin to think hard. Personally—well you are a most lovable disposition and you know that I know that nothing you have written will ever stand between our friendship . . .
>
> I hope Fegan [Bank Manager] is now satisfied that his securities are quite good and that the freeholds the Bank possesses are worth the overdraft. All the same, if you can sell Wagin and the Kimberleys my advice is to do so and come to the Philippines. There's more wealth going begging up here for anyone with capital and energy than anywhere else in the world and there are no parliamentary ins and outs to be depending on as in Australia.
>
> You mention our position in London being unsatisfactory. Well, I am in happy ignorance of what that position is. Of course I know we lost a lot at the end of the fur season. Did we also lose money on wool and skins?
>
> Many thanks for your reference to my household there. I hope you continue to see Elodie and the children frequently.
>
> Frank and Hugh are studying Spanish and getting on well here. Mother's education was completed before she left Australia and she is quite a little centre of her own here. She is now called 'The New Director of Agriculture' . . .
>
> If you come over here I can promise to fix you up with a rich and handsome Mestizo—either Spanish or Chinese cross. You takes your choice and you have the money. [F.C., Manila, to J.W.D., Perth, 27.9.11]

This letter was in transit when M.P. wrote to J.W.:

> ... A cable from Manila just received—*Macduff* arriving 5th October. Very important you give Lichauco best available cattle in view Saigon competition.
>
> Why this cable? Of course we give the best we can secure under our purchases. I have already advised Connor that he must be prepared to accept them as they come ... [M.P.D., Wyndham, to J.W.D., Perth, 28.9.11]

M.P. was even more put out when the *Macduff* did not, after all, arrive to schedule.

> This again has quite upset my programme and thrown all my fixed dates right out. I have had plants of men holding cattle out at Mantinea ever since. This of course means a lot more expense and gives us a lot of anxiety at this end, but I suppose it must continue to occur until things get properly straightened out.
>
> Connor talks a lot about his worries up in Manila but if he has worries there they are of his own making. All we want is a straight out sale for our cattle in a ready market—not this complicated game, the expensive assistance of solicitors to interpret in Spanish such legal phrases as 'first part' and 'second part' etc., and to unravel side-issues re slaughter for religious communities.
>
> The worries of which Connor complains would seem to be of his own making. I have not only those of my own making to attend to and adjust but many that are not of my making—whether it be at Argyle, on the way down or here in Wyndham. Arriving at the stud the other day I find the whole country ablaze—fire sweeping through the horse paddock and destroying much of the fencing. Not a soul at the house but Mrs McCaully and the two gins, so have to set to with the boys I have with me to save what little grass is left. Of course nobody ever sets fire to the country and everyone is quite certain it didn't originate from *his* camp.
>
> Well, I get to Ascot and there is more worry. The blacks are said to be killing up in Cragie's Gorge and generally chasing the cattle we hoped to have in good condition for the next shipment.
>
> I get to Wyndham and here are more worries. West [Manager C.D. & D. Wyndham Store] has been arrested and sends in his resignation. It is a most diabolical thing that a man can be liable

> to arrest on the words of any Tom, Dick or Harry who might make a charge against him—in this case a drunken boatswain who alleges that West stole his box of goods. I am dealing with the matter with the support of our Dr/Magistrate who also considers it disgraceful.
>
> At the same time our Hotel Manager, Thorn, is up before the Court on a charge of keeping a disorderly house. This arose over a squabble in the bar between Mick Walsh and Flinders who got into 'holts' in the bar. Flinders bore evidence of assault in two beautiful black eyes. Walsh pleaded 'guilty under provocation' but did not quite prove how he was provoked. Flinders pleaded 'not guilty of provoking' but did not quite prove it either. They were fined £1 each to keep the peace for six months. Thorn's case was dismissed. He is a very good man and the place is probably better run than it has been for years, but it is nevertheless an everlasting worry ... [M.P.D., Wyndham, to P.B.D., Wagin, 3.10.11]

A letter from M.P. to Connor at about this time gives yet another example of the poor communication between the partners:

> With reference to the horses recently despatched to you. Your cable intimated that you wanted them for the working of stock and my selection was made with this in mind rather than with a view to the Manila horse market ... I was disappointed to hear that the horses landed in such a wretched condition for they were direct off the pasture. They had not been ridden for months and were in excellent shape. The state in which they arrived must therefore have been due to conditions on the voyage to Manila.
>
> When the ship got in today I was greeted by the Captain and one of our cattle men with a repetition of the anathemas you hurled upon my head for sending these horses. You may write me what you like, Connor, but pray don't hold me up to the obloquy of the 'hoi polloi' ... [M.P.D., Wyndham, to F.C., Manila, 12.8.11]

It is hardly to be wondered that M.P. suffered a 'giddy turn' when helping to muster the scattered stock back into the Ascot paddock.

Affairs at a personal level ran on, meanwhile, more normally. The budding romance between Ambrose and Nance Tiddy had been observed with considerable interest, and progress reports were widely circulated.

Ambrose was apparently unaware of this and hoped to surprise the community on receipt of an engagement ring for which he had written to

J.W.: 'Don't get a shock old man, when I ask you to make this purchase on my behalf and charge it to my account. Enclosed pattern and size . . .'

For members of the family the shock had been cushioned some time before by letters from M.P.

> Ambrose is very well, and by the way, would seem to have fallen victim to Nurse's charms. They go riding together and enjoy long walks in the moonlight . . .

In his diary of 20 September he makes note of the engagement:

> Ambrose receiving congratulations on the conquest whereby he and Nance Tiddy agree to share the same foot mat.

Nance returned to Adelaide in mid-December, her plans for marriage dependent on the outcome of a number of ideas Ambrose was eager to investigate. Much as he was attached to his life in Kimberley, he was doubtful of its suitability as a permanent home for his wife-to-be. Further to substantiate M.J.'s contention that the north was no place for white women, was the fact of Doug Moore's mother having died of fever at Ord River only a few months after her arrival. She was buried in the station cemetery and her sorrowing daughter had since returned to England.

Both Nance and Bess had suffered attacks of fever throughout the year and were feeling the heat, noted on the day of Nance's departure as being 110°. It was little wonder that young Reg was by this time a victim of prickly heat, had gone off his food, and was inclined to be fretful.

J.W. was now urging his brother to take a trip to Manila with his family, not only for a change of air but to discuss with Connor the difficulties under which they were operating and which he still seemed unable to accept. Somehow M.P. had organized 3,000 head of cattle into the Ascot holding paddocks near the port, but this had been at considerable cost. His stockmen were now protesting against the working conditions encountered at that time of year, even the dependable Bill Jones declaring that after getting the next mob to Ascot early in December he intended handing in his resignation. Fortunately for the company he seems to have settled for taking a short holiday instead.

Roy Phillipps, in a letter to his mother, reported more brightly on the situation.

> The wet season is setting in in earnest now but we are going to ship all through the wet as we have about 3,000 bullocks in the

> Ascot paddocks only about 20 miles out so they are nice and handy.
>
> There is a young American chap here—son of Major Hartigan, the biggest solicitor in Manila. He is a great chap—about my age. Frank Connor sent him over to get some experience as they are thinking of stocking some of the Philippine Islands with Australian stock. He is going back to Manila in February as the Carnival of Flowers is on then. He says it's like the Battle of Flowers in Florence and Rome. Everyone goes masked till 11 p.m . . . It sounds exciting, does it not?

What to do with young Hartigan would seem, from the following letter, to have presented just another problem for M.P.

> . . . It gave me pleasure to make the acquaintance of the son of your friend Major Hartigan and I note what you say about the object of his stay in acquiring the practical knowledge essential to the management of a stock proposition in the Philippines . . . You say in your letter 'pay him as much as you think him worth'. Well, Connor, from a practical point of view these young chaps are really worth nothing whatever. In fact it takes twelve months before they get into the swing of things here and in most cases they think they know as much as the man who has been at it all his life. From a social point of view I will make things as agreeable for him as possible and we can organize the quid pro quo later on. He accompanies me to Argyle today. [M.P.D., Wyndham, to F.C., Manila, 1.11.11]

Of M.P.'s sudden decision to board the cattle ship *Kenkon Maru* he reports briefly:

> 23.12.11: Not a line from Connor, to my surprise, in answer to my last. After a wretched night (heat and mosquitoes) decide to go up as J.W. suggests. Loaded 502 bullocks and 97 cows in conditions of heavy rain and strong winds. Got aboard, with Bess, Reg and a milking goat at 7 a.m., and away—not envying the Wyndham people their next few weeks.
>
> The Captain of this ship is Japanese. Our waiter, Japanese from Yokohama, fanning away the flies as we breakfasted.

M.P., wife and baby were the only passengers, and no Christmas fare was served as the *Kenkon Maru* forged her way to the Philippines through gale-force winds and heavy seas. M.P. could, however, comment optimistically enough on their progress. The young fellow's rash had cleared up within a few days. He was taking his food (presumably supplied by the milking goat), better than he had for the previous few months and had made firm friends with the Japanese captain and steward.

On New Year's Day they were met by Frank Connor, and immediately plunged into the social and business involvements of the Philippines. There were elaborate luncheons and dinners at the Army and Navy Club, the Manila Club, the Hotel Metropole and the homes of business associates. M.P. found it 'quite a treat to be in civilization again'. Within a week he had resolved several pressing problems in apparently friendly discussion with Connor, Lichauco and the solicitor, Major Hartigan. The shipping, owing to signed commtments, would have to be continued over the current wet season but it seemed understood that a more realistic view must be taken in future. Furthermore, conditions of shipment that M.P. had recently been able to observe at first hand were to be improved. The heavy mortality that had been attributed to an outbreak of pleuro en route was due, he explained, to conditions of shipment under which too many of the overcrowded and untethered beasts were knocked down and fatally injured.

On this subject he reported critically to the Perth office.

> The cattle got bad treatment on the way over—they had little to eat and quite a number of them had nothing to drink after leaving Wyndham. The Filipinos looking after them don't seem to understand the basic requirements and the cattle were in such a state when they arrived that they appeared too stupid to get off the ship and up the race. They are loaded on to big floating barges, towed to a landing jetty and then run ashore into yards equipped with feeding sheds.
>
> I am confident, however that facilities for the handling of stock are to be immediately improved and that the prospects for the satisfactory continuation of business with Manila are very encouraging. [M.P.D., Manila, to C.D. & D., Perth, 23.1.12]

Urgent business necessitated M.P.'s returning to Wyndham by the next ship, but he insisted, with Connor's support, that Bess and the baby should spend the summer months out of reach of fever-carrying mosquitoes, in the exotic luxury of the Connors' Manila home.

28

Contentious Issues

January 1912–January 1913

Whether or not M.P. had by this time won his argument against shipping cattle throughout the wet season, the complaining mobs were still making in with their equally complaining drovers. At the time of his return to Wyndham, Bill Jones with Connor's protégé, Len Hartigan, had just arrived at Ascot with 1,204 head from Victoria River Downs. Roy Phillipps wrote to his mother that he and M.P. had ridden out to meet them.

> ... they certainly had marvellous luck for the day they got into the paddock it rained sixteen inches at Ascot. Parry's Creek became a torrent, flooding the plains to a depth of about five feet and all the rivers were swims ...
>
> Next evening we were attacked by myriads of flying ants which crawl all over you and leave their wings behind. Anywhere there is a light is soon about two inches deep in wings. This is not exaggeration. It's a fact ...

To this I can testify from personal experience, for even in the 1930s the days of fly-wire and insecticide still lay ahead for Kimberley. Not only flying ants but winged creatures of countless varieties, from beetles to bats, flocked to the light of every candle or kerosene lamp.

It would have been interesting to hear young Hartigan's version of his few months in North Australia, although he could hardly have found a better companion and informant on local conditions, prospects and personalities than Bill Jones. M.P. reports soon afterwards that he thought Hartigan had had quite enough of the Australian tropics and a lifestyle that could hardly have been congenial to one of his background and tastes. He was to return to Manila by the next ship, taking with him, along with a few curios, a repertoire of extraordinary anecdotes on which he could no doubt dine out for a considerable time.

M.P., missing his wife and little son but relieved that they were spared the rigours of this exceptionally torrid 'wet', remained based in Wyndham to see the mobs away while he kept in touch with the various station outposts through his Aboriginal messengers. Since Boxer, Ulysses and Big Pompey were indispensable in the Argyle and Ivanhoe stockcamps, the couriers were mainly three other well-known characters, Jabiroo, Fred and Billy Barlow. Sometimes M.P. recorded their having been held up by flooded rivers, strong swimmers though they were and with horses trained to tackle almost anything. This was a great source of concern for to be the bearer of a 'letter stick' or message was, in tribal tradition, a sacred trust.

An event the Wyndham residents looked forward to at that time was the arrival, at regular intervals, of the *Koombana* from Fremantle, for of all the ships then on the coastal run, this, with her hospitable captain and friendly crew, was the most popular. For Roy Phillipps her comings and goings were something to write about when news was otherwise so scarce. On 22 February 1912, he reported in his breezy style:

> Everything in the doldrums the last few weeks but people are all coming in for the *Koombana* now ... Patsy Durack and his wife arrived last night and Lillas will leave for South on Saturday. She has the same affliction as assails most newly weds and Patsy will be buying fizz to celebrate in a month or so. Her sister, Nellie, came in with them and is to marry Jack Martin, Manager of Ascot, on the day the boat sails.

M.P. was pleased at the prospect of parenthood for the young couple and also that his Aunt Fan now had a home in the south in which to welcome the mother-to-be. His main concern at that time was for his cousin Ambrose, whose frequent attacks of fever had so undermined his constitution that, in Dr Parer's opinion, he would be lucky to live another six months if he did not get away, for a time at least. Ambrose himself had hesitated to request an extended holiday, knowing the pressures that beset M.P. owing to a shortage of skilled men. It was now, however, at M.P.'s urging that he set off for Queensland to see his folks and to give serious thought either to getting a place of his own or to undertaking the management of a property in a more congenial locality. M.P. knew that Ambrose had had this in mind since becoming engaged, and now hastened to assure him that, much as his services and his companionship would be missed, his well-being must come first. Bill Jones had agreed to take over at Argyle on the understanding that if Ambrose did not wish to return within six to twelve months, the job would be his permanently.

As it happened, it took Ambrose no more than two months to decide that Kimberley was, after all, the best place for himself and his bride-to-be. This decision was no doubt due in part to the magnetic influence the north imposed on so many who identified with the area. His choice was rendered possible, however, by the results of a potion prescribed for him in Darwin on his way to Queensland. This was 'Dr Strangman's fever mixture', the main ingredients of which would seem to have been quinine, spirits of nitre and epsom salts, and which he and the Argyle store-room were never afterwards to be without.

While in Queensland visiting his family he made at least token investigations of prospects in the vicinity of Innisfail, Cairns, Townsville, and Charters Towers, but nothing there really tempted him. Back in Darwin awaiting a Wyndham-bound ship, he met the superintendent of a training centre for Aboriginal boys for whom he was anxious to find jobs. Ambrose, having expressed polite interest, was asked whether he could employ any of the boys at Argyle. When looking over a line-up of young people he caught the wistful gaze of a twelve-year-old named Johnnie Walker, who in time to come was to give me his own version of this encounter. He was born on Adelaide River of a white man and an Aboriginal woman, and some time before had fallen off a railway bridge and staked his head. Though not expected to survive, he had been taken by train to the Darwin Hospital. There he recovered, but in order to be kept under medical supervision was taken in at the training centre which he described as 'a kind of a half school'. He had not been happy there and had made several unsuccessful attempts to return to his family. The superintendent tried to interest Ambrose in several older boys who had been giving him trouble. Johnnie Walker's tape-recorded version of the story continues as follows:

> Ambrose looks up and down and shakes his head. Then he looks back again and points at me. 'All right,' he says, 'I'll have that little fellow over there.' They try to talk him out of it—reckon I'll only run away—clear out on him. They tell him about that accident—show him the scar, like I still got here—you know. But Ambrose make up his mind about me, like I make up my mind about him.

It was eventually agreed, at the boy's own suggestion, that Ambrose should take not only himself but his best mate, a full-blood Aboriginal named Albert.

Ambrose records in his diary how before boarding the Wyndham-bound vessel he had called on the noted anthropologist, Professor Baldwin Spencer, who had recently been appointed Chief Protector of Aborigines for the Commonwealth and was at that time in Darwin. The reason for this visit had been to assure the Protector that he would do his best to look after the boys in his charge and to train them as stockmen and general handymen. In this regard, on Johnny Walker's forthright testimony, he proved to be as good as his word.

During Johnnie's latter years on the Kununurra reserve, I translated his rambling memoirs into equally rambling verse:

It was more than fifty years ago,
Or sixty pretty near,
When Ambrose Durack picked me up
And brought me over here.
Oh, he grew me up a stockman
And he taught me how to ride
And life was mighty good the days
I travelled at his side . . .
Now I'm here in Kununurra
For there's no place left to see
That was not a long way better
How it used to be,
When we rode the fastest horses
And we threw the wildest steers
And the sound of moving cattle
Was always in our ears.
There was good times and hard times
But everywhere I'd go
They'd know that smart young stockman
Johnnie Walker-oh . . .

Much had happened during Ambrose's absence, the most memorable incident being the sinking of the *Koombana* with all hands on board in a cyclone off Port Hedland on 22 March. This disaster had a profound effect on the Kimberley people, as the 150 passengers were for the most part well-known residents returning to Broome, Derby, or Wyndham. The sinking of the *Titanic* at much the same time, though on a comparatively greater scale, lacked the personal impact of the *Koombana* tragedy in this part of the world.

Roy Phillipps wrote of it in April 1912:

> What a terrible thing, the loss of the *Koombana*—hard to believe or realise. All the chaps on her were so well-known to us. The officers on the *Moira* told us they have never been in such a storm as raged at that time. The waves came right over the cattle fittings on the top deck . . .

Doug Moore of Ord River station recalled the event in his memoirs.

> The tragedy of the *Koombana* was unforgettable. One time when I travelled on her to Wyndham we were shipping about 200 tons of railway lines to Hedland. They were then building the line to Marble bar. Just before reaching Hedland we struck a squall and the ship keeled over at an angle of 45 degrees and was quite a long time straightening up. Johnnie Rees, the skipper, said: 'There's no loading going off at Hedland. We'll hang on to those rails for ballast and drop them off coming back.'
>
> Not only the Captain but Clarke, the Chief Mate, and McDonald, Chief Engineer, all sensed that the ship was top heavy. Fortunately for them they had left that vessel by the time she capsized. She was a beautiful ship but not suitable for this cyclonic coast . . .
>
> A number of fine Kimberley people went down on her—among them George Piper, Manager of Go-Go, Mrs Sack, mother of all the Sacks in the country at that time, and all the shearers who were coming to West Kimberley.[1]

During this time M.P. had gone again to Manila, to return within a few weeks with his wife and son. With them had come Mr and Mrs Frank Connor, whose sojourn in Wyndham enlivened the local scene as nothing else had done for a considerable time. Connor, then on his way to Fremantle for a parliamentary session, and anxious to assure the constituents of his province that he was serving their interests in the Philippines, threw a dinner at the Wyndham Hotel. This was attended by thirty-one guests and was reported by M.P. as having passed off 'very sociably, ending up with a dance'.

Roy Phillipps wrote to his mother of this event, concluding with typical optimism:

> I got into Mr Connor's good books right away. He says he will take me to Manila in six to twelve months. There are plenty of new ventures on the programme up there and if I do go the old future should be pretty well assured.
>
> According to Connor things are really on the move now. Lichauco, the cattle king, has bought the *Kolya* from the Adelaide Steamship Company and it will run from here to Manila with our cattle . . .

The enterprise in which Connor had foreseen a job for Phillipps was that of transporting breeding cattle to island pastures—the same project for which young Hartigan had come in search of practical experience. It was probably with this in mind that Phillipps accepted M.P.'s offer of a job as bookkeeper and part-time stockman at Argyle. This, as his letters testify, was a novel situation for the high-spirited young man.

> Bill Jones is in charge of the camp here at present. He's a long, thin streak but a very interesting man. He was manager of Buckabunda Station near Moree and lived in the Gwydir district until 1892. You should just hear the yarns he can spin . . .
>
> I live in the house here—a bonza stone building—and live like a king—fresh eggs, cream, milk from both cows and goats, custards made from about fifteen eggs. We have a Chinese cook and gardener, and talk about vegetables! It's wonderful after Wyndham . . .
>
> The scenery is too gorgeous and grand to describe. I doubt if the novelty will ever wear off . . .
>
> I don't know whether there is anything American in my make-up, but I seem to feel a terrible force of push and impatience inside me. You would be surprised at the heights to which my castles rise as I ride along in solitude, dreaming of the day when I shall have a social position second to none and plenty of that necessary attribute—money. My hands tremble and I kick the horse along thinking I am riding my ambition until the horse stumbles and brings me back to earth . . .
>
> Well, I haven't been here long but I can cut a calf or a colt, ride a buckjumper, break in and handle a horse with the best of them.
>
> Rot, Phillipps. Shut up! . . .

As time went on, however, the novelty did begin to pall and he wrote less enthusiastically. His chances of the job in Manila had also begun to fade as rumour had it that Connor's idea of raising cattle there had been 'quashed by the American Government which is jealous of outsiders getting control of the pastoral lands!'

But this had been only one of the many avenues in which Connor foresaw intriguing developments on which he had, while in Wyndham, expounded at length to M.P. It is clear that these discussions were inclined to trigger off contentious issues of long standing. The two men were good enough friends and enjoyed each other's company on a social level but there was a stage at which their relationship obviously became competitive.

> 3.4.12: Wyndham. Rode out with Connor to inspect 571 bullocks being yarded for the *Kenkon*. Spent the rest of the day discussing with him business in general. Told him that the present position could not continue and that I fully intended pulling out if the petty subject regarding our respective merits were not entirely put aside . . .

This referred not only to the question of whether M.P.'s position as general manager in Western Australia, or Connor's as company representative in the Philippines entailed the more work and responsibility, but also to financial issues of more recent vintage. Connor insisted that the results of his activity in the Philippines fully justified his escalating expense accounts and that he was well entitled to a commission of 15s a head on cattle sold to Lichauco through the company. M.P. wrote of this to the Perth office:

> My contention is that Connor, as our direct representative and paid agent sent over by our company could not justifiably make this deduction. Connor contends that the remuneration he and the rest of us get is merely a 'Dividend Bonus'.
>
> Then there is the question of the sum being paid Connor on behalf of the Lichauco Cold Storage and which he contends has nothing to do with our company . . .
>
> I maintained that he could not enter into any enterprise that might compromise our company. He asserts that his action cannot do this and that there is nothing in the articles which prevents his embarking on any outside business. In this he may be right but the question can only be resolved at a general meeting in Perth. I have no doubt that when we get together things will be adjusted to everyone's satisfaction . . . (M.P.D., Wyndham, to C.D. & D., Perth, 20.1.12)

It was with this meeting in view that M.P. set off for Fremantle in the middle of the year. The result of these discussions is referred to in his diary:

> 20.6.12: Our General Meeting terminates today having settled everything, as far as possible, for some twelve months . . .

Among the many issues under review had been the effects of the last election in which the Wilson Government was defeated by Labor under the leadership of John Scaddan. This, as Connor had prophesied, had brought about a problem regarding the promised establishment of a freezing-works in East Kimberley, the contention now being that the growers in that area had sufficient outlets for their produce as things stood. The new Cabinet declared itself more concerned about reducing the price of beef on the metropolitan market, which they saw as being manipulated to their own ends by the 'beef barons of the meat ring'. The Government, by entering into the wholesale butchering business, had already managed to reduce the price of beef to the public by about 2d a pound, but the enterprise was already seen to be running at a loss and, as might be argued, at the taxpayers' expense. It was now proposed to tackle the problem from another angle, and try to reduce the cost of freight by establishing a State-run shipping service in place of the Adelaide Steamship Co and the Blue Funnel Line, which were then in control of trade on the north-west coast.

The C.D. & D. partners were of the opinion that this enterprise was beyond the State's resources and that the idea would soon be abandoned. Nor were they greatly perturbed by rumours, then beginning to circulate, that the American Beef Trust was planning to move into East Kimberley and the Northern Territory with a view to developing its own canning- and freezing-works. This organization was reported to the Legislative Council as being 'a danger of great magnitude, composed of a few American brigands who had cornered 31 per cent of the mutton and 46 per cent of the beef exports from Argentina'.

Connor maintained that this might even be a good thing for North Australia as increased competition would be an advantage to the growers. His public statement to this effect was soon afterwards taken up in a forceful article in the Sydney *Bulletin* of 24 October 1912:

> Up to date the Beef Trust has full control of all the meat exporting countries with the exception of Australia and Maoriland. Let them once collar Australasia and the British meat market is theirs. The Trust bosses will be able to fix the price of meat daily in London. And Connor, M.L.C., and Cattle King can't see that this would hurt anybody.

Connor's defence of the Beef Trust's reported interest in North Australia was probably a reaction to the State's having abandoned the idea of establishing a meatworks in Wyndham after so many years of promises and vacillation. He proposed at the company meeting that, in view of the mounting prejudice and political pressures, they should make further efforts to sell their northern properties and invest their money elsewhere—possibly in the Philippines, where he saw so many promising and lucrative openings. Whether or not his partners agreed with him in this, they at least raised no objection to his proposing to the State Government that, in view of its current policy of involvement in the meat trade, it should consider the purchase of the C.D. & D. properties on the basis of £2 10s per head for an estimated 50,000 head of stud cattle and 1,400 head of horses.

This proposition, which Connor was to lose no time in presenting, was acknowledged with expressions of guarded interest and the request that the offer be made in writing.

M.P.'s record of the company meeting, chaired by Connor, concluded with reference to a more personal item on the agenda.

> We enter our protest against the retention of certain monies out of our Manila contracts. I move a resolution which Connor refuses to put as it was a reflection on himself. It is not seconded but protest is entered in another form.

This would seem to have resulted in a compromise being reached whereby Connor agreed to reduce his commission on cattle sold in the Philippines from fifteen to ten shillings per head. The diary entry concludes: 'We retire and have a drink at the Palace before the big family gathering at the Esplanade.'

This was a reference to a memorable family reunion, for which J.W. had devised a special menu complete with picture of a mounted stockman and an appropriate snatch of ballad verse:

> 'Twas merry 'mid the blackwoods when we spied the station roofs,
> To wheel the wild scrub cattle at the yard.
> With a running fire of stockwhips and a fiery run of hoofs,
> Oh! the hardest day was never then too hard.

Eighteen members of the Durack family signed this memento and were to treasure it over the years to come. M.P. records it as being the first time in about thirty years that the Thylungra-reared family of four brothers and two sisters had been in one place at the same time. His sister, Bird, on hearing of Dermot's arrival from Allahabad, had hastened to join them from Melbourne, and when all six were assembled a photograph was taken to commemorate the reunion.

Among those at the dinner was Galway Jerry Durack's widow, Aunt Fan, then living in a little home with a big garden on Monger's Lake where she was raising poultry. With her for this occasion were her son Patsy and his wife, who were soon to return to the north without the eagerly awaited baby that had been, after all, stillborn[2].

During this time the brothers, sisters, and cousins moved about together from one event to another, including the races, the theatre, a Hunt Club meeting at Canning Bridge, a variety of charitable functions, and the horse sales where Dermot sought in vain for a likely polo pony. None of them, over this period, seems to have gone to bed before 1 a.m.

'The Duracks, however different in character,' my mother used to say, 'had at least one thing in common. They could all talk till the cows came home.' She would occasionally acknowledge, however, that in this respect her own family did not lag far behind. At such a reunion there was, of course, much ground to be covered, ranging from domestic issues and business concerns throughout Australia, to Dermot's version of contemporary India, the Connors' views on affairs in the Philippines, and the latest news from Denis Doherty in England.

M.P., with his wife and son, returned to Wyndham after a few packed weeks of business and social activities. He had hoped that Dermot might accompany them, to get at least some impression of the properties in which he was a shareholder. No doubt Dermot had been sadly tempted, especially since Bess was confident of his finding the polo pony of his dreams among the company stock horses, but his responsibilities were pressing and he dared not overstay his leave.

Bess, returning to the north, was already 'going home', as she had come to love the country, the people, and the station life. Her main base at this time was at Ivanhoe where Duncan McCaully and his wife were still in charge, though she often travelled with M.P. to Argyle and into Wyndham. Their son, meanwhile, having taken to his feet, had begun to express himself—even if in terms that seemed more intelligible to the Aborigines than to themselves.

By the end of the year when Bess sailed again from Wyndham, it was obvious to both black and white inhabitants that a second child was on the way. M.P. accompanied her to Fremantle on her way to Adelaide, but because of urgent company business was forced to return at once to Wyndham. As it happened he sailed north on the first voyage of the State Steamship *Western Australia*[3], of which his impressions, although no doubt prejudiced, were forthright to say the least. He described the ship as: 'An old, dirty-looking tub that gives one the impression that it has been a neglected vessel with a coat of paint put over it in a hurry . . .'

This was no doubt true for, as the C.D. & D. partners had suspected, the crippling cost to the government of securing ships for the transport of cattle from the north of the State could only be met by the purchase of old vessels never equipped for the transport of stock, but to be procured at comparatively cheap prices.

The new government venture began operations under considerable opposition from many north-western interests that had had long and satisfactory associations with other shipping companies. As M.P. predicted, stock losses, owing to unsuitable conditions, were at first fairly heavy, but facilities were gradually improved and in the process the cost of freight was, in fact, reduced. This proved in the long run to be of benefit to the vendors since it increased the price of cattle leaving Wyndham by 10s per head.

No one had then foreseen the coming of a world war which was to result in the withdrawal from the trade of the Adelaide Steamship Company. This would leave C.D. & D. with no option but to co-operate with the State Steamship Service, which had become, from my earliest memories, an indispensable fact of life.

M.P. returned, towards the end of 1912, to the familiar pattern of his bush life, once again in completely masculine company, mostly associates of many years. One name, however, that appears for the first time in his diary is that of Lake Hall, then manager of Lissadell. M.P. described him as 'an educated and interesting man with a wide experience of stock conditions throughout Australia'. It was, however, from the Aboriginal Merenji Daylight, who came with him on occasional visits to Argyle at this time, that I was to hear more of his story in years to come.

Daylight, born on Wave Hill Station in North Australia and a member of the Mudbura tribe, had become attached to Lake Hall from his earliest years. When about eight years old he had accompanied Hall from Borroloola in the Northern Territory to the Georgina River in Queensland with 2,000 head of cattle and a plant of twenty-two men. On arrival at their destination, Hall had been given the management of Glengyle Station on the Georgina where he had remained, with Daylight, for about six years. Hall had then sold his horses and gear and, with his Aboriginal companion, had set off by train for Adelaide. Here they stayed, as Daylight recalls, at 'a flash pub called the Black Bull in Hindley Street' which was owned by Hall's brother Tom. Daylight's memories of this period included his homesickness for the bush and his ecstatic encounters with several 'countrymen', two dingos, a python, and a kangaroo in the Adelaide zoo. It was in 1912 at the Black Bull that Lake Hall met M. J. Durack who, familiar with his reputation as a reliable man, offered him the management of Lissadell. With this prospect in mind, Hall and Daylight embarked for Fremantle and thence for Wyndham. Lissadell was to suit them both very well for a number of years. Daylight, for his part, had felt immediately at home in East Kimberley as had Johnnie Walker, with whom he had established a mateship that was to last for the rest of their lives. M.P.'s association with them both was also to be a more long-lasting one than he could then have imagined.

He and Ambrose, with Johnnie Walker and Alec as horse-tailers, saw in the New Year, 1913, on the road to Newry. M.P. took the conditions encountered too much for granted to make comment in his diary, but Roy Phillipps, writing at that time, tried to convey something of what wet season travel entailed.

> On New Year's Eve I left Argyle at sundown, to go to the Behn races, twenty two miles up river, near Lissadell Station. I couldn't leave 'til the last minute as Ambrose and M.P. have gone off tying up delivery dates and trying to settle a few local arguments and they left me in charge.
>
> I got to the Ord at 11 p.m.—black as ink, low, heavy clouds blotting out moon and stars. The river was a swim, creeping past dark and weird like the Styx. I expected any moment to hear a ghostly call from Charon himself. I shoved the two spare horses down the bank and into it.
>
> My horse Grady is a splendid swunmer and we made it easily enough. My boy however, was not so fortunate. He and his horse parted company midstream but both managed to climb out on the right side.
>
> Arrived at Lissadell just as the old year made his final bow. Had a nip and tumbled onto bed. It would be ridiculous to say 'into bed' with the temperature at 120° [Roy Phillipps to his mother, 12.1.13]

29

Between the City and the Bush

January–July 1913

Negotiations continued meanwhile between the company's bases in Australia and the Philippines. There was a constant adjustment of numbers, prices and dates of shipment, complicated to some extent by an increasing interplay of business tactics between Frank Connor and Faustino Lichauco.

M.P., when unable to go himself to Manila, commissioned the Wyndham agent and cattle-buyer W. R. Willesee to help straighten out the situation. Typical of these encounters is the one reported from Wyndham at the beginning of the year.

> 8.1.13: A chat with Willesee in my rooms. He informs me that Lichauco is willing to pay £5 per head for bullocks of 550 weight and to take 900 head per month.
>
> Willesee states that Connor will not close on these terms. He demands another 10/- commission which Lichauco refuses to pay. Willesee told Lichauco we made about 6/- per head. 'Oh', says Lichauco. 'C.D. & D. make 6/- per head. I make 8/- per head. Mr Connor makes 10/- per head for nothing but ride around in motor car with Kincaid and Hartigan.'

After a lively exchange of coded telegrams between Perth, Wyndham, and Manila, a new contract was drawn up safeguarding the respective rights and interests, and allowing for the separate sale of cattle for breeding purposes in the Philippines. There was no mention in this document of the contentious issue of Connor's commission, the 10s per head that he continued to draw having been arrived at by private arrangement with his company.

A clause was included to the effect that in case of dispute arising concerning the average weight of a consignment, a standard method of settlement would be resorted to. This was an interesting process in which fifty-one head were run off from the herd in question, whereupon representatives of buyer and seller selected in turn what they judged to be heaviest and lightest specimens. The remaining beast was killed and weighed and the result accepted as representing the average.

Confrontations on the Manila trading front, though sometimes acrimonious, were rational compared with those between local growers and the Government Stock Inspector named Young. The Inspector's version of the story would no doubt have shown him as a conscientious steward obstructed in his job by a band of unscrupulous would-be law-breakers. M.P. and his associates saw him as an officious nuisance. Wherever Young's name crops up in M.P.'s records the story is much the same:

> 17.1.13: . . . Called at the Three Mile to notify Inspector Young that Jack Martin cannot find the two bullocks said to be sick with pleuro and asks if Young will please come out to Ascot and show them to him. Inspector refuses to do so. Says he won't be ordered around. I then ask him to come out and show the bullocks to me. He says he has more important things to do.
> 23.5.13: . . . Met Young near Goose Hill, his gin sitting up in the buggy behind him and a cockatoo clinging to his shoulder. Asked to see the regulation by which he is holding cattle from a clean area. He said he would show me a copy if I went with him to Goose Hill. This I did but he failed to produce the evidence—said he had his own 'deliberate reasons' for his actions. On parting he asked me whether I know that I had been awarded the nick name 'Flash Mick' which he deems well chosen. Knowing him to have originated this pseudonym I congratulate him on his creative flair.

Roy Phillipps reports to his mother about the same time:

> The stock inspector is riding around on his high horse as usual, making almost everyone inoculate their cattle whether necessary or not and thereby blocking the mobs and messing up the shipping arrangements.
>
> All the incoming Victoria River bullocks are now blocked at the border of the Northern Territory for six weeks.

M.P. was relieved to take off for Fremantle early in the year, despite having to travel again by the State Steamship *Western Australia* on which he found conditions for the stock even worse than for the human passengers:

> 30.11.13: . . . The vessel is shockingly fitted up. Fyman states he can't get water for the cattle and not more than fifty have had a

> drink in the last 60 hours. I see the Captain and an attempt is now being made to carry water along in buckets.
> 1.2.13: General state of disorder. Mrs Parer complains of there being no water in the bath and is told that the silver is being cleaned and she must await the steward's pleasure. Meanwhile most of the stewards are playing cards in the smoke room.

After the usual pleasant reunions with family and friends in Perth, M.P. was away on the *Indarra* for Adelaide.

> 19.2.13: Met by Ted Johnstone at the wharf and off in his car to his comfortable home, Annandale. Bess and Reg happy and well. Bright flowers in the garden, grapes and nectarines flourishing.

On the following day he reported that Bess had entered Narma, a nearby nursing home, where a baby daughter was born at noon: 'No complications. Both bright and well.'

There followed the usual family conference regarding the child's name:

> Many suggestions forthcoming. Bess maintains that one name is enough for a girl to carry, she herself having been burdened with three. We remember sister Bird's request that the baby, if a girl, be named 'Mary'. This meets with the approval of the family on both sides. Dad Johnstone very pleased, his mother having been a Cornish woman named Mary (née Thomas).

For M.P. Adelaide was, as usual, a round of social and business activities. Lunching at the Adelaide Club with the President of the Legislative Council, Sir Lancelot Stirling[1], he discussed issues of interstate importance, including the influence of the American Meat Trust on the Australian cattle industry.

Of the stock sales which he attended with Sidney Kidman he writes:

> 10.3.13: Good prices ruling, one animal bringing £20—about 1100 lbs weight. This new business—the export of boned beef, has given a great philip to the industry, especially for the sale of indifferent stuff . . .
> 11.2.13: To the stock sales again and later shown over the Export Works, Port Adelaide, by McCann . . . Bone dust worth £4.10.0 per ton . . .
>
> Played cribbage with Dad Johnstone and billiards with Ted.

While in Perth a few weeks before, M.P. had discussed the situation of a northern meatworks with Sir Edward Wittenoom and they had arranged to meet in Melbourne to discuss the matter in appropriate circles. With this in view, he set off from Adelaide leaving his wife and children with the Johnstone family. Met at the train by his sister Bird, he embarked with Wittenoom on a series of interviews in relation to their cherished project.

It was only to be expected that the C.D. & D. partners, along with most of their Western Australian associates, should have seen Wyndham as the ideal site for a northern meatworks. Since the Commonwealth had assumed control of the Territory, however, this long-cherished dream seemed less likely to be fulfilled. They were now prepared to support the idea of a works in the Territory, preferably at Katherine, but definitely not in Darwin. The main reason for this proviso was that the track to the port was unsuitable for overlanding cattle, since it comprised at least 250 miles of inferior and tick-infested country.

M.P. and Sir Edward began their round by calling on people prominent in the meat industry who were then operating from Melbourne.

> 22.3.13: Wittenoom with me to meet Lord Whitburgh and his brother A. Borthwick at their offices. While they realise that there is a big prospect for a meatworks in North Australia, the difficulty of obtaining suitable labour in the tropics is one they do not care to face at present.
> 27.3.3: Met Joe Bradshaw this morning. We go along to Minister for External Affairs Mr Thomas accompanied by Mr Oswald. I suggest that the Commonwealth work in concert with our State Government in the erection of a meatworks in the Northern Territory.
> 27.3.13: With Wittenoom to call on Younghusband Row and Co. After lunch we meet Atlee Hunt and discuss the Territory with him.

Their next interview was with Dr J. A. Gilruth, a professor of veterinary science who had been appointed Commonwealth Administrator of the Northern Territory in April 1912. He had since set about a vigorous campaign for the establishment of agricultural, dairying and sheep-raising industries in the area, his wide-ranging plans including express train services, complete with branch lines, from Port Augusta to Darwin. He spoke eloquently of the pride he took in presiding over the dawn of a new era for a country of hitherto unrealised and inexhaustible resources.

M.P. admired his enthusiasm but was privately sceptical of the outcome of his more breath-taking schemes. He was confident, however, that as a man of genuine dedication to his task, Gilruth would be prepared to listen to experienced advice where the placing of a meatworks was concerned.

> 29.3.13: We explain the inconvenience of a Works being sited in Darwin. We ask that the question be regarded as a national one rather than the place being put up where it is bound to fail. Gilruth with some hesitancy says the Works *will* be put up in Darwin.

Despite this statement, M.P. and his friends left the interview feeling reasonably hopeful that the Administrator would give further consideration to their opinions. They were not to know that negotiations with Vestey Brothers for their takeover of large buildings in the Territory and the erection of a meatworks on a Darwin site were already in progress.[2]

M.P.'s evenings during this period were spent with Bird and Bess's relatives, the Davey family. One of Bird's closest Melbourne friends was Mrs Aeneas Gunn, of whose book, *We of the Never-Never*, M.P. had been somewhat more critical than the general public. He had known her late husband, a cousin of the colourful Joe Bradshaw who was also then in Melbourne and entering forthrightly into the current discussions. This was, however, M.P.'s first meeting with Jeannie Gunn, and he enjoyed talking with her of the characters she had portrayed. Among these was the legendary stockman 'Dan', of whose death on Ivanhoe station a year before she now heard for the first time.[3]

Back in Adelaide at last, M.P. found Bess, her sister Gert, Nance Tiddy, and the two children ready to return with him to the West. On arrival at Fremantle they sailed north without delay, travelling again by the *Western Australia* which M.P. reported as getting 'worse every trip'. The lights failed on the first night out, after which the passengers had recourse to candles and kerosene lamps. The standard of service and general cleanliness was 'appalling to say the least, fleas and bugs being much in evidence'. Wyndham, for all its shortcomings, was a welcome sight.

Ambrose was at the wharf to greet his fiancée, relatives and friends, including Father Bishoffs who had come from Broome to perform the marriage ceremony. This took place at the home of the hospitable Dr Parer and his wife within a few hours of the ship's arrival.

The bride and groom set forth next day after a rowdy send-off from the Three Mile Hotel, to be met at Argyle homestead with a joyous welcome from the Aborigines. Roy Phillipps was also delighted to greet the bride, and to relegate to her trained hands a number of health problems he had been trying to treat. Among these was one he had described to his mother not long before:

> Argyle, 21.4.13: While the musterers were away a nigger came in here with half a yard of spear in him ... The wound was over his shoulder blade but the spear head had worked down to his backbone over the ribs. It had been there a fortnight and the state of the wound can be imagined. Anyhow, I started on him with a good knife used for colts and a pair of splinter tweezers, some Condys and iodoform. I cut him about a bit but succeeded in getting the spear head out. I reckon he will die anyhow. It had been too long inside.

When Nance arrived she lost no time in applying linseed poultices to the wound, with apparent success. Her reputation was quick to spread and many, over her next ten years at Argyle, were to owe their lives to her healing skills.

M.P. was held up in Wyndham for ten days after his arrival, seeing mobs away, sending cables in all directions, and negotiating with drovers. His family was kept entertained meanwhile by old friends in Wyndham and new friends who had travelled north with them. Among these were Mr and Mrs Edward Angelo, well known throughout the north-west where Angelo was a pioneer of the banana-growing industry, a stock- and station-agent and, at that time, Mayor of Carnarvon. A genial character, generally known as 'Tubby', he was then intent on assessing the possibility of tropical agriculture in the Wyndham area, an interest in which he had been encouraged by glowing reports of Gilruth's experiments in the Territory. An investigation of the area seems to have dampened his enthusiasm and nothing came of whatever project he had in mind, but his visit sowed the seeds of a lifelong friendship between the Duracks and Angelos, and supplied the fodder for a seemingly endless succession of anecdotes that were to string on over the years but of which, unfortunately, I remember little but the laughter. No doubt one of these stories would have been of an incident of the time, briefly recorded in M.P.'s diary, concerning an encounter outside the Wyndham Hotel between Charles Edward Flinders and Inspector Young, both of whom prided themselves on their command of words. The result of this exchange was that Flinders, whom the onlookers judged to have won the ridiculous argument hands down, was issued with a summons for abusive language, fined £1, and required to apologize. Young refused to accept the written apology, popularly judged to be a literary masterpiece, whereupon it was withdrawn by the writer in language more abusive than that for which he had been fined. Despite Young's efforts to have the summons repeated, the case was declared closed.

Another fellow passenger to Wyndham at that time was the Anglican Bishop Gerard Trower[4], who had embarked on the ship at Broome to visit Forrest River Mission which, taken up in 1897, had been abandoned a few years later owing to the hostility of the Aboriginal tribespeople. A fresh start in the same locality had been made of recent months, and Bishop Trower was anxious to assess its possibilities. Delayed in getting away to the Mission by boat, he regaled the company with the story of his extraordinary life. London-born, Trower was an Oxford graduate and had been at one time Bishop of Likoma in Nyasaland. On arrival in Western Australia three years before, he had been appointed first Bishop of the North-West and his headquarters were then in the port of Broome.

My mother could recall to the end of her days an incident that he said was responsible for his entering the Church. This was a mountain-climbing accident that he claimed to have survived through an angel's somehow transferring him to a ledge of rock, from which he was seen and rescued from above.

Since Mrs McCaully, with her adopted daughter, Ina, was then on an extended visit to her family and her husband was mostly out in the stock camps, it was at the Ivanhoe homestead that M.P. now made a base for his wife and family. It suited Bess very well as she had always liked the raised bungalow with its wide verandahs. It overlooked the extensive billabong, a position deemed safer than one above the big, flood-prone river half a mile away. The kitchen and store, somewhat apart from the main house, were then in charge of a genial Chinese cook named Ah Sam, who also looked after the vegetable garden.

Dinah, who had come from Argyle with her husband Ulysses, attached herself to Bess and the children with the devotion she would display for the rest of her life. Other Aborigines to figure much in M.P.'s diaries of the time, either at Ivanhoe or moving to and fro between the stations, included Boxer, Tommy, Frying Pan, Toby, Jabiroo, Johnnie Walker, and Alec.

M.P. was seldom out of the saddle during this time, and at the pace he travelled it is hardly to be wondered that he should suffer at least one mishap.

> 16.5.13: A memorable day. Bob Vincent assisting me muster the river paddock. In the afternoon we started to take out the small cows. We had about 80 when I got a heavy fall, my horse cannoning against another beast whilst I was galloping. I was knocked senseless for about 30 minutes and brought into the station by Bob Vincent.

> A most peculiar sensation—could not recall what we were doing with the cattle, but memory slowly returned as though awakening from a long dream while riding in. Cut out 120 beasts and put them in paddock.

Occasionally, when at the homestead for a day or two, he would take the family by buggy to a pool in the nearby ranges where they could swim without fear of crocodiles. It was an idyllic spot, sheltered from the sun by an encircling, fern-draped cliff—a haunt to which the young people would return with even more delight in the years to come. Sometimes when on shorter rides he would take his son along with him.

> 21.7.13: The boy already shows considerable enjoyment of this means of transport. He is perpetually on the go and in the best of spirits. Mary also, and certainly making herself heard.

With stockmen riding to and fro and usually calling in at the homestead, there was seldom any lack of company at Ivanhoe. Where such visitors were concerned, Gert's arrival was the most exciting since that of Kit Durack several years before. Bill Jones, who had declared himself a confirmed bachelor, lost little time in proposing to her but, as he told us in later years, he soon realised that the bush life which she found pleasant enough as a novelty was certainly not for her on a permanent basis.

Rudolph Philchowski, partner with Joe Fegan in Spring Creek and mailman between Wyndham and Ord River Station, had meanwhile patched up his differences with M.P. and also made a point of calling in for longer than was necessary for the delivery of mail. Bess and her sister were intrigued to know why a man of such obvious culture and apparently aristocratic background should have resigned himself to a life of exile in the Australian bush. They hoped that by a process of careful listening and subtle questioning the secret would eventually be revealed, but this was not to be.

Another interesting visitor to Ivanhoe at this time was an American army officer named Montgomery, who had come from Manila to purchase cavalry remounts and polo ponies from C.D. & D. stations. Roy Phillipps wrote of him to his mother:

> Argyle, 6.7.13: He is a very decent chap—has been the last two years in France studying horses. All the paddocks were mustered so he could choose the horses that suited him. He picked fifty that will go to Manila soon and a couple of hundred more that are to go later on. He had a rather unique experience while staying with Mr & Mrs M.P. at Ivanhoe . . .

The story that followed is told also in M.P.'s diary:

> 25.6.13: About 11.30 last night Jim Crisp arrived on his way down from Auvergne. He reports that he found the body of a man he believes to be Philchowski at the Eight Mile, evidently killed by blacks. Jones, Montgomery, self and three boys proceed to the scene of the murder. Found the boy as described by Crisp, spear wound in back of shoulder. Held inquest. Returned verdict of wilful murder. Buried the body close by. A restless night. Dingos howling all around the grave.
> 26.6.13: Jones and Montgomery go on to Argyle. Self, Ulysses and Toby ride down the creek for a couple of miles. Saw fresh cattle tracks but no sign of the cattle. Tracks of natives to be seen about and heard their Yakki from the long grass some distance off. Returned to station bringing in some of Philchowski's things.

Next day Dr Parer, Neal Durack, Police Constables McMillan and Carr, and two black trackers arrived from Wyndham. The body was exhumed and death found to be due to a spear having penetrated a lung. Four special constables—Neal Durack, Murray Prior, Alf Martin and M. McDonough—were then sworn in to assist the police in making an arrest.

It was nearly three weeks before M.P. recorded the return of the party from 'out East of the Keep River' where they had captured an Aboriginal named Jillambin who had allegedly confessed to the crime.

On 19 December M.P. reports the arrival in Wyndham of a legal party engaged to try the case.

> Major G. T. Wood, [Resident Magistrate from Broome], young Hubert Parker for the defence and young Jack Durack [second son of the late Jerry Durack] for the prosecution. The trial lasted four hours. Charge very clear. Prisoner sentenced to death.

Roy Phillipps also gave a brief report of the episode:

> Wyndham 23.12.13: The trial of the blackfellow for the murder of Philchowski did not take long. Parker had a hopeless job trying to defend him, especially with a jury of bushmen. They found him guilty in about three seconds.

No one produced any reason for the murder and there were apparently no further questions asked at that time. It was only when researching the background for this book that I asked a group of Aborigines who had been around at the time whether Jillambin had had any motive for his action.

The story that was then unfolded with quiet objectivity seems reasonably convincing. Johnnie Walker, appointed main spokesman on this occasion, and feeling this job to be in the nature of a sacred trust, would pause to consult his companions from time to time, usually on some point of little or no importance to the main issue. At one stage I was asked to go away while they resolved the debatable question of whether the victim had turned round two, three, or four times before dropping dead. Johnnie's tape recorded version runs as follows:

> One time Philchowski got a kind of shop at Carlton Reach. We don't remember the date—before my time here anyway. He used to sell grog and he got some sort of arrangement with a couple of men for a lend of their gins—you know—for hold up travellers make it worth while call in to spend some money there.
>
> Well, M.P. get fed up this idea—teamsters too long bringing out the stores and that. He get Philchowski kicked off the place. Well that all right. Philchowski go in with old Joe Fegan, Spring Creek, then take on that mail-run.
>
> One day he camping there dinner time Eight Mile Creek and this fellow Woolambine come up. Woolambine one fella been lend'm gin when him been along Carlton Reach. Well, he reckon Philchowski old mate, like see him again—might give him hand-out tobacco, tea, sugar—like old times.
>
> Philchowski sit there reading—book, newspaper, something, we don't know. He see Woolambine come up and he make sign his hand—like that—tell him go away. Some fella reckon he sing out—'Go 'way you bloody old blackfella.'
>
> Well, Woolambine get snakey then—that not right way tribal law, s'pose you got arrangement don't matter how long ago. Woolambine go back behind that sandstone rock where his mates camped. He talk: 'Me gonna kill that whiteman.' Other fellas say: 'No. You kill that whiteman we all in bad trouble. That no good.'
>
> Woolambine don't take no notice. He sharpen up spear and he sneak close-up behind where Philchowski sitting behind tree. Then he push spear down hard along back. Philchowski jump up and yell out, turn round two, three . . . all right four time and fall down, finish. Then everybody clear out.

According to this source, Jillambin had been among those who tried to dissuade Woolambine. Jillambin spoke little or no English and when the police caught up with him on the Keep River, he had merely nodded his head in a placatory manner to all their questions. This had been taken as clear admission of his guilt, an impression that none of his companions ventured to refute.

> Every blackfella them days know you can't argue with policeman. That only waste of time—bring more trouble all round.

My informants alleged that it was at this stage that Boxer, who had some personal grievance against Woolambine, decided to take justice into his own hands. Being among the few Aborigines allowed to carry a firearm, he followed Woolambine, who somehow spotted him from a distance, scrambled to the top of a sandstone outcrop, and aimed a spear at Boxer as he approached. The weapon missed its mark but Boxer's bullet struck Woolambine in the shoulder and he dropped to the far side of the rocks. Boxer supposed him dead, and was surprised soon afterwards to hear that he was working in the stock camp on Newry station. Woolambine had meantime managed to extract the bullet and wore it as a souvenir in a little bag around his neck. He showed it to Boxer when the two met again, whereupon they shook hands and agreed to forget their differences.

There is no direct evidence of the sort of retribution often said to have followed the killing of a white man by Aborigines, but a brief comment from Roy Phillipps, written somewhat before the trial, suggests that more than one man may have suffered for this deed.

> Wyndham, 20.9.13: You will be glad to hear that Philchowski was amply avenged, though I would not say anything about it if I were you.

It is in a sense a tribute to the Aborigines that M.P. was prepared to leave his family with them and the Chinese cook, often for a week or more at a time. There were keys to the doors, but these were used only on rare occasions when the white residents were absent for more than a day or two. Otherwise the doors were open day and night, and valuables were left about on dressing-tables without a thought of possible theft.

When Lieutenant Montgomery returned from Argyle not long after Philchowski's death, he was shocked to find Bess and her sister alone in the house with the little ones, and he assumed that they would be grateful for his protection. They often recalled with amusement his declaration on retiring for the night: 'Have no fear, ladies. I am on guard.'

In fact the ladies were worried only by the fact that he kept candles, of which there was not an inexhaustible supply, burning all night.

30

The Shadow of War

July 1913–November 1914

It might then have seemed far-fetched to suppose that happenings in the distant seats of world power would directly affect the remote cattle kingdoms of North Australia. Nonetheless, Germany's transparent ambition to challenge Britain's sea supremacy and the resulting build-up of naval and military forces throughout the Empire had obviously alerted leading meat companies to a new source of demand and directed their attention to areas from which it might be supplied.

By mid-1913 prospects for the sale of C.D. & D.'s northern properties seemed propitious as never before. The wires between company representatives in Perth, Wyndham, Manila, and London fairly vibrated with references to rival businesses whose tactics, as complicated as those of so many nations, could have been properly assessed only by an astute system of espionage.

Marshall, the cantankerous representative for Bovril who had been there in 1910, was back again, riding around the stations and being as evasive as ever concerning the precise nature of his business. Also in the picture were representatives of three other well-known meat companies, and of more that remained anonymous. Two agents whose names recur in diaries and letters are those of Frederick and Searle who, although dining and wining together in Wyndham, were apparently representing rival interests. Of Frederick, Roy Phillipps wrote to his mother:

> He is a very wealthy old Scotchman with manors and grouse preserves in Scotland and is here inspecting Wave Hill with view to purchase outright—quite a fine old chap . . .

M.P. gathered that Frederick was associated with the Union Cold Storage Company, one of Vestey Brothers' many interests, but that he was also prepared to bid for properties on his own account. Of this he reports, on 19.11.13:

> Frederick asks if we will give him an offer of the stations in the event of nothing doing with the other company [presumably Vestey

> Brothers, who held an option on the purchase of C.D. & D. properties].

By the end of the year the centre of activity had switched to Sydney, where J.W. was sent to find out, if possible, what was afoot, and to represent his company's interests. The partners were prepared to sell only on condition that their properties were purchased as a 'job lot', together with Lissadell, which M.J. had agreed to include in the deal. In this decision Connor and Doherty had been outvoted by the Durack brothers, who knew they would have no difficulty in disposing of Argyle, either separately or together with Newry and Ivanhoe, which would have left them to carry on the two problem properties—Auvergne and Dunham. The bargain they were prepared to make included approximately 75,000 head of cattle, and 700 horses for £250,000 cash, 'walk in, walk out.'

From a rapid succession of letters and telegrams that often overlapped, one suspects that the issues at stake were not much clearer then than they are today. The various agents, with the exception of Marshall who refused to talk at all, seem to have had a great deal to say without revealing their companies' actual intentions, if indeed they knew what these were themselves. Armour's representative, Hodgkinson, became evasive when asked the nature of a project to which he frequently referred. Of this J.W. reports:

> He would say nothing but that his scheme embraced both Australia and New Zealand and that it would be completed by Saturday. He told me to keep myself free that night for a *Dinner* with himself and associates and I would know all.

On 10 January 1914, the day following this interview, it was announced that Copley and Co had sold Ord River Station, Sturt Creek, and Margaret River stations to Vestey's Union Cold Storage Company for a sum estimated at between £225,000 and £240,000. The same company had also negotiated a deal for the 6,000-square-mile property of Wave Hill, and was proposing to purchase still further northern holdings[1]. J.W.'s story continues:

> I could see that Hodgkinson was greatly concerned, though he never affected so. The dinner never came off. The Copley sale evidently upset his arrangements. He complains of 'wet blankets' back home who are too slow to answer cables or to *act*. Where hurried decisions are necessary all he can get out of London or Chicago is 'Wait'. Then they miss their chance and make him look a fool.

J.W. had by this time heard, in a roundabout way, that Armour's policy in America was not to purchase properties but to negotiate contracts for the purchase of fat stock, which may have been the cause of their reluctance to close the deals that Hodgkinson had proposed. What Hodgkinson himself was up to is anybody's guess, but he was obviously upset by the news of Vestey's purchase and suspected that they were now about to make a firm bid for C.D. & D. J.W.'s letter continues:

> He then said quite excitedly: 'For pity's sake don't commit yourself to sale this week. I want you for my scheme.'
>
> This he at last revealed to be the establishment of a meatworks at Katherine. I said: 'What's the use of Armour's building there? Why not Wyndham?' Hodgkinson said: 'Vesteys are there now. We would have considered Wyndham if we'd closed for Wave Hill when we had the chance . . .'

The inference to be drawn is that Hodgkinson had proposed Armour's taking up an enormous sweep of adjoining country comprising Wave Hill together with the Copley and C.D. & D. estates. This would have given them undisputed rights to enough cattle to keep a meatworks going indefinitely. When the Vestey interests got in first, he had either altered his scheme or been instructed to do so.

> Hodgkinson says Vesteys will put up a meatworks in Wyndham but Cunningham, Dalgety's man, says Marshall, for Bovril, tells him that Frederick of Union Cold Storage won't consider any place but Darwin or Katherine.
>
> Hodgkinson seems to know Vestey's every move. He must have someone on the job in London or he has interests in some way with Union Cold Storage himself. He said today: 'Don't you fellows sell out for twelve months. There's going to be a big rise in cattle by then—mark my words. If Vesteys do go to Katherine you will have Wyndham all to yourselves and the Manila livestock trade and what's to prevent a *small* works at Wyndham—say £50,000?'
>
> It is hard to dove-tail in all the odd pieces of advice and information . . .

In the process of trying to work it out, J.W. would seem to have come to the conclusion that their own business tactics were naive compared to those of more experienced and prosperous companies. He wrote to his partners at this stage, enquiring whether Vestey's option of purchase on their properties had expired.

> If not, what about asking Dalgety here in Sydney, whose confidence we have, to send a bluffing cable to Dalgety in London as follows:-
> UNABLE INDUCE C D & D GIVE OPTION BUT THINK A FIRM OFFER IN ADVANCE OF EXPIRED OFFER MIGHT OBTAIN THEIR STATIONS AND LISSADELL.

Doherty answered this suggestion by cable from London:

> 12.1.14: Armours had original option. Vestey has option fortnight longer. Vestey very keen. Armours had original option Ord River. Vestey bought this on expiration. Do not cable Dalgety London.

A lead on the confused plot is provided by a letter dated 20.1.14 from J.W. to Mrs Lumley Hill, widow of M.J.'s former partner who had written asking what on earth was going on. He told her that negotiations for the sale of the properties, including Lissadell, had been resumed by Dalgety in London after several unsuccessful bids. These efforts had again fallen through, owing to his company's decision to sell all the properties or none. Prospective buyers quibbled at the bedrock price and did not want Auvergne included in the deal. Armour's man, Hodgkinson, was now on some big scheme connected with Sidney Kidman. The letter concluded:

> We should know more within a month. If the properties that Vesteys are buying are worth the money our properties are cheap at the price offered. This much is certain—the prices are beginning to move.

On 26 January 1914 J.W. wrote his partners a final letter from Sydney.

> Now having eliminated all immediate chances I am returning home. It's no good entering into useless conjecture. We just have to sit tight and await events. Certainly most of us would have preferred to sell and I can only say I did my best. At least, if we have not sold, our places are worth much more since the Copley sale and we are much better off than a month ago. Furthermore, we know that our properties are *good*.

But if J.W. managed to find consolation in the turn of events, this was not the case with many others in his home State. An article in the *Sunday Times* dated 18 January had this to say:

> Are we at this moment losing the Kimberleys? According to the very best information we are; in fact, the whole of that immense and rich province is already gone. It is being annexed by a powerful

British company and all we are likely to get out of it hereafter is the half-a-crown per 1,000 acres rent, which will be insufficient to police and administer that huge section of the State ...

It is a million to one that the new bosses of the Kimberley meat business will establish chilling works at Port Darwin ... Port Darwin will become the great tropic port ... Not only the Kimberley cattle, but Kimberley business of all kinds will be diverted there. The stations will be supplied from the centre to which they send their stock. Port Darwin will become the capital of Kimberley.

Wyndham, on the other hand, will be suppressed, annihilated. Wyndham, the natural and embryonic metropolis of all that splended territory, will have the little it has taken from it. Wyndham and the magnificent Cambridge Gulf will be a mark on the map but nothing more ... If the Government had installed freezing and chilling works at Wyndham two years ago instead of wasting the money on a State steamer that they are now anxious to sell, the Union Cold Storage Company, which is now master of the situation, would probably have fallen in with the channel thus created ...

Chilling works at Wyndham would have paid ... Furthermore, the people whom the Government professed to be so devilish anxious about would have got better and cheaper meat ...

What is the Union Cold Storage Company? It is a huge company which was formed in 1897 ... Sir William Vestey and Edmund Hoyle Vestey seem to be the chief people in the company ... The Union Storage Company has establishments at London, Liverpool, Manchester, Hull, Glasgow, Riga, Kosloff, Kourgan, St Petersburg, Chertkovo, Griazi, Vladivostok and Moscow ...

Instead of opening up a main trade route along our north west coast to Manila, Shanghai, Hong Kong, it is probable that steamers will simply stop running between Fremantle and Wyndham. There won't be any trade and there won't be any meat ...

As a matter of fact we are dished. We may have plenty of mutton and frozen rabbit, but as for beef, well that will become a luxury like caviare. And the Government were going to play Hades and smash the alleged beef buccaneers. O Tempora! Oh Happy Jack![12]

During the latter part of this exciting period M.P., with Bess, her sister Gert, and the two children, were in the Philippines, and Frank Connor was back in Western Australia attending a parliamentary session. He had left his son Frank in charge of the Manila office but it had seemed advisable that M.P. should be there over what portended to be a critical period for the company. They had sailed on 20 December from Wyndham to Darwin where, while awaiting the departure of the *Changso* for Manila, M.P. discussed current affairs with Dr Gilruth. The news of Vestey's purchase had not yet broken, and M.P. took the fact of the Administrator's being less inclined to argue the case for a Darwin meatworks as a hopeful sign.

After a second Christmas at sea on the same route, the family arrived in Manila for the New Year festivities. M.P. was by this time well acquainted with many of the business, professional, and military hierarchy of the Islands, and was greeted by them as an old friend. He was fortunate in obtaining the use of a pleasant house on the sea-front at Pasay, complete with all available amenities and a trained staff. This included a young Filipino woman named Felice who was promptly appointed nursemaid and attached herself to the children with memorable affection. M.P.'s daily comments give some idea of the sort of life into which they entered at this time.

> 5.1.14: To see Lichauco. Much business to discuss. Caught up at the polo grounds with Lieutenant Montgomery who had three of the horses sold him last year by C.D. & D. Also with him several officers of the 7th Cavalry. Montgomery and his party motor me to the Army and Navy Club, of which they make me a member.
> 11.1.14: To church this morning where I met Major Hartigan and son Len, who has apparently happy memories of his time with us in Kimberley. We dine with them tonight.
> 13.1.14: Bess with a bad throat—can hardly speak. Took her to see an American doctor recommended by Hartigan. Says he fears it will have to run its course.
> Dine tonight with Judge Kincaid, a number of other judges and their wives.

The Lichaucos meanwhile were proving 'most affable and entertaining' and were co-operative in helping M.P. achieve one of his most cherished ambitions—the acquisition of a motor-car, or what he then usually referred to as an 'auto machine', to take back with him to Kimberley. In the process of trying out various models with experienced drivers he explored a good deal of the Philippines.

> 21.1.14: The country for a few hours after leaving Manila is mostly composed of rice fields. then sugar and coconut lands and at last, tobacco growths . . .

> We encounter interesting people in the mountain province . . . We take some photographs, one of a famous head-hunter named Beeswai, wearing, as most of his companions, nothing but a gee string . . .
> 22.1.14: We reach Vigan at 5 p.m. Everywhere evidence of decayed Spanish grandeur. Evidently there was much more prosperity here in Spanish days than to be found today . . . Hoped to make Laong this evening but, alas, man proposes and motor car disposes. We have no less than four blowouts and finally have to drive ten miles on a blown out tyre.

This was the beginning of a long love-hate relationship between M.P. and the 'auto machine', which he was to regard from this time on as an irksome essential of life.

February in Manila was a time of carnival and colourful international pageants for which the population donned masks and fancy dress and strewed the thoroughfares with confetti and flowers.

> 9.2.14: A military parade was part of today's spectacle. We watch for over an hour as it passes by—infantry and artillery, some 6,000 men headed by Major Hartigan. Many fine horses and mules though a number of soldiers I thought looked somewhat thin and tired. The fittest and most cheerful of them all were the South American blacks.
>
> The warship *Saratoga* beautifully lit up tonight and searchlights playing around the heavens. A sumptuous dinner with Lichaucos and a band playing all the time.

M.P. was kept in touch meanwhile with the situation confronting J.W. in Sydney, and before returning early in April he had some frank discussions with Lichauco on the contentious issue of Connor's commission:

> 2.4.14: Lichauco states he would not like me to think there was outside transaction between himself and Connor. He states that he told Connor that if asked, he would tell the truth of the matter.

Lichauco assisted the family, complete with 'T' Model Ford, aboard the *Kolya* and waited with a number of other friends to see them away. Among these was the young American doctor whose advice Bess had sought on a number of minor health problems, and who had become conscientiously concerned for her welfare. She gathered that he had heard from his friend Len Hartigan not so much of the pleasant experiences he recalled for M.P. and herself, as of a way of life that sounded quite intolerable. Hartigan had dwelt on the perilous isolation, the lack of amenities and the uncivilized nature not only of the Aborigines, but of the bulk of the white population. He had told of the prevalence of an often fatal form of fever, and of other ailments attributed to the harsh climate and unbalanced diet. Before their three months' sojourn was over, the doctor had been bold enough to suggest to Bess that her husband had no right to subject his family to such conditions. He also hinted that, although no doubt an admirable fellow in many respects, he was not only of a very different background from herself, but old enough to be her father. His remedy for these problems, including that of the welfare of her children, was that she should live in Manila, leaving M.P. to continue his cherished lifestyle in that outlandish country. Despite Bess's amused protestations, he urged her to think it over and to keep in touch with him until her next visit to Manila. On parting he pressed upon her a chain bracelet complete with a dangling golden heart. She put it on with a word of embarrassed thanks, but when waving good-bye as the ship moved off, the trinket slipped over her hand into the waters between them. As it happened, she was never to return to Manila or to see the young man again, but she often recalled the incident to her friends in the years to come.

Whether or not M.P. had registered any of this romantic drama, he reports their departure with a note of relief:

> 9.4.14: Bess and self pleased to be once again under weigh for Kimberley. Our stay here was rather long and I was beginning to weary of it but must say we are all in better health for the change of air and so much warm hospitality.

The devoted nursemaid, Felice, had been eager to accompany them to Australia and they to take her, but immigration problems intervened and she, too, was to remain a memory. Since Gert, owing to some family contingency in Adelaide, had returned not long before, Bess was for the first time without a woman's help with her little ones. Back in Wyndham, M.P. was in the saddle again within a few hours.

> 14.4.14: Piping hot day. Jones, Martin and Ulysses to meet us. Auto machine soon safely off the ship. Saw cattle—499 head—on board and away tonight.

The car, as Roy Phillipps reported, was the focus of immediate local interest.

> M.P. and family have arrived back from Manila bringing a motor car. As a result, talk has shifted from bullocks and live weight to

> carburettors, sparking plugs etc. [Roy Phillipps to his mother, 26.4.14]

The first motor trip from Wyndham to Ivanhoe was typical of many such journeys from that time on.

> 23.4.14: Went spinning gaily to the Twelve Mile when we skidded into some mud. Spent two hours trying to get out. Nothing to put under the jack but finally, with the aid of grass, water bags and tomahawk, we got the car lifted out and away . . . Stuck up again in Spring Creek and Jessie Creek. Much difficulty in cranking up. Covered the fifty miles in a little under ten hours.
> 25.4.14: Spent the morning cleaning the car, overhauling the machinery and screwing her up all over. Took Paddy Boyle, Ulysses, Toby and Alick for a short run this morning. Jones says he intends sticking to horseback and thinks I will come to the same conclusion before long.

A little later Roy Phillipps informed his mother:

> M.P. had a smash in his car the other day but she is mended again now with greenhide etc. He ran into a stump in the long grass and smashed the radiator and threw the family out. Still, he reckons that but a minor detail incidental to apprenticeship at the wheel.

M.P. does not admit in his diary having come to the same conclusion as Bill Jones, but the car seems to have remained for some time at Ivanhoe homestead, to be taken on short runs, while he carried out his urgent journeys between stations and into Wyndham either on horseback or buggy as before.

It did not take him long, however, to recover his confidence and with it the determination somehow to adapt himself and local conditions to a more advanced method of transport. He had always loved riding, as he would to the end of his life, but he also yearned to see ways and means of breaking down the north's problem of isolation, whether by wire, wireless, wheel, or wing. He was already following with the keenest interest news of advances in the area of powered flight, which the coming world war was to establish as a fact of life. In the meantime, he was prepared to bounce and sway over the rough bush tracks, dipping into rocky river- and creek-beds, cutting off bends by knocking down anthills, and sometimes swerving off the road to inspect surprised groups of cattle—an art in which he trained me when the cars were more reliable.

It speaks much for the stamina of those early models that they did not crack up or break down completely within a few weeks under such conditions. Needless to say, they frequently went on strike, roaring out their exasperation and huffing steam from boiling innards. They kicked and bogged in protest at being steered relentlessly into heavy sand, and at ten- to twenty-mile intervals they would slump sideways on punctured tyres. The original 'T' Model Ford, sentimentally kept by M.P. in the saddle shed at Ivanhoe, steadily disintegrated over the years.

M.P.'s reaction to the takeover of so much country by British capital rather than the American Meat Trust which had been forecast a year or so before, was not immediately pessimistic. Since all the holdings purchased by Union Cold Storage were within practical droving distance of Wyndham, and had always shipped their cattle from that port, it seemed logical that, despite rumours to the contrary, the company would favour this site for its meatworks.

The State Government had shown little interest when approached in May that year by another group of British meat-importers proposing to put up a works in Wyndham, and from this it had seemed evident to M.P. that Premier Scaddan had inside information of Vestey's holding the same thing in view. It was a bitter blow to him to learn, a few weeks later, that Vestey had signed a contract with the Commonwealth Government for the erection of a meatworks in Darwin. He did not see it, however, as portending Wyndham's 'annihilation', and since the project would obviously take some time to complete he saw C.D. & D. as continuing to purchase cattle for shipment to Fremantle and the Philippines.

The declaration of war was immediately followed by advice that the State Government was negotiating with the meat company that had approached them not long before. As a result, the chief of this concern, S. V. Nevanas, arrived in Wyndham under commission to report on the prospects for a meatworks in that port. Roy Phillipps, whose recent letters to his mother had been uncharacteristically low-spirited, was obviously cheered by the appearance of some fresh faces.

> Wyndham, 23.9.14: I feel I ought to be down taking my part in all this war business and have been trying to get a commission in the Light Horse, but things here have brightened up a bit lately. An English millionaire and his wife, private secretary and the secretary's pretty sister have arrived from Darwin in a chartered

> boat and are now fixing up preliminaries to erecting a meatworks here. Mr Nevanas is the wealthy one's name. You may have seen it in connection with some pretty big Argentine deals lately. He is a very nice man and his wife and the pretty sister are even better.

Nevanas and his party also enlivened M.P.'s daily record over this period. He took them on a tour of inspection, including a visit to Ivanhoe, where they figure in my earliest memories. Mr Nevanas certainly exuded charm to all comers, including children, and on one occasion, having encouraged me to sit on his knee, was rewarded by having a cup of hot tea spilled over his immaculate white suit. My mother often recalled her embarrassment as she hastened to repair the damage. By October the required plans and specifications, with quote of an estimated cost of £159,510, were in the hands of the government.

It seemed to M.P. and his associates that, even though the war would no doubt be over—the allies of course emerging victorious—before the project was completed, and the need for which it was intended therefore no longer pressing, it would remain to serve a purpose they had long envisioned. Vesteys could go on with their Darwin works if they liked, but it was doubtful whether, unless prepared to pay exorbitant prices, they would succeed in procuring cattle from many stations other than their own . . . in any case, C.D. & D. had so far had no trouble in renewing their contracts with holders large and small in both Kimberley and the Territory. One of these, signed by Sir C. H. Rason, Chairman of Directors of Bovril Australian Estates, in June of that year, undertook to sell them all available fat cattle, up to 4,000 head, from Victoria River and Carlton stations by the end of the year.

At this stage, the main problem for station holders was an impending shortage of labour, as one man after another answered the call to arms. It was from this time on that Aborigines came to fill a more important role in the northern stock camps. This suited them very well, for although there was then no question of their being paid in anything but the essentials of life—food, clothing and tobacco—the white man's obvious need of them increased their sense of security and self-respect, and brought more family life to the homestead encampments. Apart from this, the war made a less memorable impression on the tribal people than their sighting of Halley's comet in 1910, the sinking of the *Koombana* in 1912 and the arrival of that first motorcar in 1914. These and a few other such memorable events were to prove invaluable to me when probing Aboriginal memories which, though often more remarkable than Europeans', are less reliable where dates are concerned.

As the months went by, the war, even from snippets of news that seeped through to the station outposts, began to take on a more ominous aspect. As M.P. records from Ivanhoe on 28 October 1914:

> Ulysses back from Wyndham with mail today. The German advance has not been materially checked as we understood. The ship *Emden* continues its work, sinking and capturing British mercantile ships. It is now said to be in the Indian Ocean—but whereabouts?[3]

On one occasion the answer to this question had seemed to the startled inhabitants of Wyndham to be, 'Right here'. The alarm was given one moonless night when a mysterious red light was observed moving steadily up Cambridge Gulf. Plans for the immediate evacuation of the women and children were in hand, when the light was reported to have faded and finally blacked out. The residents were not entirely reassured until an old hand recalled having seen a similar phenomenon, which he had discovered was a burning bush blown into the water on a gust of wind.

But the shadow of war that was to loom ever more menacingly on world horizons did nothing to cloud my own first memories. According to my parents, I had begun to walk when the *Changsha* was battling its way to Manila against the head winds of the previous December. My own recollections, however begin only in later months at Ivanhoe, which locality I have always felt to be, in an Aboriginal sense, my 'spirit home'. Even before the face of my own mother, I can see Dinah's smiling countenance as she hoists me on to her shoulders and bears me off to fish, with a bent pin for a hook, from the edge of the Ivanhoe lagoon. The wriggling inches of our catch, loudly applauded by an Aboriginal audience complete with yelping but carefully tethered dogs, are a shining memory.

I remember, too, the joyous excitement of those first wet weather storms with which I felt as much at home as with the sound of cattle thundering down the race on to ships waiting at the Wyndham wharf. My father records from Ivanhoe, on 26 October 1914:

> Storm from the south-east. Over an inch of rain to replenish the lagoon. Reg and Mary enjoying it immensely. Ulysses brings in some whistling duck . . . Looks like an early wet. Much to organise before we can get away . . .

It was mid-December, and all the rivers were down in flood, before he could leave for Fremantle with his family and his precious auto machine.

He knew he now faced another turning point in his life for, with a third child on the way and all the uncertainties of the world situation, he must think seriously of establishing a home base in the comparative safety of the south.

31

PARTING OF THE WAYS

December 1914–August 1915

Perth at the end of 1914 was alive with a new sort of vitality. The first Western Australian units had by that time joined the New Zealand troops in Egypt under Sir William Birdwood, and as further countries had become embroiled there was less talk of an early end to hostilities and more enthusiastic rallying to the cause of Empire. The trend, though Australia-wide, was more dramatically evident in the Western State, where over a third of the men between the ages of eighteen and forty-four were to volunteer for the Expeditionary Forces. This was to be the cause of considerable hardship, since it left short-handed all avenues of local activity, but one division after another moved away with the wholehearted support of the community.

So far only one member of the immediate Durack family had left Australia for the front. This was Ambrose's younger brother, Fergus, who had enlisted in Queensland with the Third Field Engineers and had sailed with the first convoy from Albany, W.A., in November of that year.

Dermot had joined the 31st Lancers of the Indian Cavalry Division and, though hoping soon to sail for France, was at that time posted in Kohat. Of this he had written J.W.:

> 26.5.15: It looks as though I am stuck here for the time being as there is some trouble on the frontier. The Mahommedans are very sick about our war with Turkey . . .
>
> Re disposal of my personal effects if I don't come through—well, they don't amount to much—five ponies left in Allahabad which would probably average £100 each. My books to be given to the University in Perth or the University College in Allahabad as you see fit. I enclose a statement of my business assets which you will know how to deal with.

Much of the prevailing atmosphere of the time is conveyed in M.P.'s report of gatherings to farewell departing troops at which 'Confusion to the Kaiser' was heartily toasted, along with cries of 'Are we downhearted? No! No!'

The usual social functions had taken on a patriotic motif, emphasized with background music and decorative effects, while money-raising efforts were for wartime causes rather than for home-based charities.

A bush poet, then overseas with the A.I.F., wrote on behalf of the many stockmen who, like himself, had left the northern cattle runs to join the forces:

They have finished now with riding
Down the lonely cattle trails;
They are through with swapping stories
Watching riders from the rails.
And the moleskins and the leggings
That were sweaty, old and torn
Are discarded for the glory
Of a khaki uniform.

They won't be drafting bullocks
For many days to come,
And the noise of rushing cattle
Will yield to roaring gun.
And those nights spent by the campfire
In the stock camps near the yard
Will just be pleasant memories
To a ringer doing guard . . . [Sydney Kelly]

M.P. and his family were then staying at the King Edward Hostel in Perth, of which the proprietors, Mr and Mrs Bannon, were personal friends. They had engaged an agreeable nursemaid named May with whom they could leave the children while they went about their social and business activities, the most important of which was house-hunting. This entailed a search of several weeks, M.P. wrestling in the process with the problems of city motoring which he found to be no less exasperating than those of the outback. Whereas in the bush he had driven only by day, here he was often required to travel by night with lights that tended either to flicker and fade, or to black out completely. Punctures in city traffic were, if less frequent, at least more embarrassing than in the privacy of the bush, but most exasperating of all was being obliged to pay a fine of 25s for having minimally exceeded the speed limit of twelve miles an hour.

After inspecting many houses that they had considered either too close to the heart of the city or too far removed from it, too big or too small, over-priced or sub-standard, they purchased a home in Goldsmith Road, Claremont, for the sum of £950. A modest enough residence, it stood on an ample block of land within walking distance of the Claremont village and of railway transport to the city. They set to work at once getting the house furnished and adapted to their requirements, these including accommodation for employees on holiday from the north. Within a few weeks, M.P. was able to record on a note of obvious satisfaction:

> 10.3.15: Moved today from the Hostel to our Claremont home, this being the first place I have possessed in my own right. Bess and I very happy as we take a walk through the rooms, sitting for a while to admire them in turn. A glass of Schweppes each!

M.P., having referred to his life since 1909 as his 'Bimera', had no difficulty in naming this long-desired residence. To Bess's pleased surprise, a copper plate embossed with the name 'Bimera' was already attached to the front gate as they moved in to what would be the birthplace of their next three children.

But finding a home was only one of M.P.'s many preoccupations at that time. Since returning to Perth he had been in touch with most of the contemporary politicians, endeavouring to impress upon them the importance to the State, and indeed to the Empire, of their supporting the cause of primary production in the Kimberley district. John Forrest professed to agree with him that the heavy Leasehold Tax was a serious impediment to progress, while Johnson, Minister for Land, whom he approached for news about the Wyndham meatworks, declared that he was about to reopen the negotiations with Nevanas that had somehow been allowed to lapse.

Within a few weeks of this interview the State Government actually signed a contract with Nevanas for a construction to be put up, at an estimated cost of £159,510. Before the end of March, Nevanas was back in Perth and arrangements for the shipment of materials and construction workers to Wyndham were soon in progress. At this stage, Nevanas rivalled even Frank Connor in the eloquence with which he propounded the potential of Kimberley that was at last about to be realised. Wyndham, he declared, was soon to become an international centre of pastoral enterprise, and as such the focus of world-wide interest; and to prove his confidence he made C.D. & D. an offer of £2,500 for the Wyndham Hotel as a personal investment. This establishment, although no doubt a lucrative enough asset, had presented so many problems over the years that the company would previously have considered sale on these terms. In view of Nevanas' predictions, however, they now declared their bedrock price to be £4,500, at which the bidder withdrew for further consideration. He returned at this stage to Melbourne to proceed with the engagement of qualified staff and the purchase of materials not available in the west.

Meanwhile the contentious issue of Connor's business dealings in the Philippines had again come to the fore. Although all had agreed at the end of 1912 that Connor should receive a commission of ten shillings per head, it had become a matter of increasing uneasiness that he was operating for C.D. & D. through a private agency known as Connor & Mason. His Australian partners believed, rightly or wrongly, that this was detrimental to their interests, whereas Connor maintained that he worked his agency to their mutual advantage and with inside knowledge of the subtleties of Asian business tactics.

In April 1915 a general meeting was called, for which Doherty arrived from London and Connor from Manila. There is no detailed record of the discussions that ensued, at which the Durack brothers, with the support of their solicitor, M. L. Moss, declared that if Connor wished to continue in the same way they saw no alternative but to request his resignation from the company. Doherty, who reserved his decision until he had heard all sides of the question, finally voted in agreement with the Duracks. To Connor, this decision on the part of the schoolfriend with whom he had set up business in 1886 and had worked in close association ever since, represented a heart-breaking betrayal of trust. It no doubt grieved Doherty, too, for he was a man of loyal and kindly disposition and of generally considered judgement. In this case however, he apparently saw his first duty as lying in the interests of his family, to which Connor's activities did not appear to be favourable.

J.W., who had enjoyed a closer relationship with Connor than his brothers, was also deeply affected by the turn of events and found it hard to believe that an alternative to the break-up of the partnership could not be found. M.P.'s brief comments indicate that J.W. would have been prepared to compromise further than the rest of them:

> 16.4.15: J.W. thinks we should get Moss to yet stay the document now in progess for signatures.
> 19.4.15: To the office where we decline to accept suggestions set forth by Connor who stayed on to further discuss the question with J.W. and Moss.
> 20.4.15: Connor's frame of mind today more peaceable and he now accepts the conditions that yesterday he would not listen to. This followed the ultimatum given him this morning that he either accepts or we go to Court against him.
> 21.4.15: All papers signed today . . . Cabled Lichauco that Connor no longer with company. Our association with agency Connor/

> Mason cancelled and monies now due must be paid to Chartered Bank India & Australia. Wired Connor/Mason advising same.
>
> The atmosphere clearer generally. All feeling much relieved and looking forward to a more satisfactory situation.

The terms agreed upon were that Connor's 20,000 shares in the company were acquired by Doherty and the Durack brothers for the sum of £19,000 in the company's promissory notes payable at the expiry of ten years, a quarterly interest to have been paid in the meantime[1].

The end of Connor's association with C.D. & D. also meant the end of a colourful lifestyle that involved his commuting between business interests in Manila and his parliamentary and family commitments in Western Australia. After his split with the company, towards the end of 1915 he gave up his home in Fremantle and moved with his wife and five of their eight children to a farming property at Benger in the Harvey district, south of Perth. One son who was not with them at that time was serving abroad with the 10th Light Horse, while another two remained in Manila, presumably to carry on in the Connor & Mason agency.

Whether this business had operated so much to Lichauco's advantage in his dealings with C.D. & D. that he wished to discourage the new arrangement, or whether the change had coincided with a succession of genuine exigencies, his negotiations with the company were from this time on unsatisfactory, to say the least.

The cable informing Lichauco of Connor's resignation and the cancellation of his agency was closely followed by a message from Manila informing the company that the cattle-ship *Kolya* had been involved in an accident and would be delayed indefinitely in picking up the next consignment. A further communication stated that settlement for the last shipment from Wyndham must be delayed.

Immediately following Connor's resignation M.P. was appointed by his partners to proceed to Manila—'there to do all things which he deems necessary in the interests of the company'. He set off early in May, confident enough that a straight talk with Lichauco would clear up any possible misunderstanding. It was a time when news from the war fronts was more than ever disturbing. The landing of the Australian forces at Gallipoli, which had been hailed as a 'magnificent achievement', had been a prelude not to the anticipated triumphant advance but to an appalling and futile loss of young life. In addition to this, on the eve of M.P.'s departure came news of the sinking of the *Lusitania* by a German submarine off the Irish coast, with a loss of 1,195 lives. It was hardly, therefore, with a light heart that he took leave of his family to sail for the Philippines.

Owing to wartime conditions, he was forced to take a roundabout route via the eastern capitals, in each of which he called on family, friends and business associates. In Adelaide he was met by members of his wife's family and taken home for an exchange of news, not all of which was cheerful:

> Found Dad Johnstone in a bad way. What was thought to be a minor injury to his foot has turned gangrenous and the doctors say it must come off if he is to survive. Gert, whom I left at home in Claremont, has been wired to come back at once. Bess will miss her sadly. Was quite overcome when saying goodbye to the old man, wondering whether I will ever see that fine face again.

M.P. enjoyed a stimulating session in Melbourne with Sidney Kidman, who had recently added considerably to his pastoral empire and expressed his willingness to sell any cattle within range of their activities to C.D. & D.

Also while in Melbourne he contacted Nevanas who, although as usual optimistic, was puzzled by complications that had arisen regarding the promised transport facilities between Fremantle and Wyndham. M.P. saw this as being due to the current shipping contingencies, which had extended for himself what would normally have been a ten to fourteen days' journey to one of a month or more.

In Sydney, apart from a bewildering number of relatives, he met several old friends from the north, including Tom Hayes, erstwhile partner in Rosewood Station with Tom Kilfoyle and Jerry Durack. The merest summary of what had happened to their mutual associates since their last meeting kept them talking until M.P. almost missed his connection to Brisbane where he was met by members of the Durack and Tully families. It was here that he heard for the first time of the death of his cousin Fergus who, having been wounded at Gallipoli, had died, aged twenty-six, aboard a hospital ship two days later, and had been buried at sea.

M.P. sailed from Brisbane aboard the S.S. *Nikko*, a Japanese ship with a majority of Japanese passengers, including a group attached to the Imperial College of Japan. These he found interesting company, with much to say about the growing importance of Japan's trade relations with the United States of America and the slim chance either had of keeping for much longer out of the war. One of the Japanese, an erudite man named Dr Jessei Miura, expounded eloquently on the multifarious religious beliefs of both Occident and Orient which he feared contributed more to human distrust and animosity than to brotherly love. For himself, having sincerely studied them all, he was at that stage a professed agnostic.

Proceeding northwards through the Torres Straits, M.P. was reminded that the last time he had travelled that way had been with his brother J.W. on the *Rajputana* twenty-nine years before.

> 30.5.15: A sadness overcomes me when I think of those we then knew who have since gone to rest and of so much that has passed between that time and this.
>
> Thursday Island much quieter than when here then, the pearling industry having slumped since the war ... On through tropical waters reading Hardy's 'Far from the Madding Crowd' ...

On arrival in Manila he was greeted cordially enough by Lichauco, who hastened to assure him that the money owing to C.D. & D. had by that time been paid. M.P. was surprised to learn however that, despite Lichauco's having been fully informed of the changed situation, the settlement had been made as usual through the Connor & Mason agency. It would seem that young Frank Connor had denied any knowledge of his father's resignation and dismissed it as the absurd rumour that he might, in fact, have believed it to be.

M.P. endeavoured to explain to both Lichauco and his banker what had transpired, and that any money must henceforth be paid through the independent agent he had appointed to act for them in Manila. Of his interview with Frank Connor Junior, he reports briefly:

> 26.5.15: Called to see young Frank re disbursements from Lichauco. He says he is holding them until payment of commission owing to Connor/Mason. I told him this agency was cancelled under signed agreement with his father and the money must be paid direct to us. He says he has only my word for this statement and insinuates that this is unreliable. After which I take my leave of him.

M.P. had been informed on arrival that the *Kolya* should be ready for departure within a few days, and he anticipated returning to Wyndham by this means. Three weeks went by during which, in answer to his continual enquiries, he was told that repairs to the vessel were more extensive than had been anticipated. This meant that not only was he delayed himself, but that the cattle for the next shipment to Manila were being held up at considerable expense, and incurring loss of condition, in the Ascot paddock near Wyndham.

Meanwhile the friends he had made on previous visits extended their usual hospitality and appeared surprisingly well informed about the delicate business that had brought him there. One who claimed to have his finger on the pulse of the Philippines said he might as well give up waiting for the *Kolya* as the only thing needed to start her engines was for C.D. & D. to resume dealing through the Connor & Mason agency. It was suggested from the same source that he board the Chinese vessel *Changsha* that was about to leave for Darwin. This advice he took, with sincere thanks, though knowing from past experience that the journey would be a slow and dreary one.

> 19.7.15: Ten days at sea and more to go. My thoughts with Bess and the other dear ones at home and perhaps by this time another little mite. I count the days 'til I get to them again. Travelling held more pleasure for me in my bachelor days than now when it means long separations of this sort.

Awaiting him in Darwin was a telegram informing him of the birth of a second daughter on 6 July and wishing him a safe and swift return. The time when he could board a plane for a few days' reunion with his dear ones was still a dream of things to come, and war had disrupted even the normal coastal shipping. His quickest method of getting from Darwin to Wyndham was therefore to take a lugger due to sail with supplies to the mouth of the Victoria River in a few days time. Here the cargo would be transferred to a launch on which M.P. could continue his journey to the Auvergne Station landing-stage. During his few days in the port he spent some time at Bullocky Point where Vestey's freezing-works were by that time in progress.

> 16.7.15: The works here well advanced—about 149 men on the job and quarters for three hundred men under construction. Four bores pumping into a 40,000 gallon tank—700 gallons every twenty-four hours. The water supply does not seem to me to be too assured but a general feeling of optimism prevails and all are looking forward to the works being ready for action mid 1916. It is believed that 250 head will be treated per day.

He would no doubt have reported less objectively had he known at the time that the agreement between Nevanas and the State Government had come to an end and that the matter of a Wyndham meatworks was again under review.

The lugger journey that had seemed a simple enough undertaking was to prove a rugged experience even for one as accustomed to tough conditions as M.P.

17.7.15: Leave my luggage except for a few things at Jolly's store for shipment to Wyndham in due course. Buy a rug, net etc., and board the lugger *Venture* to experience for the first time the pleasures or otherwise of this mode of conveyance. Captain Mundo in charge, Muro the boatswain (both Malay), Song Song Chinese cook and general rouseabout.
18.7.15: Progress about twenty-five miles a day battling through heavy seas against head winds. Time passes very slowly indeed.
19.7.15: At anchor all night. Now no wind at all. Slowly on to Peron Island ... Caught a large king fish. Anchored off Cape Scott 11.30 p.m. at a place where four men, including Cousin Jerry Skeahan were killed by blacks about ten years ago.
20.7.15: Natives in three canoes meet us and barter with the crew—sea-shells for tobacco.
21.7.15: Anchored off Port Keats and round Cape Hay. About a mile out from shore a number of natives seen swimning towards us with the assistance of a log but the tide too strong for them.
22.7.15: Slept little last night—a feeling of anxiety. Natives singing out from the shore. The crew too trusting, I think, going ashore as they do at night. I try to warn them though communication is difficult. Rough passage through the Race. For the next few hours hanging onto my bunk with feet and hands. Hoping for a happier return of my birthday next year.
24.7.15: Anchored off Blunder Bay early morn. Came ashore with Mundo to usual landing place. Learn that the launch left yesterday having evidently given us up. Must now await its return from the Victoria River depot—ninety odd miles up river. From Blunder Bay to Wyndham it is only 145 miles by sea—bad luck no means of getting there that way right now ...

Four anxious, dreary days ensued 'looking in vain for the launch and trying to take refuge from the mosquitoes and flies'.

28.7.15: At last the launch arrives, loads up with cargo and we are away up river at 6.30 a.m. a strong tide in our favour. We reach the Auvergne landing, past junction of the East and West Baines at 5.00 p.m. The launch returns immediately and I walk to the house, thankful indeed to be on my home ground once more.

The 175 miles between Auvergne and Wyndham were all home ground for M.P., who set off at once by horseback, via Newry and Ivanhoe, to be met by J.W. who was then in charge of the company affairs in the port. This was a temporary arrangement as Jim Davidson had taken over the Perth office while his wife was ill, and Roy Phillipps had sailed with the 28th Battalion to Gallipoli earlier in the year. J.W. was able to bring his brother up to date with further instalments of the confusing meatworks serial.

The shipping space promised to Nevanas had been found either genuinely unprocurable or had been for some reason made to appear so. At all events, the contract had been cancelled after payment to Nevanas of 3 per cent of his estimate. The Scaddan Government had then negotiated with the Public Works Department to take charge of the construction, and some materials had already been unloaded in Wyndham. But even this was no guarantee of immediate action, since there had been complaints from the Opposition of Scaddan's having dealt surreptitiously with the Public Works Department instead of calling for public tenders as was fitting and proper. After considerable argument, a motion for again cancelling the contract was defeated, though an amendment had been added disapproving of such practice on general principle.

The affair was to react unfavourably on the Scaddan Government[2], but for the time being the matter was considered settled and the building of the works began, at long last, in August of that year.

32

Goodbye Manila

August 1915–February 1916

It was soon apparent that Connor's resignation, whilst it may have solved one difficulty, had given rise to others. With no C.D. & D. representative in Manila, negotiations became increasingly confused, Lichauco acting as though at a loss to know how to proceed—or to know whether he now wanted to do so, in any case.

After weeks of waiting for the *Kolya,* the cattle she was to have taken to Manila were at last shipped to a market that had arisen in Fremantle. Lichauco, cabled to that effect, replied at once that the *Kolya* was now on its way. At considerable inconvenience and with remarkable dispatch, a mob of 300 was got together in time for her arrival. This was 250 short of the lot that had been sent south, but M.P. thought a prompt dispatch better all round than delaying the ship while the number was made up.

His optimism was unfounded, as a cable announcing the arrival of the cattle demanded compensatory payment of £500 for the shortage, together with a cancellation of their contract. C.D. & D. replied that they would pay this only on condition that the contract was continued to its legal conclusion. This was accepted, providing the price per head was reduced by 10s. C.D. & D.'s bedrock offer of 5s less per head, plus the £500 compensation, evoked no reply.

In desperation, M.P. at last contacted his Manila friend, Judge Kincaid, asking whether he would act as their agent and inform Lichauco that they intended suing him for £4,000 breach of contract. Kincaid undertook this task, with the result that Lichauco agreed to the compromise terms laid down, and to a further extension of contract if they so desired. On this, M.P. commented somewhat tersely:

> 20.11.15: Hard to understand that having broken the contract so abruptly and unreasonably, he is now practically climbing down to renew it. His ship is to start for Wyndham tomorrow and I trust we can carry on without a further hitch. I regret, however, that we are now obliged to continue the contract after April next, by

which time I believe the prices will be considerably higher than those to which we have now agreed.

M.P. was by this time back in Perth, immersed in the usual complexity of his business and family affairs. He had not been long home when Bess, having heard that her father was not expected to live, sailed for Adelaide with the baby Betty, leaving the household in Claremont in the capable hands of May the nursemaid and Lizzie the cook, with Elodie Pombard as housekeeper. Elodie's association with the family had survived the break-up with Frank Connor, and thereafter, although mostly with the Connor family, she was also very much part of our own lives. As it happened, Grandfather Johnstone survived the last-resort amputation of a leg, and was to live on, mentally alert despite his disability, for a number of years. Bess was back within a few weeks, accompanied by her sister Nell and niece Katie Davey of Melbourne, to enjoy 'the hottest Christmas on record' with friends and family.

M.P.'s diary rambles on, recording daily activities, local politics, war news and names that recall the tangled associations of the years. Among a number in failing health for whom he was particularly concerned was Mrs Tom Kilfoyle who, then in Perth with her son Jack, was being cared for by her unmarried sisters Joe and Maggie Byrne[1]. He was worried, too, about his sister Mary whose children were being cared for during her long illness by their Aunt Bird at their home, the Nest, in Cottesloe.

Aunt Fan and her family at Leederville were also on M.P.'s visiting list. He was with them all to say farewell to Neal when he sailed with the 10th Light Horse at the end of October, taking along with him a horse he had ridden in the Kimberley stock camps. He had become engaged not long before to a girl named Imelda Sellenger, who was already regarded as part of the family. Neal was soon to be followed to the front by his younger brother Jack (J.P.), who had also joined a Light Horse regiment.

Friends and relatives away at war loomed large on all their horizons at that time. Dermot was then attached to a remount camp in Marseilles, from which post he returned at intervals to India for further horses. His letters of that period, though fairly frequent, conveyed little more than his whereabouts and the fact that he was 'still in the land of the living'[2].

Mrs Phillipps made the train journey to Claremont and thence to Bimera by horse-drawn cab to share each letter received from her beloved son with the Durack family. Together they followed him from Heliopolis to Cairo where, on 21 August 1915, he exhorted her not to worry, since 'no Turk could ever blow me out'. At the end of September he wrote cheerfully enough from Gallipoli, and again on a more serious note a few weeks later, assuring her that it was no fault of the Australian soldiers that the campaign had been unsuccessful and that they still had further fields to conquer. This was his last letter from Gallipoli, but his correspondence was indeed to continue from further fields on which, to his mother's pride and joy, he would rise steadily in military rank.

As the year drew to an end there was the customary wet-weather exodus from the north. This included Nance Durack from Argyle, on her way to Adelaide for the birth of her only child, and also Jack and Emily Skeahan who, now having a family to consider, had said goodbye to Auvergne, sold their share of Bullita Station to C.D. & D., and hoped to settle in the less remote Murchison district.

Ulysses, who had come south on the same ship, was the first to occupy Bimera's separate quarters for friends on holiday from the north. His object in wanting to make the journey was not so much to see the white man's noisy metropolis as to see how P.B. was making out at Behn Ord. The two had established a warm relationship on Argyle during the 1890s, when they had worked together in the stock camps and ridden many hundreds of miles side by side. Since P.B. had left the north in 1902, Ulysses had never ceased to enquire for his welfare and for that of his wife and the four children with whom he was acquainted only through photographs. Having greeted a number of old friends, travelled by train to the city and by ferry to South Perth Zoo, he was ready for a motor trip to Wagin. Of this more than usually trouble-free journey M.P. reports only one incident, this being an encounter with two men in search of horses that had somehow eluded them. Ulysses, having ascertained roughly where the horses were last seen, lost no time in picking up their tracks, locating, and returning them to the owners who, obviously impressed, enquired whether he wanted a job. To this he replied politely: 'No thanks. This my boss here. We havin' a holiday.'

But Ulysses showed no inclination to sit around during his three months at Behn Ord. He expected P.B. to regard him as the right-hand man he had been in their younger days in Kimberley, and in this he was not disappointed. To the end of his life he would speak of riding after sheep among the comparatively pocket-handkerchief-sized properties of the south: of farms cut into neat paddocks between made roads, an impression of which he would sketch out meanwhile with his fingers in the sand.

M.P., too, enjoyed his occasional visits to the Wagin property into which his brother had put so much energy and enthusiasm. Moving around together, they discussed their pastoral and other business projects in both north and south. Owing to their problems with the Manila market, 1915 had been a disappointing year where cattle were concerned, but Behn Ord wool had fetched more than £5,000 with an additional sum on the sale of possum furs[3]. On this latter enterprise, M.P.'s comments read surprisingly:

> 27.11.15: Heard from Doherty, London today. He sold 25,000 dozen furs and is to put a further 25,000 on the market.
> 1.12.15: Meeting with manager Hales at our wool and grain stores, Fremantle. About £4,000 credit for the furs since 30th September since when Doherty advised another £2,000 for further sales so far.

C.D. & D. had been dealing in possum skins, presumably dispatched from the Wagin area, since at least 1908, but in view of the number of furs here referred to it is possible that these included the hides of grey kangaroo and brushtail wallaby which were being traded in great numbers at that time. If this were not the case, we can only wonder that any of the genus possum should have survived to the present day.

J.W. returned from Wyndham at the end of the year to resume charge of the company office in Perth. He arrived just in time for a celebration to mark John Forrest's fiftieth year in the public service of his State. This was an occasion of special significance to the Durack family, since their venturing with cattle from Queensland to Kimberley had been largely owing to Alexander Forrest's report on the district of 1879[4]. Despite occasional business differences with Forrest, Emanuel they had always appreciated the qualities of both these families and their personal friendship had remained, for the most part, unimpaired.

M.P. and his brother called on John Forrest and his wife with two suitably inscribed books before attending a function in the town hall to celebrate the occasion.

Of this M P. records that, of the many speeches, he thought the best were those delivered by the Anglican and Roman Catholic Archbishops—Riley and Clune—the latter having been typically 'finished and ornate'. There had been references throughout to the various facets of Forrest's career as explorer, surveyor, politician, and statesman, and to his contributions to the development of his home State, among them the concepts of the goldfields' water supply, the Fremantle harbour, and the transcontinental railway.

The year ended with an emotional address to the nation by Prime Minister Hughes, asking that all denominations should unite in declaiming the horror and ultimate futility of war and join in prayer for its termination.

By that time a number of hitherto inconceivable possibilities had begun to present themselves. What if the war were to drag on until there were no further volunteers within the age limit? Was the need to conscript manpower already looming? What action could be taken in the event of invasion? Speculations of this sort generated animus for all manner of home-defence activities, and M.P. records his frequent attendance at the rifle range and Claremont recreation grounds for shooting practice, drill, and instructions in first aid.

The new year brought a cable from Lichauco wishing M.P. and his associates the compliments of the season but suggesting, as he could not say when the *Kolya* would be next available, the immediate cancellation of their contract, with no damages to be paid by either party. He was promptly informed that C.D. & D. were not prepared to terminate the contract until Lichauco had taken delivery of the two further shipments agreed upon, the cattle for which were already in hand. It was made clear to him, however, that the company would thereafter be willing to bring their contract to an end. In fact, alternative markets were already opening up at higher prices than those being offered in the Philippines, but new arrangements for shipping or droving took time and it was uneconomic to hold cattle indefinitely in the delivery paddocks near Wyndham. After considerable bargaining, the company threatened to sue for £500 breach of contract unless Lichauco would take at least one of the two shipments previously agreed upon. Challenged to prove the loss they had allegedly sustained, they declared that the cost of holding cattle, as they had done for many weeks, was more than £2,000, for which they were entitled to sue if the more generous charges were not paid immediately. This brought a final cable from Lichauco saying he would pay the £500 but was unable to do so before three months. Whether this money was ever paid is not on record, as all references to the Philippine trade stop abruptly at this stage. Nor, in view of improved prospects elsewhere, would this seem to have been a matter of great regret.

The shipping facilities to Fremantle that had caused so much inconvenience and annoyance when taken over by the State Government in 1912 had been improved by the recent acquisition of two further vessels. One of these was the *N.2*, formerly *Prinz Sigismund*, the Kaiser's private yacht, which had been captured in Brisbane at the outbreak of the war. Soon to be renamed the *Bambra*, it was more suitable as a passenger ship than for the transport of cattle, though it was used for both purposes until returned to the British Government in 1927. The other vessel was the *Kangaroo*, purchased while under construction in Glasgow, which was not only the first new ship to operate in the northern cattle-trade, but the first Australian-owned diesel-engined motor-vessel and, at 4,438 tons, the second largest British motor-ship[5].

M.P. took his family to Fremantle to welcome its arrival, and comments in his diary:

> 1.2.16: And so let us hope that we embark with this new vessel on an era of improved transport in waters soon, please God, to be again at peace.
>
> 2.2.16: Latest news—a German raider has sunk six vessels including the Clan MacTavish with all our Wagin wool—40,000 lbs—worth £5,000. It was insured, but we will lose heavily as there is a rise of thirty per cent in the wool market with even better prospects for March sales.

But for all such sharp reminders of the world situation, it is surprising to what extent M.P. and his associates had learned to live with it. There was no talk of waiting for more normal circumstances before venturing into the metropolitan real-estate market, as they did at this time, buying up blocks of bush land at absurdly low prices in anticipation of the steady spread of Perth's suburbs. Somehow or another they would ride the war out, meanwhile consolidating their position to meet the challenges of peace.

Matters of Life and Death

March 1916–October 1916

M.P., though often amused by people prone to building castles in the air, was himself an inveterate builder of this type of edifice. The time would no doubt come when improved living conditions and modern facilities would make the rearing of a family in the north more practical. He was realistic enough, however, to see this as being too far out of range to meet his own requirements. At this stage of his life, the solution to his problems appeared to lie in another direction: very soon, the war over and the Wyndham meatworks at last a going concern, they would sell the northern properties at a price that would previously have seemed improbable. He would then establish a land and estate business, or some such enterprise, in the city. He would build a fine house overlooking the Swan River and, in due course, would take his wife and children 'around the world'. Bess's fortune-telling cards had seen the fulfilment of these dreams before M.P. sailed for Wyndham on the *N.2* in March of that year, little knowing he was already trapped in a life pattern that he was destined not to escape.

This northbound journey seemed unusually significant to M.P., as the passengers included not only 200 men for the construction of the meatworks, but the geologist Dr Herbert Basedow, and party, who were to investigate inland from Derby for minerals needed by the Home Munitions Department. Anything to do with the mineral potential of the north was of particular interest to M.P., and he and Dr Basedow were soon absorbed in animated dialogue.[1]

Also on their way back to Wyndham were M.P.'s cousin M.J., his close friend Arthur Haly, then manager of Moola Bulla, and the Aboriginal Ulysses, whose three months in the south had supplied him with absorbing anecdotes for the rest of his life.

It is puzzling to find that the ship was boarded at Broome by Father Joseph Bishoffs, as when I was writing a history of missionary work in Kimberley[2], I was given to understand that he had been interned in New South Wales at the outbreak of the war. It was said that he had soon afterwards been allowed out on parole to assist the Bishop of Armidale, and that at the end of the war he had been transferred to South Africa. M.P.'s diary makes it clear, however, that if he had been interned he was by this time back in the north and deploring the decline of Aboriginal culture as forthrightly as before.

With business to attend to in Darwin relating to the company's Territory holdings, M.P. proceeded to that port before disembarking at Wyndham. The affable Mayor, Mr Percy Kelsey, drove him at once to see the progress being made on the meatworks, about which he expounded with hopeful enthusiasm. The hundreds of men engaged, earning up to £14 a week, had already brought new life to the town, and by the following year, when the works should have begun to operate, Darwin would be well and truly on the map. M.P., for all the doubts he had about the practicality of the Darwin works, could not but be impressed with the sheer magnitude of the undertaking.

> 1.1.16: One of the buildings—a two storey place, has a floor space of 350 x 65 feet. The entire works has a floor space of ten acres. The water supply still seems to present a problem though at present they are drawing 15,000 gallons a day from three or four wells. For washing down, cooling etc., they will draw water from out to sea . . . They expect soon to be killing 500 head a day.

He was surprised to find the Administrator, Dr Gilruth, rather less optimistic about the works than previously.

> He sees labour problems looming with the encouragement of irresponsible unionists. Sly-grog selling is rife and the police can't cope with it. He thinks, as before, that W.A. made a great mistake in starting the works at Wyndham—says we should have waited and profited by the mistakes that Darwin is soon to make, whatever he may have meant by that.

But about other aspects of Territory development Gilruth was as euphoric as ever. From a pastoral and agricultural point of view, he still saw no limits to its potential. Asked what he considered its average carrying capacity, he declined to specify but was sure that much of the country under his administration would carry a beast to half an acre. M.P. took his leave, wondering how Territory country of that calibre had remained hidden from him for the last thirty years[3].

Back in Wyndham he reported 'wonderful progress' on the meatworks about a mile from the town and at a pool twenty miles out which was the pumping-site where two 25,000 gallon tanks were going up. Otherwise he found the port more than usually depressing, the company hotel and store being inefficiently handled, mainly as a result of what he described as 'overindulgence in one of the commodities they are paid to dispense'.

He was also finding it difficult at this time to maintain a civil relationship with the Resident Magistrate and Medico, Dr Innis Stephen, who had succeeded the admirable Dr Parer and with whom he had been on friendly enough terms up to this time. According to my mother's memoirs, Stephen was an Englishman who had come to Wyndham after serving for some time as doctor and magistrate in the south-western port of Esperance, W.A. M.P. had listened with interest to Stephen expounding on the long-term effects of the war on human values, and even to his seeing materialism and moral corruption as being about to destroy not only Christianity but 'our so-called civilization'. It was only when Stephen became more specific that M.P. began to question his judgement. On what evidence, for instance, could he suggest that Asquith, Lord Haldane, and other Cabinet Ministers were in the pay of Germany? The question did not daunt Stephen, who saw convincing evidence in every setback to the allied cause—even, in June of that year, in the sinking of the H.M.S. *Hampshire* off the Orkney Islands. What more obvious than that these fellows should want to get rid of Lord Kitchener before he turned the tide of events in favour of the British Empire? Sometimes M.P. could attribute such statements to Stephen's being 'in a somewhat muddled state'. What he found more disturbing was that the doctor could make equally unfounded statements when apparently 'stone-cold sober'.

It was with a sense of 'blessed relief' that M.P. turned his back on Wyndham and headed for the sanctuary of the bush. What drinking there was outback at that time was discreetly handled, and usually occurred only on special occasions. For Bill Jones, who could enjoy a party with anyone and was of sociable disposition, alcohol was a pleasure but never a problem. He was at Ivanhoe homestead to greet M.P. on his arrival and to report in detail on recent happenings. There was nothing here to suggest neglect, 'muddle', or disharmony. Paddy Boyle, the genial Irish Jack-of-all-trades, had the troublesome pump working efficiently from the lagoon and a new wagon shed completed. Ah Sam, bowing and smiling blandly, set before them an excellent meal.

> 7.4.16: Everything in good order here. Ulysses quite in his element again with Jimmy Deacon, Alick and Toby in with bullocks from up river. Cattle and horses looking very well.

It is obvious however, that although the days were busy and pleasant enough, he was sadly missing his wife and family.

> 10.4.16: Ivanhoe. Finding the nights very quiet and long, my thoughts wandering to the dear ones at home in Claremont and thinking of the happy times spent here with Bess, Gert, Mrs McCaully and the children.
> 26.4.16: Argyle. Ambrose out burning around the fences when I arrived. The place looking deserted—fowls in possession of the verandah. Nance's cheerful presence much missed. The blacks anxious for news of her and the baby daughter now over a month old.

The homesteads at Newry and Auvergne were also womanless at that time, Charlie Darcy being in charge of Newry and Archie Skuthorpe, who had replaced Jack Skeahan, at Auvergne. M.P., then travelling on horseback between the properties, makes no reference to missing his car which, since Bess had taken to the wheel rather more easily than himself, he had decided to leave behind, 'pro tem'. He may even have been glad of an excuse to return for a while to the old-fashioned but comparatively trouble-free mode of transport.

On his next visit to Wyndham he presided at a dinner for the Minister of Aboriginal Affairs, R. H. Underwood, and the newly appointed Chief Protector of Aborigines, A. O. Neville. 'Party politics and other contentious issues' were eschewed for this occasion, to be taken up later at formal meetings. It would appear from M.P.'s comments that issues relating to the Aborigines were discussed somewhat warily over the next few days, Underwood and Neville feeling their way in relatively unfamiliar territory.

M.P. summed up Neville as a 'genuine seeming fellow' but with plans for assisting the people under his protection that seemed somewhat contradictory. Neville spoke movingly of the mixed and outcast people of other areas and of his hope of saving the fine, virile, full-bloods of the north from the corruptive influence of white society[4]. It was his aim to encourage the maintenance of their tribal identity in reserve areas where they could live their own lives under benign white control, and their children could go to school. M.P. was open-minded about Aboriginal education but he failed to see that the people were less likely to be corrupted by European influences if introduced to them through schooling within the boundaries of a reserve. In any case, by what means would this 'benign control' keep a people within areas which might be approved by white authority but which had little to do with the tribal areas of Aboriginal antiquity?

Much of Neville's thinking seemed to M.P. in line with that of Father

Bishoffs, which had always interested but somewhat bewildered him. The mention of this fact, however, soon revealed that Neville was forthrightly anti-mission. He was also politely critical of Aboriginal employment on pastoral properties, with the exception of Moola Bulla which, although a cattle-run where Aborigines worked much as on other stations, was a government-run reserve.

M.P. would seem to have listened patiently enough until the non-payment of wages to Aboriginal workers was brought into question. On this subject he was prepared to argue, with figures to prove his point, that the system by which not only the workers but their families, including old people and children, were kept in the necessities of life, did not represent cheap labour. A stockman's pay would not cover the cost of food, clothing, blankets, tobacco and medicine for upwards of ten dependants, and station owners could not afford to meet both wages and the cost of supplies for their extensive communities. In short, if wages were introduced, the family life that the people then enjoyed on station properties could no longer be maintained. Besides this, M.P. argued, surely Neville would agree that there was no more corruptive factor than money in our so-called 'civilized society', except the liquor that could be bought with it.

It says something for the two central figures in this discussion that they continued to converse in a friendly and mutually concerned manner until Neville's retirement from office, by that time as Commissioner for Native Affairs, in 1940.

M.P. recorded a happy return to Perth in mid-August; Bess's mother was then on a visit from Adelaide and the house at Claremont was the centre of lively social and family gatherings. He had been back only a few days when, as recorded in his diary, the *West Australian* conveyed an item of sadly disturbing news.

> 25.8.16: This morning's paper announces the tragic death of poor old Connor. It gave us all a great shock as despite our late disagreement over business matters we felt it very much—more so, in fact, under the circumstances. No details as yet but it so far appears to us to have been a case of 'felo de se'. We sent messages of sympathy to the Connor family.

This unfortunate happening was recorded at considerable length in the *Western Mail* of 1 September 1916.

> Mr Connor had arranged a kangaroo hunt and was to be accompanied on the expedition by Mrs Connor and the Rev. Father Roggero.

> At about four o'clock in the afternoon Mr Connor went into an ante room, the dimensions of which were 5' x 3', to obtain guns and a few minutes later called Mrs Connor, for what purpose cannot be conjectured. When Mrs Connor reached the room she found the door shut. In order to open the door which was defective, she had to throw her weight against it with the result that it flew open suddenly and struck Mr Connor on the elbow as he was standing behind it and apparently in the act of loading the gun. The weapon immediately went off and the whole charge entered Mr Connor's head, shattering his skull . . .
>
> Mr Connor, who was fifty-nine years of age, was a leading public figure of this State for many years. He was fond of horse racing and was equally well known in sporting and mining circles . . .
>
> On the introduction of Responsible Government to W.A., Mr Connor was elected to represent East Kimberley in the Legislative Assembly but for some years prior to his death he had been a member of the Upper House, representing the North Province . . .

This information was followed by an account of Connor's life-story from the time of his emigration from Ireland in 1895 and his setting up a store in Wyndham with Denis Doherty the following year.

> Throughout his career Mr Connor was interested not only in grazing and mercantile pursuits but in shipping and mining which alternately returned him big profits and heavy losses . . .
>
> About a year ago he purchased 'Hillside' at Benger, W.A. and made it his home. Since then he acquired other adjoining properties, his love of open air life deciding him to bring up his children on the farm.
>
> Two sons of the deceased, Frank and Patrick, are in Manila. Another son, Trooper Hugh Connor of the 10th Light Horse, was invalided home from the front only three weeks ago. His other children are Moira, Kitty, Thomas, Roderick and Peggy (aged five years).

The only aspect of Connor's activities to which there was no reference in this otherwise comprehensive article was his long association with the firm of Connor, Doherty & Durack. Members of the Durack family were, however, listed among those at the graveside in the Bunbury cemetery. These were J.W., M.J. and his wife Bertha, Jim and Mary Davidson, and Aunt Fan.

The funeral was attended by an impressive number of public figures, many of whom spoke eulogistically of the deceased. The Premier, Frank Wilson, who had replaced 'Happy Jack' Scaddan only a few weeks before, deplored the loss of one of the State's foremost citizens—'a man of virile temperament and unbounded energy who, while doing well for himself, served his adopted country faithfully and well'.

The Colonial Secretary, H. P. Colebatch, then leader of the Legislative Council, referred to the deceased's magnetic personality and forceful eloquence. 'The Legislative Council', he declared, 'will not see another Francis Connor. His colleagues will never forget his attractive features, impressive gestures, and the Irish brogue with which he illuminated and vitalized the tedium of debate.'

His friend Archdeacon Smyth spoke movingly of his lovable qualities and the ideal family life he had enjoyed. 'Would that W.A. had many politicians possessing as noble ideals. Courage he had to do and dare anything legitimate ... Honour and integrity he not only preached but practised.'

Connor's death aroused immediate speculation concerning a successor to the seat for North Province. M.P., in discussion with Premier Wilson, agreed that George Miles would be the most suitable candidate. Wilson thereupon suggested to M.P. that he might stand for Kimberley at the next election. This was a proposition that had been put to him over a number of years but which he had hitherto dismissed on the grounds that it was as much as he could do to face the problems of a 7,000,000 acre estate, without trying also to administer a district covering 121,268 square miles. He had also contended that one member of the company in politics was surely enough. From this time on, however, it is obvious that he was giving the matter more serious consideration.

It was inevitable, in any case, that political affairs should figure prominently in his diary at this time, since the implications of the conscription issue were then in the forefront of newspaper comment and public discussion. The matter had come to a head after a visit of the Federal Labor Prime Minister, William Morris Hughes, to the battlefields of France—an experience that convinced him of the need for every Australian man of military age to serve in the fighting forces. Volunteers, although an impressive number, seemed at this stage inadequate and the disturbing question of whether men should be conscripted was put to the people in October 1916. Seldom had any issue evoked such heated controversy, and certainly nothing else had ever caused such disruption both between and within the various political parties. In M.P.'s opinion, since the Empire was so obviously at stake a Bill for conscription should have been passed by Parliament, rather than the decision being put in a referendum to the people. No doubt Hughes would have agreed with him, had he not feared that there would be insufficient votes in the Senate to carry a resolution to this effect.

In the meantime so many problems had arisen in Wyndham that M.P. was obliged to return north after only a few weeks with his family. It was with a sad heart that he set off on the *Kwinana* with a 'no' vote to the referendum question ringing in his ears.

> 30.10.16: Sailed today at the same time as a transport of Australian troops for the front. What thoughts must they have entertained, knowing that the majority of their countrymen have voted 'no' in the referendum.
>
> There was a big 'yes' majority in W.A., Victoria and Tasmania, but not enough to counter opinion in the other States.

34

Wicked Wyndham

November 1916–October 1917

Know ye this Port? It's a place of some note
Where the bullocks come clamouring down to the boat;
Where no one could fancy a township could be
For the hill jams the houses right into the sea;
Where officious policemen are always a curse
And flies and mosquitoes are fifty times worse;
Where the heat and the dust and the glare from the shore
And exorbitant prices they charge at the store
May well cause the boldest of spirits to sink
Or goad you to madness, or drive you to drink.

Know ye the town where the whisky is bad
And most of the people who live there are mad;
By the sound of the sea where the salt waters meet
And the Gulf sends her waves almost into the street;
Where the Government seems to be running the show
For wherever the stranger may happen to go
There's Inspectors of this and Inspectors of that
Supervisors, Collectors—some thin and some fat.
Know ye this place? 'Tis a spot I know well
That is only a very short distance from hell.

These verses found in M.P.'s diary this year voiced sentiments he no doubt shared with the author Harry M. Skinner, the local Clerk of Courts. By the time M.P. arrived in Wyndham in November 1916 the several contentious issues he had hoped soon to sort out had become a factious entanglement of problems and personalities of which the central figure was the would-be reformer of world-wide and local shortcomings, Dr Innis Stephen. M.P. had previously observed that Stephen was prone to making unbalanced judgements, often based on peculiar flights of fancy, but the two men had not so far fallen out. By this time however, the doctor had crossed swords with most of the C.D. & D. employees, including Garvin the store manager, and Irvine who with his sisters managed the Wyndham

Hotel. In the process of making enemies, Stephen had also cultivated a few friends, with the result that the port was divided into warring camps, the rights and the wrongs of which are now impossible to assess. Garvin had apparently, on one or two occasions, sold liquor in something under the legal gallon minimum, a transgression for which Stephen, in the role of local magistrate, refused him a renewal of his licence, even after payment of a fine. Stephen was also intent on making out a case against Irvine for his employment of an Aboriginal woman named Nellie to help his sisters in the hotel.

M.P. at once approached Stephen, hoping to resolve these few issues in a reasonable manner. He records the interview as follows:

> 11.11.16: Stephen asked if I thought he was blackmailing our firm. I said I would not like to think so as our relationship had always been friendly. He then referred to the hostility of our store manager, Garvin, who had acted as secretary in framing a number of charges against him to be read at a public meeting. I said we, C.D. & D., did not associate ourselves with this affair.

Among the charges levelled against Stephen by a number of Wyndham residents were 'abusing his office as magistrate by intimidating tactics; insults from the Bench to litigants and witnesses; inconsistency and lack of discrimination; indifference to patients not among his favoured few; drunkenness and unseemly behaviour' (the *West Australian*, 20.4.17). Far from the differences blowing over, as M.P. had hoped, feelings ran so high that a Royal Commission was appointed to investigate the matter and enquiries dragged on over a period of several months. It was generally believed that the charges would result in Stephen's being dismissed from office, but since, while awaiting the outcome, neither Garvin nor Irvine could continue as managers for C.D. & D., M.P. was obliged to sign himself on as owner-manager of both store and hotel while maintaining the others concerned as his assistants. In the meantime he had no option but to take up residence in Wyndham from where, at the best of times, he had always escaped as soon as possible.

As it happened, the result of the Commission did nothing to relieve the situation, as a lawyer appointed by the Public Health Department so eloquently defended Stephen that he was exonerated of all charges and continued for the next year or more to preside over the medical and legal affairs of the East Kimberley district.

At no period of his life, either before or since, was M.P. as virtually trapped in Wyndham as at this time. Perhaps it was as well that he soon found himself involved not only in the business affairs of his company but in the social, sporting and money-raising activities of the town. Diffident at first, he seems soon enough to have become accustomed to mounting platforms and holding forth with persuasive tongue on any subject from wartime causes to local charities. Enthusiastic supporters of these activities were a number of residents of Irish background, whose names figure frequently in M.P.'s records over the years. These include members of the Walsh, Ahern, McManus, Quigley, and Bridge families, who were no doubt largely responsible for the regular visits of Fathers Creagh, Bishoffs and others from the Broome area.

It was not long before M.P. was being urged on all sides to stand for the Kimberley seat at the forthcoming elections but, involved as he was with the administration of his company affairs, he dismissed the proposition as impracticable.

It was to his great relief that a man named Sullivan was at last found to take over the store and a capable widow named Mrs Rihle to manage the hotel, with the help of the Irvine family.

Free to leave the town for the first time in several months, M.P. took a round trip to Darwin where the meatworks had at last begun to operate under the management of Vestey's North Australian executive, C. W. D. Conacher. At their first meeting in the previous year the two men had formed a mutual regard that was to stand the test of time. Australian-born in 1881, Conacher had been educated in Scotland and in 1911 had joined Vestey Brothers International Export Company as their executive representative in China and Madagascar. Transferred to the Northern Territory in 1916, he had quickly come to terms with the local conditions and looked optimistically to a bright future for the area.

The meatworks, with a capacity to treat 500 head a day, had recently begun to operate under difficulties caused by wartime shipping restrictions, high costs, and labour disputes. These, Conacher believed, would be resolved easily enough at the end of the war which, since America had now joined the allies, should not be far away. He expressed a wish to co-operate with C.D. & D. in postwar enterprises, and saw no reason for rivalry between the Darwin and Wyndham meatworks, as there should be cattle and markets enough for both.

M.P. returned to Wyndham in a more cheerful frame of mind, to be greeted by his Aunt Fan who was on a visit to her son Patsy and his wife Lillas. She brought first-hand news of Bess and family, including the latest addition, Kimberley Michael, born only a few weeks before. She also brought letters from Neal who had been wounded at the Battle of El

Magdhaba in Palestine at the end of 1916, but who had since rejoined his regiment, in which he had risen from Orderly Sergeant to Lieutenant.

Back to the familiar routine of his station rounds, M.P. was in and out of Wyndham as quickly as possible. On each visit however, he was met by increasingly earnest persuasion to stand for Parliament. He records on 18.8.17:

> Wire from Arthur Male, Broome, strongly urging me to nominate and assuring me of support in Broome, Derby, Hall's Creek and outlying areas. In Wyndham I am also promised support by O'Leary, Willesee and others. Wired J.W. asking his opinion.
> 20.8.17: Reply from J.W. urging me to stand as Nationalist candidate in deference to request of so many people.
> 22.8.17: More wires—J. J. Holmes, Aubrey McGlew (who wants to start a Derby Committee on my behalf), Arthur Haly, Rademy (Turkey Creek), and Dr Holland (in Hall's Creek today).[1] All say will leave no stone unturned in my support.

Within the next few days he had obviously decided to take the plunge.

> 16.8.17: Out from Wyndham with supporters Irvine, Potts, Barker and Dalton to the Bend of the Ord where we met by arrangement Alf Martin, Bill Jones, Percy Pretlove, Mick Walsh, Malley Gordon and Tom Adolf. Most remarkable that I should address my first meeting at the spot where, when with Bess a few years ago, I took a picture published in the 'Western Mail' Christmas number. Wired Bess to say sorry she is not here to support me but that she would be my inspiration . . . Alf Martin takes the chair—on the seat of a pack saddle, reading wires from various centres asking me to stand. I give them my manifesto and clarion call.

I was to hear of this occasion in after years from several of the participants who remembered the gathering as much for its humour as for its political significance. They laughingly recalled the chairman on his pack saddle while M.P., from the platform provided by a fallen tree, delivered a forthright address against competition from bellowing bullocks and screeching cockatoos.

Politically, it was a confusing period. Frank Wilson, with the Country Party support, had succeeded Jack Scaddan as Premier in July 1916. In April 1917, amid much controversy, the Labor party split into two irreconcilable factions, Scaddan and his supporters, who favoured conscription, having joined the opposition by forming a National Labor Party.

M.P.'s three opponents were typical of the situation. Maloney stood to represent the Unionist residents of Kimberley, but a number of these did not favour his nomination and promised their support to Cameron, who stood as an independent Labor candidate. To complicate matters further, Hollingsworth was nominated as a second Nationalist candidate.

The trade union movement that was gaining strength throughout the State had generated strikes that were impeding progress on the Wyndham meatworks. When the local wharfinger refused to unload ships from Fremantle under the conditions originally accepted, volunteers had undertaken the task—with inevitable reactions and heated back-talk from both sides. For a man of M.P.'s generally moderate disposition, it was a difficult time to embark on a political career, nor was it rendered easier by the fact that Dr Innis Stephen, whose blacklist by this time had M.P. well to the top, became a vocal participant in the proceedings.

> 2.9.17: Dr Stephen tells me with all the spleen he can muster that my committee is not sincere—says they won't vote for me and are only with me to drink my wine. He advised everyone to vote for the Labor candidate, Cameron.
> 5.9.17: Confrontation with Dr Stephen speaking to Woodland in the street. When sighting me he called out: 'That's the scoundrel over there!' When warned by Woodland that I might take him to law, he replied: 'I carry the law in my person—a stick in my hand and a pistol in my pocket.'

It was in this atmosphere that M.P. delivered the maiden speech on which he had been working over the past few days.

> 20.9.17: This evening addressed a meeting outside the hotel. About 100 people. Did not feel very nervous and think I got through fairly well. My friends congratulated me and say I exceeded their expectations.

The patriotic sentiments he expressed would certainly have lost nothing in the earnest vigour of his delivery.

> ... This is no time for party differences, no time for internal strife and strike. We must be up and doing united as a great co-operative force ...
>
> In consideration of the gallant heroes who are fighting so valiantly for our national identity to preserve our hearths and homes, we must strengthen the bonds of our Federal Government

> by supporting Conscription as a means of winning this cruel war . . .
>
> As regards local affairs I have continuously, over thirty years, been associated with the mining and pastoral industries of the Kimberley district. I attach particular importance to the construction of better roads and improved conditions of transport, . . .
>
> I wish also to speak for the importance of the pearling industry and to find means of encouraging and fostering its progress . . .
>
> I feel sure that on polling day you will express the spirit of Nationalism that prevails throughout Australia by voting Nationalist.

On the following day M.P. set sail on the *Kwinana* to visit other parts of the Kimberley electorate.

> 21.9.17: Underweigh 7 a.m. A good few passengers, including two of my political opponents Maloney and Cameron. As I moved along the deck I felt of more importance then hitherto owing to the ready recognition and cheery smiles of almost everyone I passed.

For the next six weeks, travelling by buggy, on horseback and sometimes by car, he toured the West Kimberley district, meeting and addressing the inhabitants, now already known to him, in Derby, Broome, Fitzroy Crossing, Hall's Creek and at outlying stations. It was a new experience for him not merely to discuss the tangled problems of the area, but to be asked how, if elected, he proposed to deal with them. Here as elsewhere, the war had changed many aspects of life on both a human and business level. M.P., from his association with members of the pearling fraternity in Broome, had formed some understanding of their operational difficulties and spoke forthrightly against the application of the White Australia Policy to their industry. The war had brought about a sad fall in the price of shell from the peak it had reached in 1913, and the industry was surviving meanwhile on a government subsidy. M.P. declared himself in favour of this being retained until prices picked up, as was anticipated with the coming of peace.

Whereas the 'button market' had dropped, however, that of beef and wool had risen over the same period, a state of affairs that had influenced many of the smaller land-holders to sell out at prices that would previously have seemed fanciful. There were mixed feelings about the takeover of so much country by absentee owners who would supposedly be indifferent to the needs and problems of the district as a whole. Political moves were already afoot to reduce the area held under one name to a maximum of 1,000,000 acres. In theory this seemed a prudent restriction, but in practice it was found to be easily circumvented by the division of over-large estates into smaller holdings registered under different names.

For a while it had been feared that the enlistment of such a large percentage of station workers in the armed forces would cause severe labour problems, but this too had been simply enough overcome. By 1917, while there were no more than 277 white men employed on Kimberley properties, the number of Aborigines had risen to 803 men and 560 women. It was a state of affairs that even if seen by some as a temporary expedient was to prove otherwise, and would eventually result in a significant decrease in stock losses at the hands of Aboriginal hunters.

M.P., back in Wyndham for election day, records the outcome of his strenuous campaign.

> 10.11.17: And so the anxious stretch of the last eight or nine weeks is now over and the strain relieved. While I was optimistic of the result I had no idea I would beat the Labor Candidates right here on their own ground, and with an absolute majority.

Figures

	Cameron	Maloney	Hollingsworth	Durack
Wyndham	11	51	5	69
Derby	7	8	-	73
Broome	4	31	26	274
Other Centres & Stations	13	28	-	95
Total	35	118	31	511

> 11.11.17: A ball in my honour—very convivial. FINISHED 1.30 p.m.
>
> 13.11.17: Seen off for Fremantle by many Wyndham friends. Enjoying the sea breezes and a game of bridge ...
>
> 16.11.17: Broome ... Greeted with congratulations by Cameron (Labor candidate) and had a drink with him. Having lost his deposit he tells me he is almost blown out and asks for a loan to pay his return fare to Wyndham. Hollingsworth, in the same situation, also asks me for a loan. Gave them each a cheque they assure me will be repaid ...

> Feeling a certain sadness . . . in that I am entering a new phase of life and the associations of thirty-one years in stock life must take second place, for now I become a servant and want to uphold the trust so unanimously conferred on me.

But for all the feelings of regret here expressed, the diary indicates his longing for a good excuse to spend more time with his family.

> How sad to think that our youngest member, Kimberley Michael, will be all of seven months old before I set eyes on him!

35

People and Politics

November 1917–November 1918

The year 1917, as summed up by M.P., had been one of 'changes and vicissitudes', both for the world at large and for himself. He nonetheless embarked on his new role in the political life of the State with a vigour and confidence due to some extent to the widely expressed faith in his administrative ability. He wrote of his return to Perth after a stressful twelve months' absence:

> 26.11.17: Met at Fremantle by the family. Reg, Mary and Betty are all considerably grown and the new member, Kim, quite a robust little chap. It is so pleasing to be with them all again and we make plans for outings to the hills and at the beach.

There is little evidence in his subsequent diary entries of these happy plans eventuating. The door of his Perth office, always open to friends, employees and business associates, was now open to public figures in many categories and to people seeking his advice or influence.

> 27.11.17: Meeting with Premier Lefroy and Ministers Colebatch and Underwood. Interview with Unmack for Charter Company pearlers Broome. Unmack puts forward many propositions for the industry in which he seeks my support. The Reinforcement League asks me to speak on the Conscription question.

The Commonwealth Government was again seeking authority to call up single men to whatever extent voluntary enlistments did not provide sufficient numbers. M.P. was confident that Australia would by this time agree to join Great Britain, New Zealand, and the United States in adopting this measure, and he proceeded to speak for the cause in Perth and country areas.

> 8.12.17: Reg and self by train to Wagin. Address meetings in the district with Sir John Forrest, Lynch and Stewart. Sir John, Stubbs and brother P.B. address the Wagin school. Sir John tells the young people to be moderate, just, and tolerant, not to fly off at

> tangents and to get over obstacles by means of a mental jumping pole. Very good. P.B. gives a dinner at the Wagin Hotel—more speeches.

M.P. welcomed the opportunity of congratulating Forrest on the recent completion of the transcontinental railway for which he had fought so long and so forthrightly. Both men saw the future of Western Australia, linked in this way with the other States, as being happily assured when, with the help of conscription, the war was brought to an end. Soon afterwards, M.P. recorded his disappointment at the outcome of the campaign.

> 21.12.17: Indeed a great shock to find once again a NO majority in all States except Western Australia and Tasmania.

But at least this issue was one in which he had been in agreement with most of his political associates. More difficult were matters for which his support was urged by people of different points of view. One of these pertained to the missions on the Dampierland peninsula.

> 7.12.17: Talked today on question of national reserves for Aborigines. Present—Minister Underwood, J. J. Holmes, G. Miles, A. Male and Sir Edward Wittenoom. General feeling in favour of A. O. Neville's proposal for proclaiming a large government reserve for Aborigines in which to establish a hospital and form a station which might be self supporting. He states that about £1,000 a year is paid to Beagle Bay. He wants to take over the two Catholic Missions (Beagle Bay and Lombadina) and also the Anglican Mission on nearby Sunday Island which gets £250 a year for indigent natives. Nothing beyond formal discussion . . . Minister to submit to Cabinet[1].

This proposal had been under sympathetic review by the Scaddan Government when the Liberals took over in July 1916, but this party had got in by too narrow a margin to risk offending either of the churches involved and the matter had been politely shelved.

M.P., anxious to maintain a non-sectarian front and no doubt seeing some basis for Neville's views, was approached at this stage by Archbishop Clune who had come to hear that there was what he described as a 'secret move afoot' to take over from the Pallottines in Dampierland. He spoke movingly of the devoted work and far-reaching influence of these missionaries but was well aware of the prejudice against them as enemy aliens, even in the Catholic community. Restrictions imposed upon their movements at the outbreak of the war had evidently lapsed in the meantime, providing Neville with a popular argument. The Archbishop, while himself seeing no cause for suspicion of subversive activities, realised that this was the angle most likely to concern the government and suggested that he and M.P. should discuss the matter with Senator Pearce, Minister for Defence. This they did, as M.P. faithfully records.

> 18.1.18: Clune suggests that the missionaries be interned at Beagle Bay and that no luggers go out in charge of any German without sanction from the Commandant in Perth. Pearce very courteous. He assents fully to our request and promises to send the Archbishop a copy of his order.

This would appear to have gone through, though Neville's proposal, brought before the Cabinet soon afterwards, was left in abeyance until the following year when it was finally dismissed.

The opening of Parliament at the end of January meant even busier days for M.P., followed by late-night to early-morning sittings.

Matters pertaining to the future of the Wyndham meatworks now took up a great deal of his time. How was this long-awaited enterprise, the cost of which had escalated alarmingly from Nevanas' suggested estimate of £155,150 to £723,000, to be run to the best advantage to local growers and the State as a whole? One school of thought maintained that it should be taken over by the government. Others favoured its being run as a joint enterprise by a combination of companies. To further complicate the issue, Nevanas then turned up again from Melbourne, declaring that the right to run the works was his alone. His claim was based on the fact that during the negotiations of 1914 Scaddan had written offering him management of the works. It had been taken for granted, however, that this proposition was cancelled along with his contract, and with payment of compensation. If Nevanas had a case it was certainly not accepted by Baxter, the minister in control of meat-freezing propositions, who possibly believed the rumour that Nevanas was operating for Vesteys, to whom he professed himself to be in opposition. This story did not impress M.P., who seems to have agreed that Nevanas had been given a raw deal by the State, to no apparent advantage to the undertaking. It was his view that the pastoral industry would be better served under company management than that of the government. In any case he liked Nevanas personally, and appreciated the 'good talk and excellent musical entertainment' he provided when invited to his home.

Fortunately for M.P., his wife enjoyed extending hospitality as much as she enjoyed accepting it. Life at Bimera in Claremont, and later at Binminna in Perth, included a happy succession of tea, dinner, birthday, and Christmas parties, as well as that most popular of all pastimes, the musical evening. Many of these occasions were shared with E. H. Angelo (then M.L.A. for the Gascoyne district) and his family who had come to live next door. The two families had much in common at this time, M.P. and Angelo commuting to and fro together, and their wives deploring the shocking hours of their return from late sitting at the House.

Among the more frequent visitors was Mrs Phillipps, bringing, along with gifts and goodies for the children, the latest news of her precious son. At the end of 1916, Roy had written from a London hospital where he was recovering from a wound sustained in a front line in France. Though suffering from some paralysis of the foot, owing to a damaged thigh, he wrote cheerfully as usual, supposing it was 'all in the game' and that he would soon be in shape again.

Early in 1917, having since joined the Royal Flying Corps, he wrote of attending a function at Buckingham Palace where he had attempted to 'do a line' with Princess Mary. Where romance was concerned, however, he had more success with a girl from his own State who was nursing in one of the overcrowded military hospitals in London at that time.

When Mrs Phillipps, usually so brave and bright, turned up one day in tears, my parents concluded that the worst had happened. In fact she had received a letter telling of her son's marriage to the daughter of R. T. Robinson, a prominent Perth citizen and politician. M.P. and his wife assured their distraught friend that Nell Robinson was a lovely girl and her people extremely well-to-do, but for Mrs Phillipps this did not alter the fact that another must henceforth take first place in her son's life. Roy continued, nonetheless, to write as before, his next news being that, having 'jumped over the head of ten or more pilots', he had become a Flight Commander. In 1918 he reported that he had 'scored an M.C. in the last show' and had been soon afterwards awarded the further distinction of a bar.

At about this time Neal Durack returned from the front, to the joyous relief of his mother, Aunt Fan, whose greatest worry was now for her son Jack, who was still with his regiment in Palestine. Neal Durack had been wounded several times, but if he suffered any lasting effects they had not impaired his confidence in himself as a stockman and as the prospective husband of Imelda Sellenger. He embarked for Wyndham soon after his return, eager to investigate job opportunities in Kimberley which might include a home base for himself and his wife-to-be. With Neal had returned his close friend Leslie Brockman, with whom he had joined the Light Horse and beside whom he had fought through numerous campaigns.

Towards the end of February 1918, J.W. took off to the eastern capitals on various aspects of company business, which provided a welcome excuse for contacting old friends and widely scattered relatives. His letters home tell of interviews with political figures, beef barons, and business combines. Typically, however, he gave less space to business matters than to the human contacts of his tour.

In Melbourne he had gone to see Sir John Forrest, who was there in attendance at a Treasurer's conference. The press had recently announced his being honoured by a barony, but J.W. did not find him in especially good spirits on this account. He was not enjoying his usual good health and, although pleased about the dignity bestowed on him, wished he could have accepted it in the role of Prime Minister rather than from the humbler position of Treasurer. He seemed cheered however by J.W.'s enthusiastic listing of his major contributions to the development of his home State, these including the Coolgardie water scheme, the Fremantle harbour, the Agricultural Bank and the transcontinental railway, by which J.W. looked forward to returning to Perth.

J.W. often sadly recalled this as his last meeting with Forrest, who was to die at sea in September of that year, on his way to England to take his place in the House of Lords as Baron Forrest of Bunbury.

In Sydney J.W. visited his father's cousin, Tom Durack, and went with him to watch his daughter Fanny again distinguish herself at a swimming carnival.

> 17.3.18: Fanny did 500 yards in seven minutes eight and one fifth seconds in the 100 metre baths at the Domain. She is a marvel—glides gracefully through the water and was cheered to the echo when her record was announced.

J.W. never tired of extolling Fanny's prowess as a swimmer, and her personal charm and grace, which, to our teenage amusement, did not appear to have the full endorsement of his sister Bird. I recall one occasion when his praises called forth from her an aside to my mother: 'You know Bess, she doesn't wear support.' The remark did not escape J.W. 'She doesn't need it, Bird,' he replied, and continued with his eulogy.

Also while in Sydney J.W. called on his old friend Tom Hayes, redoubtable member of the overlanding party and one of the three original partners in Rosewood Station.

> 10.3.18: To tea at Randwick with Tom, wife and two daughters, Dorothy and Pauline (seventeen and fifteen), nice bright girls. Poor old Tom, now 71, blind as a bat. The girls lead him about[2].

From Brisbane, J.W. wrote his brother of happy family gatherings.

> 28.3.18: It would take many hours to write of the Tullys alone. They are as good as gold, nearly killed me with kindness, and ran me here, there and everywhere. Poor old Uncle Pat and Aunt Sarah Tully greeted me with affectionate tears at their son Joe's house in Brisbane. They look splendid and are quite hearty. Most of the Tully clan turned up to see me. These days they all motor to and fro to their various stations out west—Joe to *Pinkilla* near *Ray*, Frank and family to *Terachie*, Uncle, and other members to *Ray*.
>
> Pat's brother Frank, in Brisbane at present, also lives at *Ray*. He is a great Home Ruler and well up in history and politics. He was loud in praise of your maiden speech, as were they all ... Will tell you *all* when we meet[3].
>
> 30.3.18: Back in Sydney and with Dan and Kit Evans to the show. Ushers Hotel full of West Australians among them Edgar and McKenzie Grant, Frank Wittenoom, Lee-Steere, Burgess, De Pledge and Copley ...

It would have been unlike J.W. to return to New South Wales without renewing associations in the Goulburn area where he was born in 1867. Having first called at the cemetery where his parents and many other relatives had been laid to rest, he visited the Christian Brothers' College where he had spent his few years of formal schooling.

> 11.4.18: Met at the old college by Brother Fitzgerald who was at school in Brisbane with brothers Pat and Jerry. He showed me photos taken in 1883 at an address of welcome given to Father Gallagher—so many once familiar faces ... teachers whose graves are now in the college cemetery. What a flood of memories as we walked around. You will recall the tombstone to the memory of Thomas Coman b.1861 d.1875 who was 'taken away lest wickedness should alter his understanding and deceit beguile his soul. Wisdom IV.II.'
>
> Called later at the presbytery to see the good Bishop Gallagher himself—more memories and anxious enquiries for everyone ...

M.P.'s journal ran on, meanwhile, in a somewhat confusing summary of political, business, and family affairs, new names cropping up among the more familiar contacts. Many of these activities awaken my childhood memories, none more so than those pertaining to Nurse Stevens, who, having delivered the last two children, had become the family friend and mainstay that she was to remain for many years[4].

M.P. would seem to have had neither space nor time to comment at length on company affairs over this period. There is reference to occasional bids for at least portions of the C.D. & D. estate, but the partners had decided to lie low until the opening of the meatworks, an event that was expected to increase greatly the value of Kimberley properties. When M.J. had been approached for the purchase of Lissadell by the Riverina pastoralist William Naughton, who had already bought stations in the district, his cousins had advised him strongly to hold on. This he had done, at least until the opening of the works was postponed from early 1918 to the following year. But he returned from Wyndham in July with the news that he had sold to Naughton for 'something over £70,000'. Never as sanguine or trusting as his cousins, he had come to the conclusion that the meatworks was a political toy and would probably create more problems for the pastoralists than it solved. He and Bertha had waited long enough to tour the world: they had no family to plan for, and the money in hand, well invested, should see them out in comfort. As a result of this 'rash decision', he was to be envied for the rest of his life as the 'wealthy member of the family'.

It was August that year before M.P. set sail for the north, his journey as a public figure by no means the relaxed interlude such trips had been in former days. At every port he was met and interviewed about local affairs. In Broome he addressed the Pearlers' Association, spoke to the schoolchildren and magnanimously granted them a half-holiday. In Derby he expounded on the war loan, the recurrent tick problem, and the roads which must be upgraded for motor transport.

Among his fellow passengers to Wyndham was Imelda Sellenger, who was met at the ship by her fiancé Neal, to whom she was married on the following day. Officiating at the ceremony was Father John Creagh, the Irish Redemptorist who had been appointed Pro-Vicar Apostolic of the Kimberley vicarate and Superior of the Pallottine Society in that district after the outbreak of war. A man of tact and good humour, he had done much to keep the missionary situation in hand over a difficult period and was able to assure M.P. that the tactics devised by Archbishop Clune and himself had so far held disruptive rumours within bounds.

Neal was by this time managing Auvergne, a problem property that, with Boxer as his right-hand man, did not appear to daunt him. It was possibly following M.P.'s example that he had, of recent months, begun to keep a diary which might, had he lived longer, have given us much otherwise unrecorded history. As it stands it tells at least something of the conditions under which many men suffered and succumbed in that rugged hinterland. Shortly before his marriage he made the following fairly typical entry:

> 10.8.18: Galloping after cattle in rough country when my horse, Dandy, fell and knocked me out. Jim and Eligha Bickley bandaged me up with strips of sheet. Rode into the station. Have broken my collarbone and two ribs. Laid up for several days—also Boxer who ran a rusty nail into his foot.

Boxer's mishap had occurred in the process of repairing the Auvergne homestead for the arrival of the bride. It was perhaps fortunate that Imelda's first experience of station life was not in the solitude of Auvergne but at Argyle with Nance Durack, the only other white woman within range, while Neal rode off on a tour of inspection with M.P., Ambrose, Boxer, and Ulysses.

M.P. was back in Wyndham when the signing of the Armistice was at last confirmed.

> 12.11.18: At about 9 a.m. I receive an urgent wire from J.W. The war is over and Perth is deliriously joyful. We here in Wyndham drank to *The Day* and proclaimed for ourselves a holiday. Cars plying between the three hotels—Wyndham, Three Mile and Six Mile but, perhaps fortunately, there is little beer in town so the crowd has been very orderly.
>
> Over to the Point where we were taken through the works, now nearing completion—yet another cause for satisfaction. We came down from the top floor in an *electric lift*. A fitting event for this great day!

36

Looking Skywards

December 1918–December 1919

The war had cost Western Australia some 6,000 young lives, amounting to 10 per cent of her population, while of the 12,000 wounded many were permanently incapacitated. It was a sad price to pay, especially for a State so largely dependent on primary production and the youth and strength to maintain it. Nonetheless the patriotic and community spirit, always a strong factor in local life, had never flagged. Good causes ranging from the Red Cross, the Victoria League and Legacy Club to Salvation Army drives and the Soldiers' Parcels and Packet Fund had set women throughout the State cooking, knitting and sewing for a wider concept of family than had fully occupied them before. Nor did the end of the war put a stop to such activities, since the needs of the boys at the front were soon replaced by those of returning veterans, many of whom were in need if not of physical help, of employment and adjustment to the postwar situation.

M.P. remarked on the many aspects of local life that had changed dramatically over the war years. Telephones were now accepted as a domestic as well as a business facility, and an expanding railway system had brought the State's southern areas into closer communication. Motorcars were becoming commonplace and motor-powered tractors had opened up new prospects for farming areas. Economically the outlook was promising and speculation was on an upward grade. Many returned men were eager to invest their savings in land-development schemes, for which both the government and the Agricultural Bank had agreed to grant credit where such was necessary to make a start.

The majority settled for modest 'cocky farms' in the comparatively closely settled south-west and eastern wheatbelt, though some had hoped to take up cattle-runs in the great open spaces of Kimberley. To these it was soon obvious that the 40,000,000 acres of more reliable country was already under leasehold, mostly to big companies, until 1948. Only two or three were determined and game enough to take up outskirt areas verging on the desert to the south and the Forrest River Aboriginal reserve to the north.

The New Year was seen by M.P. as beginning with 'an air of cheerfulness more evident than since the outbreak of the war'. Of his own life, he had been happy to record, soon after his return from the north, the birth of his third son at his Claremont residence.

> 9.11.18: The little chap made strong protest at being brought into this hard world but all is well with his mother and himself. Nurse Stevens in attendance. The children excited at seeing the baby. Reg looking very thoughtful.

The boy was christened William Aiden but, being the fifth in the family, was always known to his father as 'Quintus Superbus' rendered Quinty for short.

M.P. was becoming accustomed to juggling family affairs along with his business and parliamentary commitments, and to the pressures of party politics. The names of contemporary public figures recur in his diary day by day, most of them conjuring up for me childhood memories of big, talkative, affable men, most of whom were to remain familiar figures throughout the years to come.

> 17.1.19: Chat with Premier James Mitchell re meeting at Town Hall at which he wants me to speak. Attended meeting of Pastoral Association. Discussions with Edward Wittenoom, Angelo, J. J. Holmes and others re Fremantle freezing proposition. Still trying to devise a scheme whereby growers could enter into establishment of a company protecting both the growers' and the State's interests . . .

The Fremantle freezing proposition was another issue. It was by this time established that the Wyndham meatworks were to operate under government control but still the argument went on.

> 24.1.19: J. J. Holmes, E. Wittenoom, J. Forrest [son of the late Alexander Forrest], B. Copley, J. W. Durack, J. E. Davidson and self meet with Baxter, Minister for Agriculture in control of proposition for Government freezing. As one acting for a government professing to be out to assist the producer the Minister's attitude was one of direct hostility, implying that the government was in the box seat and would use its position for all it was worth, there being no other avenue for Kimberley producers in any case.

The pastoralists argued that the price offered by the government was £5 to £7 lower than that paid for meat in other markets. Baxter pointed out that it was more than they had obtained previously, but the growers insisted that this was beside the point since the government claimed to be supporting the interests of the producers. A cable from Doherty in London finally advised the company to settle for the proposed terms for a year at least, as postwar markets and freighting costs were still indefinite.

The Armistice that had overcome a major anxiety had by no means brought clear skies in all directions. With the passing of every month it became more obvious to M.P. that any turn of events, however seemingly irrelevant, could beget disturbing political offspring. Even the outbreak of pneumonic influenza at the beginning of that year led to parliamentary problems. H. P. Colebatch, as acting Premier and Minister for Health, had seen fit to implement quarantine restrictions which, together with a seaman's strike, served to disrupt transport, delay the unloading of cargo, and leave travellers stranded. There were bitter repercussions for Colebatch, though it was later conceded that but for the measures he adopted there would no doubt have been more than the 500 deaths from the epidemic recorded for the State.

M.P. found himself in the difficult situation of having to explain to frustrated representatives from Broome, Derby, and Wyndham that, to comply with the regulations, vessels must be unloaded and away before low tide left them high and dry. At the same time he was earnestly impressing on Colebatch the importance of better postal facilities and improvements to the coastal shipping service.

As always, the breaking down of isolation for the north was a major consideration with M.P., and he faithfully recorded every hopeful reference to the possibilities of air travel.

> 25.2.19: This morning's paper reports that aerial expert, General Sykes, speaking in London, says that Wyndham should be first Australian port of call in flights from England via Cairo, India and Singapore—thence to Normanton and along the railway system to Melbourne.
>
> Please God I live to see the day when the first plane from overseas sets down on Australian soil.

With a view to touring his electorate he was then having his Dodge car fitted up on what he described as 'the Abbot's buggy principle', equipped with duplicate parts and a number of ingenious devices for getting a vehicle over river beds, through sand, mud, and other obstacles to outback motoring. He was meanwhile driving his wife's car, in which he experienced his usual variety of odd mishaps.

> 9.2.19: Door of the car swung open this morning and caught the gate as I was going through. Tore off portion of the door and damaged the hinge.
> 28.2.19: Returning home this afternoon when a man on a bike ran into me, damaging the radiator and hurting his hand. He was on the wrong side of the road and had his head down on account of the wind. Took him to the hotel, got him a brandy and drove him to his home with his bike.

M.P. had originally planned to travel overland on the approximately 2,000-mile journey from Perth to Wyndham, taking with him a man named Bolton as mechanic and chauffeur. Having been persuaded that this would be a hazardous and time-wasting venture, he decided to bring Bolton and the car along with him to Wyndham by ship. They sailed on the *Kwinana* at the end of March, in overcrowded and uncomfortable conditions of which M.P. did not spare the details:

> 7.4.19: ... For evidence of dirt, neglect and mismanagement commend me to the State steamers ... the comfort of the passengers in no way considered but their toleration is commendable!

Whether Wyndham was more or less 'wicked' as a result of its increased population and activity, he does not say. By the time of his arrival the men engaged to erect the works, including a number of Greeks who were making via Darwin for the canefields of Queensland, were moving out as others engaged to process the cattle were moving in. The port was a hub of activity, and M.P. was plunged headlong into the negotiation of stock numbers and delivery dates with Arthur Haly and Malcolm McGhie, who were in charge of the forthcoming operation.

There was still so much to be done and so many problems to be overcome that M.P. was doubtful whether the works could open on the appointed date. He feared that further disturbing news of industrial trouble in Darwin might foreshadow similar problems for Wyndham, where strikes were already threatening. A stop-work meeting at Vestey's works in protest at an increase in the price of bottled beer had been followed by hundreds of Unionists marching on Government House and demanding to see the administrator. Gilruth had handled the situation firmly, with the result that the crowd, before dispersing, had burned his effigy. He had since gone on leave and it was considered doubtful that he would return.

Meanwhile in Wyndham the schoolchildren were confidently rehearsing a concert for the projected opening. M.P. paid them his usual visit and delivered a typical address.

> 26.4.19: I spoke on the meaning of Anzac Day and of how Australia is no longer an isolated sub-continent but very much part of the outside world to which it grows closer with the advent of powered flight.

A round of the stations with Bolton at the wheel of the 'Khaki Cloud', as M.P. called his Dodge, brought him in touch once more with his bush associates. Bill Jones based at Ivanhoe and Ambrose at Argyle had ably represented him during his extended absences, while the other stations were being capably carried on by Charlie Darcy at Newry, Neal Durack at Auvergne and Jim Crisp at Bullita.

Darcy had recently married Gertrude Hyland, member of a family famous in the circus business, whose mother and sister Maud were then visiting her. M.P. was fascinated by the stories, not only of their performances throughout Australia but of those overseas[1]. He was relieved to know that there was again a white woman in residence at Newry, as he had been concerned for the isolation of Neal's young wife, to whom a daughter, named Auvergne for the remote station of her origin, had been born in Wyndham at about that time.

The opening of the meatworks, an event he had looked forward to for so many years, was not after all delayed.

> 29.5.19: *Der Tag!* Haly, Jones and I select a big red bullock, the *first to be knocked down* and of which I get the horns and hide as a memento. Large crowd present but no ceremony. Heaviest beast killed today went 960 lbs—the average 761 to 764 lbs. Haly, Jones and self celebrate the occasion with a glass of wine.

He remained in Wyndham for the next ten days carefully observing and recording the teething problems of the new enterprise.

> 2.6.19: At Works. Killed fifty head by 11.00 a.m.—too many for the boning department to keep up with. Good average weight—none condemned.
> 4.6.19: With Jones, McGhie and Haly re price adjustment for loss of weight from holding cattle more than three days—about 5 lbs a day per beast. Finally agree to allow 4 lbs loss per day.
> 19.6.19: Entertain members of the Engineering Department to celebrate the running of the big Diesel engine which was started

up today. The wheel is 18' by 4' diameter—makes fifty-five revolutions to the minute.

Everything now ready for overland trip. Leaving with Bolton tomorrow.

This tour of his electorate that he had planned and looked forward to for some time proved to be something of a nightmare experience. The 'pull-me-out', a new gadget in which he had placed considerable faith, would seem to have achieved little if anything more than an old-fashioned push from the rear:

23.6.19: Struggled on to the Dunham. Encountering many hold-ups. Looked over the deserted homestead and the family graves. Sad memories.
25.6.19: Delayed in sand. Two hours crossing the Little Bow. Hands bleeding from hauling ropes on the pull-me-out . . . Wired Bess from Turkey Creek. Worried that she is at present without help and not well. She replied reassuringly.
27.6.19: Very hard going and feel tired out. Car smashed into a heap of stones concealed in long grass. Bolton dismantles it near Frog Hollow Station. We have no tea. The packet must have jumped out of the tucker box over rough going. Get some at last from passing drovers.
29.6.19: Bolton still hammering away . . . Took walk along creek and came upon graves of Muggleton and McKenzie. Am overcome with sense of loneliness. Too many sad memories . . . Certainly a long and weary wait.
2.7.19: Jack Tweed, teamster, turned up and undertakes to tow car behind his donkey wagon to Alice Downs, Bolton going along with him. I borrow a horse from drover Burness though hands almost too sore to handle the reins.

Nonetheless he obviously made better progress on horseback than by automobile, and over the next few days visited the scattered station communities from there to Hall's Creek.

3.7.19: After bitterly cold night cross Ord River to Alice Downs about twenty-eight miles. Tom Cole and family there—Mrs Cole with new baby. Also there Bert Bridge, Bert Ogden, Flanders and Sellers. Bolton there with car still all knocked about.
4.7.19: Very cold. Hands sore. Met Walter Darcy with Booty's bullocks—550 head—good mob . . .

> 5.7.19: Arrived Moola Bulla. Many natives, children and problems here. Nothing much doing at tannery. Large tank leaking. Horses low. Fair garden . . .
> 7.7.19: Drove with postmaster Tuckett to Hall's Creek.

Here he was hospitably greeted by two pioneer Australian Inland Mission Sisters, Rogasch and Middelton, who treated his blistered hands and cooked him the first square meal he had enjoyed since leaving Wyndham. While waiting for Bolton to arrive with his 'Khaki Cloud', he inspected the remains of his father's Ruby Queen crushing-plant—relic of the goldrush of 1886. The main shaft had been long since burned out but there was still much material that he believed could be salvaged for station use.

When Bolton at last arrived with the car, fitted with a new main shaft, he and M.P. set out again upon the road. There were inevitably further crises encountered on the remainder of the journey to Derby, the most mysterious being at Yeeda Station where the car, for no apparent reason, refused to start. Arrangements were being made to have her towed to the port when the trouble was diagnosed: 'Bolton had forgotten to turn the petrol on!'

M.P. was welcomed, mostly by old friends, at all the stations en route. He enjoyed congenial and (as he hoped) fruitful discussions on local affairs, culminating in a formal reception in Derby and participation in a race-meeting and carnival.

His final reference to the 'Khaki Cloud' was when he boarded the S.S. *Charon* for return to Perth:

> 22.7.19: Have given McGlew authority to sell the car which I leave with the blacksmith Hylitt undergoing further repairs.

He arrived home only a day before the opening of Parliament. It was a busy and exciting time for him on many levels. Politically there was enough to keep him fully occupied, as was there also in company affairs, where prospects for meat, wool and real estate seemed brighter than for some time past. Whatever their associated problems, the Wyndham Works were at long last a *fait acompli* and he was confident that terms would improve as initial difficulties were overcome and the economic situation became stabilized.

He had been delighted to find that among those gathered to greet him on his return were Mrs Doherty, her daughter Bylly, and son Roy. Although M.P. was in constant touch with Denis Doherty by letter and cable, there was much he had not heard of this family of recent years. He now learned that Bylly, youngest of the three girls, had distinguished herself during the war as an intrepid ambulance driver both in England and France. She was to entertain us in years to come with stories of her adventures over this period which, for all their tragic aspects, she managed to infuse with a lively humour that was typical of her family.

Roy had attended a military college, but after his wartime experiences in France he had no interest in following a soldier's career. He was attracted rather to the comparatively free and easy prospects that were supposedly offering 'down under'. His father suggested his going into the Perth office at least until he had learned something of the colonial ropes, but Roy soon made it clear that he had no taste for acrobatics of this kind. He was more interested in investigating possibilities in the pearling industry, or maybe the wool business of which he had learned something from his father.

The Dohertys also brought news of their two elder girls, Katch (who had taken up practice as a physiotherapist) and Vergne (who had embarked on a legal career, and was later to be the first woman admitted to the Inner Temple in London).

Roy Phillipps, now proudly referred to by M.P. as 'the Major', was a frequent visitor, accompanied by his young wife and his mother, now apparently reconciled to his marriage and on affectionate terms with her daughter-in-law. To M.P.'s surprise, Roy did not enthuse about the possibilities of air travel.

> 4.8.19: Roy states that as a result of his experience he discounts the popular view that flying will soon be a commercial proposition. He thinks the cost will be prohibitive.

Roy had hoped to take up a property in Kimberley, but his father-in-law, R. T. Robinson, then Minister for Industries, soon convinced him of the impracticality of this dream and directed his attention to more civilized areas. Before long he announced that they had purchased a sheep property in the Riverina district of New South Wales, for which they left Western Australia soon afterwards[2].

M.P. had been elsewhere when the first aircraft, a Bristol Box Kite piloted by J. J. Hammond, had landed in Perth in 1911. He records sighting a plane in flight for the first time in August 1919: 'It soared aloft of the city under the command of Major Norman Brearley . . .'

This enterprising young man, born in Geelong, Victoria, had come to Western Australia with his parents in 1906. He had served with the Royal Flying Corps from 1916 to 1918 and at the end of the war purchased two Avro 504 aircraft from surplus Government stores. These he had shipped from England, hoping to awaken public interest in the potential of aircraft for civilian use. With this in mind, he had set up a hangar at the Belmont Race Club, where he was permitted to use a part of the ground as his airfield. By that time married to the daughter of M.P.'s parliamentary associate, Sydney Stubbs, Brearley believed he could make a reasonable living from ten-minute joy-rides until better uses for his aircraft opened up. M.P.'s account of his first aircraft sighting continues:

> My impression, watching the graceful movement of this machine was that it looked a very simple matter and that one would be perfectly safe aloft.
>
> I met Bess with the family and together we went along to see Major Brearley give an exhibition of flying at the Cricket Association grounds. During the first landing with Mayor W. Lathlain as passenger the machine caught in the electric wires and was practically put out of action. Nothing daunted, Brearley sped away by motor-car to his Belmont hangar and soon returned with his other machine, giving a fine display of flying and stunts in the air before gracefully descending to the ground.
>
> Soon afterwards Brearley returns to Belmont, meeting with another slight accident in his ascent, one of the wings coming in contact with the wires.

M.P.'s meeting with Brearley ,a week or so later, after a demonstration flight at the Claremont Show Grounds, was the beginning of a long and eventually fruitful association.

Another major talking-point of that time was Premier James Mitchell's proposal for the intensive development of a dairy industry in the south-west by the settlement of co-operative groups of thousands of small farmers. In order to demonstrate the practicality of the idea, he invited a party of parliamentarians, including M.P., to accompany him to the eastern wheat-belt, where ten years before he had been instrumental in making land available to fifty unemployed men. The success with which most of them had met and the flourishing condition of their properties impressed the visitors, and appeared to convince them that a similar scheme on a larger scale would help solve many pressing economic and human problems.

M.P. made good use of his few days in the Premier's company by enlisting his support for ideas to benefit M.P.'s own electorate. He also took the opportunity of airing a company grievance about the government's resumption of the 60,000-acre Ascot property near Wyndham. Just as C.D. & D. had needed this as a holding area when shipping cattle, so it was now required for holding cattle for the meatworks. With this, the company agreed. What they protested about was the resumption of the land together with improvements, including living-quarters, yards, fences, and wells, without any compensation whatever. Mitchell advised that the company's best course was to go to law against the Crown, a step eventually taken.

The ensuing legal debate, faithfully reported by the *West Australian* of 30 August 1919, is an excellent example of legal phraseology at its most tautological. According to the Land Act of 1898, the government had power to resume any land leased from the Crown with right to purchase and the lessee was entitled to compensation of interest on the purchase-money paid. The long argument devolved on the interpretation of the word 'interest' in the context of the Act, the Hon Justice Burnside coming at last to the conclusion that the petitioners were entitled to their minimum claim of £883 15s 0d.

It can be seen that the fact of M.P.'s being a Member for the Kimberley district by no means limited the areas of his political involvement. He was at this time speaking for the rights of women to sit in Parliament and for amendments to the outdated Land Act, and was participating in heated debate regarding the Claremont Mental Hospital. The only proposition concerning these and many other issues that would seem to have been unanimously approved was for an increase in the Members' salaries.

It is not surprising that M.P. had been looking around for some time for a home more conveniently situated for his political and business affairs. In August of that year he was advised by his friend Timothy Quinlan[4] of a big house on an extensive block of land with a splendid view of the Swan River, not only for sale and within walking distance of Parliament House and the C.D. & D. office, but literally within a stone's throw of a boys' college and a girls' convent school.

The house had been built in 1896 by George Parker, a lawyer and member of a prominent Perth family which included founding members of the exclusive Weld Club and the W.A. Turf Club. The asking price was £3,000, which the company's bank manager, Mr Fegan, considered extortionate, but Timothy Quinlan, a shrewd business head, advised otherwise. In August the house was purchased and the strenuous process of moving from Claremont to Perth embarked upon.

It was not without regret that M.P. left 'the house we have lived in since March '15, where Betty, Kim and Quinty were born and of which Bim and I have many happy memories'. There is no doubt, however, of his satisfaction at having found such an ideal location for his many involvements.

He had not long moved into the new premises when his spirits were lifted sky-high by an event he had often wondered whether he would live to see. On 10 December 1919, Ross Macpherson Smith with his brother Keith and Sergeants Bennett and Shiers arrived in Darwin after a twenty-eight day journey from England in a Vickers Vimy flying-machine! M.P., meeting with Brearley a few days later at a Government House function to welcome the visiting Generals Birdwood and Monash, spoke enthusiastically of the achievement which he saw as a great boost to the concept of air-travel within Australia. His earnest enquiries for the progress of his young friend's flying activities resulted in a discussion of which Brearley himself was to write in later years:

> The landing area beside the Belmont Race Course was something of a problem. It was rather far out from the City and at times it was boggy and given to flooding when the river ran high.
>
> Whenever I flew over Perth I looked down on a nice cleared grassed area—a park-land rectangle west of the Causeway, and the blue Swan River formed its southern border. Two hundred yards across the grass to the north it was edged with private homes on high ground and by Government House and its gardens . . . Strange as it may seem, from 1920 to 1923 it became Perth's unofficial and only airport.
>
> Now and then I made discreet inquiries as to the possibility of using part of the Esplanade foreshore, which was Council land, as a flying field.
>
> Then an authoritative figure, that grand pioneer pastoralist of Kimberley, M. P. Durack, loomed up to play a large part in this phase of my life. Tall and straight-backed with his Spanish grandee beard and softly modulated voice, he was a rather awe-inspiring figure. At that time he was a Member of Parliament for the Kimberley and had a town house just beside the area I wanted to use.
>
> With his far-seeing imagination, 'M.P.' could see that the possible future development of flying could help to solve some of the communications of that vast and distant area in which he was particularly involved.
>
> At a Government House party he asked casually if I would like to erect a hangar at the foot of the Durack garden, which provided easy access to the foreshore. Even though it was public land I gratefully accepted his offer and immediately organized a contractor

to move the hangar from Belmont. Within a week I flew both Avros across to the new field and set up shop in the city . . .

So what is now Langley Park beside the Swan River became my flying headquarters without official permission until 1924, when the Federal Government had built Maylands Aerodrome! [From *Australian Aviator* by Sir Norman Brearley C.B.E., M.C., A.F.C., F.R.A.E.S. with co-author Ted Mayman, Rigby, 1971]

37

A Man Who Lived Three Lives

December 1919–December 1920

Moving into the town house marked the beginning of a new sort of life for us all. Here the comparatively scattered bungalow-type homes of outer Perth had been, for the most part, replaced by statelier two-storey residences, and the nearby Claremont 'village' by the equally nearby 'metropolis' of Perth. In Claremont we had been as close to the Swan River as we were here, but there we had walked down bush tracks to curving beaches lapped by shallow waters that held no threat to the paddler or would-be swimmer. We had romped and picked wild flowers in virgin bush (now long since taken over by closely built-up suburbs). There was no bush in reach or sight of our new home, and what beach there had been was nowhere then in view. A stone wall kept the river in its place except for rare occasions when flood-waters set it free to deluge the esplanade.

We children were unconcerned by such differences. We loved the big back garden wth its grape-vines and fig trees, and Major Brearley's hangar where his friendly mechanic, Harry Critchley, kept a generous supply of boiled sweets. My brother Reg and I had already embarked on our education at the Claremont State school, and we had no difficulty in adapting to the institutions run by the Christian Brothers and the Loreto nuns.

We soon became acquainted with, and interested in, our neighbours, many of them interrelated descendants of early colonial families and in some respects more typical of Queen Victoria's era than that of her grandson George V[1].

For as long as I can remember my father said that he lived three entirely different lives at much the same time. There was his life 'up north', his life in the city, and the life of his dreams, which he would often recall to us in fascinating detail over the breakfast table. Many of them involved adventures with horses, cattle, crocodiles, and northern characters. It was not, however, only in sleep that he was projected from the city to the bush, for every mail brought letters from Wyndham and the stations which required his close attention.

A letter he received from Neal Durack at about this time indicates that life in the north, particularly on the more remote frontiers of Auvergne and Bullita, was as precarious as ever and that the relationships between white men and bush Aborigines had undergone little change.

> Auvergne Station NT. 3.12.19.
> You will of course have heard that Jim Crisp was killed at Bullita, apparently by the Auvergne Sandstone blacks.
>
> They suspect it was a nigger called Monkey and another called Emu who had been killing cattle. Crisp went after them but his rifle jammed on the first shot and a spear got him in the side. He rode 300 yards before he fell off his horse. He sent his boy for water then pulled the spear out leaving the head in. When the boy got back from the river he was dead.
>
> A police party of five whites and ten good boys are at present chasing the murderers. The party consists of Heathcote (returned soldiers), Lake Hall, Jim Howarth, Tom Dare and George Campbell. The boys are Springheel and Freddy (Auvergne), Daylight and Toby (Lake Hall's boys), Jimmy Mulga (Crisp's boy), Pompey and Ungin (Bullita boys), Sambo and Jacky (Wilson's boys).
>
> I gave the party twenty-six head of fat horses, all shod, four rifles and ammunition, and as much tucker as I could spare . . . I am sad to think I couldn't go with them as of course it was impossible to leave Imelda here alone. I thought of taking her to Newry and joining them but the road is too wet to travel by buggy and I have to play the Old Buffer and miss all the sport . . .

In later years I recorded the following Aboriginal version of this story, my informants including Daylight, who was one of the police party involved:

> Jim Crisp been managing Bullita that time. They bin out branding when one boy come galloping back to camp. Sang out: 'Boss, Boss—big mob blackfella killing cattle over that way.'
>
> Jim Crisp get a good horse and tell Paddy and Pompey and old Ungin get horses too. They ride straight on, only bush blackfellow spot them from hill. They talk: 'Guddea! Guddea!' That 'white man' blackfella language. They duck down and wait along gorge and when Jim ride through they drop him—spear along back. Jim sing out: 'Oh boy! Oh boy!'

> Ungin sing out: 'Hey! Boss bin get a spear. Let that mob blackfella go. We gotta go back Boss.'
>
> Yes, he got a spear all right. He singin' out for water. They take him to river but he die there where they make him grave.

Another version ran thus:

> Jim Crisp was a thin man of about thirty-five. Quiet when the action around him was quiet, he changed dramatically to a cursing, yelling demon of energy in the branding pens or the cutting out camps . . .
>
> Jim's death was the end of the old story of the white men's interference between the bush Aborigines and their women. He had taken to himself a bush girl from another local tribe, and from then on he was marked down. One morning he awoke to find the young lubra gone . . . He caught a horse and started in pursuit. As he urged his horse forward on the tracks, he had picked up a spear plunged between his shoulder blades. He died in agony and alone! [*Turn Again Home*, G. W. Broughton, Brisbane, 1965]

Whether Crisp died in pursuit of cattle-spearers or woman-stealers, he certainly left a handsome half-caste son to bear his name, whom I was to meet at Ivanhoe Station in later years.

Early in 1920, M.P., travelling with H. P. Colebatch and Ben Copley, made his first transcontinental rail journey from Perth to South Australia and thence to Melbourne, the object being to represent W.A. interests at a meeting of meat producers and exporters.

> 1.2.20: The Nullarbor Plains are indeed well named—a monotonous, treeless landscape from Kalgoorlie to Ooldea. A few families at the dreary railway depots and a few miserable natives at the sidings . . . Dead rabbits along the track . . .

The meeting, convened at Melbourne's Menzies Hotel, brought together a high-powered collection of politicians, meat-growers, and exporters from all over Australia and New Zealand. The chair was taken by Sir Owen Cox, live-wire member of many businesses and political projects, including the packing and shipping of refrigerated meats. He was also closely associated with Prime Minister W. M. Hughes in reforming the businessmen's committee in support of the Nationalists. Hughes had made himself available to answer questions, which he seems to have done by throwing the ball back into the producers' court. He dismissed the current drop in prices and other difficulties as temporary matters of postwar adjustment. Asked if he could take steps to prevent the Queensland Government commandeering meat supplies and fixing prices detrimental to the other States, he declared it was all in the producers' hands and they must stick together.

It is clear from M.P.'s diary jottings that the formal meetings were not his only preoccupation during this time.

> 6.2.20: With Copley to Johnson Bros tannery. Discussion on employment of Chinese labour and Union objections re same ...
> Promised to send crocodile skins to Johnson.

For a number of years M.P. had talked of the industrial possibilities of crocodile hides for the production of goods, including suitcases, handbags, belts, and even furniture. For as long as I can remember he had carried his precious panoramic camera in a crocodile case, and he had had made to order for the hall and study of his new home a handsome timber and crocodile sofa and chairs, which had already become a popular talking-point. Perhaps the reason why these items of furniture remain unique is that they are more interesting than comfortable.

> 7.2.20: To Shepparton freezing works. Talk with manager Graham. Net return last year £24,000. Later to fruit-canning factory associated with closer settlement scheme run by a co-operative society and employing about 400 hands. Thence around the Settlement—some thirty square miles—about four thousand people. Took details for James Mitchell.
> 9.2.20: Today with Dr Gilruth to the Veterinary College where he was formerly professor. He reports serious trouble with the Darwin works and doubts Vesteys can carry on[2].
> 10.2.20: With W. Angliss and Copley to the works. Angliss (who has by this time opened offices in London and Liverpool) informs he killed last year 1,250,000 sheep and 30,000 cattle, employs about 1,000 men at £4 to £4.10.00 per week. Discussed possibility his leasing Wyndham Works from Government and co-operating with producers. We could supply 25/30,000 head yearly, and more if a satisfactory price arranged.
> 11.2.20: With Bert and Nell Davey and family [his wife's relations] looking at musical instruments and catching up on family news.
> 16.2.20: To Federal House with George Miles. Interviewed members re iron deposit show. Saw Senator Pearce re meeting the Prime Minister with respect to the North-West Railway Development

> League. Pearce strongly in favour. Minister Watt, Treasurer, also sympathetic. He realises the development of the north is a Commonwealth obligation[3].

M.P. had been back in Perth only a few days when he set off for Kalgoorlie with his brothers J.W. and P.B. Always interested in the possibilities of mining, they became from this time on more actively involved in speculative ventures. A new boom in gold prices, accelerated by wartime inflation, was then eagerly anticipated and had drawn a number of prominent interstate members to the field. M.P.'s comments give some idea of the prevailing optimism.

> 13.2.20: A lot of people we know are putting up here at the Palace Hotel. A thrill of excitement animates the company and one hears nothing talked of but mining prospects and shares.

Together the brothers toured the mines, interviewed owners and prospectors, and gave notice of application for goldmining leases. Before leaving Kalgoorlie, M.P. was elected a director of a show known as *Ives Reward* in which he had become a shareholder. The report on samples submitted to the government geologist was opened eagerly soon afterwards. '31.3.20: Result of assay out this evening. Another dream exploded. Alas for the fever of gold!'

This entry precedes one of the few gaps since M.P. began keeping his remarkable record in 1886. On a few occasions when suffering from severe bouts of fever he had missed several days, but only once before (in 1906) anything over a month. Health problems were given little space in his diaries, and it is with a hint of impatience that he records having been put out of action by a carbuncle on his neck and resultant migraine. He was subsequently found to be suffering from diabetes, and from this time on paid at least token attention to his diet, if not to the advice that he should try to slow down.

He took up his pen again on 8 May to record having set out on the S.S. *Gorgon* with a party comprising representatives of the Federal and State Governments and the press, on a tour of the north-west. This expedition was covered for the *West Australian* by Charles Frost who, writing under the pen name of 'Nomad' explains the undertaking as having been proposed by George Miles to further his campaign for a north-west railway service.

> The expedition comprised Mr G. Hobler, Commonwealth Railway Engineer; the Minister for Education and two other Legislative

> Councillors, two members of the Assembly, representatives of 'The Age' and 'The West Australian'; three chauffeurs, and the same number of cars.

The party included M.P.'s good friends George Miles, Hal Colebatch and Brearley's father-in-law, Sydney Stubbs. It was a congenial group, accompanied on the ship to Derby by the newly appointed Governor, Sir Francis Newdegate, who was suitably welcomed at the various ports of call.

'Nomad' describes the 1,500-mile overland journey from Derby to Wyndham via Hall's Creek and Turkey Creek in considerable detail.

> The cars must have carried added weight when the expedition, full of gratitude and good cheer, started out from Derby to face the ordeal of the road . . . Margaret River is wider than the Fitzroy with a double channel and full of the softest, deepest sand conceivable. The head chauffeur says: 'My car can do anything except climb a tree or dig a well,' and he proceeds to put on its sandshoes. These are a Kimberley patent—broad fringes of stiff leather linked crosswise by steel bands buckled round the tyres so as to give them more than double the width. They are an adaptation of the snow-shoe principle. The welcome 'coo-ee' comes over the bank and the Margaret River manager, with half a dozen black stockmen, arrives to assist the car propellers. All the blacks but one were fully clothed, the exception being stark naked except for the narrowest of loin strips and a three-inch fig-leaf pendant.

M.P.'s account of the journey was more matter of fact. He was however obviously delighted by the enthusiastic reaction of his companions to the rugged beauty of the landscape and the wonder of its wildlife. He also appreciated their keen interest in the problems and potential of the country.

'Nomad' described how, on arrival at Ivanhoe, the party was greeted by great flocks of white cockatoos, galahs, and whistling duck that came crying and swirling in on the homestead waterhole. He also reported M.P.'s having made it clear that this was sacred ground for his feathered friends, and no shooting was allowed[4].

So far the party's progress had been exceptionally trouble-free. The only problem reported to have arisen was at Argyle.

> Mr M. P. Durack, M.L.A. for Kimberley, who has guided the party so far, can accompany us no further and no-one else knows the upper Ord track. M.P. solves the difficulty. He will take the party

> to Ord River Station, borrow a horse there and ride the ninety-five miles back to Argyle alone. That point settled, and the station Stud Book with its twenty-six years of bloodstock breeding overhauled, the expedition encamps luxuriously on the station verandah and is lulled to rest by a choral symphony with orchestral accompaniments of long tubes of hollow timber supplied by a corroboree of Argyle blacks in the dry bed of the Behn.

The party, as reported stage by stage, continued overland to Perth. M.P. regretted being unable to accompany them and expressed himself with some feeling after seeing them on their way.

> 4.6.20: With deep regret I part with the good friends and companions of the last month. The days from Derby I shall remember for all time. Good fellowship and harmony prevailed to the fullest degree and we enjoyed every moment of the run through. Our three drivers—Atkinson, Stocker and Yates, were experts in their field and the cars proved to my surprise quite equal to the heavy task imposed.

Having returned from Ord River Station on a borrowed horse, he set off again on his station rounds accompanied by Roy Doherty who, after the return to England of his mother and sister, had come north to see the country of which he had heard so much from his earliest years. He had thought he might take on the sort of job Roy Phillipps professed to have found so enjoyable, but three months were enough to convince him otherwise. After recovering from a bad bout of fever, he claimed to have tried hard to understand the country and its inhabitants. He was at last forced to admit, however, that the rugged lonely landscape held no charm for him and that he found its people, black and white, curiously blind to the fact that the country they enthused about was the end of the earth, not the centre, as their tedious talk implied[5].

M.P. found that the long awaited meatworks were operating under difficulties caused by inexperienced workers and strikes for higher pay. Those who, like himself, had favoured the enterprise being under company rather than government control were having second thoughts, as talk of Vesteys abandoning the Darwin works became established fact. The result of the union leaders' determined campaign was after all to render the works an uneconomic proposition, and their resultant closure threw hundreds of men out of jobs. East Kimberley pastoralists could see that the W.A. Government might also find itself hard pressed to continue on an economic footing, but it could hardly close down while any alternative remained. Government control was therefore perhaps the safer proposition, at least until prices stabilized and the workers came to terms with reality.

It was at this stage that M.P. became involved in a search for oil that was to absorb much of his time, and to sustain his spirits for many years to come. His interest in this activity was awakened by a returned soldier-prospector named Walter Okes, who had found what he believed to be indications of oil at the junction of the Ord and Negri Rivers. Geological specimens from the area, assayed as 'glance pitch in basalt', were considered extremely promising, and M.P. drew up an agreement of partnership to be known as the Okes-Durack Kimberley Oil Company N.L.

Before the year was out he had returned to Melbourne where, after conferring with the appropriate Federal members and ministers, he secured an oil-drilling lease and proceeded to Sydney to interview the influential Sir Owen Cox, whom he had encountered earlier in the year. This led to his receiving a message from the Prime Minister to the effect that the Federal Government would assist, pound for pound, up to £25,000.

Cox himself was keen to buy Okes out at a sum that could well have tempted the struggling prospector. M.P., however, found himself unable in conscience to encourage the deal, since he saw the £10,000 offered as being of small account, were their expectations to be realised.

With the possibilities of oil doing for Australia what it had done for the U.S.A., the news soon hit the headlines, and M.P. was eagerly questioned on the subject wherever he went. His response inevitably struck a positive note.

> If this work goes ahead as we all anticipate, W.A. will be a different country before a few years are out. Of course the whole of Australia will be affected and for this reason we anticipate a certain amount of assistance from the Federal Government, as well as the State. If we obtain oil in commercial quantities our lease will be extended to twenty-one years. Wyndham is a fine deep water port and if we get going properly it is certain to become a big gateway to developmental trade with the East—Australia's natural market. [*Herald*, Melbourne, 26.7.22][6]

The year 1920 took M.P. not only twice interstate but several times between Fremantle and Wyndham, while fitting in the commitments of his political life. While at home he kept in constant touch with Norman Brearley whose barnstorming activities were steadily building up public confidence in the dependability of flight. More than that, they had contributed to the Federal

Government's growing interest in the development of flying in Australia, and to the consideration of a structured programme for civil aviation at a Commonwealth level.

M.P. was also involved by this time with the Reverend John Flynn, director of the Australian Inland Mission, who was already discussing the idea of a Flying Doctor Service within radio contact of outback towns and settlements, thus spreading 'a mantle of safety' over Australia's isolated areas. From this time on, 'Flynn of the Inland' was a familiar figure in our lives, and Mother and her friends worked together for fêtes and concerts to assist his cause.

M.P. moved the Address in Reply at the opening of Parliament on 6 August, of which the *West Australian* reported in its editorial:

> It is satisfactory to learn that the Member for Kimberley, whose acquaintance with the problems involved in the settlement of these distant parts of the State is of practical and extensive character, has faith in the efforts and energy with which the Government is directing itself to their solution. Not merely the north but the whole State is fortunate in representatives of the calibre, knowledge and enthusiasm which distinguish men like Mr Angelo and Mr Durack in the Assembly and Mr Holmes and Mr Miles in the Council, with whose assistance the Government is not likely to make any serious problems in the formation and prosecution of a policy of northern development.

Be that as it may, M.P. was not always in accord with the Nationalist Party of the time. It was in that year, when the Farmers & Settlers Association enlarged its platform and changed its name to the Primary Producers Association, that he and Angelo (then M.L.A. for the Gascoyne district) transferred their allegiance from the Nationalist to the Country Party.

The arrival of Denis Doherty and his daughter Katch on a visit from London towards the end of the year was a stimulus to much animated conversation, at least some of which was of interest to young ears. One subject that never failed to intrigue us was the prospected oil boom that would solve everyone's problems and open up to us the wonders of the world. What were we not going to do when we struck oil? One plan was to procure a yacht and sail the world at our own pleasure and in our own time. I recall this dream being discussed quite seriously for several years, and its becoming the subject of heated argument concerning who would and who would not be invited to accompany us. Our near neighbour, John Kirwan, an old friend of the Connor, Doherty, and Durack families, and at least as imaginative, contributed the idea of our purchasing a castle on the Bosphorus near the Dardanelles, which he described as being an idyllic retreat for contemporary millionaires.

For the younger members of the family, a memorable incident of this year was our being awakened one morning in November by a high-pitched wail, which was followed soon afterwards by the appearance of Nurse Stevens with beaming face and a mysterious bundle in her arms. This we soon found was a baby brother, to be named David after the Prince of Wales who had charmed the ladies of Perth on his recent visit.

This happy event coincided with the sad news of Neal Durack's death by drowning in the Ord River. The story, as gradually unfolded, was that he had recently attended a race-meeting at the Victoria River Depot, where he had found himself the surprised winner of £500. His wife, who was expecting their second child, was then in Wyndham where she was to board the next ship south within a few days. Anxious to see her away with this unexpected windfall, Neal rode off with two companions, determined to reach Wyndham before the ship sailed. The wet season had already set in and at Ivanhoe they found the Ord had come down in flood. Neal's mates advised that it was madness to attempt crossing before it had subsided, but Neal, being a strong swimmer with a strong motivation, jammed his winnings tightly under his hat and plunged in. When he disappeared suddenly midstream it was thought that he had been taken by a crocodile, but his body was found soon afterwards, caught up in a tree some distance downstream. The cause of his drowning, though attributed to cardiac failure, may well have been connected with the injuries he had sustained during the war and in the stock camps of his home country.

He had been highly thought of in both contexts, and it is heartwarming to know that as a gesture of friendship and sympathy for his family the cheques and notes that had been swept away were repaid in full by his bush associates[7]. There were glowing tributes to his memory in the press:

> Neal Durack was one of the best known and best liked men in the Tenth Light Horse. He achieved a good deal of fame as a member of the Third Brigade Scouts, a body of picked bushmen. Theirs was an onerous and dangerous job in which initiative and resourcefulness were essential. A typical bushman and expert horseman, the deceased not only had these qualifications but was exceptionally game ... 'He was one of the most cheerful men under fire', said Colonel Olden, Commander of the regiment. 'He

> always had a smile and kept everyone in good spirits . . .' [*Sunday Times*, 5.12.20]

H. P. Colebatch was reported as saying:

> When the Ministerial party visited Kimberley this year we met Neal Durack at Argyle Station. He was as fine a specimen of manhood as one would ever see and it is sad to think that one so well equipped for carrying on development in the Kimberley should go in this way in his 30th year.
>
> When a young man who has passed through the perils of the Palestine Campaign is thus overtaken in the course of his day's work, we realise the difficulties and dangers still associated with station life in the north. [The *West Australian*, 1.2.20]

M.P.'s diary of the year, for all its optimistic interludes, ends after all on a note of sadness.

> So finishes 1920, shadowed for us all by the tragic death of young Neal—a bright and promising life cut short in its prime. I doubt that poor Aunt Fan will recover from his passing. The wonder is she has survived so many heart-breaking losses. Have never seen her look so frail[8].
>
> I felt a good deal of sadness too on saying goodbye to Doherty who was here with daughter Katch and has just returned. He is not in robust health and doubts he will be able to return to Australia again[9].
>
> On the brighter side is the arrival of a healthy little son, christened David Johnstone Durack by the Reverend Father Moss . . .
>
> Prospects for our growing family should be bright if oil is found up north, as is at present indicated. Doherty has taken some samples home for the Anglo-Persian Oil Company and we eagerly await results.
>
> I wonder what the coming year will reveal in this respect, and also as regards the future of aerial transport. There is a great future in store for this State if both these dreams can become reality.

Epilogue

I had anticipated ending this chronicle with my father's death in 1950, but the records so meticulously kept from the formation of the company fifty-three years before contained more material than I had bargained on. Without the deletion of a great deal that was of at least some historical interest, this book would have become unwieldy. I have therefore drawn it to a conclusion at a stage my father saw as the beginning of a new era of postwar expansion, of pastoral and mineral development, new modes of travel and communication, and the fulfilment of many other long-cherished dreams.

Readers who have had the stamina to follow the rambling saga to this point can set it aside knowing that at least some of M.P.'s hopes were to be realised. He had rightly foreseen an era of air travel and radio communication that was to bring Australia closer to the outside world and to solve some major problems for her outback areas.

By 1921 Norman Brearley's flying activities had built up both public and political confidence, and towards the end of that year he was awarded a government contract to form the first regular airmail service in Australia, covering a coastal route of 1,200 miles between the ports of Geraldton and Derby.

Accompanying his young friend on the inaugural flight was for M.P. one of the highlights of his life, and I recall the excitement of seeing the three Bristol aircraft taking off from the Esplanade at the back of our house. Nor can I forget the shock of hearing the following day that one of the planes had crashed near Geraldton, killing the pilot and mechanic aboard. This sad beginning did not long delay the successful development of the airline which was to contribute so much to the advancement of the State. Needless to say, M.P. was from that time on an inveterate air-traveller.

In the fullness of time Brearley's pioneer air service was sold out to Ansett-Australian National Airways, and the west coastal service then running between Perth and Darwin was taken over by MacRobertson-Miller Airlines, of which my late husband was a founder-partner.

At a down-to-earth level, the 1920s brought roads and river crossings to improve conditions for motor transport and trucks, which took over station carrying from the slow-moving camel teams. This was to some extent owing to M.P.'s political influence. He felt strongly, however, that the problems of the north were not properly understood by a southern-based government and that the North Province should be administered by a separate body.

It soon became clear from his diaries that although he enjoyed the active part of his political life, he found it more difficult, as the novelty wore off, to sit through long speeches and debates of little relevance to his own electorate, which sometimes continued into the small hours of the morning. He frequently protested 'the pettiness of party politics', but his decision not to stand for reelection in 1924 had probably more to do with his increasing involvement in the search for oil.

This became ever more important, for the opening of the local meatworks, seen for so long as a solution to his company's problems, had come at a time when Britain was obtaining ample supplies of meat from sources closer to hand. Vesteys, while retaining their North Australian properties for what might lie ahead, were then concentrating on meat production in the Argentine, but other Kimberley cattlemen had no such option.

The world economy steadily recessed and with it prices for Australian beef. It was as well that oil-exploration provided a sustaining ray of hope until postwar demands brightened the horizon in other directions.

Early in 1950 the news of the actual tapping of oil by the West Australian Petroleum Company (WAPET) was hailed by M.P. as a justification of his optimistic prophecies. He did not live to hear that the supply was soon found to be inadequate for commercial purposes, and it was not until 1966 that a workable oilfield was at last declared at Barrow Island near the port of Onslow.

The subsequent tapping of considerable quantities of natural gas and increased drilling activities on the north-west shelf continues to enhance the possibility of oil's becoming a major source of income to Western Australia.

It is somewhat ironical that, of all the minerals M.P. hoped to find, he seems never to have considered the possibility of there being diamonds under the hoofs of the horses he rode and the cattle he mustered for so many years.

I would like to continue this chronicle until the time of his death and the disposal of the company properties, but if this proves beyond my capacity I have at least outlined the story in an epilogue to *Kings in Grass Castles*.

Suffice it here to say that M.P. was to meet with more adversity than prosperity in his 'new era', but even when the company fortunes sank to bedrock along with the world economy, he continued, as his motto exhorted him, to 'Travel hopefully and trust in God'.

References

Chapter 1: An End and a Beginning, 1898

M. P. Durack receives news of his father's death. Patsy Durack in retrospect. Background to formation of Connor, Doherty & Durack. The contentious tick question. M.P.D. in the Territory awaiting removal of the tick quarantine barrier.

1. *Macartney, John Arthur and Mayne, Edward Graves*. J. A. Macartney was born in County Cork, Ireland, in 1834, the son of an Anglican clergyman of aristocratic lineage, who migrated with his family to Port Phillip in 1848. After some experience in the legal profession in Victoria he took up a property on the Ovens River in 1854.

   In 1857 he went into partnership with E. G. Mayne of Beechworth, with whom he pioneered the Waverley run near Rockhampton. The partners explored much of Queensland and the Northern Territory and took up a number of major runs in both areas. These included Diamantina Gates, a large property on the Diamantina River in Western Queensland. The Mayne River, a tributary of the Diamantina, was named after Edward Mayne.

   In 1884 they took up from the South Australian Government Florida Station in Arnhem Land and Auvergne Station near the West Australian border. Both properties were of an unwieldy size, Florida alone covering 10,000 square miles and including about 300 miles of coastline. They soon found these remote holdings impossible to control, mostly on account of repeated attacks from Aborigines who hunted and speared the cattle and threatened the lives of the stockmen. Tom Hardy, who had brought the cattle to Auvergne in 1885 and remained as manager, was soon afterwards fatally speared in a raid on the homestead. His was the first of a succession of violent deaths on this property. The partners no doubt considered themselves fortunate when they managed to sell the remaining stock and land rights of Auvergne to Connor and Doherty in 1896.

   The Macartney-Mayne partnership was dissolved in 1884, though some properties continued to be held in both names. In 1887 Macartney went into a second partnership with H. L. Heber-Percy, nephew of the fifth Duke of Northumberland. Macartney was at various times associated with the ownership of thirty-five stations covering an estimated 30,000 square miles and carrying half a million head of cattle. From the early '90s onwards his fortunes, like those of many pastoralists of the time, went into a decline. He took on a mail contract and was later employed as station manager on various properties. He was married in 1861 to Anne Flora Wallace-Dunlop, and died in 1917, being survived by four daughters and two sons. His autobiography, *Rockhampton Fifty Years Ago, Reminiscences of a Pioneer*, was published in 1909.

Edward Mayne was unmarried, and apparently left no record of his pioneering life.

2. Various species of tick have been observed in the district from the beginning of white settlement. The species *Ixodes bovis*, identified in 1894 as the cause of redwater fever, was thought to have been introduced into North Australia in 1876 by cattle imported from Timor to serve the cable station at Darwin. The first outbreak of redwater occurred in the Darwin area in 1880, but was not related to tick until the insect had taken a strong hold of large areas in the Northern Territory and Queensland. The species in question was no doubt brought into East Kimberley with the first cattle overlanded from Queensland, and spread to West Kimberley with mobs being driven to Derby for shipment in the early 1890s.

Chapter 2: A World Without Time, November 1897–July 1898

Hold-up with cattle in Northern Territory. M.P.'s Territory associates. Ban on South African trade. Negotiations with Queensland buyers. Burketown meatworks burned down. M.P. in Camooweal. Meeting with Nat Buchanan. Cattle taken Birdsville Track to South Australia.

1. *Charles Biondi* is believed to have had two daughters by a previous marriage in Italy, and to have written to them from time to time of his Australian cattle station. It is said that one girl was in an opera company in Milan, and that while on tour in Australia she wrote to her father that she was on her way to visit him. Disconcerted by this news, Biondi allegedly enlisted the help of his friend Tiny Dean, the local policeman, who dressed him up as smartly as possible and took him to Camooweal. There he met his daughter and told her that it was impossible for her to venture further on account of the wet season.

His other Italian-born daughter, reputedly married to a Macquarie Street specialist, is also said to have attempted to visit Anthony's Lagoon but was met by her father at Newcastle Waters and dissuaded from proceeding further.

2. *Redford* still cherished hopes of opening up new country, and believing that rich grazing lands were to be found in Central Australia, he set out in 1901 for Tennant Creek, hoping to organize such a venture. However, when making south he was drowned in the flood waters of Corella Creek, on the banks of which his lonely grave is still to be seen.
3. *Buchanan, Nathaniel.* Born Dublin in 1826, he came to Sydney with his parents and family in 1837 and settled in New England district. He joined explorer William Landsborough in 1859 and became first manager and partner in the Landsborough River Co to pioneer Bowen Downs station on the Thomson River in Queensland. In 1863 he married Catherine Gordon of nearby Ban Ban station, and abandoned Bowen Downs in 1867. In the early '70s he was given contracts to take cattle to far western fringes of Queensland. In 1878 with the help of the Gordon brothers he stocked Glencoe station with cattle from Aramac in Queensland, pioneering the first stock route into the Northern Territory. In 1883 he took 4,000 head of cattle to stock Ord River station for the Melbourne firm of Osmond and Panton, thus being the first with cattle into the Kimberley district. He also opened the Murranji track in the Northern Territory. In 1883 he and the Gordon brothers took up Wave Hill on the Victoria River. In 1892 he blazed the so-called 'Buchanan's track' to the Murchison goldfields. His last big expedition, of which an incident is recorded below, he made at the age of seventy, travelling from Tennant's Creek to Sturt Creek in an attempt to find a route from the Barkly Tableland into Western Australia. He died on a small farm near Tamworth in 1901, just three years after his encounter with M. P. Durack in 1898.

Coming upon the brief reference to Buchanan in his diary for 27 June 1885, M.P.D. later made the following notes:

> ... Buchanan and I had met on several occasions before but never did I get to know him as I did that night. It may have been my intense interest in his many daring exploits that encouraged him to 'let himself go' ... One story that stands out most vividly in my memory was of a time not long before, when he was making north from Oodnadatta, intent on striking

from Tennant's Creek, across the practically unknown partly desert country in Flora Valley near Hall's Creek. He set out with 7 camels, 6 horses and two men but on reaching Tennant's Creek his companions, being warned of the risk they were taking, 'funked on it' and refused to accompany him. The only man he could find to go along with him was a stalwart young native named Jack who claimed to know something of the country he wished to traverse. The local residents tried to dissuade him from setting out with no-one but this partly Myall native, but he humorously waved their fears aside.

A few days on from Tennant's Creek the Aboriginal began to show signs of uneasiness and declared: 'No more water that way. 'Spose we go that way we two-fella die.'

Buchanan had never been baulked in an undertaking of this kind and was well prepared to meet any emergency. He lived frugally at the best of times, never smoked or drank alcohol and even when in civilization limited himself to a pint of water a day to keep in training, as it were, for his next exploratory venture. Acting on previous experience, he had equipped himself on this trip with a pair of handcuffs which he contrived, in a playful demonstration, to slip adroitly around the native's ankle, having previously fastened the chain to the heavy camel saddle.

Strange though it may appear, black Jack, on realising his predicament, quickly became reconciled to his captive state and for the next seven or eight days rode on quite cheerfully shackled to the leading camel. At Sturt Creek, about 360 miles from Tennant's Creek, Buchanan released him, knowing that he would not dare to return alone over a desert waste inhabited by strange tribes.

A few more days' travelling brought them safely to Flora Valley where Buchanan was happily reunited with his son Gordie and two brothers-in-law, Hughie and Wattie Gordon.

Buchanan had also many tales to tell of his life-long friend Donald McIntyre of Dalgonelly, to whom he was then on his way. McIntyre though an early pioneer of Northern Queensland was regarded as a poor bushman and when he failed to return to his homestead one evening as he had intended, flare lights were set up on the stock yard posts to act as a guide. Approaching the gate at last he mistook the flares for the campfires of possibly hostile blacks and riding back a short distance he sat holding his horse through a bitterly cold night. His disgust on realising that he had been within a stone's throw of a warm bed may be imagined.

He was forced to submit to a good deal of banter concerning this incident in the years to come.

Chapter 3: Golden Opportunities, July–September 1898

With Cobb & Co, from Camooweal. Townsville meatworks. Brisbane contacts. M.P. meets family members in Sydney. Brotherly discussions. Federal referendum. Goulburn contacts. Tick Commission in Perth. Visit to the goldfields. Tick embargo lifted for East Kimberley. Family affairs. A romantic meeting.

1. These verses, inspired by M.P.'s reminiscences, were published in *The Bulletin* in the 1950s. They brought forth a number of letters from readers who recalled the legend of this mysterious lone woman.

RED JACK

She rises clear to memory's eye
From the mists of long ago,
Though we met but once in '98
In the days of Cobb & Co.

'Twas driving into Hughenden
With mail and gold for load
That I saw Red Jack the wanderer
Come riding down the road.

Red Jack and Mephistopheles—
They knew them far and wide
From Camooweal to Charters Towers,
The route they used to ride.

They knew them round the Selwyns where
The Leichhardt has its source,
Along the winding cattle ways—
A woman and a horse.

And strange the tales they told of them
Who ranged the dusty track:

The great black Mephistopheles
And the red-haired witch Red Jack.

She claimed no name but that, they said
And owned no things but these:
Her saddle, swag and riding-kit,
And Mephistopheles.

And often travellers such as I
Had seen, and thought it strange,
A woman working on the line
That crossed McKinlay Range;

Had seen her in the dreary wake
Of stock upon the plains,
Her brown hand quick upon the whip
And light upon the reins.

With milling cattle in the yard
Amid the dust-fouled air,
With rope and knife and branding-iron—
A girl with glowing hair.

'Red Jack's as good as any man!'
The settlers used to own:
And some bold spirits sought her hand
But Red Jack rode alone.

She rode alone and wise men learned
To set her virtue high,
To weigh what skill she plied her whip
With the hardness of her eye.

I saw Red Jack in '98
The first time and the last,
But her face brown-gaunt, and her hair red-bright
Still haunt me from the past.

The coach drew in as she rode in sight;
We passed the time of day,
Then shuffled out the mail she sought
And watched her ride away.

And oh! her hair was living fire,
But her eyes were cold as stone:
Red Jack and Mephistopheles
Went all their ways alone.

Mary Durack

2. In 1966, on the invitation of the Parish Priest, Father T. Bartley, I attended Sunday Mass at this little church. Almost everyone in the congregation, including the celebrant, was in some way related to, or had been associated with, my family. Afterwards a ninety-five-year-old parishioner who mistook me for my Aunt Mary, with whom she had been to school in Goulburn, led me out to look down on the Costellos' Tea Tree station homestead in the valley below, to which John Costello and his wife had been thankful to return when their far-flung enterprises finally failed.
3. The *Kalgoorlie Miner*, established by Hocking Brothers in 1895, mouthpiece for the eastern goldfields, was by that time one of the most widely read newspapers in the colony.
4. The Dohertys' house was on the delightful river site now occupied by the Claremont Yacht Club, at the end of Victoria Avenue.

Chapter 4: Problems and Personalities, October 1898

Return to Wyndham. Opening of new hotel. Matters of the heart. Homeward track. The brothers at Argyle. Local identities. Relatives at Dunham and Lissadell Stations. The Kilfoyles of Rosewood.

1. *Duncan McCaully*. F. C. Booty, writing of McCaully in later years, recalled that he was generally known as 'the Scrub Bull'. 'Something about the man reminded me of Falstaff—an unconscious swagger that suggested ancestry from some old soldier of fortune . . .' [F. C. Booty, *The Pastoralist & Grazier*, 16.6.27]
2. *Jim Campbell*. Three writers of Northern Territory history who have had something to say of Jim Campbell are Ernestine Hill in *The Territory*, Tom Ronan in *Deep of the Sky*, and Jack Makin in *The Big Run*. 'Campbell', Makin writes, 'was far from being the Robin Hood of the north as he has so often been portrayed . . .'
3. R. W. Durack sold Kildurk Station to the Commonwealth Government as an Aboriginal station in 1973.
4. *John Byrne*, Mrs Tom Kilfoyle's father, migrated from Ireland to New

South Wales. He arrived with his three brothers in 1849 to join their father who had been deported from Ireland for high treason in 1833 and had since been granted a ticket of leave. John Byrne was married in Sydney in 1852, and when his wife died in 1876 giving birth to her tenth child, his eldest daughter Catherine (Mrs Kilfoyle) took over the upbringing of the four younger members of the family. Their father died two years later; however the family, though widespread, remained closely knit.

In 1882 Jim and Michael Byrne went to work at Thylungra on the invitation of their father's friend, Patsy Durack. Mick Byrne with two other stockmen, Connors and Livingstone, set off with a mob of horses for Argyle Station. Jim sailed for Wyndham with M.P. and J.W.D. on the *Rajputana* in 1886.

In 1887 Will Byrne arrived in East Kimberley and between them the brothers took over the Six Mile Hotel out of Wyndham. There they were joined by their four sisters. Catherine married Tom Kilfoyle in 1891, and Mary-Anne married G. W. Mayhew of Darwin in 1895.

Thereafter the family played an active role, first in East Kimberley and the Northern Territory, and later on the goldfields and wheatbelt of Western Australia. The association of the Byrne, Kilfoyle, and Durack families has stretched from 1840 until the present day.

Chapter 5: Dreams and Realities, October 1898–July 1899

Mustering in 'the wet'. A shipment cancelled. Romantic correspondence. Photography. Visit to Ord River Station. A manager's problem. Aboriginal cattle-spearers. Death of Annie Durack at Dunham Station. Two women speared at Argyle. Shipping cattle from Wyndham. Two proposals of marriage. A cross-branded horse. Evading the tick barrier. Letters to employees. A mysterious telegram.

1. A bush jingle, the first three verses of which were sent to me by Mrs Burston, a niece of Bob Button, the first manager, tells something of the story:

   A smartish young fellow named Button,
   Brought up on horses and mutton,
   First managed the Ord
   And the country explored—
   In the bush he was what they called 'sudden'.

Barefooted Hedley succeeded,
Put up improvements much needed;
But the old man at Stawell
Did not like them at all
So barefooted Hedley was weeded.

McLellan next rode for a fall,
His yarns were exceedingly tall,
He bustled around,
Galloped over the ground,
And swore that he'd branded them all.

2. Part of a tape-recorded statement by Johnnie Walker, Kununurra Reserve, 1978.
3. *Pumpkin*, *Boxer*, and *Ulysses* were generally regarded as a family, though Pumpkin hailed from Cooper's Creek, Western Queensland, Boxer from the Mt Isa area, and Ulysses from the upper Ord. Pumpkin, at his own insistence, had come to Kimberley with Patsy Durack in 1887. Not long afterwards the eight-year-old Boxer had come across from Queensland with his mother and a man called Wesley Lyttleton, then on their way to the Hall's Creek goldfields. Pumpkin, so the story goes, took a fancy to the boy and acquired him in exchange for a good packhorse and a tin of jam. What became of Boxer's mother is not recorded, but Wesley Lyttleton soon returned from the goldfields and worked thereafter on Argyle. Ulysses, orphaned in a punitive expedition on Ord River station in 1890, was brought to Argyle by Duncan McCaully and was also taken charge of by Pumpkin who reared him, together with Boxer, in the early Queensland traditions of stockmanship. Boxer—*Warramunga* to his countrymen—spoke several languages, including the local Miriwung, into which tribe he was formally initiated. He was acknowledged in later years as a 'dreamer' of song cycles and corroborrees connected with Miriwung mythology, which he bequeathed to his two younger friends, Johnnie Walker and Daylight. They include the long song cycle of *Moolarli*, a spirit hero to whose magic the formation of the Ord River gorge was attributed.
4. *Cockburn-Campbell*. The Cockburn family (originally de Cokburn) were among the most ancient land-holders in Scotland. They also owned large estates in England, including the Barony of Langton in Berwickshire of which they became possessed after the Battle of Bannockburn in 1314. From that time on, members of the family were prominent as soldiers, sailors, diplomats, statesmen, and lawyers.

In 1627, Charles I created Sir William Cockburn 1st Baronet of Langton, which estate was sold by the 7th Baronet in 1793. General Sir James Cockburn, 8th Baronet, became Under Secretary for State in 1806 and was later appointed Governor of Curaçao and Bermuda. The 9th Baronet, Admiral Sir George Cockburn, 1772-1853, commanded the siege of Cadiz in 1810. He took Napoleon to St Helena in the *Northumberland* in 1815, remained for a time as Governor of the island, and was later appointed Lord of the Admiralty. Cockburn Sound, near Fremantle, and Mt Cockburn near Wyndham, were named after him.

Sir William Cockburn, D.D., 10th Baronet, Dean of York, married a sister of Sir Robert Peel. He was succeeded by Sir Alexander Cockburn, 11th and last Baronet, famous as an orator, statesman, and lawyer and who became Lord Chief Justice of England. He married a daughter of Sir Alexander Campbell, 1st Baronet of Gartsford, Ross-shire.

When his son Alexander succeeded his maternal grandfather, becoming 2nd Baronet of Gartsford, he was required to take the second name of Campbell. He entered the army and was military secretary to his father-in-law, then Governor of Bombay. He came to Australia in 1858 to act as Superintendent of Police, and two years later was appointed Government Resident at Albany. He died in 1871, and his eldest son died soon after succeeding to the title. He was succeeded by his brother Thomas, who migrated to Queensland in 1857 and worked for a time as chainman with the Gregory brothers. He came to Western Australia in the late 1860s and began farming at a property he called Langton Park near Mount Barker. He was married in 1870 to Lucy Anne Trimmer, grand-daughter of Captain Sir Richard Spencer, R.N., first Government Resident at Albany, Western Australia. In 1879 he settled in Perth where he became half owner and managing editor of the *Western Australian Times* (soon afterwards renamed the *West Australian*). He was nominated President of the Legislative Council in 1890. A patron of the arts and an astute commentator on current affairs, he was described as 'one of the ablest, most diligent, most capable and most statesmanlike of the political writers in this colony'.

He died in 1892 and was succeeded by his eldest son Alexander Thomas Cockburn-Campbell, 5th Baronet, who came to Wyndham in about 1898, served for a short time as Clerk of Courts, and later worked on East Kimberley and Northern Territory stations as stockman and drover. In 1918, after his marriage to the only daughter of the explorer Alfred Giles, the couple went to Waterloo Station in the Northern Territory. Lady Cockburn-Campbell died on Rosewood Station in 1926, leaving three sons, Thomas, Urban, and Alexander, of whom the eldest succeeded to the title on the death of his father in 1935.

Information about the colourful history of the Cockburn family is to be found in *The House of Cockburn* by Thomas H. Cockburn-Hood, published 1888. See also Sir Alexander and Sir Thomas Cockburn-Campbell, Bonnie Hicks, *Early Days*, Vol. VI, Part VI, The Royal Western Australian Historical Society, Journal and Proceedings, 1967.

Chapter 6: A Bid for Empire, July–December 1899

Expanding prospects. End of a romance. Engagement of Mary Durack and J. E. Davidson. J. D. Moss visits Kimberley. Arthur Richardson cycling around Australia. M.P. in the Territory. Inspects Victoria River Downs with view to purchase. Buys cattle from Northern Territory stations. Interviews manager of Goldsbrough Mort in Melbourne re purchase Victoria Downs. Visits Tasmania. Calls on W. S. Osmond, owner Ord River station, re purchase of cattle.

1. See *The Bicycle in Rural Australia, A Study of Man, Machine and Milieu*, by James Douglas Fitzpatrick, Oxford, 1980.
2. *Robert Watson* succeeded to the management of Victoria River Downs in 1896 on the death of his brother Jack, whose bizarre exploits and foolhardy pranks had earned him the somewhat satirical nickname of 'The Gulf Hero'. R. Watson's wife was the first white woman to take up residence at the station, and their infant son, George, was the first white baby in the district. M.P. makes no mention of 'Mrs Bob's' being at the station in October 1899.
3. Osmond had originally named Ord River Station Plympton Saint Mary, after his birthplace in Devonshire, England, to where he was returned for burial.

   He bequeathed his considerable fortune, including Ord River and The Sycamores, to his unspecified 'next of kin'. A dispute arose between a woman in Devonport who claimed to be his niece, and a cousin who declared her to be illegitimate. The case was referred to the Supreme Court of Victoria, and a Commission was set up to take evidence in England. After a law-suit lasting three years and costing £20,000, a decision was made in favour of the niece.

   The fact that his Australian-based nephew Frederick Booty was not mentioned in this regard indicates that communication between them had broken down to the extent of neither acknowledging their relationship.

Chapter 7: Turn of the Century, January 1900–May 1901

Marriages of Mary Durack and J. E. Davidson, Black Pat Durack and Susan Downes, M. J. Durack and Bertha Levinson. Experiment with carrier pigeons. Local personalities. Western Australia votes to enter Federal Commonwealth. M.P. explores unoccupied country. P.B. leaves to be married. Christmas at Argyle. Murder of Galway Jerry Durack at Dunham Station. The accused tried in Perth.

1. *The Martin family*. Jack and Alf Martin, sons of Alfred Martin of South Australia, were later joined in the Kimberleys by their three brothers, William, Archibald and Frank.

   Jack Martin, born 1872, became manager of Legune (originally Leguna) Station, Northern Territory, for Bovril Estates. He married Nellie Mulligan (sister of Lillas who married Patsy Durack in 1910). Jack was accidentally killed at Parry's Creek, near Wyndham, in 1924.

   James Alfred Martin (*Alf*) was originally employed by C.D. & D. in Fremantle. He came to Kimberley in 1901, working as stockman and drover for the same firm until he took over the management of Carlton Station for Bovril Estates in 1909. In 1926 he became manager of Bovril's Victoria River Downs, which post he filled until his retirement in 1945. (See *The Big Run*, Jock Makin, Adelaide, 1971.) He married Beatrice Edwards, and the couple reared a family of five sons and three daughters on Carlton and Victoria Stations, Mrs Martin starting her children's education by correspondence. After their retirement Mr and Mrs Martin settled for some years at Katherine. When Alf's health began to fail, they came to Perth where he died in 1950. Mrs Martin died in 1965.

   William Henry Page Martin, born 1879, came north soon after his elder brothers and took over a carrying business, operating with a mule team between Wyndham and the outlying stations. He died alone, of fever, between Wyndham and the Dunham Station in April 1908. He is buried at the Dunham Station beside Jerry Durack and his two daughters. He was unmarried.

   Archibald Martin, born 1881, came to Kimberley after his return from the Boer War. He went into partnership with young Patsy Durack at

Cow Creek Station near the Dunham, and later became secretary of the Wyndham Road Board, which position he held for many years. He married Hilda Nugent and they had a son and daughter. Mrs Archie Martin died in Perth in 1951, and her husband in 1960.

Frank Martin, born 1886, came first to West Kimberley where he was inspecting land for Bovril Estates. A boab tree near Kalumburu Mission bears his name and the date 3.8.1915. He formed Northcote Station which was later abandoned and the cattle shifted to Legune. He later managed a station named Speewah which had been left to his brother Archie's son Alan by its original owner J. B. Dillon, 'The Silver King', a relative of the Duracks. He was unmarried, and died in the 1960s.

2. '*Forty-five years in the Great Nor-West of Western Australia*,' by Charles Edward Flinders, set down by J. F. Christie. Unpublished. Copy in Battye Library, Perth.
3. In the years to come my sister Elizabeth and myself were to find Charles Edward Flinders both amusing and interesting company. We enjoyed his caustic comments on local life and characters, and his memories of days gone by. When we left Wyndham for England in 1936 he gave us a letter of introduction to his sister Gertrude and her husband Walter Raphael. They proved to be a charming and hospitable couple residing in a fine mansion in Cambridgeshire where they bred racehorses, entertained lavishly, and mingled with the élite of the British counties.
4. The Federal Referendum, held July 1900, resulted in a vote of 44,100 to 19,000 in favour of Western Australia entering the Commonwealth. The East Kimberley figures were 60 in favour of Federation and only 1 against. In West Kimberley 97 voted for and 34 against.
5. See *Deep of the Sky*, a biography of Jim Ronan by his son, Tom, London, 1962.
6. Letter to me from C. Lacy Good, Forster, N.S.W., 29.3.1960. A further extract from this letter is quoted in Chapter Sixteen. Copy of full text in Battye Library.
7. Besides the attack on Jerry Durack and his son there was the well-known case of the police trackers Pigeon and Captain of West Kimberley who turned outlaw in 1894. Another was that of Major, trusted employee of Jack Kelly of Texas Downs, of whom more in Chapter Twenty.

Chapter 8: A Bride in Kimberley: May–December 1901

Fifteen years in Kimberley. Encouraging prospects. F. Connor re-elected for East Kimberley. P.B. returns with wife Eva. A bride's impression of the north. Black Pat and wife leave Kimberley. J.W. leaves for Kalgoorlie. Letters from J. J. Durack in England.

1. *William Stretch*, with three partners, Foster, Weekes, and Lewers, took up Denison Downs on Sturt Creek in 1887 and started out from Normanton, Queensland, with 750 head of cattle. They arrived with 550 head in October 1888. An educated man and a brother of the Bishop of Newcastle, Stretch had married the cultured Miss Gratton Rivers of Euroa, Victoria, who later joined him at Sturt Creek. Weekes was said to have been formerly an artist in Montmartre.
2. *Jack Skeahan junior* credited Louis Dagenhardt with having taught him to work with tools and timber from his earliest years, and having been conscientious of his welfare in other regards. After Jack Kelly and Bob Sexton took up Bedford Downs in 1910 Dagenhardt arranged with them to employ young Skeahan while he was taught to read and write by Billy Miller (otherwise Linklater, well known as a composer of colloquial ballad verse), who was then cooking on the station. From Bedford, Skeahan went to Ning Bing to work for Billy Weaber, with whom he took several droving trips to the Queensland market. From this he graduated to a droving team of his own, and for some time had two plants on the road, earning a reputation for good organization and outstanding reliability.

   He married an Aboriginal woman named Rosie, and they reared a sturdy family.

Chapter 9: South African Sojourn, January–August 1902

M.P. calls on Sir John Forrest. Death of Alexander Forrest. The 'meat ring'. M.P. with sister Bird sails for South Africa to investigate market for Australian beef. Visits Durban, Pietermaritzburg, Ladysmith, Port Elizabeth, Cape Town. Sets sail for England.

1. In 1903 a monument to Alexander Forrest was erected on the corner of Barrack Street and St George's Terrace, Perth. From that time on M.P., when passing to and from his Perth office in Howard Street, would never fail to lift his hat in token of his respect.
2. This is not surprising, since C.D. & D. and Forrest, Emanuel were

often linked in accusations of manipulating a 'meat ring' and purchasing beef at a pittance from struggling Kimberley growers to sell at inflated prices to southern butchers.

3. An agreement had been entered into in 1901 whereby C.D. & D. were to supply to William Henderson Fell & Donald McInnes (of Bourke Street, Melbourne) 6,000 heifers, which were to be shipped to South Africa and sold, the proceeds to be divided between the contracting parties.
4. Other accounts reveal Britain's mishandling of Boer encampments at this time, with resultant suffering and loss of life.

Chapter 10: The Distressful Country, March–June 1902

M.P. and his sister Bird sail from Cape Town to London. Met by brother Jerry (Dermot) Durack. Visit Northern Ireland to meet Connor and Doherty families. A tour of Ireland. Impressions of a sad country.

1. This name, given Jerry by his Irish friends, was from this time on adopted by his family, to distinguish him from various other relatives of the same name.

Chapter 11: A Traveller's Tales, June–August 1902

M.P. in London with brother Jerry (Dermot) and sister Bird. The coronation of Edward VII postponed. Sightseeing in London and Cambridge. F. Connor negotiates trial shipment of cattle to South Africa. Business negotiations and social contacts in London. M.P. and Bird tour France and Switzerland, and return to Fremantle.

1. *Sir Edward Horne Wittenoom* had been Agent-General in London from 1898 to 1901, when he was succeeded by his brother-in-law, H. B. Lefroy. Wittenoom was at that time director of Dalgety & Company.
2. J.W. pursued the matter further on his visit to France in 1907. A firm of genealogists found evidence of several of the name Duroc having emigrated to Ireland after the Revocation of the Edict of Nantes in 1685, which rendered their relationship to Napoleon's Marshal, in any case, rather remote. From the same source J.W. procured a copy of the Duroc family crest which he bore back to Australia in triumph and in all good faith. One branch of the family had it stamped on their

cutlery, while M.J. had it copied in stained glass for the front door of his city home.

In the 1930s it came to the attention of Irish historians that the Duracks in Australia believed themselves to be of French origin. The family history (later summarized in Chapter One of *Kings in Grass Castles*) was then brought to light, leaving no doubt that the name derived from the ancient Gaelic O'Dubraic which in time (stripped of the aspirate 'b') came to be rendered as O'Duraic, O'Durack and finally, (deprived of the prefix by Henry VIII) as Durack.

Descendants of Patsy Durack, if anxious to claim some French ancestry, might do so through his mother's name, since the Dillons came to Ireland at the time of the Anglo-Norman invasion, a mere eight centuries ago.

Chapter 12: The Traveller Back to Base, October 1902–December 1903
M.P. returns to Kimberley. C.D. & D. flexible policy. Hopes dashed for South African trade. P.B. and wife leaving the north. Boxer visits the metropolis. New arrivals: Charlie Eich and wife, Rudolph Philchowski, W. J. C. Jones. Letter to J.A. A broken contract. Tom Scanlan begins work on short cut across range (Duracks's Folly). The Copley case. Damages to C.D. & D.

1. On his electioneering tour of West Kimberley in October 1917, M.P. called on the Bell-Blays at Ellendale where he was pleased to find them happily settled.

   > The place is about 25 miles off the road—area about 10,000 acres, fenced and carrying about 2,000 sheep—all the result of their own labour. They now owe only about £650 on the place and netted £400 last year.

2. *Rudolph Philchowski*. A possible clue to Philchowski's background is given by Mrs Elsie Withey of Northbridge, New South Wales, who wrote to me in November 1972 after reading *Kings in Grass Castles:*

   > William Carr-Boyd, the explorer of whom you write, was my father's cousin. I have been wondering whether the mailman you mentioned might also have some connection with our family. A cousin of my mother's married a German Count who was German Consul in Sydney at the time of their marriage.

> Owing to his bad temper he was unable to keep his position. He was a clever man and spoke many different languages and was a wonderful pianist. He went over to Western Australia where he obtained, and lost, a good position on account of his temper. The next his wife heard of him, he was killed by the blacks. His name was Hans Weickhardt. I wonder if the 'postie' you speak of could be the same man.

In reply to my letter asking for further details, Mrs Withey wrote again:

> Hans Weickhardt married Margaret Potts (Mother's cousin) on a German warship. The bride walked on a red carpet strewn with rose petals. They had two children, Margueretta and a boy, Erdhard. I was in my teens when I met them and now I am ninety-three and a half years old. (I was born in 1879.) I'm sorry I don't know the year they were married, or when he was Consul. I think his wife died about 1924.

As Rudolph Philchowski does not come into the family records before being employed as a stockman on Argyle in 1902, it would hardly have been possible for him to have been the mailman referred to in *Kings in Grass Castles*. It is possible, however, that there may be a link between Hans Weickhardt and Philchowski who, as told in a later chapter, was speared by blacks in 1913. It is, of course, well known that many men who came to North Australia with pasts to live down operated under assumed names.

3. Some years later, Roy Phillipps, then book-keeper at Argyle, wrote of Bill Jones to his mother in Perth:

> 12.9.12: The manager here at present is Mr W. J. C. Jones—a long thin streak but a very interesting man. He was manager of Buckabundi station near Moree and lived in the Gwida district for about twenty years until 1892.

4. *John Healy* was an Irish tutor employed by Grandfather Patsy Durack at Thylungra, 1874–1884.

Chapter 13: Propitious Stars, December 1903–April 1905

A good time for C.D. & D. Family affairs. Francis Connor on the political front. Social diversions. Opening of the Kalgoorlie water supply. Decline of the gold boom. P.B. selects land near Wagin. M.P. back to Kimberley.

Death of Tom Scanlan. Completion of Durack's Folly. Men without wives. Differences with Philchowski. Constable Parker taken by crocodile. Local problems discussed. Overland movement of cattle from East Kimberley to eastern States.

1. *Sydney Capel Piggott*, foundation member of the Pearlers' Association and chairman of the Broome Roads Board, who had succeeded Alexander Forrest to the West Kimberley seat in 1901.
2. About a year later Connor withdrew his support from Daglish over a move for the Government purchase of the Midland Railway. His ministry fell to a non-Labour government under C. H. Rason.
3. Argyle homestead was built on the banks of the Behn River which disappeared under the waters of the Ord River dam in 1972.
4. Roy Phillipps, a C.D. & D. employee of later years, writing to his mother from Wyndham describes 'the Folly' thus:

   > I had a good trip down from Argyle—left about 10 a.m. and got to Granite Creek that night for camp and started over Durack's Folly about sunrise. This is a bridle path up the sheer face of a precipice. It is a very wild and picturesque spot in the mountains with a lonely grave at the foot of the climb.
   >
   > The scenery here is too gorgeous and grand to describe. You travel through rugged mountain passes for about 10 miles then you get out on the open plains of long waving grass. I travel with 4 riding horses, four packs and one boy. I doubt if the novelty will ever wear off.

5. *The Bushman's Mulga Wires:* quoted from the first and probably only number of *The Spinifex Gazette*, 29 November 1906, a handwritten collection of local, anonymous, and mostly scurrilous, items circulated for the amusement of residents.
6. *Jacob Kuhl* was a German who had been attracted to the Hall's Creek gold-rush in 1886. He later set up a pub at the Three Mile but abandoned this business when his wife, taking their young daughter, eloped with one Tom Chapman. They made local history by riding over 400 miles of wild and mountainous country between Wyndham and Derby, on a direct route over the King Leopold Ranges. Thereafter Kuhl was employed in various capacities by C.D. & D. and Jack Kelly of Texas.

   A tale told of him is that he used to bore holes in the raised floorboards of C.D. & D.'s store, through which he drained grog from casks into his own bottles. On one occasion he went to sleep in the process and woke to find that he had drained the cask dry, letting the precious liquor soak into the ground.

His death in Perth on 6 March 1930 is noted by M.P.:

> Poor old fellow—a link with Wyndham's very early days. He came to the Kimberleys in the early gold rush about June 1886 and lived in the North except for the last year or so. The disappearance of his wife and daughter from their Three Mile Hotel caused quite a sensation at the time.

Chapman, who eloped with Mrs Kuhl, was himself one of the most colourful characters of the north at that time and was said to have numbered among the notorious 'Ragged Thirteen'. I once wrote to my cousin, Patsy M. Durack, asking for his version of this stock-thieving group, and received the following reply:

> Argyle Station,
> 5.6.32
>
> ... You ask about the 'Ragged Thirteen'. This was more of a myth than a reality. I have met a number who claimed to belong to it—many more than thirteen of them—and all I know was that they were a b—lot of horse-thieves. Chapman, the man who stole Jack Kuhl's wife, was the ring-leader of the real thirteen.

7. There are no alligators in Australian waters but the term was frequently used in the north to distinguish the large salt-water *Crocodilus porosus* from the smaller fresh-water species *Crocodilus johnstoni*. The latter feeds on fish and small mammals, and seldom grows to more than seven or eight feet. The former grows to an average of eighteen feet and is often considerably more. They are a menace to stock, and have been known to claim a number of human victims.
8. The cause of this disease was traced in the early 1950s to a leguminous plant named *Crotalaria Retusa* (commonly known as 'Rattle-pod') which horses would eat when better fodder was scarce.
9. The cattle were sold at prices ranging from £3 17s 6d to £6 6s 0d per head.

Chapter 14: A Girl in a Man's World, May–December 1905

Kathleen Durack arrives at Argyle. Visits Lissadell with M.P. Becomes engaged to young Patsy Durack. M.P.'s correspondence with Miss Vera Angier. Denis Doherty on visit to Kimberley and proposes London agency. Arrangements re purchase Dunham Station. Formation of Bullita Pastoral Company. M.P. names creek Kildurk. Visits Waterloo Station. Death of owner Tom Deacon that year. M.P. negotiates re border with Mrs Deacon. Visits Kilfoyles at Rosewood Station. Royal Commission on Aborigines (W. E. Roth). M.P.'s correspondence re same. Spearing of Hugh McKenna. Murder of four white men on board J. Bradshaw's launch *Wunwalla* off Port Keats.

1. *Bullita Station*. The Bullita lease has been considerably reduced over the years from that of the original area.
2. Grandfather Patsy Durack had stipulated that his nephew Ambrose was to receive 635 head of the cattle started overland in 1881. While managing Argyle, Ambrose was agisting his cattle on Dunham Station by arrangement with young Patsy and his mother. M.P., writing to J.W. in September 1905, states:

   > I think we can make use of this place [the Bullita block] as a kind of fattening reserve for the end of the year shipments . . . Ambrose has his cattle now in hand at lower or top end of Dunham with a man looking after them . . . The intention was to have started them over direct for the Baines but he is holding them pending further inspection . . .
   >
   > I intend getting Chambers over shortly to run a line straight out east from the corner of Kilfoyle's northern block, the point of contact with our southern Newry block being already defined. He has merely to run a line east 36 miles. This will pretty well define our position with respect to line between ourselves and Deacon, as well as defining country between ourselves and Rosewood. We have some very fine country right on the back of the Keep but not very accessible from the Newry side—the country rough to get across . . .

3. Doug Moore, a young Englishman (the son of a solicitor in Hull), who had been influenced to come to Australia by appealing pictures of sheep and cattle stations, had come to Kimberley not long before to be book-keeper for the Ord River Station. He was in regular touch with the family at Argyle and had formed a warm friendship with M.P.

In his latter years he set down his reminiscences which were made available to me by his widow after his death in 1977. Concerning the death of Tom Deacon he writes as follows:

> When Bill Maybury and I got to the Stud [Ivanhoe Station] we found that Tom Deacon of Waterloo Station had been dead 24 hours and not buried so Bill and I stayed and sunk the grave—the hardest ground I have ever used pick and shovel on . . . The heat was terrific and Bill had no shirt on. He got terribly sunburnt and was in great pain for the next few days. Meanwhile someone had gone up the track in search of M. P. Durack and when he turned up eventually the corpse was put on a buckboard and the blacks pulled it down to the grave at a trot. M.P. then read the burial service. Mrs. Deacon and Sophie, her adopted daughter, were there . . . Mrs. Deacon afterwards married Amos Skuthorpe of the family of famous horsemen.

4. The Kilfoyles had corresponded with Tom's relatives in County Galway since 1896 when Grandfather Patsy Durack, then on a trip to Ireland, had brought them welcome news of this long-lost Australian branch of their family. A cherished packet of letters was left to me by Tom Kilfoyle's son Jack. The first, to Tom and his wife, was from his sister Kate Carolan, dated November 1896.

> My Dear and loving Brother and Sister,
>
> It causes me feelings of inexpressible joy to get your address (which I so long sought for) from P. Durack Esq., and also to learn from him that you were getting along so well and lucky to get such a nice respectable companion. Mr. Durack is never done talking of her and he says you have a very nice little boy.
>
> I had nearly despaired from ever hearing from you as I wrote for your address several times to me Brother John and he did not send it to me but told me you would scarcely ever get me letter if I had your address itself as the post was not going out there . . .
>
> Now I expect that when you get this letter that you will send me your photographs as nothing would please me better except to see your personal presence as I hope yet to see. I expect you will come for a tower [sic] of pleasure as Mr. Durack is presently. He is an awful nice man and he is telling us all about the

country and how you live. We were surprised to learn that it took such a long time for ye to go out there with all your cattle. He told us that the wheel of his waggon broke down going out there and that you made a new one and he has it at his place yet.

He never speaks of poor Johnny Durack [speared on Rosewood Station in 1886] but he cries. We were all in sorrow he was killed for he was so good and dutiful to his Mother. May the Lord have mercy on his soul. He gives a great character of Long Michael' as he calls him. He says he is very well to do. He seems to be a fine man by his photo that he had with Sister Peggy's [Margaret Kilfoyle *nee* Durack] photo and her family's . . .

Dear Brother it was a sudden shock to us all to here the sudden death of poor John a man of such an age and he so Affectionate and good natured. We never wrote a letter to him but he answered it by the return of post and he was deeply regretted by all the day that he was prayed for in the Church . . .

Dear Brother would you think it advisable for any of the three boys we have still at home to go out to that country. They are very sturdy and sensible, and we would let James go if you gave us any encouragement.

My dear sister I expect if Thomas don't answer this letter you will take the interest of doing so as Mr. Durack said you are as good a natured woman as he ever spoke a word to . . .

From your Sister.

Kate Carolan to Thomas Guilfoyle [sic].
Glenvanish, Mt. Shannon, Co. Galway.

The reply to this letter encouraged correspondence from younger relatives. Letters of gratitude from one and another testify that the association was a fairly expensive one for Tom and his wife.

I never can forget your kindness and I cannot express my feelings to you for to think of me and my family . . . Not one single person or friend that heard of your action but applauded you for it. Dear Uncle and Aunt you done what was fair for to send it to me. My father felt bad the bill was not sent to him but I have no doubt if you done so I would be without it . . . Dear Uncle I think it a pity to have my Aunt—a woman so nice as her in such wilderness shut out from society and from

> her Chapel. You ought to let her into town and not leave her in such a lonesome place. I wish to God you and Aunt and little Jack came to Ireland. I will bring you to Lisdoonvarna . . . It is a place where people go for health and pleasure and exchange of air . . .
>
> Your loving niece,
> Julia Brody.

A later letter from Mrs Brody expresses further gratitude and offers repayment in kind:

> I and my family will pray for you both and little Jack and I will do more than prayers. I will get you all enrolled in the Immaculate Conseption of the Blessed Virgin and St. Joseph's Union so that each of you will have your share of four thousand Masses every year. I will pay for ye as long as God leaves me alive it only costs a shilling and a half penny for each person during the year . . . I am sending ye my own card to see the instructions—let each of ye say the little prayers on the back from the first of next March to gain the indulgence . . . I will also make a Novena for you in the end of August . . . and you can offer it up for any intention you like . . . I am sending ye those little medals for ye protection . . .
>
> I was glad you send the nice postcard of the Black Men. Indeed we would think it very strange there was such quere people living. We would be almost afraid to look at them in a picture. I wonder how ye put up with such creatures. Just the same we enjoyed them great . . .
>
> I never can stop thinking of you to be in such a wild lonely place . . . You ought to get a house in town where you could go to Mass and little Jack could go home at night from school . . .

A letter to Jack Kilfoyle from his cousin Babie Brody is dated November 1905.

> I cannot tell you how sorry I was to hear you have been sick. Mother used to be troubled about ye. She knew something should have happened ye or ye would have answered our letters. I could not tell ye how glad she was to have ye joined St. Joseph's Union . . .
>
> My brother Michael (the shop boy) got a great fit last Xmas.

> *Pneumonia* was the name of the fit he had. When we heard of the fit you had every one we told it to said God should have a hand in you. I hope ye will be soon finished at school and we would be delighted ye to come to Ireland . . .

A letter from Julia Brody written in October 1909 conveys condolences to Mrs Kilfoyle on the death of her husband and provides on request a few biographical details.

> You asked me about poor Uncle's age and I can give ye a good idea of it for he was born in the next townsland to Currakyle where I am living . . . He was born in Derrynarna in the year 1842 in the parish of Toomgrancy and Scariff in the County Clare. He left Ireland for Australia in 1856. He was then fourteen years of age and by that he would be 67 years when he died . . . This might not correspond with the dates he gave down for he may not know his correct age he going away so young . . . Hoping this will be of help to ye for the fixing of his estate . . .

5. This letter continues as follows:

> I do not know anyone yet who offered any practical solution to the whole question. Is it better that they should depart as a bygone race? Is it better that they and their culture should be preserved in entirety? Or is it best that they should be elevated on the social plane to be eventually absorbed into the white race?
>
> History tells us that the first proposition is inevitable. To preserve them as a race complete with their own culture is a course which never appears to have been considered very seriously or given much encouragement. Missionaries have gone out and, I have no doubt, with the best of intentions, but I have often thought have neglected to bring along one most important factor—the influence of womankind . . .*

* Sisters of the St John of God Order joined the Pallottine Society in the missionary field in West Kimberley in 1907. They have since carried on over an extended area and have been joined of recent years by the Sisters of St Joseph. Our Lady of Missions and Loreto Orders. The Benedictine missionaries at Kalumburu on the Drysdale River, north of Derby, were joined by Spanish Sisters of the same Order in 1931.

> If a body of people, male and female, could be got to interest themselves in the native question, owing no allegiance to any particular denomination, working for the good that begets good, then I think much might be done ... How can we expect the native to harmonise the teachings of those diversified bodies all of which more or less introduce the element of bias? ...
>
> We know instances when the cross between European and Australian native have given us the highest type of manhood ... and we know of instances where the cross has resulted in a depraved form of humanity—although in justification of the latter we should consider the desperate position into which the half-caste is driven ... [M.P.D., Fremantle, to J.W.D., Perth, 13.2.05]

6. Historical research of later years indicates that Roth's assessment was not far from the truth.
7. They were not so much 'dressed up as men' as doing a man's work in helping their white companions to handle their cattle. The so-called 'Kombo' (or 'Combo'), the man who maintained a steady association with an Aboriginal woman, was generally looked down on by men who associated casually with any number of women.
8. I recall the matter still being discussed thirty years later, the police contending that the chains were as light as possible and that it was better to attach them to the neck of a prisoner than to restrict the use of his hands and arms.
9. A letter from Jerry Skeahan's brother Patrick, replying to J.W.'s letter of condolence, reflects not only family sentiment but something of an attitude towards the Aborigines which was fairly common among outback residents.

> J. D. Springs,
> *Adavale*, Queensland.
> 20.1.06.
>
> Dear Jack,
>
> I beg to thank you kindly for your sympathetic letter re poor Jerry's sad end. I got a wire the day before Xmas from Sydney and as Mother was not well I did not tell her til some days later. You can judge of my Happy Xmas with a secret like that all to myself, especially when anyone mentioned his name ... When I think that I shall never see him and of his lonely grave it is all too hard to write about. I had a faint hope after

receiving the wire that there had been some mistake but the account was wrong only in detail . . .

I consider that the Government is much to blame for the repeated outrages in the West, by keeping an inadequate police force and by connivance at the depredations of the niggers. If the State protects the Blacks (!) in all justice they (the State) should be held responsible for their actions. By all accounts if you use arms against the Blacks in Westralia and the Police get wind of it you are likely to be shipped 1,500 miles to Perth and there tried for your Life . . .

Well Jack, I've neither seen or heard from you for many years but I was very pleased to see by the papers that you boys have some good properties over there.

Mother sends her kindest love. The poor old soul is getting very feeble but she can still walk about a little. She had Masses said for Jerry in December before the sad news reached us and when she heard it at last she did not take it at all as you would expect. She said she was quite prepared for it.

A most singular thing—the night he was killed I had something like a nightmare—jumped out of bed and said, 'God Almighty—Jerry is dead!' A man sleeping close by said—'You're dreaming Patsy.' 'I know,' I said, 'but what are all those b— Afghans doing here?' I never jumped out of bed like that before or since. Of course it was only a dream but a strange thing, wasn't it?

Yours faithfully,
P. J. Skeahan.

10. *Joseph Bradshaw* was among the most picturesque personalities in the north at that time. For a number of years First Mate on a British India vessel, he was said to have had considerable private means and to have been a member of the Melbourne Stock Exchange and the Royal Melbourne Yacht Club.

In 1890 he purchased the pearling schooner *Gemini* (generally referred to as *The Twins*) and set off with his young wife, his brother Fred, his cousin Aeneas Gunn (of *We of the Never-Never* fame), a French store-keeper, a West Indian Negro, two Spaniards, a Hebridean sailor, and a Chinese cook to survey the northern coast in search of a property. They selected a site on the wild reaches of the Prince Regent River and set up a station they called Maragui, to which they brought

4,000 sheep from Victoria River Downs—driven to Wyndham by Aeneas Gunn and shipped to their destination. After a valiant struggle to gain a footing in the area, they were defeated by marauding blacks and wild dogs, by the general unsuitability of the country for sheep-raising and by a crippling tax on the importation of sheep from the Northern Territory into Western Australia.

In January 1894, after further investigation of the coast, Bradshaw took up 4,800 square miles of country between the Victoria and Fitzmaurice Rivers. The remaining sheep were shipped and driven back to the Territory and others were purchased from Goldsbrough, Mort & Co., then owners of Wickham River Station. Meanwhile Bradshaw had gone to Melbourne where he purchased the 'steamerette' *Red Gauntlet*, filled her up with supplies, and returned to Darwin. In April of the same year the two vessels *Red Gauntlet* and *The Twins* set sail for the Victoria. The sheep fared no better in the new locality than on the Prince Regent River, and Bradshaw soon turned his station over to cattle.

M. P. Durack called there on a number of occasions and had pleasant business contacts with the Bradshaw brothers and their first manager Aeneas Gunn, under whom the property seems to have prospered reasonably well in its earlier years. When visiting during the early 1900s, M.P. copied notes from the station diaries made available to him by the book-keeper. Extracts from these may be of interest:

> *April 8th, 1894*: Steamer *Red Gauntlet* and schooner *Twins* left Pt. Darwin for Victoria River. The complement of the *Red Gauntlet* was J. Bradshaw (owner), R. Lindsay (master), R. Woolhouse (engineer), D. Darrock (mate), Ah Pan (cook), Sales (deckhand), and the Negro Johnson (fireman). *The Twins* was manned by A. Gunn (master), J. Larian (mate), Ivan Egeroff and D. Buchanan.
>
> *—16th, 1894*: Vessels anchored in Blunder Bay. *Red Gauntlet* grounded in Shoal Reach and *The Twins* collided with her, doing considerable damage.
>
> *—17th, 1894*: Temporary station formed at base of the Dome.
>
> *—26th, 1894*: Bradshaw with horses purchased from Auvergne and accompanied by Larian and black boy named Nim, proceeded up Victoria and Gregory Rivers to the sheep at Gregory Crossing. Here they were attacked by blacks. The boy Nim was killed and Bradshaw narrowly escaped.

June 2nd, 1894: J. Bradshaw reached the sheep in charge of H. Young and party. All right but several sheep had died from poison . . .
August 1st, 1894: J. Bradshaw took geologist, H. Y. L. ('Geology') Broun and party to Victoria River to make deep drilling exploration on behalf of the Government. [He found goldbearing ore down to 500 ft, but in marginal values only.]
Sept 4th, 1894: J. Bradshaw with Capt. Lindsay explored Fitzmaurice River.
—24th, 1894: The Twins proceeded up the Shaw River (renamed the Bradshaw by 'Geology' Broun) and anchored at a place called by the natives Kumallay (renamed Youngford as H. Young rode his horse across). Here all material and stores brought from the Dome was landed. The sheep shorn at large billabong four miles distant—wool brought in boats to *The Twins* and taken by A. Gunn to Darwin. Many sheep dying of poison.
May 27th, 1895: Messrs. Mulligan & Ligar brought in whale boat to the station in half dead condition, having been attacked by natives some days before, but managed to reach Auvergne Station and brought down the Baines in a boat and thence here to await transport Darwin.
—30th, 1895: Young with an armed party proceeded to T.K. [Tom Kilfoyle] Camp to ascertain the fate of Mulligan's waggons and loading. Found a large number of white men assembled so returned to the station.
June 5th, 1895: Took Mulligan & Ligar to S.S. *Victoria* in Blunder Bay. J. Bradshaw in Melbourne purchased all the herd cattle and horses on Willeroo Station from R. C. Cooper.
Sept 2nd, 1895: Took delivery from G. E. Scott (Cooper's manager) of 880 cattle and 27 horses. Stock brought on by drover J. McPhee.
Nov 8th, 1895: The Government Resident and party visited the station.
Jan, 1896: The station moved this month to a high bank on the North side of the Bradshaw River. Shepherd Antonie Bolan died while out with sheep. J. Bradshaw sold *Red Gauntlet* to Burns Philp & Co., Thursday Island.
Sept 15th, 1896: Shearing—1553 sheep shorn, yielding 18 bales wool.
Oct 16th, 1896: The Twins arrived with 17 rams and a paraffin

and coal prospector, Aikins. Got 20 bulls from Goldsbrough Mort Station.

Jan 8th, 1897: Terrific storm struck Darwin damaging *The Twins* which was anchored there.

June, 1897: J. Bradshaw returned from Melbourne. Came to Blunder Bay in S.S. *Victoria*. Met the *Wunwalla* with Nasmith, Desmond and others as passengers.

July, 1897: Shore 662 sheep for 9 bales wool.

Jan, 1898: Fred Bradshaw took up 2,000 miles of country continuous to the north boundary of J. Bradshaw's present run. It is proposed to work the two stations as one.

April 1898: J. & F. Bradshaw with about 50 tons of cargo for various stations arrived with the *Cygnet* at Holdfast Reach where the *Wunwalla* met them. A month spent delivering the various cargoes at their destinations with launch and a barge purchased from Stevens.

May 11th, 1898: J. Bradshaw held a court at the Victoria Depot under a box tree.

May 20th, 1898: Erected police station at Burmaione on Timber Creek four miles from Depot. Constable O'Keefe to be in charge.

June 25th, 1898: Mrs Pound, the station housekeeper, died and was buried in the horse paddock. She came from Queensland with her husband in a dray. Pound was paid off and went with H. Young to the Katherine.

Sept 2nd, 1898: M. P. Durack, managing owner of Auvergne and other stations, visited here.

March, 1899: The wet season culminated in an exceptional flood which drowned nearly half the remaining sheep. All hands working up to their neck in water till midnight. Flood waters 2 ft. deep in house. Staff vacated and camped for 10 days on a stoney rise in the horse paddock.

April and May, 1899: Only 114 surviving sheep shorn today. Fred Bradshaw and party to Darwin to bring out a blood stallion and mare which J. Bradshaw purchased in Melbourne from Yuille & Co.

Sept 29th, 1899: M. P. Durack arrived—fired a shot on the other side of the river. J. Bradshaw and two boys took the dinghy down and brought him to the station. Jack Skeahan waiting on the other side. Negotiation re bullocks which

Skeahan to take delivery of. A plough and earth scoop rented at £2.10 per month for four months for Auvergne from Bradshaws. *Oct 25th, 1899*: J. Skeahan took delivery cattle from Young—94 bullocks.

June, 1900: M. P. Durack and J. Skeahan arrive and stay for the night. Bradshaw agreed charter launch for Auvergne at £3.0.0 per day.

April 8th, 1901: Jimmy, one of the murderers of Jack Larsen, was executed this morning at 7 a.m. All the blacks on the place were mustered as a warning to see the execution. The body was left hanging until after breakfast when it was cut down and buried beneath the scaffold. Mr Little [J.A.G. first official Post Master in Darwin acting as Sheriff] distributed tobacco among the blacks who were onlookers.

The launch left for Port Darwin taking Sheriff Mr. Little, Corporal Waters, Captain Mugg and a number of visitors.

Chapter 15: More Traveller's Tales, December 1905–October 1906

M.P. and Denis Doherty sail for London. Winston Churchill speaks at Western Australian dinner. M.P. visits the United States and Canada, then sails for Japan and China, returning via Manila, Timor, and Darwin to Wyndham.

1. *Sir Walter James*, a leading lawyer in his home State, was then Agent-General for Western Australia in London. He had entered Parliament in 1894, and was State Premier 1902–04.
2. G. S. *Yuill*, born in Aberdeenshire in 1868 and at this time Australia-based, had irons in many fires. His subsequent involvement with members of C.D. & D. is referred to in later chapters.
3. *Denis Francis Durack* (born 1869) was, it was later established, the son of Grandfather Patsy's first cousin John Joseph (born 1842), son of James John (born Magerareagh 1820), younger brother of Michael and Darby Durack who emigrated to Australia in the 1850s.

Chapter 16: A Stockman's Story, March 1906–January 1907

Frank Eipper from Scone, N.S.W., arrives in East Kimberley. He writes to his family of conditions and people encountered while working as a stockman on Argyle. M.P. returns from abroad at the end of the year and reports Eipper's drowning in the Behn River on Christmas Day.

1. The letters from Frank Eipper here quoted were made available to me by his great-niece, Mrs Sabina Flanagan of Rose Park, South Australia.
2. Extracts from letter to me from C. Lacy Good, Forster, N.S.W., 29.3.1960:

> My people went from here to W.A. in 1897, I being 13 at the time and was sent to Christian Brothers' College, Perth where I palled up with Patsy Durack whose father had a cattle station in Kimberley and this didn't convey much to me—didn't know where it was then. Leaving school I was put into an office—which I detested—and later, as Mother and Father had gone to the Barbados, I got out. A boy friend working in Forrest, Emanuels told me a station owner who had been at the office wanted a boy, why not see him? He, himself, was going to Victoria Downs; following his advice I got the job with Tom Kilfoyle. Getting off the gangway at Wyndham the first one I met was young Patsy Durack. Date 1900.
>
> From Wyndham I was sent out to Kilfoyle's training camp—Wyndham races being due in a week or so—4 miles out from the Six Mile Hotel. There I did a little quiet riding on one of the 2 horses being trained. After the meeting we picked up a mob of cattle Kilfoyle had bought from 'Black Pat' Durack, who was selling out Goose Hill and going south to Geraldton. 'Black Pat' was in charge of the cattle, Kilfoyle having gone on to Rosewood. Camping in Buttons Gap one night a terrific storm broke out. I was on watch at the time, a proper New Chum, and several times during flashes of lightning found myself in the middle of the mob which was milling around. I rode into the camp and called Pat and said I couldn't see a thing—his reply—'get back and do the best you can, if you can't see how the b . . . h . . . do you think I can!'

[The section of this letter relating to the death of J. J. Durack at the Dunham Station is quoted in Chapter Seven.]

> I left Rosewood a month or two after [the death of J. J. Durack] and got a job at Ivanhoe breaking in some cattle brought down from the Dunham on to that piece of land on the Dunham Station side of Carlton Reach. The Wet being due, I had a boy and a couple of months rations in case the rivers came down. They did, both the Dunham and Ord, one night, just after me

sending the boy to Ivanhoe for mail or orders, result some weeks before I could get across either, on my pat, keeping the niggers up on the ranges. Duncan McCaully, his wife and small daughter were there then. Some 40 years later I happened to mention to our Shire Clerk's wife—he had been Shire Clerk at Gunning at some period—that I had been in East Kimberley when she said she had had a girl friend who went as companion to a Mrs. Durack in Kimberley, who had married a man named McCaully, how he had died and she had come back to N.S.W. and the daughter was a nurse—she didn't know where.

Another time I attended a muster on Dunham Station. Mrs. Jerry Durack and son Frank aged about 2 were there. I had a bad spell of fever there, but Mrs. Durack was very nice and pulled me round. The first part of my stay on Argyle P.B. was manager until he went south to start sheep, I didn't know where. Then your Father came on the scene. I think he had been to England and was on Argyle up to my leaving. Ambrose and I worked together most of my time. Others that worked with us or I met were Charlie Whittacre, manager at Newry, Jack Skeahan, Auvergne (who married Miss Woodland a girl friend who came up with your cousin Kattie—a very nice girl), Jerry Skeahan—murdered on Bradshaw's launch—and Sir Alec Campbell. I also met all the Lissadell Duracks at different times, also at Tom Deacon's Waterloo Station I met a very game woman, Mrs. Tom Deacon, the blacks being bad out there then.

My father having retired from Civil Engineering bought a wheat and sheep place at Wagin and asked me to come down and help him for a while, so I left Argyle and went to Wagin to find P.B. on Behn Ord and my people knew them well. I often went over to Behn Ord. I wasn't at Wagin very long, came to N.S.W. where I married an Irish girl in 1910 name of Kelly, (O'Kelly of West Meath at some period). We had a small orchard about 60 miles from Sydney. One day, on a Mosman ferry, I ran into P.B. He was over here at the Sheep Show.

In 1915 I sold the farm to volunteer in the 1914–1918 flare up. Tried for Air Force, couldn't get in so we went to Wagin and I joined the 44th Battalion in Perth. Not having any youngsters my wife came to England when I cabled her and I was there. She joined the Women's Legion and transferred to Australia Base post office in London while I was in France.

After the Armistice I managed to get 6 months 'non-military leave' as it was called, in a motor repair shop in Chester. A grandmother and aunt lived in Neston a few miles away. A wonderful 6 months—we saw most of Cheshire, North Wales, Liverpool etc. We came home per troopship bringing a small boy aged 7 from a poor London suburb with us. Discharged in Perth, came to N.S.W. and bought an orchard 30 miles from Sydney where we stagnated for 28 years.

Meeting with a bad accident I found I could not work the property so sold and retired to a beautiful little place on Wallis Lake, Forster, on the mid north coast.

Before leaving Perth I heard Mrs. Jerry Durack was living there so my wife and I called on her, my wife being very pleased at having met one of the hardy old pioneers. Later I heard she had passed on . . .

The little boy we brought from England is now a good Aussie with a family of his own and is Chief Valuer in the Rural Bank in Goulburn . . .

3. *Emily Woodland* was a sister of Tom Woodland, then manager of Newry. In 1908 she married M.P.'s cousin Jack Skeahan, then manager of Auvergne.

Chapter 17: Allied Interests, January–April 1907

Competition for Kimberley cattle. Rising overdraft. J.W. in charge of business in Fremantle and Perth. His serious illness and departure for England with Mr and Mrs F. Connor. Purchase of a company car. C.D. & D. confer with Emanuels and Copleys re mutual problems. Promise of government funds for erection of Wyndham meatworks. Wreck of the S.S. *Mildura*. M.P. returns north for few months. Business and social activities in Perth. Family affairs. Death of James Matthew Durack at Camooweal. M.P. visits Murchison district. Summary of New Year prospects and problems.

1. *Grace Palotta* made her Australian debut in 1900 when she appeared with the J. C. Williamson Company at Her Majesty's Theatre in Melbourne. This was in the London hit show *Floradora*, in which she played the part of Lady Hollywood. In about 1907 she joined Hugh J. Ward's group which, having toured India and China, returned to Australia in 1909, playing, among other pieces, the popular *A Bachelor's Honeymoon*.

Chapter 18: J.W.'s Year Abroad, February–November 1907

J.W. sails on the *Scharnhorst* with Mr and Mrs F. Connor. Disembarks at Colombo and thence to India to visit J. J. (Dermot) Durack at Allahabad. Sightseeing in India. From Bombay to Suez. From Egypt to Naples. Touring in Italy, Switzerland, and France. In London with F. Connor. Friendly encounters include Mrs Denis Doherty and family. Cultural and business activities. Meets G. S. Yuill. To Ireland with F. Connor. Visits his father's birthplace in Scariff. To New York on the *Lusitania.* Meets American relatives. Panic follows bank smash. Washington contacts. Captain Pentacost of the *Saxonia.*

1. J.W. held a life subscription to this magazine which he delighted in sharing with other members of the family. When applying for membership he had given his occupation as 'pastoralist', a term not known in the United States to be synonymous with 'rancher'. He ever afterwards received his copies addressed to 'The Rev J. W. Durack'.
2. *Dr (later Bishop) J. Gallagher* had been headmaster of St Patrick's College, Goulburn, N.S.W., where J.W. and his brother M.P. went to school.
3. *Annie Besant* was a disciple and biographer of Mme Blavatsky, founder of the Theosophical Society, and herself founded the Central Hindu College at Benares in 1898. In 1916 she established the Indian Home Rule League.
4. *J. E. Redmond*, 1856–1918, was an Irish political leader; a supporter of Parnell, and Chairman of the Combined Irish Party; a strong supporter of the Bill for Home Rule.
5. *A. Birrell*, 1850–1933, was an English essayist and public official. Chief Secretary for Ireland, 1907–1916, his works include biographies of Charlotte Brontë, William Hazlitt and Andrew Marvell.
6. *Amy Castles* was one of a large musical family of Irish-Australian background. Born in Melbourne in 1882, she began her career by performing in amateur productions of Gilbert and Sullivan. Before long she was appearing in England and on the Continent, to enthusiastic audiences. In 1906 and 1907 she was singing at command performances for King Edward VII and Queen Alexandra.
7. *Patrick Scanlan* married Grandfather Patsy's sister Bridget. Mary Scanlan (Patrick's sister) married John Costello, brother of Mrs Patsy Durack.
8. *Pat Tully* married Grandfather Patsy's sister Sarah.
9. J.W. corresponded with *Walter Durack* until the latter's death in 1918, after which he kept in touch with Walter's daughter Lucille,

Brooklyn-born in 1905. After J.W.'s death in 1936 a tenuous link was maintained until 1978, when my sister Elizabeth visited Lucille Durack Ayres, by that time a widow, in her New York apartment. The two distant cousins found much in common in family backgrounds and interests. Strangely enough, however, whereas the Durack family in Australia had increased considerably, there was not by that time a single person of the name in the New York telephone directory.

10. *Williamina Fleming* was born Williamina Stevens in Dundee, Scotland, 15 May 1857. In 1877 she married James Orr Fleming; the next year they migrated to the United States. She entered Harvard College Observatory in 1879 as a temporary employee and two years later was given a permanent position. She was one of the first to work with stellar spectra as recorded on photographic plates, and discovered by this means two meteors, ten novas and more than two hundred variable stars. She was made an honorary member of the Royal Astronomical Society of London and received the Guadalupe Almendaro medal of the Sociedad Astronomica de Mexico. Her works include two books on aspects of stellar photography. She died in Boston on 21 May 1911. (*Encyclopaedia Americana; Dictionary of American Biography.*)

Chapter 19: Of Schemes and Dreams, January–May 1908

The Wyndham meatworks project again delayed. J.W. returns from abroad with G. S. Yuill of Sydney. A time of indecision for the company. The partners talk of breaking up but decide to carry on. Doherty to open a wool-buying office for C.D. & D. in London. M.P. and sister Bird visit Eastern States capitals. Meeting in Adelaide with the Johnstone family. Business and family contacts in Melbourne, Sydney and Brisbane. M.J.D. buys stud in N.S.W. and engages G. W. Broughton to accompany the stock to Wyndham. Bird Durack decides to go her own way. M.P. returns to Perth and sails north.

1. *The Yuills* were related to the Anderson and Skelton families, who were shipowners at Peterhead from the eighteenth century. The Andersons of the Orient line were of these families. Alan Anderson, Controller of Admiralty shipping and Sir Kenneth Anderson, of the Department of the Ministry of Shipping, were cousins of G. S. Yuill. On his visit to England in 1907 they had all gathered to attend the wedding of Yuill's only daughter to the Earl of Portarlington.
2. *William Johnstone*, S.M, was born in Adelaide in 1843. His father, from

Annandale, Scotland, had married a Cornishwoman named Mary Thomas. Their son William was educated at Albert House Academy and St Peter's College, and, after a brief but nearly fatal experience with a Government survey party exploring north of Oodnadatta, he entered the office of the official Assignee where he soon rose to the position of Chief Clerk.

In 1882 he became Clerk of the Adelaide Local Court and is credited with much of the subsequent efficient book-keeping and indexing of that establishment. In 1892 he was appointed a Special Magistrate of the province and Stipendiary Magistrate of the Local Court of Port Adelaide and associated courts.

Many cases he dealt with related to seamen absconding from foreign ships, and others coming under the Worker's Compensation and Customs Acts. These excited considerable public interest and he was credited with a clear perception of the law in solving many difficult and complex problems.

In 1904 he was placed in charge of the Local Courts of the Mount Gambier district. At the time of his meeting with M.P. Durack in 1908 he was Returning Officer for the electoral district of Victoria and Albert, Representing Officer for the Destitute Poor Department, and Visiting Justice to Mount Gambier.

At the age of twenty-one he had married the eighteen-year-old Sarah Cherry, who had migrated from Lancaster, England, with her parents, brothers and sisters in 1853. They had two sons and five daughters, of whom Bessie was the youngest. At the time of M.P.'s first visit to the family, their eldest son William was Locomotive Inspector in the Railway Department, and the other son, Edward A., was a partner in the electrical engineering firm of Unbehaun & Johnstone of Adelaide and Perth.

3. *William Angliss*, born in England in 1865, migrated to Australia in 1884 and eventually opened a butcher's shop in Melbourne. As time went on, his enterprise expanded into a chain of meat stores throughout Australia, and into many other fields of business, industry, and finance. He held a seat in the Victorian Legislative Council from 1912 to 1952, and was knighted in 1939. M.P. was to keep in touch with him throughout the years.
4. *Fanny Durack's* supporters were indignant that she was not selected for the Olympic Games in Stockholm in 1912, the grounds being that no woman had ever been included in an Australian team for overseas competition. There were angry protests from women's clubs throughout

Australia, and money was donated to cover her expenses. The selection committee finally backed down and sent Fanny Durack and Mina Wylie with the male members of the team. The two girls made a sensational debut in world swimming, Fanny Durack being the first Australian woman to win an Olympic gold medal. She died in 1955, leaving a name as one of the greatest figures in Australian athletic history and a pioneer of women swimming champions.

5. *W. F. Buchanan* was to die in Sydney in 1911 aged eighty-seven, leaving one son and four daughters.
6. *Gordon W. Broughton's* great-grandfather, William Broughton, had embarked with the first fleet in 1787. He served in various government capacities in Parramatta, Norfolk Island, Tasmania, and Sydney, where he was made Acting Assistant Commissary General for N.S.W. and its dependencies. His marriage in 1810 connected him with two other well-known pioneering families, the Kennedys and the Humes.

   His grandson, Gordon Broughton, was brought up in the country districts of New South Wales and worked as book-keeper on Lissadell Station from 1908 to 1910. In the latter years of his life he wrote to me about my book, *Kings in Grass Castles*, telling me of his experiences in East Kimberley, Western Australia. A voluminous correspondence developed from this introductory letter, and Broughton was at last persuaded to write his story for the Jacaranda Press, Brisbane, who published it under the title of *Turn Again Home* in 1965. It tells not only of his boyhood in New South Wales and experiences in the North, but his subsequent adventures in the Far East when he joined an American lumber company in the Philippines.

   He served with the Australian Imperial Forces in World War I and later became a licensed surveyor, a qualified engineer, and finally an associate member of the Australian Institute of Engineers.

Chapter 20: 'Land of Expanse and Romance': May–October 1908

M.P. returns to Kimberley. Hears of Pumpkin's recent death at Argyle. Kit Durack and brother Fergus at Argyle. They visit Auvergne station. G. W. Broughton records his impressions of station life in East Kimberley. Death of Alec Keelar from fever. Aboriginal, Major, of Texas Downs Station, turns outlaw. Various versions.

1. *Turn Again Home*, see Reference 6, Chapter Nineteen.
2. It would be interesting to know in which category Broughton would

have placed Sam Muggleton, whom he describes as 'a rugged character', who rode one day into Lissadell beside a wagon drawn by eight draft mules. Also in the party were two Aboriginal women, mounted on good horses, 'their feet bare in the stirrup irons', and who were, he learned, Muggleton's 'personal black velvet'. Further references to Sam Muggleton in Chapter Twenty-five.

3. This version, given to me by Mrs Jack Kelly, was published as an article entitled 'Major the Outlaw' in the *West Australian* of 14 May 1932.
4. Yet another version of the story is given by Doug Moore, then book-keeper at Ord River Station, in his unpublished memoirs:

> I knew Major well. He was a civilized native—in fact the only one I have ever shaken hands with. I met him on the track one day and he showed me the way to a yard I was looking for, then held out his hand and said 'goodbye' cordially. I heard a bit later that the day before Major had had a row with Kelly and cleared out with a couple of rifles and ammunition and made for Growler's Gully. He teamed up on the way with Nipper and Debbie and they stole a bag of flour and another firearm from Scotty McDonald's camp. When Scotty moved on he left half a bag of flour mixed up with half a bottle of strychnine in his camp. Major found the flour all right but was too shrewd to fall for it. He sifted through and soon found signs of the poison. He then went into ambush, shot Scotty on his return to the outstation and cleared out up the Osbourn River . . . Soon afterwards he killed Davis and Fettle, took their tucker and more firearms and cartridges.
>
> By the time I got to Wyndham the whole country had been warned about Major and his associates and we were all armed and on the lookout for their tracks. Many innocent natives—if there were any—were probably shot at this time as all the police in the district were on the job. The outlaws were so hard pressed and hungry, with the police on their heels, that the remains of Nipper's piccaninny that they had eaten were found in one of their camp fires . . . After they were rounded up and shot, the gin Knowla who was with them was taken to Hall's Creek where she remained at the police station for years. It was this woman's child that was eaten when they were hard pressed . . .

For the Aboriginal version of the story see *Rebels & Radicals in Australia*, by Bruce Shaw, Allen and Unwin, 1981.

Chapter 21: The Link with London, June–December 1908
M.P. in East Kimberley, concerned with C.D. & D.'s business problems and prospects. Communication between Denis Doherty, London, and partners in Australia. Sale of Victoria River Downs Station to Bovril Australian Estates. C.D. & D. exporting sheep and possum skins to Leeds. Kit Durack departs from Wyndham to get married. Camels replacing other carrying teams. Death of Tom Kilfoyle. M.P. sails from Wyndham to Fremantle.

1. This is no doubt a reference to G. S. Yuill.
2. Top-making is a step in the manufacturing process before the wool is converted into yarn. Top-making wool, being of an average kind, was more common to Western Australia than the more stylish and unusual spinner's variety.
3. *Frances (Fan) Cherry* (Mrs F. M. Drew) was born in Port Wakefield, South Australia in 1872. After completing her nurse's training in Adelaide she was for two years with Lord and Lady Tennyson at Government House in South Australia, and again with them when Lord Tennyson was Governor-General in Melbourne. She had been in Western Australia for a few years when she met the Durack family. Her first experience in this State was nursing typhoid-stricken miners on the goldfields, and she had that year joined the Silver Chain District Nursing Service established by Mrs Muriel Chase in 1906. Nurse Cherry covered her nursing rounds at first on foot and then in a sulky, and as the organization grew she became its Acting Superintendent. Always closely identified with the needs of the community, she was to become widely known and loved for her skilled and unselfish service. Predeceased by her husband, she died in 1941, being at that time Superintendent of the Silver Chain Cottage Homes in North Perth.

Chapter 22: Of Hopes and Apprehensions, January–August 1909
M.P. with F. Connor to Busselton. M.P. to Adelaide, contacts Johnstone family. Bess Johnstone's account of their association and budding romance. M.P.'s proposal accepted. Religious problems discussed. M.P. returns to Kimberley. Correspondence with his fiancée. Some apprehensions. Father F. X. Gsell in East Kimberley. He and M.P. survive an accident. Young Paxton dies of fever at Lissadell.

1. *Gordon Buchanan* was the son of Nat Buchanan, born 1865. He took up the Flora Valley Station in 1887, and was the author of *Pack-horse and Waterhole* (Sydney, 1934).
2. *Sir Jenkin Coles*, born in 1842, had had a varied career, his activities before entering politics in 1875 including service in the mounted police and being an auctioneer and stock salesman. In this capacity he had dealings with M.P.'s father and other relatives. He represented Wooroora, South Australia for thirty years, and was Speaker in the House of Assembly from 1890 until the year of his death—1911.
3. *Father Francis Xavier Gsell* was five years exploring his vast domain in this way before establishing the Bathurst Island Mission in 1911. He was created Bishop of Darwin in 1938 and retired ten years later, to be succeeded by Bishop J. P. O'Loughlin. He was soon afterwards awarded the O.B.E. and the French Legion of Honour. He has told his own story in *The Bishop with 150 Wives* (Sydney, 1956)—the title deriving from the fact that he purchased young Aboriginal girls from their elderly promised husbands so that they might be cared for and educated at the mission school. The arrangement was accepted as a transaction in keeping with tribal law. Bishop Gsell died in Sydney in 1960, aged eighty-eight.

Chapter 23: A Dream Come True, August–December 1909

M.P. to Adelaide. Overcomes religious obstacles to marriage. Wedding in Adelaide and thence to Melbourne. Interesting contacts and entertainments. Interlude in Tasmania and back to Perth. Welcome to bride from family and friends. M.P. and wife to Behn Ord, Wagin with P.B. Bride and groom leave Fremantle bound for India in the *Königin Luise*.

1. Of *Edward Johnstone*, who was to become a prominent figure in the Australian business world, Bess Durack wrote as follows:

   > My brother Ted had a great friend named Albert Unbehaun, and by the time they left school in the early 1890s they were both interested in electricity which was just beginning to be put to domestic use. Albert's father, who was Post Master General in Adelaide, called on Dad and persuaded him to allow Ted to join his son in becoming apprenticed to the electrical section at the G.P.O. We had a workshop at the back of our garden and the two boys used to work there in the weekends.

> I'll never forget our joy and excitement when they installed electric bells at our front door and in the dining and bedrooms. Until then we had a bracket with four bells hanging from it in the kitchen and a handle with a knob to pull at the front door. It seemed like magic to simply press a button and set the bells ringing.
>
> The boys also installed the first electric light I remember seeing in their shed.
>
> When our friends came and saw these wonders, they got the boys to do the same for them. In this way they were kept busy in their spare time and were able to open a joint savings account. So from small beginnings they worked up the firm of Unbehaun & Johnstone, which was to become well-known throughout Australia. ['Memories', B.I.M. Durack, written June 1963]

2. *John Morton Craig* was head of the W.A. Stock Department for thirty years, and was responsible for the eradication of sheep scab. His association with the Durack family continued until his death in 1924.
3. Bess Durack completed the story of Fanny Dango and Sam Mackay in her 'Memoirs' (see Reference 1, above):

> Sam eventually divorced his wife and married Fanny, who used to call him 'my big, handsome Sam'. They had one son, Peter, whom his mother idealized. She was also very kind to Keith and Elsie, and encouraged the latter, a beautiful girl, to go on the stage. Elsie was successful in this field and had many admirers. When in London she nearly married a duke, but settled instead for the actor Max Montisole. In later years Elsie and Max came to live in Western Australia and ran a weekly radio session which was popular and entertaining.
>
> Max died about five years after his arrival in Australia, and in the meantime Sam had also died leaving Fanny a wealthy woman . . . When I last saw her in July 1963 she was on her way to England after seeing the last of poor Elsie in Melbourne. Fanny was then eighty-two, still charming and pretty, and with a remarkable memory. She clearly recalled our first meeting when we had supper together with my Miguel and her 'big, handsome Sam', both of whom had left us widows years before.

4. The *Königin Luise* belonged to the North German Lloyd line then

running from Bremen and Southampton to New York in summer, and to Australia in winter. She was scrapped in Italy in 1935.

Chapter 24: New Horizons, December 1909–May 1910

M.P. and wife aboard the *Königin Luise* to Colombo, thence to India. With brother Dermot Durack at University of Allahabad. They discuss company business. M.P. receives commission from South Australian Government to report on trade possibilities with Asian countries. Sightseeing expeditions. Discussing import of Australian products in Rangoon, Singapore and Philippines. Negotiations for import cattle with Faustino Lichauco of Manila. Return Singapore to Fremantle.

1. The drovers Thompson and Shoosmith who set off with the first mob of cattle on this lonely route were speared by Aborigines within that year (1910).
2. The result of M.P.'s enquiries in Manila were detailed in his letter to the South Australian Government:

> Manila has a population of some 300,000 and offers some encouragement to exports from North Australia. The majority in Manila and the Island of Luzon are Christianized and without taboos in the eating of meat within the limitation of their pockets.
>
> On the presentation of your Commission I was accorded every assistance by the American authorities. The Director of Agriculture, Dr Nesom, assured me of their desire to import stock from Australia.
>
> In company with Dr Nesom I called on the Acting Governor, Commander Gilbert, who further assured me that the Government was only too anxious to deal with a country with which they enjoyed a most friendly relationship.
>
> At Alabang, about twenty miles from Manila, the Government is now engaged in extensive experiments with a view to exterminating all diseases in the Island. It appears that of recent years their herds have become decimated through the introduction of stock from Hong Kong and French Indo-China which carried rinderpest and other diseases. Satisfactory results have followed their experiments in controlling this problem and the Government hopes to be able, within a few years, to re-stock

the Islands, for which purpose they now see North Australia as being the best field from which to draw.

Luzon has similar climatic conditions to North Australia. This, in addition to our existing immunity against tick fever and our close proximity to the Philippines—viz., only about 1800 miles from Port Darwin—recommends itself strongly to the Philippine Government.

The fact remains, however, that there are certain disadvantages associated with the reception and slaughter of North Australian cattle. The facilities for such are inadequate. The present matadors, or slaughter yards, are near the main centre of the town. Hong Kong and French Indo-China importations are all of a quiet, domestic nature, one man being sufficient to hold the animal, while a second hits it on the back of the head. The impracticality of this method where North Australian cattle are concerned can be easily understood . . . Northern pastoralists should therefore be prepared to meet some opposition and to overcome it with good sense and diplomacy.

The Government has now undertaken the erection of sheds for the reception of stock from abroad and they also intend to erect abattoirs for the treatment of cattle under Australian methods.

The official figures give the live importation into Manila as 36,305 cattle, mainly from French Indo-China, and the number of animals slaughtered in Manila as 28,379. In addition to the live import there is the frozen meat supply which for the last nine years has averaged over 9,000,000 lbs . . . at a cost landed of about £5 per head.*

I wish most respectfully to tender my thanks to the South Australian Government for the valuable assistance their Commission afforded me and hope this report will help to indicate the present prospects of the pastoral industry and that it may encourage the Government in the erection of a meat works in North Australia. This would encourage Northern pastoralists in opening up that vast area of magnificent country capable of carrying millions of sheep and cattle. [M.P.D., Perth, to the

* This was no doubt a reference to the trade built up by Sidney Kidman who had secured a contract with the Philippine Government for the export of canned meat from a works in Queensland.

Minister controlling the Northern Territory of South Australia, 12.5.1910]

3. The Lichauco family was of Mestizo (or mixed) background, in this case Filipino and Chinese.

Chapter 25: Cat Among the Pigeons, April–July 1910

Interest in Manila trade. Prospects sale C.D. & D. estate to Bovril & Co. M.P. and wife in East Kimberley. Mrs M.P. records her first impressions. Arrival of Lichauco agents and first shipment cattle to Manila. Bovril agents inspect stations and possibility of meatworks. C.D. & D. make offer for Lissadell Station. C.D. & D. purchase Dunham and Fossil Downs Stations. Fossil contract cancelled on death of W. MacDonald. Threat to prohibit entry Australian cattle to Philippines.

1. *Frank (Frederick Francis Burdett) Wittenoom* and his elder brother *Edward Horne Wittenoom*, were sons of the Rev John Burdett Wittenoom, first chaplain to the Swan River Colony. In 1874 the brothers began sheep farming in the Murchison district and in time became owners of a number of fine sheep properties in the north-west of the State. They were involved not only in the development of stock and stations, but with affairs in the fields of politics, company direction, and community activities of all kinds.
2. *Bang-tail muster:* a precise count of stock rather than a rough estimate. This was carried out by trimming the tail of each beast counted.
3. *Ali Bey Abdelaley (1856–1939)* was an Indian of the merchant class in Bombay. As a young man he fought in the border wars under Lord Frederick Roberts of Kandahar. He is said to have come to Australia in connection with the horse trade and often spoke of having been in Cooktown, Queensland, during the devastating cyclone of 1907.

   When, or for what reason, he came to the Kimberley district is not recorded, but his name appears in the diary of Tom Kilfoyle of Rosewood in 1907. From January 1909 he figures continually in the records of Argyle Station as stockman, homestead and mustering-camp cook and Jack-of-all-trades. From this time on he was Ambrose Durack's devoted companion and helper. In 1923, when Ambrose left Argyle for Renmark, South Australia with his wife and daughter, Ali Bey accompanied them. The inscription on his headstone in the Renmark cemetery reads:

Ali Bey
of Bombay
Died 19th July 1939
Aged 83
A faithful servant and loving
friend.

4. *W. S. Osmond:* M.P.'s visit to Osmond when he was near the end of his life and living in Stawell, Victoria, is described in Chapter Six.
5. *Frederick Booty.* Of Booty's four part-Aboriginal children, the eldest, Annie Tulevera, was born about 1900. It was probably on the trip from which he returned in early 1911 that he left her at the Sacred Heart Convent in Perth, where she remained until her marriage to Cedric O'Donovan in 1940. The three younger children, Laura (later Mrs Frederick Russ of Gibb River Station), Eva (Mrs David Bickley) and the only son, Oliver, were educated at Beagle Bay Mission. Booty held and worked Lambo until his death in 1946.

   A letter he wrote to Tom Cahill in November 1911 somehow found its way into the C.D. & D. files. Cahill's interest in Ruby Plains after Bob Button's death would seem to have been looked after by Booty who wrote as follows:

   > Dear Cahill—I am sorry I missed you in Sydney when there last as we had quite a foregathering of old Kimberley hands. It is good to hear that you came out all right when leaving Queensland and that you are gathering a family around you as well as gathering money.
   >
   > Of the old hands here, few remain. I hang on, being loathe to get out of the old rut until I can get better terms than so far offered. I still have Frog Hollow for sale cheap, and hope it will go off soon.
   >
   > You ought to have a good delivery from Ruby Plains though there were some heavy losses there this year. Matters have been going from bad to worse there for some time although the Old Fellow [Bob Button] did not say much . . . He worked very hard and although not a good hand at money matters he set a fine example of battling and minding his own business, and his honesty is a matter of history . . .

6. *Sam Muggleton.* I was to hear much of Sam Muggleton in later years from Ernie Chapman, son of an Aboriginal woman and a white

stockman who, although of the same name, was apparently not the Tom Chapman who eloped with the wife and daughter of Jacob Kuhl (see Chapter Thirteen).

Ernie recalls that he was 'picked up' at Eva Downs by Booty and Muggleton when they were purchasing Territory cattle for Coojabring. Ernie, then a small boy, became devoted to the two men but was especially attached to Muggleton, with whom he worked for a while at Frog Hollow. At the time of Muggleton's death, Ernie had been droving for Jack Kelly of Texas Downs and was nightwatching cattle en route to Wyndham when a man galloped up with the news of Muggleton's death, and also that of Jack McKenzie the day before. Ernie recalls looking up in his grief to see the blazing light of a shooting star, which he later learned was Halley's comet. The date of this sad happening must therefore have been 11 May 1910.

7. Bess Durack's 'Memoirs' proceed from this stage to tell of the various Wyndham doctors she recalled.

> *Dr Parer* was, I consider, the best doctor we ever had in Wyndham. He was always immaculate and attended to his duties well. I believe his people were Spanish. He was dark complexioned and had big brown eyes that could flash or become as soft as a doe's. During his reign in Wyndham both he and his wife became loved and respected and to me it was never the same place again when they left.
>
> *Dr Adams* came next. He was a stocky little man with reddish hair and beard and was very eccentric. He let people know he was 'a woman hater' and I never heard one woman say she *liked* him, although on occasions he proved himself a good doctor. He slways wore khaki clothes, the coat up to the neck with studs. To sit next to him or even meet him in the street, one was overcome with iodoform! The bushmen all said he dry-cleaned himself in it.
>
> When in Wyndham we sat at the same table with him for meals which was unpleasant in more ways than one. He never asked for things to be passed to him but stretched over one to get them! One day at luncheon, a bushman at another table was drinking his soup somewhat noisily. When the waitress came to take his plate he said: 'Golly, that was good soup!' The doctor quickly said: 'So we've *all* heard!' Naturally we all laughed

and he looked around without a smile and said: 'I was not meaning to be amusing.'

The little home that was always so wonderfully kept by the Parers soon became neglected and the surgery lost its sparkle.

After him came *Dr Innis Stephen* who was even more eccentric. He was an Englishman and brought a monkey with him! He wanted to have it in his cabin when coming from Darwin but the Captain objected and ordered the stewards to tie it up in one of the holds. The doctor was very indignant and ended up sleeping in the hold himself! Two or three days after being in Wyndham the monkey got away and climbed the Bastion, the hill behind the town. Everyone came out to watch the fun. Several natives were the first to catch up with it and the doctor, perspiring and out of breath, stood still and shouted: 'If one of you b—natives puts a hand on him, I'll shoot!' So they ran away and the doctor was left to catch it himself. This took him nearly an hour and he was exhausted by the time he got back. He had a wife in England who joined him after a couple of months. She was a very nice woman with a beautiful English complexion, but Wyndham soon proved too much for her. Naturally, she objected to having a monkey living in the house and at last told the doctor he would have to choose between them! He evidently chose the monkey, as Mrs Stephen left Wyndham on the boat a couple of days later and the residency went back to its haphazard bachelor regime!

Dr Cotton came after Innis Stephen. He was very tall and slight (6' 4") and was more professional than the others, dressing always in immaculate white clothes and helmet. He was quiet and didn't fraternize with anyone very much. One night when driving with Jim and Marie Davidson to the pictures at the Meatworks we approached a white post about 8 ft high, marking a culvert, and Marie said: 'Pull up Jim, and give Dr Cotton a lift.' To Marie's indignation we all had a good laugh.

8. *The brothers Duncan and Donald MacDonald* engaged a manager named Jim Leahy to look after Fossil Downs and some time later Sidney Kidman acquired a half-share in the property for £85,000. Donald MacDonald's two sons were meanwhile being reared on sheep properties in New South Wales. In the early thirties, the younger of these, another William, put the money he had inherited on his Uncle Duncan's death

into buying out Kidman. He soon became sole owner of Fossil Downs, and came north to work the property. Married in 1938 to Maxine Darrow of Sydney, he built a fine new house on the property and proceeded to develop the estate. He died in 1963, leaving his widow and two daughters to carry on.

Chapter 26: Propositions and Promises, July 1910–January 1911
Manila market in jeopardy. Doherty reports talks with R. Tilden Smith. Argyle and Lissadell cattle to Queensland. F. Connor in Wyndham. Discussions re meatworks with Government Survey Party. Tilden Smith urges C.D. & D. to join Cypress Pine Syndicate. Opinion of Adrian Despeissis sought. Mrs M.P. to Adelaide. M.P. in charge at Argyle. Joins wife in Adelaide. Proposition re meatworks partnership from Tilden Smith. Son, Reginald, born to M.P. and wife.

1. This was one of several unsuccessful attempts to introduce new blood into the company herds. Imported stud did not easily become acclimatized, and most soon fell victims to pleuro or tick-fever.
2. As it happened, Dr Will Durack was to die tragically at Marble Bar later that same year, aged only thirty-eight. He was the first definitely to diagnose leprosy in the north-west and to recommend a course of action that was not taken seriously until the 1930s.

Chapter 27: Full Steam Ahead, February 1911–January 1912
Obstructions on two fronts. F. Connor to Philippines. M.P. returns to Western Australia with wife, nurse and infant son. Consecration of Bishop J. P. Clune. Interviews with politicians. M.P. and family to Wyndham. Price Connigrave and party on scientific survey. Reopening of Manila trade. Death of W. F. Buchanan. P. M. Durack agrees to take half-share of Ellen Vale with C.D. & D. The Dunham abandoned. Partners at cross purposes. Engagement of Ambrose Durack and Nance Tiddy. M.P., wife and son to Manila.

1. *Roy Phillipps' mother*, who answered to the masculine-sounding name of Cecil Raymond Phillipps, was to become a close friend of M.P. and family. She was of obviously genteel upbringing and a bright and fluent conversationalist, but she made little reference to her background, presumably in Narooma, a district of New South Wales. It is known

only that she appeared to be familiar with life on the land and was an excellent horsewoman. It was generally assumed that she had been widowed shortly before the birth of her only son in Sydney, after which she had come to Perth, obtained a secretarial position, and devoted herself to his well-being and education at Perth's exclusive High School (later Hale School). What her story was we will never know, but a reference in one of Roy's letters, from which a page is missing, suggests that she may at one stage have apologized for not enlightening him. This, written from Wyndham on 14.7.14, reads as follows:

> ... about my early history. There is nothing I could know that will ever alter my love for you Mother dearest, as I realise only too well how patient you have been with me at different times and all that I owe to you alone.

Roy's widow and family, who have generously made his letters available, are also in the dark about his paternity.

2. Roy Phillipps to his mother, in a letter dated 21.1.12:

> Connigrave and party arrived back safely after a lapse of six months and have some marvellous photographs. The expedition seems to have come up without a bob, relying on 'the wealth of flora and fauna' to buy them out of here. They're owing money all over town.

3. Recalling thus his own situation when in his early twenties, he was prompted to write to J.W. at about this time, requesting that he take out an insurance policy payable when his boy was twenty-five years of age: 'I think when a young chap has reached that age, if he has anything in him he should be able to put £1,000 to some good use!'

   The fact that he had a similar thought for his two daughters meant that my sister and I were able, in 1936, to embark on a meat-boat from Wyndham for a limited, but significant, voyage of discovery, during which we visited the U.K., Ireland and the Continent.

4. W. F. *Buchanan* was born in Dublin in 1824 and came to New South Wales with his parents and four brothers in 1837. He and his elder brother, Nathaniel, were among the most remarkable pioneers of the Australian pastoral industry. Both famous as horsemen, bushmen, and overlanders, W.F. was the most successful in a material sense. He left his heirs a pastoral empire and a considerable fortune. (See Reference 3, Chapter Two, for information about Nathaniel Buchanan.)

Chapter 28: Contentious Issues, January 1912–January 1913

M.P. returns to Wyndham. Wet weather conditions. Ambrose Durack brings Johnnie Walker and Albert to Argyle. Sinking of the *Koombana*. F. Connor in Perth with partners. They discuss effects of new Labour Government policy. Beginning of the State Steamship Service. A family reunion. M.P. and wife return to Wyndham. Mrs M.P. to Adelaide. First State Steamship *Western Australia*. Arrival of Lake Hall and Aboriginal, Daylight.

1. *Doug Moore's memoirs*—see Reference 3, Chapter Fourteen.
2. Their only son Neal was born in 1923. He was killed in a car accident in 1974. Their daughter Patricia (Patsy) died in 1936, aged eight.
3. *The S.S. Western Australia* was originally built for the Tsar of Russia. Then named the *Mongolia*, it was used as a hospital ship in the Russo-Japanese war. In 1912 it was bought by the W.A. State Governnent from the East Asiatic Co of Denmark, whence it arrived at the end of that year. It was used on the north-west coast only until the middle of 1916, when it was taken over by the British Admiralty as a Quaker-staffed hospital ship operating between France and England.

Chapter 29: Between the City and the Bush, January–July 1913

Contracts with Manila. Arguments with stock inspector. M.P. to Adelaide. Birth of his daughter Mary. M.P. in Melbourne re plan for meatworks in the Northern Territory. Interview with Dr Gilruth, Administrator of N.T. M.P. meets Mrs Aeneas Gunn. Returns to Wyndham with family. Marriage of Ambrose Durack and Nance Tiddy. Mr and Mrs E. H. Angelo and Bishop Trower in Wyndham. Mrs M.P. and family at Ivanhoe Station. Rudolph Philchowski speared on Ivanhoe. Trial of Aboriginal Jillambin, Wyndham. Aboriginal version of Philchowski's murder.

1. *Sir Lancelot Stirling* K.C.M.G.,1849–1932. A politician and a sportsman, who bred horses and merino sheep. He entered the House of Assembly for Mt Barker, W.A. in 1881 and in 1901 became President of the Legislative Council, a position he held until his death. He started polo in South Australia, and was also Master of the Adelaide hounds.
2. By 1912 the Commonwealth Government appeared to have accepted the idea of undertaking the installation of a meatworks in Darwin. Later that year the Department of External Affairs was advised of the projected visit of a Mr Frederick who was representing an 'English

syndicate'. Frederick came first to Darwin where he interviewed Gilruth and inspected possible sites before moving on to survey other sites at Wyndham and Wave Hill. Frederick thereafter wired External Affairs, intimating that while inclined to favour Wyndham as the best site for a meatworks, he could induce the unnamed firm he represented to build in Darwin if the Government would lease the site and give 'moral support' to the undertaking.

On 28 July 1913 Gilruth was officially informed that the cabinet had decided to permit Frederick's syndicate to proceed with the work along the lines laid down by Gilruth. [From: C.S.I.R.O. Divisional Report No 64/1, by F. H. Bauer, 1964]

3. In real life 'Dan' was known to have been Dave Suttee, Victorian-born and of Scottish descent, who came to the Territory from Queensland in 1896. After being for some time head stockman on Victoria River Downs he was engaged for the same position on Elsie Station by Aeneas Gunn. After Gunn's death in 1903, Suttee became joint manager of the Elsie with one Herbert Bryant.

   When the Elsie was sold and amalgamated with Hodgson Downs, Dave Suttee became a stockman on Ord River station. In January 1912 he rode into Wyndham to meet the mailboat and, according to Roy Phillipps, 'left a few days later with a sore head, same being the effects of about a gallon of rum'. He went to sleep near a creek about four miles from Ivanhoe homestead and was found dead there the following day.

   Twenty years later when my sister and I were on Ivanhoe station, Suttee's grave on Capsize Creek was to become a familiar feature on the moonlight walks.

4. *Bishop Trower* resigned from the north-west diocese in 1927, after which he became Vicar of Chale on the Isle of Wight. He died in 1928.

Chapter 30: The Shadow of War, July 1913–November 1914

Lively interest in North Australian properties. J.W. reports from Sydney on complicated activities. Purchase of extensive holdings by Union Cold Storage. Critical comment. M.P. and family in Manila. Purchase of 'T' Model Ford. Problems of modern transport. Vesteys sign contract for meatworks Darwin. S. V. Nevanas reports to Government re meatworks, Wyndham. War news disturbs.

1. It was announced soon afterwards that this company had also purchased Flora Valley near Hall's Creek.
2. This is a reference to Jack Scaddan, then State Premier, who had considered the establishment of a State Shipping Company of more importance than that of a meatworks in Wyndham.
3. *The Emden* was destroyed off Cocos Island by the Australian naval cruiser *Sydney* on 9.11.14.

Chapter 31: Parting of the Ways, December 1914–August 1915
State Government signs contract with S. V. Nevanas for construction of meatworks, Wyndham. General meeting C.D. & D. partners. F. Connor resigns from company. M.P. to Manila. Returns to Darwin and informed of birth of second daughter, Elizabeth. Thence by supply lugger to Victoria River. J.W. in Wyndham. Nevanas contract cancelled. Meatworks now in hands of Public Works Department.

1. There was to be no simple conclusion to this agreement. On 9 August 1916 Connor signed an indenture stating that he owed his wife the sum of £4,200, for the recovery of which she threatened him with legal action. She had, however, according to this document, agreed to refrain from proceedings on condition that her husband assigned to her the money payable on the thirty-eight promissory notes of £500 each by Doherty and the Durack Brothers in ten years' time.

   This document, dated only two weeks before Connor's death, may have been drawn up as a means of protecting his wife from probate on his estate. He had, however, become involved in a number of precarious mining ventures of which she may have become impatient.

   Owing to unforeseen financial problems for the company, a new arrangement was agreed upon with Mrs Connor in 1924 by which she was paid £7,999, the remainder to accrue in 1931. As it happened, she died in 1929, after which, owing to the current depression, payment was again brought forward.

   In the meantime, the deaths of Denis Doherty, J.W. and P.B. Durack had further complicated the issues involved and led to a protracted Court case which went on from 1939 until 1944.

   At the end of the war, as a result of greatly improved markets, the company was at last able to pay its debts, including money owed to the bank and the Connor family. Shortly before his death in 1950,

M.P. disposed of the 80,000 company shares to the New Zealand Loan Company for a gross sum of £260,000.

2. As a result of this episode, the Country Party withdrew its support from the Scaddan Government. In July 1916 a coalition of the Country Party and Liberal Opposition passed a no-confidence motion which forced the resignation of the Labor Party.

Chapter 32: Goodbye Manila, August 1915–February 1916

Dealings with Manila become confused. M.P. in Perth and wife to Adelaide. News from the war front. Ulysses visits Behn Ord. Sale of possum furs abroad. John Forrest fifty years in service of State. Termination of Manila trade. New State ships for north-west trade. Sinking of cargo ship *Clan MacTavish*.

1. *Mrs Tom Kilfoyle*, *nee* Byrne, died at the end of that year. Her funeral brought together many of her widely scattered family, including her brother Michael, her sister Mrs Mahew and husband Jack from Darwin, as well as her two unmarried sisters, Josephine and Margaret. The presence at the funeral of M.J. and his brother J. B. Durack was a reminder of the marriage relationship between the Durack and Kilfoyle families, their father's wife Margaret (Mrs Darby Durack) having been an elder sister of Tom Kilfoyle. Among the pallbearers were Mrs Kilfoyle's partner in Rosewood Station, Mr. J. J. Holmes. M.P. was also a pallbearer, having been longer and more closely associated with both Tom Kilfoyle and his wife than other family members.
2. A letter written when on leave in England in 1917 told of his marriage to Diana Wentworth, a member of the well-known New South Wales family of that name. A son, Patrick, was born to them in 1920. At the end of the war he returned with his wife to India where he remained for some years as Principal of the Allahabad University. He resigned from this position in 1922 and thereafter lived for the most part in Dublin, where he died in 1955.
3. The many varieties of possum in Australia are herbivorous, differing from the carnivorous opossum of America. The export of possum skins to London, Paris, and New York had been going on from all parts of Australia since the 1890s. In 1906 it was recorded that more than 4,000,000 brushtail possum skins had been marketed abroad, sometimes being sold as 'beaver' or 'Adelaide chinchilla' and sometimes, when suitably clipped and dyed, as 'skunk'.

The original Game Act of 1892 was revised in 1912/13 to discourage the unrestricted killing and trapping of possums, but 'open seasons' of a few weeks were declared from time to time and a government royalty of 3d per skin imposed. Even under these conditions, it is interesting to note that in 1919, 2,500,000 skins were recorded as having been exported from Queensland alone; in 1922, 199,000 from Western Australia and in 1931/32, 1,000,000 from New South Wales.

From this time on the number of possum furs reported to have been marketed declined significantly. Where Western Australia was concerned, this was not only the result of a national awakening to the importance of wildlife conservation but also of the Depression, the extended release of farmland and the resulting forest clearance this involved, as well as of the effects of a protracted drought.

The Fauna Conservation Act of 1950 brought about the legal winding-down of the possum fur trade throughout Australia.

4. M.P.'s diary of 2.9.16 contains the following reference to this remarkable man:

> J.W. and I today attended the unveiling of Mr Alexander Forrest's monument which has been removed from its former position outside his old home to the corner of St George's Terrace and Barrack Street. My memory of Alex Forrest goes back to my first visit to Perth many years ago. I then called on him in the Lands Office and he assisted me in taking up a certain area on what is now Ivanhoe.

5. The *Kangaroo* was to operate on the coast until 1938, when it was sold to a Shanghai firm and renamed *Norah Moller*. It was sunk by a Japanese aircraft in the Sunda Straits in 1942.

Chapter 33: Matters of Life and Death, March 1916–October 1916

M.P. returns north. Father Bishoffs embarks at Broome. M.P. in Darwin sees progress on meatworks construction. Interview with Administrator Gilruth. Meatworks proceeding in Wyndham. Station activities. R. H. Underwood, Minister for Aboriginal Affairs and A. O. Neville, Aboriginal Protector in Wyndham. M.P. returns to Perth. Death of Francis Connor. The conscription issue.

1. A day-to-day description of the activities of this party, with photographs and a synopsis of the geology of the area, was published in 1918:

Narrative of an Expedition of Exploration in North-Western Australia, by H. Basedow, Adelaide, South Australia.

2. *The Rock and the Sand* by Mary Durack, London, 1969.
3. The best country in the Territory, and that only in very limited areas, would probably carry a beast to thirty or thirty-five acres.
4. From *The Rock and the Sand* (see Reference 2, above):

> He [Neville] saw that the mixed-blood people, left to breed haphazardly and to grow up in their rubbish-tip camps with little training or education of any sort, would soon become a serious problem, not only to themselves, but to the whole of Australia. Contemptuous of the school of thought that dismissed them as being incapable of improvement, he pointed out that many, both in country areas and the far outback, despite their lack of opportunity, were playing an extremely useful role. The fact that some had already been successfully absorbed into the white community, to the extent that no one ignorant of their history was aware of their native blood, indicated that the Aboriginal strain was not inclined to throw back and that future trouble could quite simply be averted by an upgrading of their education and a forthright programme of assimilation. 'We are', he declared with cheerful confidence, 'going to merge the native race into our white community.'
>
> The mating of Aboriginal with half-caste, or even half-caste with half-caste, which perpetuated the dark strain, was to be kindly but firmly discouraged. Instead there was to be a progressive breeding out of the Aboriginal by the pairing of half with quarter-caste or preferably with white. Why, after all should the Mendelian law not be applied to the solution of a human problem?
>
> Since Aboriginal women begot children by the white or the mixed blood much more readily than by the black, it seemed expedient to segregate the full-bloods in areas where their racial decline could follow its apparently inexorable course. This did not mean, however, that they were not to be encouraged to maintain their pride of race—a much simpler matter away from the degenerating influences of the closely settled areas.

Chapter 34: Wicked Wyndham, November 1916–October 1917
Factious issues in Wyndham. Royal Commission charges Dr Innis Stephen. M.P. takes over hotel and store. Stephen exonerated. M.P. to Darwin—meets C. W. D. Conacher. Birth of second son, Kimberley Michael. M.P. persuaded to stand for Kimberley electorate. Contemporary politics. M.P. tours electorate—wins by outright majority. Sails for Fremantle.

1. *Dr Holland* had come from Perth to attend one of the Darcy brothers who had been seriously injured in a fall from his horse some six weeks before. When it became clear that only immediate surgery could save his life, the local postmaster undertook to operate on instructions relayed by telegraph from Dr Holland in Perth. The report in the *West Australian* of 11 August indicated that the operation was successful:

   > The case is remarkable. It stands to the credit of the surgeon that he was able, by messages, to give such directions . . . Perhaps even more remarkable is the fact that Mr Tuckett should have been able to carry out those instructions with the instruments he had to hand. It also reveals the heroic fortitude of the patient who allowed Mr Tuckett to operate without anaesthetics. The brothers Darcy must be built of tough material . . .

   Dr Holland left by ship as soon as possible to follow up the case, but by the time he reached Hall's Creek the patient had died.

Chapter 35: People and Politics, November 1917–November 1918
M.P. returns to Perth in political role. Contentious issues—conscription, the Dampierland Missions, the Wyndham meatworks. Roy Phillipps writes from abroad. Neal Durack returns from the front. J.W. travels interstate—sees Sir John Forrest, Tom Hayes, Fanny Durack, the Tully family of Queensland, old friends at C.B. College, Goulburn. M. J. Durack sells Lissadell to W. Naughton. M.P. goes north again. Neal Durack married in Wyndham. Armistice signed.

1. Neville's proposal entailed making a clean sweep of the three struggling missions and starting afresh on a 'sound economic basis'—a move in which he saw nothing to be lost and much to be gained. It would put an end to sectarian bickering, to complaints about inadequate subsidies, to fear of subversive activities, and to the wholesale mixing of

part- and full-blood Aborigines that was going on in that region. [*The Rock and the Sand*, see Reference 2, Chapter Thirty-three]

2. *Tom Hayes* died at his home in Hazeldene, Randwick, in December 1929, aged eighty-two years. In 1931 Jack, son of his erstwhile partner Tom Kilfoyle and then owner of Rosewood, became engaged to his daughter Dorothy. The engagement was broken off some time later, after which Dorothy Hayes sued Jack Kilfoyle for £10,000 damages for breach of promise. Kilfoyle was eventually required to pay only £800 to cover Court costs and the aggrieved girl's trousseau. I was amused to find the ample newspaper coverage carefully preserved in Jack Kilfoyle's own scrapbook.
3. *Pat Tully*, born in County Galway in 1830, came to Australia in 1853, went to Ballarat goldfields and stood with Peter Lalor and his men at Eureka Stockade in 1854. As told in *Kings in Grass Castles*, he went to Goulburn where he met and married Grandfather Patsy's sister, Sarah. They followed other members of the family to Western Queensland in 1874 and took up a property adjoining Thylungra Station. On this station, originally named Wathagurra and later known as Ray, they reared a family of three sons and four daughters. Pat Tully died at Ray in 1922, aged ninety-two, and his widow died not long afterwards.
4. Bess Durack, in her latter-day 'Memoirs', wrote feelingly of this good friend:

> Sarah Stevens often told us that she was born in East London, 'within the sound of Bow bells'. She trained as a nurse in London and came to Western Australia about 1904. After working for some time in a hospital at Laverton, on the goldfields, she came to work as midwifery nurse for Dr Dixie Clement in Perth.
>
> Reg and Mary were born in Adelaide but Nurse Stevens came to me at our home in Claremont when Betty was born in 1915 and stayed and helped me for some months. She then went into partnership with Sister Connor in a nursing home in Shenton Park. That was where Kim was born in 1917.
>
> In 1919 she gave up the nursing home and helped with our big move to Adelaide Terrace in the city and came to live with us. Her being with us from then on made it possible for me to go up north with Miguel from time to time. David, who was born in that house in 1920, became her special favourite though

she bestowed loving care and devotion on us all.

In 1926 she returned to her people in England, saying sadly as she went off that she might not come back again. It was a joy to us all when she wrote after a three months' absence that she was coming 'home'. She had a great love of literature and was a splendid reader. In the days before radio or TV she entertained us all by her rendering of Dickens, Scott, Dumas, Jane Austen, the Brontës, and the rest of them.

She died on 23 August 1945, beloved by us all.

Chapter 36: Looking Skywards, December 1918–December 1919

The price of war. Changes and prospects. Birth of M.P.'s fifth child, William. Politics and business. Pneumonic influenza. M.P. goes north. Industrial trouble Darwin. Opening Wyndham meatworks. M.P. and mechanic Bolton tour Kimberley electorate. Many difficulties. M.P. returns south. Mrs Doherty, son and daughter in Perth. Roy Phillipps returns with wife. Major Norman Brearley gives flying displays. C.D. & D. in case against the Crown. M.P. purchases house in Perth. Brearley has flying headquarters in back yard.

1. *The Hyland Circus* was a family affair well known throughout Australasia and abroad from the late 1890s to the outbreak of war. It was formed by John Thomas Hyland, who had owned a cattle property in Queensland and had trained his daughters as trick-riders, acrobats and trapeze-artists. Evelyn Hyland married A. A. M. Coverley, who was member for Kimberley from 1924 to 1953.
2. The Phillipps family later moved on to a grazing property near Moree, New South Wales. Roy continued to fly until killed on a night-training flight in 1940. He left two daughters and a son. His World War I experiences, as told in his letters, figure in *Lords of Death*, a book about the young Western Australians who served at Gallipoli and in France, by Suzanne Welborn, Fremantle, 1982.
3. This may well have been due to the influence of his friend Edith Dircksey Cowan who in 1921 was to become the first woman member of Parliament in Australia. Born in Geraldton W.A. to Kenneth and Mary Eliza Brown in 1861, she married James Cowan, Registrar of the Supreme Court, in 1879. The mother of four children, she was a foundation member of the Women's Service Guild of W.A. and of the

National Council of Women, and she was involved in community efforts of all kinds. During the war she worked for Red Cross voluntary aid societies and for many other patriotic causes, and after the war for the rights of the returned soldiers. She was one of the founders of the W.A. Historical Society in 1926 and, together with her daughter Dircksey, encouraged me from my teenage years to interest myself in Australian history.

4. *Timothy Quinlan* had come to W.A. with his parents from Ireland as a small boy. Orphaned in the mid-1860s, he had been adopted by J. T. Reilly, an enterprising and generous pioneer of the young colony. In 1883 he married Teresa Connor, daughter of Daniel Connor, a self-made Irishman with whom he formed the firm of Connor & Quinlan. The two men were among the few wealthy Irish Catholics in the State, owning both farm and city properties, including a number of shops and hotels in the heart of Perth.

   Quinlan had been for a number of years a member of the Perth City Council and had represented West Perth in the Legislative Assembly. His daughter, Gertrude Teresa, married John Kirwan (later Sir John) who had been for thirty years editor of the *Kalgoorlie Miner*. The Quinlan and Kirwan families shared a house close to the Durack residence in Adelaide Terrace.

Chapter 37: A Man Who Lived Three Lives, December 1919–December 1920

Move to new locality. Jim Crisp speared Bullita Station. M.P. to meeting producers and exporters, Melbourne. Discussions with Prime Minister and many others. M.P. and brothers to the W.A. goldfields. M.P. accompanies political party on tour of Kimberley. Wyndham meatworks operating. Formation Okes-Durack Oil Company and Freney Kimberley Oil Company. Prospects for Civil Aviation and Flying Doctor service. M.P. joins Country Party. Denis Doherty from England. Birth of M.P.'s fourth son, David Johnstone. Neal Durack drowned Ord River.

1. Whenever I pass the old home at 263 Adelaide Terrace, long since business premises, I am overcome with memories such as are told here in verse.

   The inclusion of a third sister is poetic licence: in our time only two of George Parker's sisters, Misses Bessie and Louisa, still occupied the house next door.

There is the house we lived in when I was growing,
The house I dream in, climbing the dim stairs,
Raising the long windows on to the river,
The long blinds on to the street that was ours—and theirs.

The veiled sisters—Miss Annie, Miss Louisa,
And Miss Matilda—we watched them and heard them talk
As they came out of the straight, dark house they haunted,
On the stroke of the hour for correct ghosts to walk.

We knew it was four p.m., less half a minute
When we heard the knock-knock of the bolts—there were
two and a chain;
The door whined and slammed like a dog barking
And the key turned in the lock with a yap of pain.

The latch of the gate clacked at four precisely,
And the parasols went up with a ghosty fuss,
As they stepped abreast in the shade of big Cape lilacs
To drop ghost cards on other ghosts—or on us.

'How the town has changed,' they would say, 'and not for the
better!
When last we were in there was scarcely a *soul* we knew.
So *difficult* for you,' they told my mother,
'With growing daughters, and not to know who's who!'

The rattle of tea in the silver service signalled
A ritual raising of veils with a genteel flutter,
The flaking of kid, like skin from skeleton fingers
That clinked on cups and toyed with the bread and butter.

'We were so careful always about strangers
But even *then* we might easily have made a mistake.
One of us *nearly* married the son of a draper
And another *almost* went off with a charming rake!

'Once we were all *three* in quite a flutter
Over some fellow the *Governor* had entertained.

We heard in the nick of time he had been transported.
Some said it was politics—but *the fact remained!*'

Such hair-breadth escapes from living! Ghost feathers shivered
And gossamer shrouds shook in remembered shock.
Miss Annie, Miss Louisa and Miss Matilda—
Safe—in the big, dark house with the double lock.

Mary Durack

2. After leaving Darwin under stress a year or so before, Gilruth had visited the U.S.A. for the Commonwealth Government and on his return had officially resigned as Administrator. Soon afterwards a Royal Commission had been appointed to enquire into the administration of the Northern Territory. Judge Ewing reported that Gilruth and his associates had not exercised their powers with sufficient firmness, discretion and justice. He also found the Commonwealth at fault in its lack of policy towards northern development.
3. The North West Railway Development League had been formed by George Miles, M.L.C. for North Province. The scheme entailed establishing a railway some two to three hundred miles inland, connecting with the north-west ports by branch lines. The Prime Minister and his Treasurer were reported to have been somewhat startled by this 'Napoleonic project'. It was discussed for many years but the hope of associating it with an oil-boom and an increased demand for pastoral produce was not realised. The 1920s proceeded steadily into the Depression, and the 1930s into World War II. The war years brought about a much improved road system that encouraged the use of updated motor transport, including station-wagons, buses, trucks and road-trains. An extended railway system is nonetheless still discussed.
4. During his time in Parliament, M.P. was to be responsible for the passing of a bill for the protection of bird-life in the Kimberley district.
5. *Roy Doherty* soon afterwards returned to Perth and took up Eulina Station, a sheep property in the Kalgoorlie district, with his cousin Jim Cable. Before long he left this place and tried his luck in a search for sandalwood. He was employed for a while in the company's wool and grain stores at Fremantle, and on the outbreak of the Second World War found a post in Perth's military barracks. This he claimed to have been the best position he ever occupied. A man of attractive and genial personality, with a quick wit and a keen zest for life, he seems

never to have realised his apparent potential in Australia.

6. At about the same time as the Okes-Durack company was formed, a Broome pearler named M. F. Freney, one of the original directors of Okes-Durack, took out a mining lease in Kimberley. Before long the Freney Kimberley Oil Company, of which M.P. was a director, was formed, leading geologists were engaged, and drilling began.
7. Imelda's second child, a daughter named Nancye, was born in April 1921.
8. Aunt Fan, Mrs Jerry Durack, died at the home of her daughter Molly (Mrs Leslie) Brockman in Beverley, W.A. in September 1921.
9. D. J. Doherty returned to Perth with his daughters Auvergne (Vergne) and Bylly after the death of his wife in 1930, and remained there until his death in 1935. In my memory, Doherty was an entertaining, ebullient personality to the end. His daughters Vergne and Bylly ran the C.D. & D. office until the wind-up of the company in 1950. Their elder sister, Katch, remained in England and practised for many years as a physiotherapist in London and the Channel Islands.

Index

Also by Mary Durack

KEEP HIM MY COUNTRY

When 19-year-old Stan Rolt strikes out for the Northern Territory, determined to manage an ailing family cattle station, he plays into the hands of his manipulative grandfather. Intending to spend two years at Trafalgar Station, he stays fifteen, his soul captured by the harsh but haunting country of the Kimberley. Try as he might, he can't seem to escape its clutches, even though it killed his father and threatens also to bring him down. He is held there by the dependence of the people, black and white, and the memory of a tragic love affair that still haunts him . . .

. . . for anyone with Australia in their blood it is compulsory reading.
THE AGE

A powerful novel in a man's world of mustering, horse-breaking and crocodile hunting with an interlude of idyllic and tragic love. Leaves one with a lasting memory of white men and black working together in a strange wild country.
TIMES LITERARY SUPPLEMENT

Salty humour and a deep respect for those who come to terms with an uncompromising outback.
CANBERRA TIMES

Bantam Paperback
ISBN 1 86325 166 9

PILGRIMAGE

A journey through the life and writings of Mary Durack

Edited by Patsy and Naomi Millett

Though best known for two family histories that have become literary classics, *Kings in Grass Castles* and *Sons in the Saddle*, Mary Durack's great talent extended to fiction, short stories, drama and verse.

This long-awaited collection of her favourite works, including material never before published, provides a rare glimpse into Mary's extraordinary experiences, from her Kimberley days on the family properties and her time with her own family in Broome, to her city home in Perth.

Mary writes with insight, compassion and humour of outback legends and the many bush characters whom she knew and loved—of their far-reaching wisdom and struggle to adapt to a changing land.

Pilgrimage is an enduring record of a way of life that is fast disappearing and a testament to an exceptional writer.

Bantam Paperback
ISBN 1 86325 243 6